Implications for Entrepreneurship and Enterprise Development in the Blue Economy

Lukman Raimi
Universiti Brunei Darussalam, Brunei

Jainaba M. L. Kah
Office of the President, Gambia

IGI Global
PUBLISHER of TIMELY KNOWLEDGE

A volume in the Practice, Progress, and Proficiency in Sustainability (PPPS) Book Series

Published in the United States of America by
IGI Global
Business Science Reference (an imprint of IGI Global)
701 E. Chocolate Avenue
Hershey PA, USA 17033
Tel: 717-533-8845
Fax: 717-533-8661
E-mail: cust@igi-global.com
Web site: http://www.igi-global.com

Library of Congress Cataloging-in-Publication Data

Names: Raimi, Lukman, 1971- editor. | Kah, Jainaba M. L., 1970- editor.
Title: Implications for entrepreneurship and enterprise development in the blue economy / Lukman Raimi, and Jainaba M.L. Kah, editors.
Description: Hershey, PA : Business Science Reference, 2022. | Includes bibliographical references and index. | Summary: "This book discusses the concept of the blue economy dealing with safeguarding the oceans and presenting huge opportunities for the coastal countries economy by promoting positive exploitation of the ocean's resources while urging the users to sustainably provide basic human needs such as clean water, food security, massive jobs, and habitable shelter for the people"-- Provided by publisher.
Identifiers: LCCN 2021059265 (print) | LCCN 2021059266 (ebook) | ISBN 9781668433935 (hardcover) | ISBN 9781668433942 (paperback) | ISBN 9781668433959 (ebook)
Subjects: LCSH: Environmental economics. | Coastal ecology--Economic aspects. | Marine resources--Economic aspects. | Coastal ecosystem health. | Marine ecosystem health.
Classification: LCC HC79.E5 I51127 2022 (print) | LCC HC79.E5 (ebook) | DDC 338.9/27--dc23/eng/20220128
LC record available at https://lccn.loc.gov/2021059265
LC ebook record available at https://lccn.loc.gov/2021059266

This book is published in the IGI Global book series Practice, Progress, and Proficiency in Sustainability (PPPS) (ISSN: 2330-3271; eISSN: 2330-328X)

British Cataloguing in Publication Data
A Cataloguing in Publication record for this book is available from the British Library.

Practice, Progress, and Proficiency in Sustainability (PPPS) Book Series

Ayman Batisha
International Sustainability Institute, Egypt

ISSN:2330-3271
EISSN:2330-328X

Mission

In a world where traditional business practices are reconsidered and economic activity is performed in a global context, new areas of economic developments are recognized as the key enablers of wealth and income production. This knowledge of information technologies provides infrastructures, systems, and services towards sustainable development.

The **Practices, Progress, and Proficiency in Sustainability (PPPS) Book Series** focuses on the local and global challenges, business opportunities, and societal needs surrounding international collaboration and sustainable development of technology. This series brings together academics, researchers, entrepreneurs, policy makers and government officers aiming to contribute to the progress and proficiency in sustainability.

Coverage

- Global Content and Knowledge Repositories
- Strategic Management of IT
- Socio-Economic
- Outsourcing
- Sustainable Development
- Intellectual Capital
- Global Business
- Knowledge clusters
- E-Development
- Green Technology

IGI Global is currently accepting manuscripts for publication within this series. To submit a proposal for a volume in this series, please contact our Acquisition Editors at Acquisitions@igi-global.com or visit: http://www.igi-global.com/publish/.

The Practice, Progress, and Proficiency in Sustainability (PPPS) Book Series (ISSN 2330-3271) is published by IGI Global, 701 E. Chocolate Avenue, Hershey, PA 17033-1240, USA, www.igi-global.com. This series is composed of titles available for purchase individually; each title is edited to be contextually exclusive from any other title within the series. For pricing and ordering information please visit http://www.igi-global.com/book-series/practice-progress-proficiency-sustainability/73810. Postmaster: Send all address changes to above address.

Titles in this Series

For a list of additional titles in this series, please visit: www.igi-global.com/book-series/practice-progress-proficiency-sustainability/73810

Handbook of Research on Monitoring and Evaluating the Ecological Health of Wetlands
Ashok K. Rathoure (Akone Services, India)
Engineering Science Reference • © 2022 • 370pp • H/C (ISBN: 9781799894988) • US $295.00

Blockchain Technologies for Sustainable Development in Smart Cities
P. Swarnalatha (Vellore Institute of Technology, India) and S. Prabu (Vellore Institute of Technology, India)
Engineering Science Reference • © 2022 • 285pp • H/C (ISBN: 9781799892748) • US $215.00

Impacts of Climate Change and Economic and Health Crises on the Agriculture and Food Sectors
Vítor João Pereira Domingues Martinho (Polytechnic Institute of Viseu, Portugal)
Engineering Science Reference • © 2022 • 420pp • H/C (ISBN: 9781799895572) • US $195.00

Handbook of Research on Resource Management and the Struggle for Water Sustainability in Africa
Innocent Simphiwe Nojiyeza (University of Zululand, South Africa) Oliver Mtapuri (University of KwaZulu-Natal, South Africa) Prosper Bazaanah (University of Johannesburg, South Africa) and Edzisani Ellen Netshiozwi (Office of the Chief Justice, South Africa)
Engineering Science Reference • © 2022 • 437pp • H/C (ISBN: 9781799888093) • US $295.00

Innovative Strategic Planning and International Collaboration for the Mitigation of Global Crises
Gabriela Antošová (University College of Business in Prague, Czech Republic)
Information Science Reference • © 2022 • 327pp • H/C (ISBN: 9781799883395) • US $195.00

Handbook of Research on Changing Dynamics in Responsible and Sustainable Business in the Post-COVID-19 Era
Cristina Raluca Gh. Popescu (University of Bucharest, Romania & The Bucharest University of Economic Studies, Romania & The National Institute for Research and Development in Environmental Protection (INCDPM), Romania & National Research and Development Institute for Gas Turbines (COMOTI), Romania)
Business Science Reference • © 2022 • 512pp • H/C (ISBN: 9781668425237) • US $315.00

Achieving Sustainability Using Creativity, Innovation, and Education A Multidisciplinary Approach
Ziska Fields (University of Johannesburg, South Africa)
Information Science Reference • © 2022 • 260pp • H/C (ISBN: 9781799879633) • US $215.00

IGI Global
PUBLISHER of TIMELY KNOWLEDGE

701 East Chocolate Avenue, Hershey, PA 17033, USA
Tel: 717-533-8845 x100 • Fax: 717-533-8661
E-Mail: cust@igi-global.com • www.igi-global.com

Editorial Advisory Board

Table of Contents

Detailed Table of Contents

the chapter analyses the proposal to adopt the International Tribunal on the Laws of the Sea (ITLOS) and other alternative propositions.

With the emergence of economic globalization, the concept of the blue economy has evolved from fisheries to a wider context that comprised all kinds of biological and mineral resources, maritime trade, shipping, energy, and tourism. Intensive economic exploration of water areas is changing ecosystems, affecting biodiversity, and threatening sustainability. The transformations are felt globally in a form of climate change and environmental degradation, but the Arctic has appeared to be particularly vulnerable. Using the case of China, this chapter attempts to contribute to the convergence of economic benefits of exploring the Arctic with the urgent need for the protection of a fragile Arctic environment. The authors discuss how China's involvement in the Arctic-related activities can benefit the sustainable development of the blue economy in the region.

For policy enrichment, this chapter discusses the opportunities available to maritime nations in the blue economy and explicates the roles of policymakers in achieving an improved economy by encouraging and attracting foreign investors and grants, which is a catalyst to achieving a blue economy. First, the author argues that the transition to the blue economy has encouraged maritime nations to look inward and diversify their economies by harnessing ocean resources and other economic potentials. Second, the proximity to the seas and oceans has made maritime nations realize the possibility of converting ocean resources to boost their national GDPs. However, this opportunity comes with enormous responsibilities. Third, policymakers must ensure proper conservation and management measures so that living creatures in the exclusive economic zones (EEZ) are not endangered. Finally, maritime nations need to exercise their jurisdiction for the protection and preservation of the marine environment.

The blue economy provides a unique opportunity to policymakers in Nigeria to diversify the economy by exploiting ocean resources to attract foreign direct investment and generate foreign exchange. The chapter adds to the existing body of knowledge by discussing the nexus between the blue economy and foreign direct investment (FDI). Three key issues were articulated in the chapter. First, the blue economy has the potential to provide an opportunity for Nigeria to develop and exploit the diverse ocean resources while protecting and conserving endangered marine resources. Secondly, the transition to a blue economy presents some challenges; hence, the policymakers need to develop ocean governance and policies for strengthening its realisation. LastlySecond, the blue economy enhances wealth creation and youth employment in different ocean-related industrial activities such as shipping, shipbuilding

The eco-responsible concept presents a new vision for the rational and sustainable exploitation of oceans, lakes, and rivers in the development literature. Arguably, the blue economy is very often cited as an example of a new development paradigm with the capability to fight against poverty, improve food diversification, and create added value in coastal countries of the African continent. To differentiate themselves and ensure long-lasting growth, established companies in Gabon have embraced sustainable development through several actions, some of which are CSR projects and interventions. This chapter presents a model of CSR action that impacts SDG 1 and shows how a vulnerable community has benefited from a project to improve its well-being and that of other populations.

Foreword

Implications for Entrepreneurship and Enterprise Development in the Blue Economy discusses important issues of entrepreneurship in the Blue Economy, which serves to enrich existing definitions of a blue economy with more insightful inputs from multidisciplinary lenses, and to produce more valuable research materials that are focused on the blue economy for universities and industries in order to aid basic and applied research. Additionally, to that, the presented works provide some veritable measures for evaluating blue economy progression and compliance.

Each chapter is designed in such a way that treats a particular part of the whole puzzle, and all together they highlighted very important elements of the blue economy. Starting with theoretical discussions, this book integrates some case studies of specific countries and zones. Moreover, it discovers and stimulates further arguments and debates on other economic indicators that are linked to the blue economy, such as sustainable development, foreign investments, poverty, corporate social responsibility, and empowerment of woman in blue entrepreneurship.

As this book provides both, theoretical and practical framework, it can be considered an important resource book for libraries, academicians, and policymakers fostering the sustainable development through blue economy.

Eglantina Hysa
Department of Economics, Epoka University, Albania

Preface

The blue economy is a widely used concept in policy and academic circles in developed and developing countries. However, people have a peripheral understanding of the phenomenon. Considering the unique value that the blue economy portends for the survival of people, planets, and profits (3Ps), there is an urgent need for rigorous conceptual, policy-focused, theoretical, and empirical studies on the subject from multidisciplinary perspectives. At the moment, there are several conflicting understandings of the blue economy, but there is no universally accepted definition or veritable measures. The blue economy comes with humongous economic opportunities and sustainability challenges. How ready are coastal and noncoastal countries? Do policymakers in coastal countries fully understand and appreciate what a blue economy entails? To mitigate the abuse of the oceans in coastal countries and promote the principle of sustainable development through the blue economy, there is an urgent need to enhance the knowledge of multiple stakeholders.

The book titled *Implications for Entrepreneurship and Enterprise Development in the Blue Economy* intends to bridge the knowledge gap of academics and practitioners by focusing on concepts, prospects, theories, practices and strategies, and challenges of the Blue economy. The book explores the blue economy from a variety of contexts, along with highlighting contemporary issues facing marine nations and coastal states. The book consists of 12 chapters. A brief description of each of the chapters is as follows:

Chapter 1, contributed by Lukman Raimi, Jainaba M.L. Kah and Muhammad Usman Tariq, discusses the definitions of the blue economy, its measurements, and theories purposively to provide a better understanding of the diverse issues that surround the blue economy, including governance.

Chapter 2 by Saheed Adebowale Nurein, explicates the opportunities and challenges of enterprise development in the blue economy from the perspective of a developing economy of Nigeria struggling threats of climate change and other sustainability issues.

Paul Olatidoye anchored Chapter 3, which focuses on connections among the blue economy, food security and food sustainability. He underscored that the vast sea resources in the blue economy, when optimally managed, utilised and conserved, could ensure sustainable food supply and the attainment of food security.

Chapter 4, authored by Seda Yıldırım and Merve Kaplan, analyses the impact of invasive alien marine species on the seafood market, marine biodiversity and countries from the Mediterranean region in the blue economy. This chapter is a call for caution and collaborative surveillance by the international community and coastal countries.

Chapter 5, **written by a lawyer and seasoned lecturer**, Abayomi Al-Ameen, reviews the draft High Sea Treaty (draft HST) and the on-going deliberations and proposals in the different aspects of the document. with the aim of identifying the potential postratification challenges that may be faced in the implementation of the draft HST and recommending adoption of the International Tribunal on the Laws of the Sea (ITLOS) and other alternative propositions.

Gao Tianming and Vasilii Erokhin in Chapter 6 discuss the convergence of economic benefits of exploring the Arctic, particularly how China's involvement in Arctic-related activities can benefit the sustainable development of the blue economy in the region.

Chapter 7, written by Taoreed Alaba Amodu, explores the nexus of the blue economy and foreign direct investment in Maritime Nations, especially China. The chapter argues that the transition to the blue economy offers maritime nations the opportunity to convert ocean resources to boost their national GDPs and attract FDI.

Chapter 8, authored by Moshood Abiola Sanni, similarly examines the linkage between the blue economy and foreign direct investment in Maritime Nations with a specific focus on how Nigeria could diversify its economy by exploiting ocean resources to attract foreign direct investment and generate foreign exchange.

Muriel Lendoye, in Chapter 9, considers the mutually reinforcing influence of the tripod of the blue economy, sustainable development goals (SDGs) and corporate social responsibility (CSR) on the rational and sustainable exploitation of ocean resources to solve the socioenvironmental problems of poverty, food inadequacy and unemployment in vulnerable communities in Africa with a growing population.

In Chapter 10, Raheem Shefiu explains how the blue economy's entrepreneurial potentials, especially the exploitation of ocean resources, could be catalysts for the alleviation of extreme poverty and hunger, the provision of employment and other economic opportunities, including the progression toward sustainable development in Nigeria.

Chapter 11, authored by Dr. Nima Norouzi, analyses the positive or negative impact of environmental accounting on greening the economy, especially in different socioeconomic environments.

Finally, Raheem Shefiu in Chapter 12 examines the gender implication of the blue economy on women's entrepreneurship. The author explicates the laudable contributions of women in marine and coastal areas to onshore enterprises such as fisheries, aquaculture, processing and trading of marine products, including their role in ocean resource conservation and disaster-risk reduction initiatives, among others.

Lukman Raimi
Universiti Brunei Darussalam, Brunei

Jainaba M. L. Kah
Office of the President, Gambia

Acknowledgment

I would like to extend my appreciation to all the chapter contributors, whose intellectual inputs, relentless efforts, and resources made the completion of this edited book possible within the set timelines.

We extend thanks to the reviewers who provided scholarly reviews for all the chapters. It is apt to report that their expertise, critiques and insightful comments and suggestions have enhanced the quality of the final chapters.

We are also highly indebted to the editorial advisory board members for their assistance, cooperation, and invaluable comments that enhanced the quality of this book. Great appreciation is extended to Dr. Eglantina Hysa, Associate Professor, Department of Economics, Epoka University, Albania, who wrote a foreword for this book. Additionally, the editors are grateful to the IGI Global team and development editor for consistent follow-up, encouragement and professional guidance right from the beginning of the book project.

This acknowledgement would be incomplete without appreciating Dr. Hj. Masairol Hj. Masri, Professor Muhammadou Kah, Professor Ahmed Khalid, Dr. Wardah Azimah Haji Sumardi and Dr Quazi Sakalayen, who provided valuable moral support. The concluding acknowledgement goes to our families, friends, and academic colleagues. Their patience, cooperation, encouragement, and understanding are stimulants for the timely completion of this book.

Chapter 1
The Discourse of Blue Economy Definitions, Measurements, and Theories:
Implications for Strengthening Academic Research and Industry Practice

Lukman Raimi
https://orcid.org/0000-0002-5329-8715
Universiti Brunei Darussalam, Brunei

Jainaba M. L. Kah
Office of the President, The Gambia

Muhammad Usman Tariq
https://orcid.org/0000-0002-7605-3040
Abu Dhabi School of Management, UAE

ABSTRACT

This chapter discusses the definitions, measurements, and theories of the blue economy for strengthening academic research and industry practice. A critical literature review provided four insights. First, the definition of the blue economy connotes a responsible utilisation, management, conservation, and preservation of the ocean in a manner that aligns with triple themes of sustainable development. Second, the best measurement of the blue economy is the coastal governance index (CGI) that has 24 indicators and 43 subindicators. Third, the prospects of the blue economy include the creation of sustainable ocean industrialization, boosts for traditional industries, new employment opportunities, food and nutritional security through aquaculture, a boost for SDGs, and improved economic growth, among others. The challenges of a blue economy include lack of national legislation and protocols on ocean economic activities, threats of overuse of ocean and its resources, sea pollution, ocean security, and international conflicts on maritime delineations. The chapter concludes with implications.

DOI: 10.4018/978-1-6684-3393-5.ch001

INTRODUCTION

Oceans constitute more than 70% of the Earth's surface, which translates to almost 99% of the 'living space' on the planet (European Commission, 2012). Moreover, reliable reports estimated that 80% of the volume of global trade is undertaken on the oceans because they are linked to global supply chains and global markets (UNCTAD 2016; World Bank, 2017). The oceans, seas and waterways provide ecological, economic, and social benefits, which are combined to guarantee continued existence not only for humans but also for other living things (Costanza, 1999). To mitigate the abuse of oceans in coastal countries and promote the principle of sustainable development, the term 'blue economy' was developed to escalate the compelling issue of unsustainable use of oceans (Smith-Godfrey, 2016). The former US Secretary of State, John Kerry, counseled that "protecting our oceans is not a luxury. It is a necessity that contributes to our economy, our climate, and our way of life. Working together, we can change the current course and chart a sustainable future" (Spalding, 2016, p1).

Currently, the blue economy is a widely used sustainability concept in academia and policy circles. A quick Google search produced 965 million results in 0.59 seconds – a further indication that the concept has become a frontburner issue of interest to global governments and multiple stakeholders. Commonwealth (2021) describes the blue economy as an emerging concept that obligates better stewardship over the ocean otherwise or blue resources. Scholars and international organisations have noted that the blue economy, otherwise called the blue ocean economy, ocean economy, marine economy, and sustainable ocean economy, emerged as a pragmatic response to existential threats, environmental risks and ecological scarcities posed by the reckless use of the oceans and unsustainable exploitation of ocean resources by illegal, unreported and unregulated (IUU) fishing fleets, distant water fishing nations (DWFNs) fleets and other ocean users (United Nations, 2014; Lee, Noh, Khim, 2020; Okafor-Yarwood, 2022). Based on the point above, the blue economy was mooted by the international community to safeguard the oceans on one hand and present huge opportunities for coastal countries on the other. As important as the concept is, people across a wide spectrum, including academics, have a different understanding and perspective about the phenomenon. Consequently, different stakeholders within global blue economy ecosystems have divergent focuses, intents and interpretations about the blue economy – a situation that may create potential conflicts and conceptual misgivings due to different stakeholders' preferences or interests (Voyer et al., 2018; Lee et al., 2020).

For several decades, national development policies and business policies on real estates, tourism and social interventions have consistently favoured noncoastal agricultural areas, with little concern for coastal areas, which has heightened regional disparities (Crane, et al, 2018; Irazábal, 2018; Khan et al., 2020). Renewed interests in the economic development and wellbeing of coastal countries and small island states across the globe are positive development, as they would experience accelerated economic growth and improved livelihood. Moreover, the World Economic Forum (2017) underscored the importance of coastal countries and ocean economies, stating that 83 countries are more ocean than land, and an additional 54 countries are more than 80% ocean. However, at present, only 20 coastal countries are recognised and ranked in the coastal governance index (CGI), including Norway, Spain, the United States, France, Japan, New Zealand, the Philippines, Canada, China, South Africa, Vietnam, Indonesia, South Korea, Brazil, Mexico, India, Nigeria, Chile, Peru, and Russia (The Economist, 2015a).

Should these countries and states embrace the emerging blue economy, it comes with humongous opportunities and foundational challenges. How ready are the coastal and noncoastal countries? Do policymakers in coastal countries fully understand and appreciate what a blue economy entails? Unfortunately, most coastal countries have refused to organise themselves as 'ocean states' (World Economic Forum, 2017). At the level of international foreign policy relations, however, sustainable ocean governance principles were enriched in the UN Conference on Sustainable Development, millennium development goals (MDGs) and sustainable development goals (SDGs). All these development blueprints collectively articulated social, economic, and environmental sustainability in the use of Earth's humongous resources (Costanza, 1999; Silver et al., 2015). Additionally, the institutional readiness of coastal and noncoastal countries to embrace the opportunities inherent in the blue economy concept is still in doubt and unclear. Worse still, every new economic model comes with opportunities and challenges. With particular reference to the blue economy, apart from the Work Bank's policy papers and the United Nations' international laws, the emerging opportunities and challenges of the blue economy have not been properly articulated. This further justifies the need for more conceptual, policy, and empirical research to fill the vacuum.

More importantly, coastal countries require enabling laws, protocols and governance policies on blue economies. Europe is passionate about the blue economy, unlike other continents. Europe's blue economy governance policies include the European Commission's Blue Growth initiative, the Europe 2020 strategy on maritime oceans, seas, and coasts, the European Commission's Integrated Maritime Policy (2007), the Marine Strategy Framework Directive (2008) and the EU's maritime research and innovation (European Commission, 2012). Similarly, United Nations agencies such as the United Nations Conventions on the Law of the Sea (UNCLOS) and the International Maritime Organisation (IMO) have developed a global regulatory framework that explicates best practices and policies on the management of the oceans and exploitation of their resources for economic activities (European Commission, 2012; Smith-Godfrey, 2016). However, coastal countries that are members of the United Nations are expected to develop their respective national policies and strategies to regulate the use of ocean resources and curb unsustainable economic activities. This has not been adhered to by many countries. Similarly, there are four competing issues on the human–ocean nexus that need to be redressed and restructured in line with the sustainable development agenda: (a) oceans as natural capital, (b) oceans as good business, (c) oceans as integral to Pacific Small Island Developing States, and (d) oceans as small-scale fisheries livelihoods (Silver et al., 2015). Considering the importance of the blue economy for the survival of people, planets, and profits (3Ps), there is a need for rigorous conceptual, policy-focused, theoretical, and empirical studies on the subject from multidisciplinary perspectives. This chapter responds to this need by discussing the concept of the blue economy and its definitions, measurements, and foundational theories to strengthen academic research and industry practice in developed and developing contexts. Apart from the introduction (Section 1) above, there are ten sections in this paper. Section 2 explains the methods and approach. Section 3 focuses on the literature review that covers subsections such as blue economy definitions, measurements and theories. Section 4 explicates the prospects of adoption of a blue economy and implementation challenges of progression towards a blue economy. Section 5 concludes with a contextualisation of the findings, practical implications, limitations, and policy recommendations.

METHODOLOGY

We adopted qualitative research in this chapter. The interpretivist paradigm was adopted to provide deeper insight into the discourse of the blue economy and its measurements, theories, prospects and challenges. To achieve the objective of this chapter, we sourced numeric and nonnumeric data on the blue economy from scholarly articles, texts, policy documents, working papers, and online resources of international organisations. We employed the use of content analysis to review, integrate and synthesise the extracted textual information. According to Denscombe (2017), content analysis is a logical procedure for quantifying the contents of texts, writings, interviews, picture speeches, books, correspondences and other verbal data. We found it useful because it allows the texts, words and other visual and verbal data to be compressed, classified, summarised and tabulated into fewer content categories for meaningful and useful interpretation in research (Saunders et al., 2016). For more clarity, we follow a three-stage process explained further below.

1. **Stage 1: Data sourcing** - At this stage, we sourced the required numeric secondary data on the blue ocean economy to address our chapter objectives. For data sourcing, we previewed explored Science Direct and Google Scholar, from which over 100 relevant articles were selected. The selected articles provide insights into the blue economy, green economy, theories and prospects and challenges of the blue economy.
2. **Stage 2: Data development and conversion** – At this stage, we compiled insightful pieces of information based on relevance, recency and suitability in readiness for analysis data.
3. **Stage 3: Data analysis** – At this final stage, the insightful pieces of information were critically reviewed, appraised, synthesised and contextualised using a content analysis. This methodological approach is supported by (Jepson, 2009; Williams & Shepherd, 2017).

BACKGROUND

The thematic issues in the literature that underpin this chapter are systematically and sequentially discussed hereunder with relevant takeaways for governments, academics and policymakers in the blue economy.

Conceptualisation of the Blue Economy

Currently, there are divergent and conflicting understandings of the blue economy, but no universally accepted definition or veritable measures. However, a number of scholars, practitioners, and international bodies have attempted to define and measure the concept. It is believed that the definition of the blue economy expands the ideals of the green economy by prioritising ocean problems, solutions, and the collaborative role of stakeholders/participants (Silver et al., 2015). In addition, the blue economy promotes positive exploitation of ocean resources while encouraging the users of ocean resources to sustainably provide basic human needs such as clean water, food security, massive jobs, and habitable shelter for the coastal population (Pauli, 2010). Moreover, Lee, Noh and Khim (2020) posited that the blue economy is a strategy for conserving and safeguarding the oceans and water resources in coastal countries across the globe from two inherent conflicts: (a) pursuit of economic growth and industrial development; and (b) protection of oceans and their vast resources from reckless exploitation. The World Bank (2017) views the blue economy as the sustainable use of ocean resources for the pursuit of economic growth, improved livelihoods, and jobs while preserving the health of ocean ecosystems. Additionally, a blue economy or ocean economy refers to a sustainable ocean economy where the environmental risks and ecological damage unleashed on ocean through reckless economic and industrial activities are mitigated, reduced and managed to restore the health of the ocean (The Economist, 2015). Bari (2017) defines the blue economy as the decoupling of socioeconomic activities away from an environmentally degrading approach to a better approach that optimises the array of benefits derived from marine resources to citizens. Summarizing the valuable definitions above, the policy thrust of the blue economy is the need to optimally balance the economic, social, and environmental dimensions of sustainable development with regard to the use of the oceans and their vast resources to increase long-term benefits for small island developing states and coastal least developed countries across the globe (World Bank and United Nations Department of Economic and Social Affairs, 2017). The working definition of a blue economy contextualised by this chapter is an ocean-oriented economy that seeks to manage, conserve and safeguard the oceans and their vast resources for the pursuit of economic growth, sustainable ocean industrialisation, wealth creation, job creation and sustainable development.

Blue Economy versus Green Economy: Convergence and Divergence

This section examines the convergence and divergence of the green economy and blue economy. The extant literature reviewed established a convergence rather than a divergence in the two sustainability concepts. According to the United Nations Environment Programme (2021), the term green economy denotes a new economic sustainability model, which is characterised by low carbon, resource efficiency and socially inclusive features. The sustainability features of a green economy help reduce environmental risks and avert ecological scarcities that unsustainable human consumption, exploitation and industrial production have forced on the people and planet. The six strategic pillars that drive the green economy include (a) climate change, (b) resource saving and management, (c) circular economy, (d) environmental protection, (e) ecosystem protection and recovery, and (f) water conservation and natural disaster prevention (OECD, 2011). Comparatively, the blue economy is defined as an emerging concept that encourages better stewardship by countries over the blue ocean and its vast resources to actualise the Sustainable Development Goals (SDGs), especially SDG14 'life below water', as well as close linkages between the ocean, climate change, and the wellbeing of the present and future generations, including equity and public participation in marine and coastal decision-making (The Commonwealth, 2021).

From the two definitions above, it is obvious that the concept of the blue economy complements the green economy. In other words, the definition of the blue economy merely expands the green economy but priortises ocean problems, prospects and solutions (Silver et al., 2015). Bargh (2014) opined that the green economy and blue economy be combined. Both sustainability concepts advocate the triple themes of sustainable development in the face of imminent extinction and existential threat posed by industrial activities and unsustainable consumption to humans, animals, plants and other living creatures. Furthermore, UNEP (2015) explained that the blue economy converges with the green economy because it is an extension of the green economy into the oceans and seas. The UNEP would continue to develop the "Green Economy in a Blue World Capacity Building Initiative" with its partners, including the Regional Seas Conventions and Action Plans, because the Green Economy for Oceans is an emerging issue to which many member states are asking for technical support. The UNEP is poised to provide technical support on how oceans and coasts transit towards a green economy through innovative sectoral approaches within the context of sustainable development. Moreover, the Green Economy Coalition (2021) explains that a green economy emerged because the existing economic system is unfit and weak to achieve a good balance of triple themes of sustainable development. The green economy hopes to redress the serious challenges of climate change, biodiversity loss, growing inequality, and other systemic interconnected global crises facing humanity.

The green economy being the first to emerge in the development literature is expanding faster in European and other knowledge-based economies because of the successful adoption and application of the "green revolution" principle and technologies such as green agriculture, green products, green energy, green technologies, green business and green industries (Bogdan et al., 2014). In view of convergence in definitions and objectives, this chapter is of the view that both addressed existential threats – the green economy focuses sustainable consumption and production on land, while the blue economy focuses sustainable consumption and production on water. Overall, both concepts could be potent drivers for the achievement of the Sustainable Development Goals (SDGs). The SDGs comprise 17 goals, 169 targets, and 230 indicators systematically packaged as a blueprint for eradicating poverty and global hunger, protecting the environment and fostering peace and inclusive societies, among others (Bello-Bravo & Lutomia, 2020).

Measurements of the Blue Economy

In social and management sciences, the use of measurements, metrics and indicators are quite important for making informed decisions on events and phenomena. Scholars asserted that measurement of a social construct is the first step that leads to control and eventually to improvement; whatever cannot be measured obviously cannot be well understood and controlled, and whatever cannot be controlled cannot be improved (Karlsson, Trygg & Elfström, 2004; Priven et al., 2014). An important question for governments, policymakers and blue economy advocates is: How can the governments of coastal countries and international bodies measure progression toward a blue economy? The extant literature has established that a green economy is premised on six strategic pillars, namely, climate change, resource saving and management, circular economy, environmental protection, ecosystem protection and recovery, (f) water conservation and natural disaster prevention (OECD, 2011). Over time, these pillars have been used to measure and assess the progression and compliance with green economy ideals. Are these measurements adequate and appropriate for a blue economy? A blue economy would remain green if sustainable ocean commercialisation and industrialization are ensured by governments and other stakeholders (Golden et al., 2017). Considering the distinct nature of the blue economy, the best measurement of a blue economy is the Coastal Governance Index (CGI). The CGI is the initiative of the Economist Intelligence Unit, commissioned by the David and Lucile Packard Foundation and California Environmental Associates IN 2015 (The Economist, 2015a). The goal of the CGI is to provide governments, private investors, nongovernmental organisations and multiple other stakeholders with a basis for understanding ocean management, governance, conservation and compliance with maritime regulations for better decision-making and stimulation of investment in the ocean economy. Operationally, the CGI, as a quantitative index, measures the effectiveness of coastal and fisheries governance, particularly the extent of government regulation and management across 20 ocean economies. It has 24 indicators and 43 sub indicators that cut across six thematic categories: (a) policy and institutional capacity; (b) business environment for coastal activities; (c) water quality; (d) minerals and energy; (e) land; and (f) living resources (The Economist, 2015a). The veritable indicators and sub indicators of CGI are depicted in Figure 1 below.

The rankings of the 20 officially recognised coastal countries in the CGI reports for 2015 and 2019 are shown in Table 1 below. While several counties occupied different positions in 2015 and 2019, the United States was ranked 2nd in both years, and South Africa also maintained 8th in both years. Despite the political visibility of Russian among the comity of nations, I was ranked 20th position in both years – an indication that the country's governance of the ocean and its vast resources are not productively

Figure 1. Six thematic categories of CGI (adapted from The Economist, 2015a)

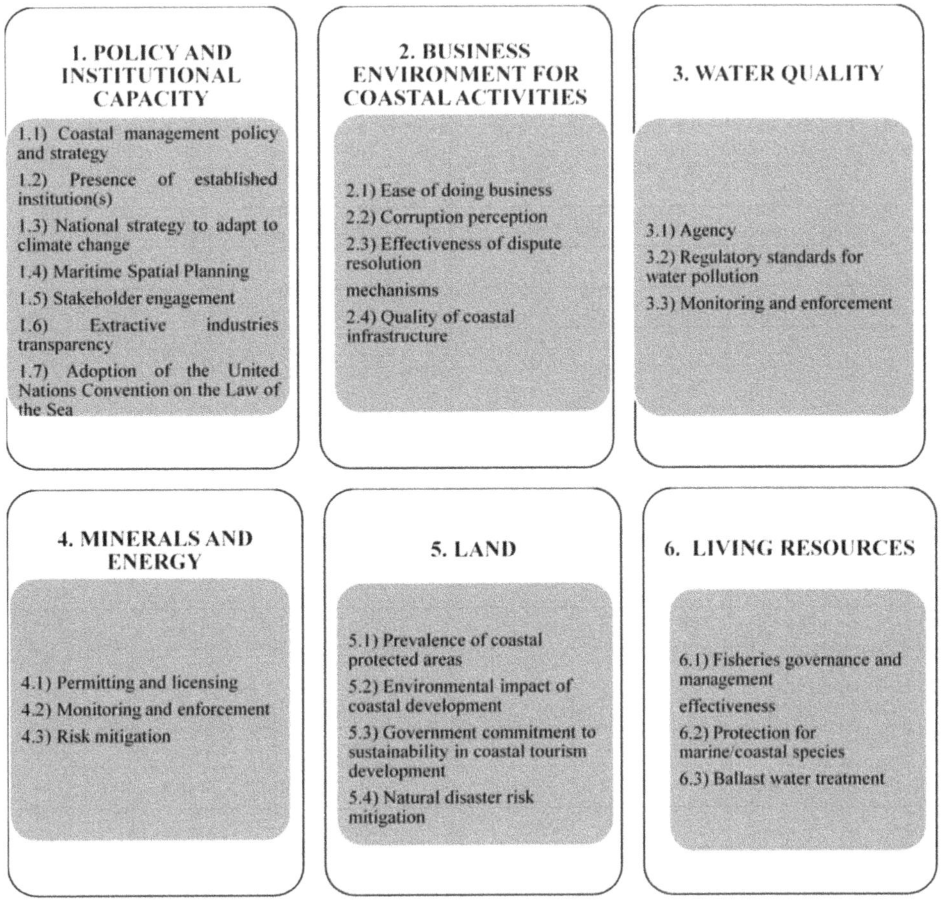

managed, conserved and preserved based on the 24 indicators and 43 sub indicators that cut across six thematic governance issues. According to the World Ocean Initiative (2018), the scoring and ranking of coastal countries on CGI based on their performance across six thematic areas in the index clearly show that many countries still have a long way to go with regard to governance readiness in relation to exploitation, conservation and sustainability of coastal natural resources. The report further reiterated that many coastal countries (US, France, Japan, Canada, Peru, China, Mexico, the Philippines, Chile and Indonesia) have made commendable progress on coastal sustainability, but Nigeria and Russia have not truly made progress in the last four years.

In rounding up the section, it is instructive to note that apart from the CGI, the coastal countries and small island states require national and regional coastal governance indexes as a baseline for evaluating and monitoring internal and external elements of coastal management processes. A national or regional baseline index would provide a framework for understanding the strengths of the national coastal governance system for consolidating the gains of the blue economy. Understanding the weakness of the blue economy would also aid improvement and corrections (Scherer & Asmus, 2021).

Table 1. Coastal Governance Index (2015 and 2019)

SN	Countries	Score (2015)	Rank (2015	Score (2019)	Rank (2019)
1	Norway	79	5	89.5	1
2	Spain	80	4	80.3	7
3	United States	85	2	85.4	2
4	France	82	3	83.3	5
5	Japan	78	6	83.4	4
6	New Zealand	86	1	84.4	3
7	Philippines	59	14	71.4	15
8	Canada	78	7	78.6	9
9	China	61	12	73	13
10	South Africa	68	9	75.7	10
11	Vietnam	57	15	65	17
12	Indonesia	57	15	72.6	14
13	South Korea	72	8	80.2	8
14	Brazil	67	10	73.1	12
15	Mexico	60	13	74.1	11
16	India	56	17	61.6	18
17	Nigeria	50	19	48.7	19
18	Chile	67	10	82.3	6
19	Peru	55	18	69.5	16
20	Russia	42	20	44.6	20

Source: The Economist Intelligence Unit (2015, 2019)

Theories of the Blue Economy

Green theory provides a theoretical underpinning of a blue economy. Green advocacy or greening of the earth is a normative argument that supports sustainable behaviour by persuading individuals and corporations to be concerned with the environmental and economic sustainability of their consumption and production activities in society (Eckersley, 2010; Zhao et al., 2020). Greening of the earth, water and vegetation supports the triple themes of sustainable development, which is the hallmark of sustainable development goals (SDGs). The SDG agenda comprises 17 goals, 169 targets, and 230 indicators with the mission of eradicating poverty and hunger in the world, protecting the environment and fostering peace and inclusive societies, among others (Bello-Bravo & Lutomia, 2020). Variants of discussions around sustainability, sustainable development, sustainable lifestyle, sustainable diets, and sustainable finance (Hagbert & Bradley, 2017; Sareen & Haarstad, 2018; Raimi, Olowo & Shokunbi, 2021). A green approach to economic, social and environmental management would accelerate the actualisation of the SDGs. A development process becomes sustainable when it integrates economic and social development with environmental protection (Mohammad 2010). Economic sustainability refers to integrated economic management that safeguards and sustains human and material resources for creating long-term sustainable values through optimal use, recovery, and recycling (University of Gävle 2018b).

Social sustainability, on the other hand, refers to a social security approach that improves the wellbeing of current and future generations through access to basic social services such as healthcare, education, transportation, housing, and recreation, including security (Glasson & Wood 2009; Michael & Peacock 2011). Environmental refers to productive conservation of the waters, the soil, and the ecosystem and reduction of externalities impact on the natural environment and humanity (University of Gävle 2018a).

Green theory logically advocates the use of green policies for the regulation of consumption and production with a view to preserving the ecosystem, safeguarding the rights of the people, ensuing social justice, encouraging responsible citizenship, good governance/democracy and eco-clean environments, among others (Dunne, Kurki & Smith, 2010; Eckersley, 2010). The various green concepts that abound in the literature and policy documents emphasise the need for countries and stakeholders to imbibe sustainable consumption and production with regard to utilisation of earth resources so that future generations would be safeguarded and protected from extreme resource scarcities, existential threats and environmental risks (Henriksen et al., 2012). A new business model that supports the transition to a blue ocean economy is green business model innovation (GBMI), which emphasises the conservation of natural resources and prudent utilisation for economic growth and sustainable development (Danse et al., 2020; Méda & Atewamba, 2020). The GBMI is therefore an operational process that fundamentally changes key parts of the traditional business model for an inclusive integration of economic value (making profit) and ecological value (reduces the ecological footprint from a lifecycle perspective). In addition, the greener the BMI is, the higher the potential for creating radical eco-innovation and sustainable use of resources (Henriksen et al., 2012).

MAIN FOCUS OF THE CHAPTER

Issues, Controversies, Problems of Blue Economy

Undoubtedly, the creation of a blue economy in coastal countries and small island states, as discussed earlier, would accelerate the sustainable use of oceans, seas and their vast resources for economic growth, jobs and improved livelihoods and progression towards the actualisation of SDGs. However, these plethora of benefits are hampered by some surmountable problems and challenges that governments and stakeholders of blue economies should tackle frontally.

The first major challenge to the blue ocean economy is climate change's devastating backlashes in the forms of retreat, migration, loss of lives and property in coastal countries and small island states. The blue economy and emerging economic activities cannot endure the adverse effects of climate change unless the issue is frontally approached. Climate change has increasingly forced islanders and ocean communities to relocate and migrate to other areas to cope with threats to their lives and livelihoods (Gharbaoui & Blocher, 2016). Coastal flooding, violent storms and oceanic waves are major challenges with significant human and economic costs for coastal countries and states along the coastlines around the world. These issues need to be carefully looked at, against the backdrop of the estimation that by 2070, approximately 150 million people and $35,000 billion of assets will be exposed to flood events (Wenhai et al., 2019).

Second, the pervasive issue of settlement of maritime boundary delimitation disputes among coastal countries is another major challenge. Hussain et al. (2017) mentioned Bangladesh's maritime boundary delimitation disputes with Myanmar in 2012 and India in 2014 to exercise sovereign rights to 118,813 sq.

km of waters thereby paving the way for a hitch-free progression toward a blue economy. Several other coastal countries, such as Nigeria and Turkey, have lingering disputes on maritime boundary delimitations.

Third, the blue economy and the ideals of SDGs do not clearly align. This may pose serious operational challenges to coastal countries. Lim et al. (2020) noted that it is difficult and vague to identify the scope and boundaries of the blue economy and UN's SDGs. A literature survey conducted on articles from 1998 to 2018 revealed that the blue economy is strongly associated with SDG 14 (Life Below Water), SDG 15 (Life on Land), SDG 16 (Peace, Justice and Strong Institutions) and SDG 17 (Partnerships for the Goals), but in reality, blue economy stakeholders prefer SDG 3 (Good Health & Well-Being) and SDG 8 (Decent Work & Economic Growth). This lack of clarity extends to the inability to delineate the key stakeholders, their interests and roles in the implementation and harmonisation of both development agendas in coastal countries.

Fourth, the challenge of regional, national and international maritime security and surveillance in a blue ocean economy needs to be critically examined. This is critical and expedient to protect the oceans, the people, economic and industrial activities terrorists, international piracy and illegal wildlife trade, illegal unreported and unregulated (IUU) fishing, illegal logging, and illegal mining (Hussain et al., 2017; United Nations, 2021).

Related to the challenge of security above is the threat of ocean and marine life sustainability. The Food and Agriculture Organisation (FAO) reported that reckless commercialisation of the ocean across the globe has led to overfishing and endangering of some marine species. The incidence of overfishing has exceeded the ideal threshold by approximately 33 percent, while illegal fishing across the world's oceans is estimated at approximately 11 million to 26 million tonnes of fish, valued at $26 billion to $35 billion annually (United Nations, 2021).

SOLUTIONS AND RECOMMENDATIONS

As solutions, this section discusses the prospects/benefits of a blue economy to aid implementation and transition by coastal countries to a blue economy. The inherent benefits of the blue economy are humongous and mind boggling, when fully understood, adopted, and implemented by the government of coastal countries and small island states. Some of the benefits of the blue ocean economy based on insights from the literature systematically discussed below.

First, the blue ocean economy has the prospect of boosting traditional ocean industries such as fisheries, tourism, and maritime transport. For fisheries, a total of 350 million jobs worldwide are linked to the sector. At the same time, the blue economy would accelerate the emergence of new industrial activities such as offshore renewable energy, aquaculture, seabed extractive activities, and marine biotechnology and bioprospecting. Currently, Commonwealth (2021) estimated the global ocean economy to be worth approximately US$1.5 trillion per year.

Related to the above is the creation of a sustainable ocean industrialisation where all economic activities, such as shipping, commercial fishing, and the oil, gas, minerals and mining industries, are conducted in a manner that balances the long-term carrying capacity of ocean ecosystems (The Commonwealth, 2021). The blue ocean economy is also a boost to traditional ocean industries such as fisheries, tourism, and maritime transport. The blue economy is also a goldmine for the exploitation of gas hydrates as energy resources and the extraction of marine genetic resources for biopharmaceutical or industrial uses, including acquiring space for building telecommunications cables (Ramirez-Llodra et al., 2011).

Second, new employment opportunities would spring up in the maritime sector shipping, commercial fishing, oil and gas, minerals and mining industries in coastal countries and small island states with vast ocean resources. The new employment opportunities present a huge opportunity for these countries to tackle the problems of unemployment, unsustainable use of marine resources, food insecurity, poverty and economic growth (The Commonwealth, 2021). In addition, Economist (2015) reiterated that the emergence of blue economy would allow governments of coastal countries to play a notable key role in driving economic growth through their new national ocean development plans that, if well implemented, could turn the ocean into a "new" source of jobs, innovation and competitive advantage.

Third, the blue ocean economy driven by a blue ocean charter would help coastal countries and small island states develop an integrated approach to building a blue economy that values inclusiveness and diversity and inclusion in workplaces by accommodating overlooked sectors and undeserved segments of society, such as artisanal fishing, women and young people (The Commonwealth, 2021).

Fourth, the blue ocean economy would boost access to food and sufficient nutrition by the 'ten billion people' estimated to live on Earth in 2050 (van Ginneken & de Vries, (2016). The Food and Agriculture Organisation [FAO] (2018) noted that approximately 820 million people worldwide suffer from hunger, while every third person is malnourished. To redress the problem of food poverty, sustainable food production that impacts all four pillars of food security – availability, access, utilisation, and stability is recommended. Hopefully, the blue ocean economy could help tackle food poverty through its aquaculture potential. According to Commonwealth (2021b), aquaculture has a strong influence in redressing food and nutrition security, sustainable economic development, marine resource management, and health issues in Commonwealth countries and beyond. Aquatic fish and plants cultivated annually constitute almost half of all global fish consumption. Moreover, the aquaculture sector in 2015 alone produced 76.6 million tonnes of fish valued at US$157.9 billion, 29.4 million tonnes of plants (US$ 4.8 billion) and 41 thousand tonnes of nonfood products such as pearls and shells, valued at US$ 208.2 million. A more coordinated blue ocean economy would generate more aquatic fish and plants to meet the protein needs of the growing population in the world.

Furthermore, adoption of a blue ocean economy is one of the effective and efficient pathways towards the actualisation of the Sustainable Development Goals (SDGs), particularly SDG14, which focuses on 'life below water'. Drift toward actualisation of the SDGs therefore prepossesses that governments and ocean users be concerned about the future health and productivity of the ocean and its vast ocean resources because the ocean constitutes more than 95% of the Earth's living space, hosting more than 220,000 known species and 2 million unknown species of plants and animals.

Overall, a blue economy would provide social and economic benefits for current and future generations by restoring, protecting and maintaining the diversity, productivity, resilience, core functions, and intrinsic value of marine ecosystems through the use of clean technologies, renewable energy, and circular material flows/recycling of materials (World Bank, 2017; World Bank and United Nations Department of Economic and Social Affairs (2017). These benefits would further stimulate the creation of new ocean-oriented services such as carbon sequestration, coastal protection, waste disposal and biodiversity.

Conclusion, Limitations Implications, and Future Research Directions

The chapter sets out to discuss the concept of the blue economy, definitions, measurements, and theories for the purpose of strengthening academic research and industry practice in developed and developing contexts. A critical literature review provided four insights into the blue economy. First, the definition

Figure 2. Prospects/benefits of a blue economy

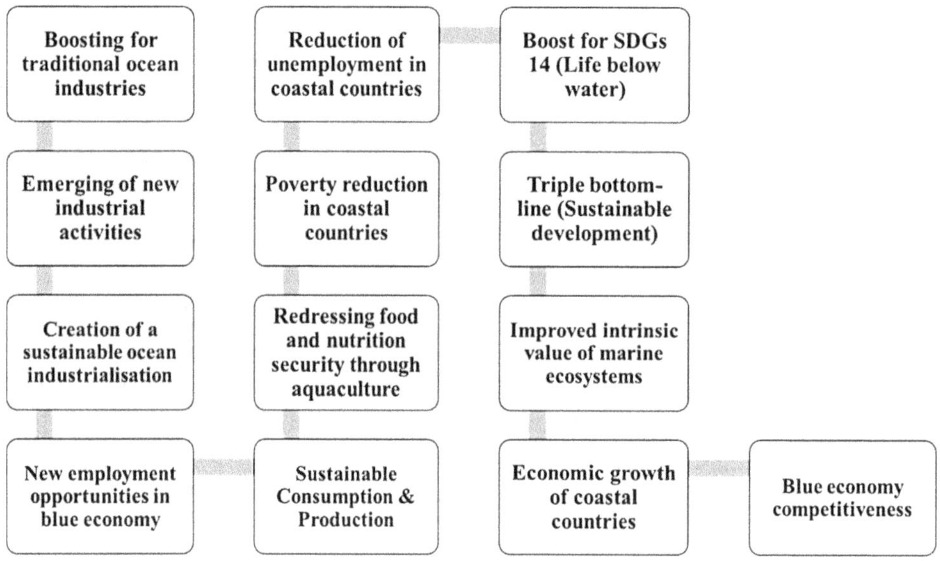

of the blue economy is rooted in the green economy and green theory. Second, the best measurement of the blue economy is the coastal governance index (CGI), with 24 indicators and 43 sub indicators developed by the Economist Intelligence Unit. Third, the prospects of the blue economy include the creation of sustainable ocean industrialisation, emergence of new industrialization and boosts for traditional industries, new employment opportunities, food and nutritional security through aquaculture, boost for SDGs 14-17, and improved economic growth of coastal countries, among others. The challenges of transition to a blue economy include lack of national legislation and protocols on ocean economic activities, threats of overuse of ocean and its resources, sea pollution, ocean security and international conflicts on maritime delineations.

The discourse yielded several policy and research implications that would strengthen academic research and industry practice. First, the policy implication of the discourse is that if policymakers in coastal countries, as a matter of urgency, need to harness oceans and their resources through proper planning and intersectoral coordination by leveraging public–private partnerships for investment and management. This would enable blue economies to build strong economic foundations for generating sustainable incomes to meet the growing socioeconomic needs of their citizens living along the coastlines and small islands. Second, policymakers managing the CGI need to add more countries to the index. Despite several coastal countries and small island states in Africa, only South Africa and Nigeria were recognised, assessed and ranked. Additionally, Brunei Darussalam is a coastal country; it is missing from the list, but some ASEAN countries were recognised. Third, the ideals of the blue economy and SDGs need to be aligned by governments and other stakeholders to avoid working at cross purposes in the blue economy-SDGs context. Furthermore, policymakers and academics need to understand that the transition to a blue economy is not just about market opportunities; it is an inclusive economic paradigm that comes with huge responsibilities. To consolidate the blue economy, policy makers in coastal countries should put in place strong governance and regulatory structures to ensure sustainable consumption and utilisation of blue resources in compliance with climate change action plans. Further conceptual, theoretical and empirical research may explore the effects of ocean piracy, terrorism, and territorial water disputes, including the role of international maritime regulations in curbing interstate competition on the sea and industrial pollution of the oceans.

REFERENCES

Bargh, M. (2014). A blue economy for Aotearoa New Zealand? *Environment, Development and Sustainability*, *16*(3), 459–470. doi:10.100710668-013-9487-4

Bari, A. (2017). Our oceans and the blue economy: Opportunities and challenges. *Procedia Engineering*, *194*, 5–11. doi:10.1016/j.proeng.2017.08.109

Bello-Bravo, J., & Lutomia, A. N. (2020). Supporting Sustainability for a Decent Work and Economic Growth in Ghana. In Decent Work and Economic Growth, Encyclopedia of the UN Sustainable Development Goals. Springer Nature Switzerland. doi:10.1007/978-3-319-71058-7_120-1

Bogdan, A., Istudor, N., Gruia, R., Tobă, G. F., Bulz, N., Gâf-Deac, I., Chelmu, S., Găvan, C., Prică, I., & Paşalău, C. (2014). New holistic approach of bioeconomics and ecoeconomics theories, practical bridging from the green economy to blue economy, trough new integrated and innovative paradigm about "bioeco-geo-economy". *Procedia Economics and Finance*, *8*, 83–90. doi:10.1016/S2212-5671(14)00066-5

Conger, T., & Chang, S. E. (2019). Developing indicators to identify coastal green infrastructure potential: The case of the Salish Sea region. *Ocean and Coastal Management*, *175*, 53–69. doi:10.1016/j.ocecoaman.2019.03.011

Costanza, R. (1999). The ecological, economic, and social importance of the oceans. *Ecological Economics*, *31*(2), 199–213. doi:10.1016/S0921-8009(99)00079-8

Crane, B., Albrecht, C., Duffin, K. M., & Albrecht, C. (2018). China's special economic zones: An analysis of policy to reduce regional disparities. *Regional Studies, Regional Science*, *5*(1), 98–107. doi:10.1080/21681376.2018.1430612

Denscombe, M. (2017). *EBOOK: The Good Research Guide: For Small-Scale Social Research Projects.* McGraw-Hill Education.

Dunne, T., Kurki, M., & Smith, S. (Eds.). (2010). *International Relations Theories: Discipline and Diversity* (2nd ed.). Oxford University Press.

Eckersley, R. (2010). Green Theory. In International Relations Theories Disciplines and Diversity (2nd ed.). New York: Oxford University Press.

European Commission. (2012, August). *Blue Growth Study - Scenarios and drivers for Sustainable Growth from the Oceans, Seas and Coasts*. European Commission, DG MARE. https://webgate.ec.europa.eu/maritimeforum/system/files/Blue%20Growth%20Final%20Report%2013092012.pdf

Food and Agriculture Organisation, International Fund for Agricultural Development, United Nations International Children's Emergency Fund, World Food Program, & World Health Organisation. (2018). The State of Food Security and Nutrition in the World 2018. Building Climate Resilience for Food Security and Nutrition. Rome: FAO.

Gharbaoui, D., & Blocher, J. (2016). The reason land matters: Relocation as adaptation to climate change in Fiji Islands. In *Migration, risk management and climate change: Evidence and policy responses* (pp. 149–173). Springer. doi:10.1007/978-3-319-42922-9_8

Glasson, J., & Wood, G. (2009). Urban regeneration and impact assessment for social sustainability. *Impact Assessment and Project Appraisal, 27*(4), 283–290. doi:10.3152/146155109X480358

Golden, J. S., Virdin, J., Nowacek, D., Halpin, P., Bennear, L., & Patil, P. G. (2017). Making sure the blue economy is green. *Nature Ecology & Evolution, 1*(2), 1–3. doi:10.103841559-016-0017 PMID:28812613

Green Economy Coalition. (2021, June). *The 5 Principles of Green Economy*. https://www.greeneconomycoalition.org/news-and-resources/the-5-principles-of-green-economy

Hagbert, P., & Bradley, K. (2017). Transitions on the home front: A story of sustainable living beyond eco-efficiency. *Energy Research & Social Science, 31*, 240–248. doi:10.1016/j.erss.2017.05.002

Henriksen, K., Bjerre, M., Maria Almasi, A., & Damgaard-Grann, E. (2012). *Green Business Model Innovation-Conceptualisation report. Nordic Council of Ministers.* Nordic Innovation Publication.

Hussain, M. G., Failler, P., Al Karim, A., & Alam, M. K. (2017). Review on opportunities, constraints and challenges of blue economy development in Bangladesh. *Journal of Fisheries and Life Sciences, 2*(1), 45–57.

Irazábal, C. (2018). Coastal urban planning in the 'Green Republic': Tourism development and the nature–infrastructure paradox in Costa Rica. *International Journal of Urban and Regional Research, 42*(5), 882–913. doi:10.1111/1468-2427.12654

Kahle, L. R., & Gurel-Atay, E. (Eds.). (2014). *Communicating Sustainability for the Green Economy*. M.E. Sharpe.

Karlsson, M., Trygg, L., & Elfström, B. O. (2004). Measuring R&D productivity: Complementing the picture by focusing on research activities. *Technovation, 24*(3), 179–186. doi:10.1016/S0166-4972(03)00111-1

Khan, T. M., Bai, G., Fareed, Z., Quresh, S., Khalid, Z., & Khan, W. A. (2020). CEO Tenure, CEO Compensation, Corporate Social & Environmental Performance in China. The Moderating Role of Coastal and Non-Coastal Areas. *Frontiers in Psychology, 11*, 3815. PMID:33551900

Lee, K. H., Noh, J., & Khim, J. S. (2020). The Blue Economy and the United Nations' sustainable development goals: Challenges and opportunities. *Environment International, 137*, 105528. doi:10.1016/j.envint.2020.105528 PMID:32014791

Michael, Y. M. A. K., & Peacock, C. J. (2011, January). Social sustainability: A comparison of case studies in UK, USA and Australia. In *17th Pacific Rim Real Estate Society Conference, Gold Coast* (pp. 16-19). Academic Press.

Mohammad, M. T. S. H. (2010). Principles of sustainable development in Ibn Khaldun's economic thought. *Malaysian Journal of Real Estate, 5*(1), 1–18.

OECD. (2011, May). *Towards green growth A summary for policy makers*. Brochure of OECD Meeting of the Council at Ministerial Level, Paris, France. https://www.oecd.org/greengrowth/48012345.pdf

Okafor-Yarwood, I., Kadagi, N. I., Belhabib, D., & Allison, E. H. (2022). Survival of the Richest, not the Fittest: How attempts to improve governance impact African small-scale marine fisheries. *Marine Policy*, *135*, 104847. doi:10.1016/j.marpol.2021.104847

Pauli, G. A. (2010). *The blue economy: 10 years, 100 innovations, 100 million jobs*. Paradigm publications.

Priven, V., Sacks, R., Seppänen, O., & Savosnick, J. (2014, June). A lean workflow index for construction projects. In *22nd Annual Conference of the International Group for Lean Construction: Understanding and Improving Project Based Production, IGLC 2014* (pp. 715-726). Academic Press.

Raimi, L., Olowo, R., & Shokunbi, M. (2021). A comparative discourse of sustainable finance options for agribusiness transformation in Nigeria and Brunei: Implications for entrepreneurship and enterprise development. *World Journal of Science, Technology and Sustainable Development*, *18*(4), 325–350. doi:10.1108/WJSTSD-05-2021-0051

Sareen, S., & Haarstad, H. (2018). Bridging sociotechnical and justice aspects of sustainable energy transitions. *Applied Energy*, *228*, 624–632. doi:10.1016/j.apenergy.2018.06.104

Saunders, M., Lewis, P., & Thornhill, A. (2016). *Research Methods for Business Students* (7th ed.). Pearson Education.

Scherer, M. E., & Asmus, M. L. (2021). Modeling to evaluate coastal governance in Brazil. *Marine Policy*, *129*, 104501. doi:10.1016/j.marpol.2021.104501

Silver, J. J., Gray, N. J., Campbell, L. M., Fairbanks, L. W., & Gruby, R. L. (2015). Blue economy and competing discourses in international oceans governance. *Journal of Environment & Development*, *24*(2), 135–160. doi:10.1177/1070496515580797

Smith-Godfrey, S. (2016). Defining the blue economy. *Maritime Affairs: Journal of the National Maritime Foundation of India, 12*(1), 58-64.

The Commonwealth. (2021a). *Blue economy*. Commonwealth Secretariat. https://thecommonwealth.org/blue-economy

The Commonwealth. (2021b). *Aquaculture*. Commonwealth Secretariat https://thecommonwealth.org/aquaculture

The Economist. (2015a). *Coastal Governance Index 2015*. An index and study by The Economist Intelligence Unit. https://www.oceanprosperityroadmap.org/wp-content/uploads/2015/05/EIU_CGIndex_WEB-revised-June-4.pdf

The Economist. (2015b). *The Blue Economy: Growth, Opportunity and a Sustainable Ocean Economy*. https://www.oceanprosperityroadmap.org/wp-content/uploads/2015/05/2.-State-of-the-Blue-Economy_briefing-paper_WOS2015.pdf

The Economist. (2019). *Coastal Governance Index 2019*. An index and study by The Economist Intelligence Unit. https://www.oceanprosperityroadmap.org/wp-content/uploads/2015/05/EIU_CGIndex_WEB-revised-June-4.pdf

United Nations. (2021). *Illegal wildlife trade/fishing/logging/mining. Interagency task form on financing for development.* https://developmentfinance.un.org/illegal-wildlife-tradefishingloggingmining

United Nations Environment Programme. (2016). *Green Economy – Towards Greener and more inlusibe economies.* https://www.unepfi.org/fileadmin/documents/greeneconomy_flyer.pdf

United Nations Environment Programme. (2021). *Green Economy.* https://www.unep.org/explore-topics/green-economy

University of Gävle. (2018a). *Ecological sustainability.* https://www.hig.se/Ext/En/University-of-Gavle/About-the-University/Environmental-Work/What-is-sustainable-development-at-HiG/Ecological-sustainability.html

University of Gävle. (2018b). *Economic sustainability.* https://www.hig.se/Ext/En/University-of-Gavle/About-the-University/Environmental-Work/What-is-sustainable-development-at-HiG/Economic-sustainability.html

van Ginneken, V., & de Vries, E. (2016). Towards a Seaweed Based Economy": The Global Ten Billion People Issue at the Midst of the 21st Century. *Journal of FisheriesSciences.Com, 10*(2), 1–11.

Wenhai, L., Cusack, C., Baker, M., Tao, W., Mingbao, C., Paige, K., Xiaofan, Z., Levin, L., Escobar, E., Amon, D., Yue, Y., Reitz, A., Neves, A. A. S., O'Rourke, E., Mannarini, G., Pearlman, J., Tinker, J., Horsburgh, K. J., Lehodey, P., ... Yufeng, Y. (2019). Successful blue economy examples with an emphasis on international perspectives. *Frontiers in Marine Science, 6*, 261. doi:10.3389/fmars.2019.00261

Williams, T. A., & Shepherd, D. A. (2017). Mixed method social network analysis: Combining inductive concept development, content analysis, and secondary data for quantitative analysis. *Organizational Research Methods, 20*(2), 268–298. doi:10.1177/1094428115610807

World Bank. (2017, July). *What is the Blue Economy?* The World Bank. https://www.worldbank.org/en/news/infographic/2017/06/06/blue-economy

World Bank and United Nations Department of Economic and Social Affairs. (2017). *The Potential of the Blue Economy: Increasing Long-term Benefits of the Sustainable Use of Marine Resources for Small Island Developing States and Coastal Least Developed Countries.* World Bank.

World Economic Forum. (2017). *83 countries are more ocean than land.* https://www.weforum.org/agenda/2017/10/global-ocean-governance-all-at-sea/

World Ocean Initiative. (2018). *Economist Intelligence Unit reveals leaders and laggards on coastal governance.* The Economist Newspaper Limited. https://ocean.economist.com/governance/articles/economist-intelligence-unit-reveals-leaders-and-laggards-on-coastal-governance

Zhao, Q., Zhu, Z., Zeng, H., Zhao, W., & Myneni, R. B. (2020). Future greening of the Earth may not be as large as previously predicted. *Agricultural and Forest Meteorology, 292*, 108111. doi:10.1016/j.agrformet.2020.108111

KEY TERMS AND DEFINITIONS

Academic Research: This describes the scientific and structured approach of conducting research. The academic research cycle consists of problem identification, defining objectives, formulation of hypotheses, data gathering, data analysis and testing hypotheses, and reporting of findings.

Blue Economy: This describes an ocean-oriented economy that seeks to conserve and safeguard oceans and water resources for sustainable development.

Developed Countries: These are high-income countries with well-developed industrial bases and infrastructural facilities, enabling an environment for businesses and a high human capital index including strong governmental institutions.

Developing Countries: These are low-income countries with high reliance on natural resources, a weak industrial base, poor infrastructural facilities, a lack of an enabling environment for businesses and a low human capital index, including weak governmental institutions.

Emerging Economies: These are developing countries that progressively manifest some characteristics of developed countries but have not fully meet the standards. They attained this enviable status because of engagement with global markets and steady transition from natural resource-driven economies to becoming newly industrialized countries.

Green Economy: This describes an economy that aims at balancing economic prosperity with a reduction in environmental risks and ecological scarcities on the basis of six sustainability pillars, namely, climate change, resource savings and management, a circular economy, environmental protection, ecosystem protection and recovery, water conservation, and natural disaster prevention.

Industry Practice: This refers to the norms of the world of work, including the rules and ethics of the workplace. The way jobs and tasks are carried out in corporate organisations.

Measurement: This refers to the process of evaluating, comparing, assessing, and determining the size, quality and magnitude of a concrete item or a phenomenon based on standard criteria and quantification of attributes.

Sustainable Development: This describes an inclusive development paradigm that addresses the economic, social, and environmental needs of the present generation without endangering or compromising those of the upcoming generations.

Theory: This refers to a tested proposition or statement of fact that enables a phenomenon to be described, explained, predicted, and/or controlled in research.

Chapter 2
Opportunities and Challenges of Enterprise Development in the Blue Economy:
A Developing Economy Perspective

Saheed Adebowale Nurein
https://orcid.org/0000-0002-9828-4923
American University of Nigeria, Nigeria

ABSTRACT

There has been rapid expansion on the blue economy activities driven by the increase in the global population, technology, climate change, trade, and economic growth. However, developing economies such as Nigeria are still struggling with identifying the untapped opportunities and curbing the existing threats and challenges to achieve a sustainable blue economy. The attention of this review focuses on highlighting the opportunities and challenges of enterprise development in a BE, specifically in the context of a developing economy such as Nigeria. The aim of this review is to create more awareness on the opportunities and challenges facing enterprise development in BE in a developing economy and proffer basis for further research. This study recommends that Nigeria government should focus on creating home-grown innovation and improve governance in the economy to address the challenges crippling its BE to create and achieve a sustainable enterprise development.

INTRODUCTION

Though, the notion "Blue Economy" (BE) which is also known as blue growth, the ocean economy or the marine economy originated during the 1992 Earth Summit in Rio but gained momentum two decades later at the 'Rio+20 United Nations Conference on Sustainable Development' in 2012. Since then, numerous governmental bodies, non-governmental organizations (NGOs), international institutions, and multinational companies have move into the BE space as they see it as a model that will bring sustainable growth through the creation of innovative economic opportunities, alleviation of poverty,

DOI: 10.4018/978-1-6684-3393-5.ch002

Table 1. Established and Emerging Blue Economy Activities Globally

ESTABLISHED	EMERGING
1. Fisheries 2. Ports 3. Shipping 4. Seafood processing 5. Offshore oil and gas 6. Shipbuilding and repair 7. Marine manufacturing and construction 8. Marine business services 9. Maritime and coastal tourism 10. Dredging 11. Education and research & development on marine	1. Marine aquaculture 2. Offshore wind energy 3. Deep and ultra-deepwater oil and gas 4. Marine and seabed mining 5. Ocean renewable energy 6. Marine biotechnology 7. Maritime safety and surveillance 8. Sophisticated technical marine products and services

Source: Attri (2016).

improvement of sustainable livelihoods and food security, as well as serving as a tool to improve other Sustainable Development Goals (SDGs) (Keen et al., 2017; Purvis, 2015; Lee et al., 2020; Voyer et al., 2018a). Specifically, the earliest adopters of the BE concept are the Least Developed economies and the Small Island Developing economies because they view their huge ocean influences as new source of economic opportunities (Purvis, 2015; Keen et al., 2017). The European Union also viewed the BE as an integral part of its economic growth since the 2012 European Union's Blue Growth Agenda (Eikeset et al., 2018). Moreover, the African Union also referenced the BE concept in its 2014 Agenda 2063, which serves as the main framework for their policies to transform the continent's socio-economic development (Pretorius & Henwood, 2019). Thus, the BE is of great importance in this current situation where there is resource constrained globally and the threat climate ecosystem.

The BE encompasses all economic activities that directly depend on the natural resources from the ocean. These economic activities are categorized into ocean-based activities and ocean related activities. Meanwhile, ocean-based activities comprise of activities carried out in the marine, which include shipping and marine transportation, fisheries and aquaculture, seabed mining, marine tourism, offshore oil and gas, marine construction, and offshore energy wind-farms; while ocean related activities comprise of activities that make use of the produces from the ocean (e.g., marine chemicals and biotechnology, seafood processing), as well as produced products and services used for ocean-based activities (e.g., port construction, shipbuilding and repair, maritime law, maritime insurance, and communication, (UNDP, 2018). Moreover, there have been rapid expansion on the ocean economics activities driven by the increase in the global population, technology, climate change, trade, and economic growth (Attri, 2016). Also, it has been projected that by 2030 numerous ocean-based businesses have the prospect of out-performing the global economy growth based on value-added and employment, and where the contribution of the BE to the global economy could have been over three trillion United States Dollar (Attri, 2016). The sturdy BE growth is specifically projected in seafood processing, port activities, shipbuilding and repairs, offshore energy, and marine aquaculture.

There are established and emerging BE activities in most countries globally. These are listed in the table below.

However, despite the upsurge interest, there is no consensus on the best definition for BE and no relatively little tangible guidance on how to achieve it (Bennett et al., 2019; Mulazzani & Malorgio, 2017). While the Food and Agriculture Organization of the United Nations (FAO, 2016) views BE "as a cohesive approach for environmentally compatible, integrated and socioeconomically sensitive management of aquatic resources including marine, freshwater, and brackish water environments" (Moffitt & Cajas-Cano, 2014), the World Bank defines the BE as the "sustainable use of ocean resources for economic growth, improved livelihoods, and jobs while preserving the health of ocean ecosystem" (World Bank, 2017). The European Union view it as "all economic activities related to oceans, seas and coasts" (Eikeset et al., 2018) and as "the long term strategy to support sustainable growth in the marine and maritime sectors as a whole." (Arbow, 2019; Hadjimichael, 2018). The African Union view the BE as "sustainable economic development of oceans using such technics as regional development to integrate the use of seas and oceans, coasts, lakes, rivers and underground water for economic purposes, including, but without being limited to fisheries, mining, energy, aquaculture and maritime transport, while protecting the sea to improve social well-being" (Africa Blue Economy Strategy, 2019). Thus, outside the seeming linking of BE initiatives to ocean-based activities and resources, no consensus yet built on its vision and parameters which has resulted in a disjointed efforts and varying degrees of cohesiveness with the initial concept or with each other (Eikeset et al., 2018; Silver et al., 2015; Voyer et al., 2018). This is because for some interested parties their focus is on sustainability of the BE, while others is about using the blue Economy to maximize economic growth (Bennett et al., 2019; Eikeset et al., 2018; Mulazzani & Malorgio, 2017).

BACKGROUND

Africa is one of the parties that embraced the BE concept and adopt its narrative towards maximizing the economic growth of the continent. The governments of African countries are gradually effecting an ocean-based economy as a way to generate economic growth through improving social welfare and equity, as well as reducing ecological and environmental challenges on the continent (Pretorius & Henwood, 2019). Out of the fifty-four countries in Africa, thirty-eight of them are coastline and under maritime zones in African jurisdiction (AMCEN, 2019). Moreover, with the lake zones covering 240,000 sq. km, approximately, and the transboundary river basins covering sixty-four percent of the continent's land area, Africa is heavily rich in both living and non-living natural resources which include water, wildlife, fish, flora and fauna, hydrocarbons and minerals (Pichon, 2019). African countries transport ninety percent of their imports and exports through water, which stresses the better geographical opportunity for African countries to improve their regional and international trade (Africa Blue Economy Strategy, 2019). The BE of Africa is estimated to generate US$ 4 trillion annually, which can be compare to the GDP of all East Asian countries. However, despite the existence of the blue economy and enormous natural resources that creates enough openings for diversification of economies in Africa (Pichon, 2019), the continent is still afflicted with poverty, as forty-six percent of its population still lives in extreme poverty (Nagy & Nene, 2021). This high poverty rate increases the susceptibility to environmental degradation and climate change in the continent (United Nations, 2016). The human health and welfare have been deteriorated by the protracted human-made dilapidation of ocean and aquatic resources, and this has affected the majority of the population in Africa as it is responsible for twenty-eight percent of its disease burden (Voyer et al., 2018a).

Africa has revealed a wider awareness of its significance globally due to its direction towards adopting BE approaches (Nagy & Nene, 2021), which has created room to establish regional, bilateral, and international partnerships and cooperation (United Nations, 2016). Though, there is need for Africa to map out its own pathway and coordinate policy that will identify, define, and understand what will be of progress and prosperity for its continent, with the aim of inspiring innovative ideas and practices that will improve ecological and human development (Roy, 2019). While achieving this in line with the AU Agenda 2063, Africa has the opportunity to create a BE narrative that fit in to the continent's societal needs, co-operations, and development goals which are imperative in moving forward in the 21st century.

The attention of this review focuses on highlighting the opportunities and challenges of enterprise development in a BE, specifically, in the context of a developing economy such as Nigeria. This enterprise development lies with the opportunities and challenges of creating businesses, attracting investment, investing knowledge and time, building business connections, and creating employment in Nigeria's BE. The aim of this review is to create more awareness on the opportunities and challenges facing enterprise development in BE in a developing economy and proffer basis for further research. The remaining part of this review focus on the overview, opportunities, and challenges of BE in Nigeria, discussion as well as the conclusion that proffer suggestions to improve enterprise development in BE in developing economy, such as Nigeria.

LITERATURE REVIEW

Overview of the Nigeria Blue Economy

The coastline of Nigeria is about 420 nautical miles (approximately 778 km) which borders the Atlantic Ocean in the Gulf of Guinea. (Fairbridge, 2004; Finkl, 2004; Nwilo & Badejo, 2006). Nigeria also has an exclusive economic zone (EEZ) of 200 nautical miles (370 km) which deciphers to a maritime area of 84,000 square nautical miles (288112 km^2), with an important and diversifying marine natural resources (Hamisu, 2019). In addition, the coastline and coastal zone of Nigeria is perhaps the most heavily populated and one of the most significant economic axis in Africa (Sexton & Murday, 1994). The coastline area is categorized into two coastline geographical zones which include the western coast and the eastern coast (Danladi et al., 2017). The Nigeria coastal length is divided into five distinct morphological regions which include Strand Coast, Arcuate Delta, Western and Eastern Delta Flanks, Barrier Lagoon Coast, and Transgressive Mud Coast (Fairbridge, 2004; Finkl, 2004). Out of the thirty-six states in Nigeria, nine of the states are coastaline states which include Edo, Akwa Ibom, Rivers, Cross River, Bayelsa, Delta, Ogun Ondo and Lagos. The total population of these States is about fifty million, which is proportion of twenty-five (25%) of the total population of Nigeria (Omole & Isiorho, 2011).

Opportunities for Enterprise Development in Nigeria's Blue Economy

Despite that the highest percentage of Nigeria's economic activities rely or are derived from the ocean resources, Nigeria's BE capabilities are yet to be fully harnessed. Specifically, maritime transport for trade took the largest share of the ocean activities in Nigeria as over ninety-five percent (95%) of its trade by volume as well as over seventy percent (70%) of its value are transported through ships and controlled by seaports and the offshore oil and gas (NIMASA, 2018). The Nigerian BE has been imperative and beneficial significantly to the country's whole economy through exploiting, distributing and exporting the country's ocean natural resources. As estimates of $6 billion and $8 billion are contributed annually

Table 2. Blue Economy activities in Nigeria

S/N	CATEGORY	ESTABLISHED	EMERGING
1.	**Commerce and trade**	**Shipping;** International shipping and its associates are essential to the Nigerian economy in which 95 percent of the country's imports are by the sea. **Ports;** Nigerian economy benefits from a variety of commercial facilities which are cargo handling, bunkering, warehousing, technical services, cargo discharge, marine security, handling and stevedoring and inter-island terminal and quays. Demand for processing and transshipment facilities as well as fuel supplies and its associated commodities.	
2.	**Food, Nutrition, and Health**	**Fishing;** The fishing sector is critical for both the generation of national income and fish products, leading from fishing activities to revenue generation and food security.	**Aquaculture;** The demand for fish globally is anticipated to efflux in the years coming, the majority of it would emerge from aquaculture in which many of that production capacity took place in the ocean. **Mariculture;** Virtually mariculture is not practicalizing (is not taking place) in Nigeria, but now the country is developing an interest in it. **Biotechnology;** This is harvesting the marine natural resources, processing and developing new pharmaceutical drugs, chemical products, enzymes, and other industrial products and processes.
3.	**Energy and Raw materials**	**Marine minerals;** The mainly marine mineral resources activities which contribute tremendously to the Nigerian blue economy is offshore oil and deposits	**Marine renewable energy;** There are great possibilities for the development and existence of offshore wind farms and wave, and Ocean Thermal Energy Conversion (OTEC) in Nigeria within the near future.

Source: Nigeria's Maritime Industry Forecast 2018 - 2019 (NIMASA, 2018).

by the maritime freight and offshore oil and gas, respectively, to the overall economy; fishing activities also contribute $1 billion annually to the overall economy (NIMASA, 2018).

The BE activities in Nigeria are also classified into established activities and emerging activities. The activities which include marine minerals, ports, fishing and shipping, fishing are regarded as established activities, while biotechnology, aquaculture, marine renewable energy and mariculture are regarded as emerging activities (NIMASA, 2018). These activities are fully described in the Table 2 below.

Threats and Challenges to Enterprise Development in Nigeria's Blue Economy

Threats

1. Piracy and Armed Robbery

The high rates of piracy and armed robbery incidents in the Gulf of Guinea (where Nigeria coastline lies) has become an increasing worry in the maritime industry and seriously threatening the activities of

BE in this part of the world (NIMASA, 2018). These incidents have caused substantial effects in the BE sectors through hindering the growth and unsettling businesses in the maritime industry. African states lack sufficient infrastructure and capabilities to guarantee coastal protection and maritime security, in which both are crucial for a creation of a sustainable BE (Rustomjee, 2018).

2. Illegal, Unreported and Unregulated (IUU) fishing

Illegal, Unreported and Unregulated (IUU) fishing (in which one-fifth of the global fisheries captured is estimated to have been derived from) is another greatest threat disturbing BE activities globally (Rustomjee, 2018). Cases of IUU fishing is common in the coastline of Africa and specifically on the Africa's western coast, in which Nigeria's coastline lies (Rustomjee, 2018). Countries (including Nigeria) in the western region loses $1.3 billion per annum to the IUU fishing, especially the unlicensed foreign industrial vessels operating and causing malicious human economic and social effects in the region (Hamisu, 2019; Rustomjee, 2016).

3. Eutrophication

Eutrophication which is caused through amassing of nutrients and moves to the sea from sewage discharge, agricultural erosion and industrial waste water is another threat to BE activities. Eutrophication produce algae bloom that change the seawater's turbidity and decrease the force of the light moving into the deeper layers of the water, while triggering permanent and temporary harms to the ocean natural resources, and consequently having effect on the activities of the BE.

4. Climate Change

Effects of climate change have also threatened the activities of the BE due to the incessant proliferation of atmospheric carbon emissions that caused substantial ocean warming. Increasing ocean temperature is typical to Nigeria setting, however, this can cause stratification, changes in the ocean's physical properties, changes in the sea currents and rise in sea-level, which then generate increasing effects on the ocean resources (Kadafa, 2012; Visbeck et al., 2014).

5. Anthropogenic Factors

The anthropogenic factors which include unmaintainable exploitation of resources, land-based sources and marine operations pollution, as well as obliteration and alteration of the marine and coastal habitats which is caused by invasive species and coastline development activities are the most extreme in threatening BE activities in Nigeria (Ibrahim, 2018).

6. Oil Spillage

Oil spillage due to oil industries activities, which causes an undesirable effect to the marine environment of the oil producing areas through destruction of their ecosystem is one of the major threats affecting activities of BE in Nigeria (Kadafa, 2012).

Challenges

The challenges hindering a sustainable BE in Nigeria evolves round six main strategic problems that relate to the following:

1. Political

The Nigeria's BE has been a fragile concept due to the absence of all-inclusive political consensus on the nature of the country's fiscal federalism. There have been problem and a long-drawn conflict over who controls revenue of inland waterways since two decades ago, which implies the inherent of conflict between the state governments and federal government over control of resources. The inability for coastal states to control their coastline and natural water resources has led to ineffective management of Nigeria's waterways primarily situated in the South South, South East and South West of the country.

2. Economic

Port activities in Nigeria has decreased due to the high cost of Nigerian ports which is costlier than that of neighbouring countries such as Tema Port in Ghana or Port Novo in Benin Republic. This has decreased the potential tax revenues from the ports and reduced the potential employment that could be created in a more effective and less expensive administrative setting. The high implicit and explicit cost of making use of Nigeria ports is stifling the growth of maritime activities and holding down the development of Nigerian BE. The evidence of shrink in port patronage is depicted from the decrease in ships that moored in Nigeria between the period 2012 to 2017. While numbers of service boat fell from 21,726 vessels as of 2012 to 12,243 in 2017, which shows 271% in reduction; amount of ocean going ships drop from 6,369 in 2013 to 4,175 in 2017, indicating 52.6% fall (Nigeria Bureau of Statistics, 2018).

3. Social

Maritime business in Nigeria has been a perilous entrepreneurial activity due to the high incidence of drug peddling, human trafficking, smuggling, and piracy. Many port securities officials have allowed illegal activities rankle because for fear of their lives, and while also taking a pre-arranged share of the proceeds. The high existence or effect of wharf gangs have given room for an inverse ecosystem in the marine industry which is socially hazardous involving drugs, illegal guns, gambling and prostitution. Thus, lack of communal productivity, and the problems of education, entrepreneurship reward and social aspiration has been worsened by the deprived social circumstances of maritime communities.

4. Technology

Adoption of technology has been an imperative feature of the developing BE, as using machines is a compelling requirement to eradicate the evident of multi-point human interface corruption that transpires in shipping operations. Port turnaround time and corruption level caused by high levels of human discretion have improved through digitalizing standard operating procedures (SOPs) and applying electronic monitoring and inspection technology. Though, inefficient, mismanagement and corruption are still paramount in Nigeria ports due to inadequate application of technology in ship processing. Also, a survey conducted (through Maritime Anti-Corruption Network (MACN) and Convention on Business Integrity (CBi)) showed that despite the knowledge of the SOPs in the port activities, most ports users basically avoided them to create opportunities for arranged expedition in the port processing. This lean towards preferring human arrangement that gives room for operational opacity as a tradeoff for lucidity which may be reasonably cheaper based on timely delivery and service quality.

5. Environment

The environment of Nigeria ports is in poor condition and cultivates weak moral culture and obdurate hygiene. There is lack of maintenance of port infrastructures and high pollution of marine shorelines through industrial contamination and as well as waste products usually dumped inside the dock waters by refuse disposal vendors and port users. These have created difficulties for environmental sustainability.

6. Legal

Though Nigeria have a comprehensive and strong laws and procedures guiding its maritime services, but have issue with its enforcement. Most disciplinary sanctions and encouraging incentives which could have inspired healthier port behavior have not been effective, primarily because the economic rewards of violating SOPs is find more fascinating by port officials than given sanctions for violations.

DISCUSSION AND RECOMMENDATION

From the highlighted opportunities, threats and challenges, it can be deduced that Nigeria needs comprehensive and holistic approaches to harness these opportunities and curb the threats and challenges affecting enterprise development in its BE. One of the major holistic approaches is for the Nigeria government to improve in the governance of its BE to mitigate and manage the concerns of failing or potential businesses in the BE. To an extent, an effective ocean governance will unbridle the full capabilities of the oceans towards achieving its desired goals in a sustainable BE. Thus, there is need for the Nigeria government to improve the ocean governance framework which will guide the path towards attaining an effective enterprise development in its BE and achieve best practice that can be emulate by other countries.

The proposed BE framework adapted from the United Nations Economic Commission for Africa report (UNECA, 2016), shown below in Figure 1 illustrates the tools, concepts, and pillars of the BE; and also depicts the established opportunities when a holistic, inclusive and intersectoral-linked development spaces are created by the system; where governance or transparency, social equity and environmental sustainability are equally vital as economic growth in measuring development (United Nations, 2016). Nigeria government need to adopt this BE framework because it promotes an inclusive, systemic, integrated, participatory, ecosystem-based and dynamic approach which reduces sectorial barriers at the governance and activity level, while economic, environmental and social factors are included and attained in all BE activities. This will also promote enterprise development and increase employment opportunities in Nigeria's BE since effective innovation to achieve sustainable economic system depends on actively engaging different stakeholders in numerous sectors and in all levels of the society.

Also, to prioritize the use of ocean resources in BE, numerous options on transformative innovation policy need to be explore by the government, which is imperative in accomplishing any transformation

Figure 1. Blue Economy Framework (adapted from UNECA, 2016)

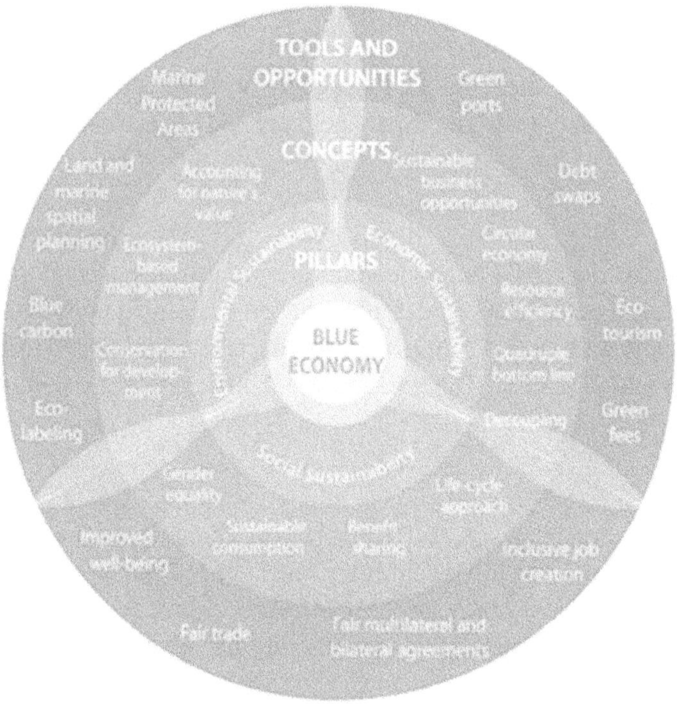

level and sustainability development (Fartash et al., 2008; Kemp et al., 1998). The innovation policy should focus on improving research development and create national systems of innovation that will lead to green development where the government can capitalize on clean technology to regulate the climate change, reduce pollutions, as well as clean up the environment. In addition, these policies will also lessen inequalities by creating employment opportunities and improve enterprise development as a result of growth and income distributional measures (Fagerberg, 2018; Wenhai et al., 2019).

Moreover, there are other possible drastic measures that can be taken to specifically curb the challenges hindering a sustainable BE in Nigeria. First, there is need to revisit Nigeria's fiscal arrangement so as to provide the states greater autonomy on their domestic marine resources, which would then facilitate the generation of private capital investments required by coastal states to enhance the quality of marine ecosystems and develop the local BE in sustainable ways. Though, providing more fiscal autonomy to coastal states might seems radical, however, to attain greater and rapid growth in the BE, it is essential to decentralize its policies and regulations and encourage private sector engagement, which will lead to stronger localization of economics activities, better privatization of infrastructure, and improve enterprise development. Second, it is imperative to improve the physical state of communities around the ports may be by compelling port operators to donate to a community trust fund through a community charge on port activities. Also, sustainability programmes should be initiated in the port, which would involve support for clear waters and clean port communities. Third, increase the use of technology in the port to lessen human intervention by circulating SOPs to captains and crew of berthing ships through their emails, using many point CCTV cameras to surveil personnel and cargo, daily update of the digital register of all port officials, and using cargo scanners as first line method of inspection before human intervention.

CONCLUSION

This review has highlighted the opportunities, threats and challenges which hindered enterprise development in Nigeria's BE and proffer possible way out for a sustainable BE. The aim of this review is to create more awareness on the opportunities and challenges facing enterprise development in BE in a developing economy and proffer basis for further research. From this review, it can be deduced that Nigeria's BE can generate larger revenues far better than it does now, assist the country significantly in diversifying the economy and improve enterprise development if there is a thorough description of the maritime economic activities. Moreover, there is also need to create coastal maritime activity budget lines at state and federal levels; make use of a single central database to record all activities under the BE; and bring some marine activities into a comprehensive national plan which will detail the required set of activities to attain clear goals. These activities include waterway management and waste management, coastal state beachside revenue generation, marine transportation, fishing and hydro-energy generation.

Furthermore, emphasis on how policy and informal institutions can be used to regulate human behaviour and improve enterprise development in BE required further research. Such studies need to explore empirical dimensions to improve implementation of people-centered and environmental policies that focused on the existing BE practices.

In conclusion, the threats and challenges of BE outlined in this review as affect businesses and people every day and hindered enterprise development in Nigeria, this stress the need for researchers and policymakers to develop innovative frameworks while pursuing experimentation using different policy practices. Thus, it is suggested that Nigeria government should focused on creating innovation locally and improve governance in the economy to address the challenges crippling its BE to create and achieve a sustainable enterprise development. As this study create more awareness on the opportunities and challenges facing enterprise development in BE in a developing economy, further research can empirically examine the critical success factors of enterprises in BE so as to proffer solution to the challenges hindering the performance of these enterprises in the BE.

REFERENCES

Africa Blue Economy Strategy. (2019). Available online: https://www.au-ibar. org/ sites/ default/ files/ 2020-10/sd_20200313_africa_blue_economy_strategy_en.pdf

AMCEN. (2019). *Seventeenth Regular Session of the African Ministerial Conference on the Environment (AMCEN), UNEP—UN Environment Programme*. Available online: http://www.Unep .org/ events/ conference/seventeenth-regular-session-african-ministerialconference-environment-amcen

Arbow, T. (2019). *Washington Maritime Blue and the Blue Economy: Using diversity and inclusion to advance social justice in the maritime industry* (Doctoral dissertation).

Attri, V. N. (2016). *An emerging new development paradigm of the blue economy in IORA; A policy framework for the future. Chair Indian Ocean Studies, Indian Ocean Rim Association (IORA)*. University of Mauritius.

Bennett, N. J., Cisneros-Montemayor, A. M., Blythe, J., Silver, J. J., Singh, G., Andrews, N., Calo, A., Christie, P., Di Franco, A., Finkbeiner, E. M., Gelcich, S., Guidetti, P., Harper, S., Hotte, N., Kittinger, J. N., Le Billon, P., Lister, J., Lopez De La Lama, R., Mckinley, E., ... Sumaila, U. R. (2019). *Towards a sustainable and equitable blue economy*. Nature Sustainability.

Danladi, I. B., Kore, B. M., & Gül, M. (2017). Vulnerability of the nigerian coast: An insight into sea level rise owing to climate change and anthropogenic activities. *Journal of African Earth Sciences*, *134*, 493–503. doi:10.1016/j.jafrearsci.2017.07.019

Eikeset, A. M., Mazzarella, A. B., Davíðsdóttir, B., Klinger, D. H., Levin, S. A., Rovenskaya, E., & Stenseth, N. C. (2018). What is blue growth? The semantics of "Sustainable Development" of marine environments. *Marine Policy*, *87*, 177–179. doi:10.1016/j.marpol.2017.10.019

Fagerberg, J. (2018). Mobilizing innovation for sustainability transitions: A comment on transformative innovation policy. *Research Policy*, *47*(9), 1568–1576. doi:10.1016/j.respol.2018.08.012

Fairbridge, R. W. (2004). Classification of coasts. *Journal of Coastal Research*, *201*, 155–165. doi:10.2112/1551-5036(2004)20[155:COC]2.0.CO;2

FAO. (2016). The State of World Fisheries and Aquaculture 2016. FAO.

Fartash, K., Jahangirnia, M., & Sadabadi, A. A. (2018). Three frames for innovation policy: R&D, systems of innovation and transformative change. *Research Policy*, *47*(9), 1554–1567. doi:10.1016/j.respol.2018.08.011

Finkl, C. W. (2004). Coastal classification: Systematic approaches to consider in the development of a comprehensive scheme. *Journal of Coastal Research*, *201*, 166–213. doi:10.2112/1551-5036(2004)20[166:CCSATC]2.0.CO;2

Hadjimichael, M. (2018). A call for a blue degrowth: Unravelling the European Union's fisheries and maritime policies. *Marine Policy*, *94*, 158–164. doi:10.1016/j.marpol.2018.05.007

Hamisu, A. H. (2019). *A study of Nigeria's blue economy potential with particular reference to the oil and gas sector.* World Maritime University Dissertations. 1234. https://commons. wmu.se/all_ dissertations/1234

Ibrahim, H. D. (2018). *Harnessing the potentials of blue economy for sustainable development of Nigeria*. Academic Press.

Kadafa, A. A. (2012). Oil exploration and spillage in the Niger Delta of Nigeria. *Civil and Environmental Research*, *2*(3), 38–51.

Keen, M.R., Schwarz, A.-M., & Wini-Simeon, L. (2017). Towards defining the Blue Economy: practical lessons from Pacific Ocean governance. *Mar. Pol.*

Lee, K.-H., Noh, J., & Khim, J. S. (2020). The blue economy and the united nations' sustainable development goals: Challenges and opportunities. *Environment International*, *137*, 105528. doi:10.1016/j.envint.2020.105528 PMID:32014791

Moffitt, C. M., & Cajas-Cano, L. (2014). Blue growth: The 2014 FAO state of world fisheries and aquaculture. *Fisheries (Bethesda, Md.)*, *39*(11), 552–553. doi:10.1080/03632415.2014.966265

Mulazzani, L., & Malorgio, G. (2017). Blue growth and ecosystem services. *Marine Policy*, *85*, 17–24. doi:10.1016/j.marpol.2017.08.006

Nagy, H., & Nene, S. (2021). Blue Gold: Advancing Blue Economy Governance in Africa. *Sustainability*, *13*(13), 7153. doi:10.3390u13137153

NIMASA. (2018). *Nigeria's Maritime Industry Forecast. Emerging opportunities and Challenges.* Author.

Nwankwpala, H. O. (2011). Coastal aquifers of Nigeria: An overview of its management and sustainability considerations. *Journal of Applied Technology in Environmental Sanitation*, *1*(4).

Nwilo, P. C., & Badejo, O. T. (2006). *Impacts and management of oil spill pollution along the Nigerian coastal areas*. Academic Press.

Omole, D. O., & Isiorho, S. A. (2011). Waste management and water quality issues in coastal states of Nigeria: The ogun state experience. *Journal of Sustainable Development in Africa*, *13*(6), 207–217.

Pichon, E. (2019). *The African Union's Blue Strategy*. European Parliamentary Research Service. Available online: https://www. europarl. europa. eu/RegData/etudes/ ATAG/2019/635574/ EPRS_ATA(2019)635574_EN.pdf

Pretorius, R., & Henwood, R. (2019). Governing Africa's blue economy: The protection and utilisation of the continent's blue spaces. Studia Univ. *Babes-Bolyai Studia Eur.*, *64*(2), 119–148. doi:10.24193u bbeuropaea.2019.2.05

Purvis, M.-T. (2015). Seychelles blue economy Strategy. *Island Stud.: Indian Ocean*, 14–19.

Roy, A. (2019). Blue Economy in the Indian Ocean: Governance perspectives for sustainable development in the region. *Observer Research Foundation Occasional Paper*, (181).

Rustomjee, C. (2016). *Developing the blue economy in Caribbean and other small states*. Academic Press.

Rustomjee, C. (2018). *Green shoots for the African blue economy?* Academic Press.

Sexton, W. J., & Murday, M. (1994). The morphology and sediment character of the coastline of Nigeria: The Niger delta. *Journal of Coastal Research*, •••, 959–977.

Silver, J. J., Gray, N. J., Campbell, L. M., Fairbanks, L. W., & Gruby, R. L. (2015). Blue Economy and Competing Discourses in International Oceans Governance. *Journal of Environment & Development*, *24*(2), 135–160. doi:10.1177/1070496515580797

UNDP. (2018). *Leveraging the Blue Economy for Inclusive and Sustainable Growth.* https://www.undp.org/content/dam/kenya/docs/UNDP%20Reports/Policy%20 Brief%20%202018%20-%206-%20%20 Blue% 20Economy%20for%20Inclusive%20and%20Sustainable%20Growth.pdf

UNDP. (2018). Policy Brief. *Harnessing the Blue Economy for Sustainable Development in Nigeria.* Retrieved from; https://www.ng.undp.org/content/nigeria/en/home/library/poverty/policy-briefharnessing-the-blue-economy-for-sustainable-develop.html

United Nations. (2016). *Africa's Blue Economy a Policy Handbook*. Available online: https://wedocs.unep.org/bitstream/handle/20.500.11822/30130/AfricasBlueEconomy.pdf?sequence=1&isAllowed=y

Visbeck, M. (2018a). Ocean science research is key for a sustainable future. *Nature Communications*, *9*(1), 690. doi:10.103841467-018-03158-3 PMID:29449661

Voyer, M., Farmery, A. K., Kajlich, L., Vachette, A., & Quirk, G. (2020). Assessing policy coherence and coordination in the sustainable development of a Blue Economy. A case study from Timor Leste. *Ocean and Coastal Management*, *192*, 105187. doi:10.1016/j.ocecoaman.2020.105187

Voyer, M., Quirk, G., McIlgorm, A., & Azmi, K. (2018a). Shades of blue: What do competing interpretations of the Blue Economy mean for oceans governance? *Journal of Environmental Policy and Planning*, *20*(5), 595–616. doi:10.1080/1523908X.2018.1473153

Voyer, M., Schofield, C., Azmi, K., Warner, R., Mcilgorm, A., Quirk, G. (2018). Maritime security and the blue economy: Intersections and interdependencies in the Indian ocean. *J. Indian Ocean Reg.,* 1–21.

World Bank. (2017). *What is the Blue Economy?* Available from: https://www.worldbank.org/en/news/infographic/2017/06/06/blueeconomy

Yang, Y. (2019). Successful blue economy examples with an emphasis on international perspectives. *Frontiers in Marine Science*, *6*, 261. doi:10.3389/fmars.2019.00261

Chapter 3
Blue Economy, Food Security, and Food Sustainability

Olawale Paul Olatidoye
https://orcid.org/0000-0002-6926-9724
Yaba College of Technology, Nigeria

ABSTRACT

Blue economy refers to the economic activities geared towards advanced sustainable management and conservation of maritime resources and coastal resources and sustainable development in order to foster economic growth. The challenges of meeting the food demand of the world's rising populations require sustainable food supply chains anchored on coastal communities and sustainable food production. Moreover, marine resources are vital to ensuring food security, accounting for two-thirds of the world's fishery production, 80% of the world's aquaculture production, and per capita supply of fish is 65% higher than the world average. As the world population grows, the volume of food needed in the future will depend on these intrinsic factors and human choices. The chapter explores the current status of sea resources and proposed some ways forward based on existing opportunities and challenges using secondary data to accelerate the sustainable use of the sea resources and analyzes some of the human actions that may affect the sustainable future of the food supply chain, food waste.

INTRODUCTION

The issue of food security has been a major field of activity for long because several Nations of the world are food insecure as the agricultural system is backward, and worsened by high global food prices especially in Africa. Food now accounts for large share of family budgets for rural poor and urban families. Food and Agricultural Organization (FAO) in several forums have said that several countries may face imminent food crisis as the world food situation was in difficult situation or position. It is a known fact that food remains the most important due to its centrality to human existence; hence ruthless expenditure on food has reshaped human history leading to wars, migration of people and slowing down the growth of nations. The recent deliberate or premeditated increase in prices of food leading to increase in violence has necessitated a call for sober reflection. This major field of activity including unrest and

DOI: 10.4018/978-1-6684-3393-5.ch003

political instability has taken central stage among world leaders thereby the concern increasing for the ability of Nations of the world to feed its over 6.5 billion people (FAO, 2007).

Consequently, various groups and individual Nation of the world have resulted to combative food security campaign to correct or redress the difficult or unpleasant set of circumstances in order to provide food at affordable prices to all. About 750 million people were reported to be food insecure in about 70 countries with low income while Asia Nations were reported to undergo a 30% drop in the number of hungry in Food security survey carried out in 2005 but the South and Central America with the Caribbean had a slightly varied report. The current challenge today is the high food prices which may eventually bring about increase in food security and widespread food crisis in many Nations of the world. This global food crisis is brought about by factors such as climate change, population explosion, increased demand for bio-fuels, low crop yield, increase in oil prices which bring about producers and traders loss.

Food security is known to center basically on food availability and access to and utilization of food. The fact food security depends on robust food systems that encompass availability issues, access and utilization of food. Also, the challenges of meeting the food demand of the world's rising populations require sustainable food supply chains anchored on resilient resources and coastal communities, sustainable food production, developed markets, and open and fair trade; Moreover, marine resources are vital to ensuring food security, accounting for two-thirds of the world's capture fishery production, 80 percent of the world's aquaculture production, and per capita supply of fish is 65 percent higher than the world average. The long-term goal of food sustainability is to produce enough food to maintain the human population'. Hence, food security defined as the condition achieved when food systems operate in a way that all people, at all times, have physical and economic access to sufficient, safe and nutritious food to meet their dietary needs and food preferences for an active and healthy life (FAO 1996). Food systems are usually stressed when there is reduction in Food security which are usually caused by climate change and environmental changes such as conflict, inconsistent international trade agreements and policies and there combination. The effects of rising ocean temperatures, ocean acidification and destruction of habitat destruction are now seriously affecting the quantity and quality of fish and other marine animals and consequently livelihoods animals that depend on it. Furthermore, effects of other marine activities hinder the productive potential and sustainable use of the seas and oceans. Water quality and security challenges in the context of climate change and environmental management also require attention, since industrialization, expanding and intensifying food production are putting pressure on water resources, which affects human health and food security. However, due to lack of institutional capacity and given the socio-cultural context, the sustainability of the sea resources is now facing critical threats. Hence, paper aims to explore the current scenario of sea resources using secondary data, to accelerate the economic growth through the sustainable use of the sea resources and analyzes some of the human actions that may affect the sustainable future of the food supply chain, including diet, obesity, food miles, food waste, labor issues, availability and quality of ground water for irrigation. Apart from studying the present status of sea resources, the paper proposed some way forwards based on existing opportunities and challenges for promoting sustainable development in the world.

The World Ocean

Oceans and seas cover over two-thirds of Earth's surface, contribute to poverty eradication by creating sustainable livelihoods and decent work, provide food and minerals, generate oxygen, absorb greenhouse gases and mitigate the impacts of climate change, determine weather patterns and temperatures, and serve as highways for seaborne international trade. With an estimated 80 percent of the volume of world trade carried by sea, international shipping and ports provide crucial linkages in global supply chains and are essential for the ability of all countries to gain access to global markets (UNCTAD 2016). The fundamental importance of Worlds Ocean to life on planet Earth cannot be overemphasized as the ocean is known to cover about two-thirds of the Earth's surface representing 71%. The relationship of human with the oceans, and how people use and exploit ocean resources is evolving in important ways. Oceans are increasingly becoming a source of food, energy, and products such as medicines and enzymes, there is also now a better understanding of the non-market goods and services that the oceans provide, which are vital for life on Earth. Scientist have also reperted that oceans are not limitless and that they are suffering from increasingly cumulative human impacts. Oceans that are not healthy and resilient are not able to support economic growth. The ocean also known to regulate the climate and provides very large or wide natural resources for human benefits such as food, raw materials, energy, transportation and seascape for recreational and/or religious practices (Visbeck, 2018a). Oceans are known to provide some essential services for human existence such as oxygen for breathing, absorbing the excess heat and recycling the water we drink and providing protein food all year round (Djavidnia et al., 2014). In addition, ocean is also responsible for regulating climate and atmospheric gases, waste recycling and providing natural ecosystem and natural animal species for sustaining human life (Costanza et al., 1999; Fisher et al., 2009). Ocean is also reported to have contributed about 21 trillion US$/year to human welfare (Costanza, 1999). More recently, a conservative estimate of the total asset value of the oceans, restricted to renewable economic activities and thus excluding offshore oil and gas, put the annual "gross marine product" of the ocean at 2.5 trillion with the total asset base of the ocean put at 24 trillion, meaning that the ocean ranks as the world's 7th biggest economy (WWF, 2015).The Ocean also benefits human with the means of transportation, linking cities and countries around the world. Maritime transport is considered to be the backbone of the world economy accounting for over 80% of the world trade (UNCTAD, 2016). The ocean also provides an enormous source of potential renewable energy resources. Offshore Wind Farm (OWF) can be constructed and developed for an alternative power generation for the benefit of mankind (Pelc& Fujita, 2002). In the process of exploring the above benefits, the ocean receives a huge amount of pressure from humans. Human activity has already been affecting all parts of the ocean body with so many stressors such as pollution and overfishing (McIntyre, 1995). Increasing global population, rapid industrial development, and growing human wealth are all factors contributing to the increase of pressure on the ocean. Climate change, non-sustainable resource extraction, land pollution, and degradation of habitat have also become a threat to the health and economic productivity of the ocean in most of the developing and emerging economic countries of the world (Visbeck, 2018b). Figure 1 shows the benefits Oceans and Seas to Mankind with prevailing pressure from Man (Visbeck, 2018).

In the face of these threats to the ocean, there is an increasing need for the sustainable use of ocean resources while at the same time securing the economic and social objectives. The understanding of the economic growth based on the exploitation of marine natural resources of living resources (fisheries) and non-living resources (petroleum resources) in preventing their degradation, overuse, and pollution (Park et al., 2014). In addition, the use of ocean benefits can be in agreement with sole aim of improving oceans management in a sustainable way of exploration of the ocean resources, sustainable management of ocean resources to support livelihoods with sustainable economic policy in a more equitable benefits sharing and ecosystem resilience in the face of climate change, destructive fishing practices and external pressures (Techera, 2018). Hence, for sustainable interaction between ocean and human, marine policymakers must understand that there is a need to support and analyze the economic and social aspect

Figure 1. Interaction between Human activities and ocean ecosystem and their threats
Source: Visbeck, (2018).

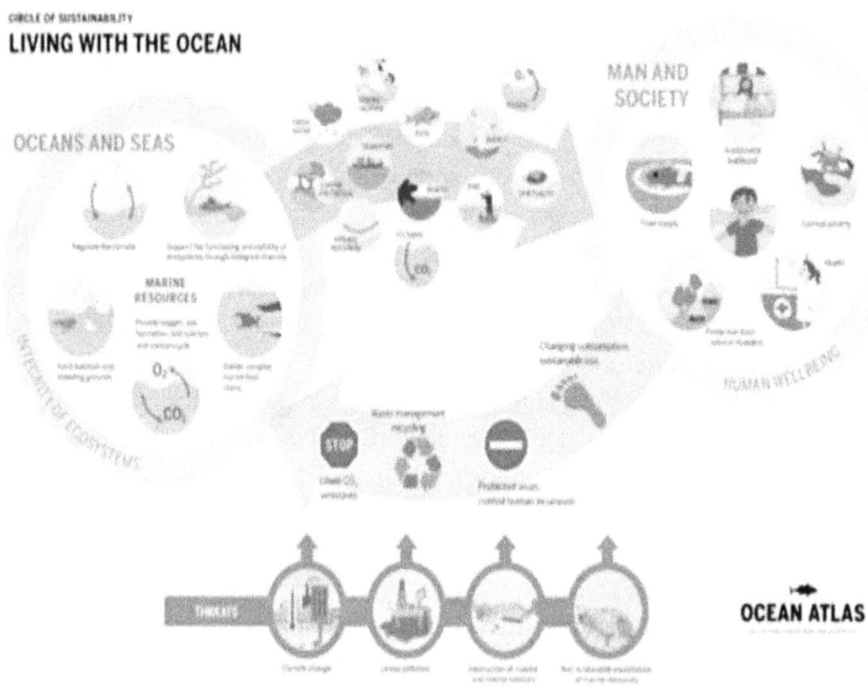

of marine activities as a blue economy component for sustainable development (Morrissey, 2017). The ocean is an important source of economic opportunities for several activities for tourism, transportation, aquaculture and mariculture, seawater utilization and biodiversity conservation (Choi, 2017).

Defining the Blue Economy

Blue Economy or ocean economy is a recent word coined from a conference on held in Rio de Je Janeiro by the United Nations on Sustainable in 2012 where a separation was made between socio-economic development and environmental degradation. The definition of the term has now been extended to include economic and trade activities where it has been extended to include the marine ecology or environment, conservation and sustainability in maritime sector management. There have been several definition put forward to define the concept of blue economy as there is no unified or single means of defining blue economy. However, several definitions have been put forward for Blue Economy or Oceans Economy and emphasis in this write up will seeks to find a definition easy to read and digest, manage, and measure. In The Economist, specifically the Intelligence Unit of 2015in a report on “The Blue Economy: Growth, Opportunity and a Sustainable Ocean Economy”, a working definition of Blue Economy is stated as follows: “A sustainable ocean economy emerges when economic activity is in balance with the long term capacity of ocean ecosystems to support this activity and remain resilient and healthy”. Therefore, this section gives a broad range of opinion from contributors in the emerging literature on the blue economy. Choi, (2017) opined that blue economy is a mean by ocean is identified as a new economic way of bringing both wealth and environmental protection to the people and implementing new desirable biological economic relationships. Choi, (2017) also gave the Chinese perspective about the concept of blue economy as a means of new biological-economic knowledge and relations in creating new spatial rationalities with a view of changing how we perceive sea space and relations in that space. Furthermore, Blue Economy concept is seen as means of sustaining aquaculture, mariculture, tourism, ocean transportation, seawater utilization, renewable ocean energy, ecological restoration, and biodiversity conservation. Blue Economy is observed as a means of opening up activities taking at sea space for the accumulation of benefits and the products obtained from such activities. Blue Economy is also believed to entails degree of resources exploitation, sustainability of ocean management and relationship between bio-economics and politics (Foley, 2017). Also, Blue Economy to be involved in balancing sustainable economic benefits with long-term ocean health in a manner which is consistent with sustainable development and its commitment to intra- and inter-generational equity (Keen et al., 2018). The Blue Economy can also be viewed as involving initiatives aimed to improve oceans governance through the sustainable use of ocean resources, the better coordination of management across scales and time and the protection of ocean's cultural and natural integrity (Keen et al., 2018). The concept of sustainability involves generation of lower greenhouse gas (GHG) emissions and sustainability of the oceans so as to provide feed for both animals and humans.

Blue Economy was designed to improve human wellbeing and social equity with the main aim of reducing environmental risks and ecological scarcities and bringing about low carbon emission, resource efficiency and social inclusion which is also espoused in the United Nations Environment Programme of Green to Blue Economy7. This desired outcome is based on the needs to develop and increasingly world population world located in the oceans through improved human wellbeing and social equity. Hence, from the definitions given above, blue Economy could then be defined as the sustainable industrialization of the oceans for the benefit of mankind" creating a balance between activities such as trade activities, legislative and regulatory), ecological environment which is the support system and livelihoods and food of the community. The balance created by this system should have the tendency to be measured effectively and can be calculated.

"Oceans" is defined as the operating environment which is differentiated from the land where traditional activities take place. These activities are now being transferred to a non-traditional operating environment: the oceans. Benefit allows the measurement of all the elements involved which is a measurement of effectiveness that covers humans, systems and operations.

Hence, working concepts of the Blue Economy allows for the effectiveness of its application to be measured in calculable terms. However, based on the aforementioned conception, Blue Economy concept is made up of five (5) main components.

- Ecosystem resilience
- Economic sustainability
- Community engagement
- Institutional integration
- Technical capacity

The first three components are derived directly from the Blue Economy's roots in the sustainable development literature (Keen et al., 2018). And these components can be represented in Fig. 2, below.

Table 1. Components of Blue Economy

Activity Type	Ocean Service	Industry	Drivers of growth
Harvesting of living resources	Sea food Marine biotechnology	Fisheries Aquaculture Pharmaceuticals, Chemicals, marine derived bio-products	Food security Demand for protein Research and development for healthcare
Extraction of non-living resources, generation of new resources	Minerals Energy	Sea bed mining Oil and gas Renewable Desalination	Demand for freshwater Seaborne trade growth; International regulations
Commerce and trade within the oceans	Transport and trade Tourism and recreation	Shipping (boat and ship repairs, safety and training, marine engineering) Port infrastructure and services Coastal and maritime Coastal development	Growth in seaborne trade; International regulations Global tourism growth Coastal urbanization Domestic regulations
Response to Ocean health challenges	Ocean monitoring and surveillance Carbon sequestration Coastal protection Waste Disposal	Technology, R & D and Education Bleu Carbon Habitat protection and restoration Assimilation of nutrients and wastes	R & D in ocean technologies Growth in Coastal and Ocean protection and conservation activities

Adapted from: World Bank (2017).

Challenges of the Blue Economy

The Blue Economy encompasses economic activities that depend on the sea, often associated with other economic sectors, including tourism, maritime transport, energy and fishing. Blue growth supports the sustainable growth of the maritime and marine sectors as the oceans and seas are engines of the global economy and have great potential for growth and innovation. Throughout history, the sea has always been present in the economic activities of all civilizations as a food resource, a means of transportation and commercial trade. In recent years the term Blue Economy (BE) has become a concept closely related to maritime resources and developed economies in the oceans. Its growing expansion and the emerging needs of a circular economy (CE) herald challenges in both new and established treatments and materials (Cristiani, 2017). CE is understood as an economic model oriented towards the elimination of waste generated, efficient use of resources, recycling and recovery (Mah, 2021; Shojaei et al., 2021). The BE aims to promote economic growth, improve life and social inclusion without compromising the oceans' environmental sustainability and coastal areas since the sea's resources are limited and their physical conditions have been harmed by human actions (European Commission, 2020) .

PRINCIPLES FOR A SUSTAINABLE BLUE ECONOMY DEVELOPMENT

Blue Economy or Blue Growth is a term which represents sustainable economic activity in the maritime sector and the use of the sea and its resources for sustainable economic development. The largest ecosystem on the planet has been reported to be oceans and seas with coastal areas and a precious part of our natural heritage which are important to the livelihoods and food security of several people around the world. These marine environments has been placed under severe or undue pressure from human activities

Table 2. Definitions of some terms

Concept	Definitions and related concepts	Authors
Blue Economy	The sustainable use of ocean resources for economic growth, the improvement of livelihoods and the health of ocean ecosystems	World Bank (2013)
	The rethinking concept of industrial processes and searching for a viable biological solution that reduces contamination	Costa et al., (2019)
	It has become synonymous with generating wealth from activities related to the oceans while protecting and supporting marine ecosystems.	Phelan et al.(2020)
	It is a mean of preventing biodiversity loss while stimulating economic development thereby integrating environmental and economic interests.	Schutter and Hicks (2019)
	It is the mainstream of national development and can integrate land and sea-based socio-economic sustainable development.	Kathijotes(2013)
	It refers to the commercially sustainable development of the ocean	Kaczynski(2011)
	It has emerged in the last two decades from various forums, but above all from within the policy and practice of environmental development.	Hoegh-Guldberg et al., (2015)
Blue growth	Emerging from national and international marine policy, it aims to promote the growth of ocean economies and at the same time holistically manage marine socio-ecological systems.	Caswell et al(2020)
	It aims at achieving economic growth based on the exploitation of marine resources with the aim of avoiding their degradation, excessive use, and pollution	Boostra et al., (2020)
	It refers to the holistic management of complex marine socio-ecological systems, dynamic and complex system that covers all industries and regions.	Burgess et al., (2018)
Marine economy	It is a dynamic and complex system that covers all industries and regions.	Qi and xiao (2019)
	It is a new economic form that emphasizes a new development concept, a new operating mechanism and a management model	Wenwen et al., (2016)
	A heterogeneous innovation system with ensuring relevance to the spatial and functional development of European regions.	Bentlage et al.,(2014)
Ocean economy	Is a subset and complement of the evolving development paradigm emphasizing sustainable greener and more inclusive economic pathways	UNCTAD (2014)
	It is an important factor for global economic growth and development, with excellent opportunities, challenges and risks	Potgieter(2018)

Martinez-Vazquez et al., (2021)

due to the fact that they several provide both jobs and nutrition to the teeming population and nutrition over the long term. They are also threatened due to several fragmented and uncoordinated activities. Hence, there is the need for the governments, organizations and coastal communities to develop a more coherent, integrated, fair, and science based approach to managing the economic development of the oceans. Moreover, several schools of thought opined that we are an integral part of the marine ecosystem which requires adequate planning and implementation of these economic activities with care, balancing the desire to improve human living standards and wellbeing so as to sustain ecosystem health. Public and private sectors require active leaders to steer the Blue Economy in a sustainable direction with the aim of delivering on commitments already made – globally, regionally, nationally and locally. Hence, in order to ensure that the economic development of the ocean contributes to true prosperity and resilience of today and the near future, the following principles for a Sustainable Blue Economy is hereby suggested . These principles for sustainable development therefore, provide a distinctness of outline of a Sustainable Blue Economy and a roadmap to help us achieve it. They are general purpose which can be used by government, private bodies, international agencies and civil society which can be applied to any part of the oceans, seas and coasts. These Principles for a Sustainable Blue Economy must be practiced by all actors and to embed these actions into marine policy and activities for use all around the world.

Sustainable blue economy is a marine-based economy that performs the following functions:

- Provides social and economic benefits for current and future generations, by contributing to food security, poverty eradication, income, employment, safe health and political stability.
- It can also restore, protects and maintains the productivity, resilience, core functions, and intrinsic value of marine ecosystems – the natural capital upon which its prosperity depends.
- Is based on clean technologies, renewable energy, and circular material flows so as to ensure social and economic stability within the limits of one planet.

However, sustainable Blue Economy is based on active and effective (inclusive) stakeholder engagement and participation. Also, well informed decisions are based on scientifically sound information to avoid harmful effects that undermine long-term sustainability. When adequate information and knowledge are missing, actors take a precautionary approach, actively seek to develop such knowledge, and refrain from undertaking activities that could potentially lead to harmful effects.

To create a sustainable blue economy, the following set of goals must be achieved:

- **A consistent, clear, and measurable goals and target must be set:** All actors (governments, economist, and business men) must come up with relevant and measurable goals and targets to provide planning, management and activities with a clear direction while conflicts and contradictions must be avoided at all cost
- **All the set goals and targets must be assessed and their performance indicators communicated:** The set goals and targets must be monitored and progress reports communicated in a transparent and accessible manner to the general public and all the critical stakeholders.
- **A level economic and legislative playing field with adequate incentives and rules must be provided:** All private agreements (International and national laws) and Economic activities (taxes and subsidies fees) should be continuously designed and enforced so as to support a Sustainable Blue Economy.
- **Marine space resources should be planned and managed effectively using inclusive methods and ecosystem approach:** All relevant uses of marine space and resources must be accounted and managed through precautionary, adaptive and integrated processes that ensure the sustainable healthy use of the sea while also taking into account human activities on land. Such processes must be accountable and equitably transparent in order to be responsive to present and future human uses and needs.
- **Develop and use standards guidelines and best practices that support a Sustainable Blue Economy:** All actors —including governments, businesses, non-profit enterprises, investors and consumers—must develop or apply the global sustainability standards, guidelines, best practices, or other behaviors that are relevant to them. For organizations, application of such standards should not only ensure that their activities are conducted in a responsible way, but also improve their own performance and competitiveness, today and in the future.

- **Land-based maritime economies are interlinked and many of problems encountered in marine business begins on land:** Land-based maritime ecosystem impacts must be solved and all parties involved must work together to promote and achieve sustainable green economy on land.
- All actors in a Sustainable Blue Economy have a responsibility to participate in the process of implementation, and to reach out across national, regional, sectorial, organizational, and other borders, to ensure collective stewardship of our common marine heritage.

A Sustainable Blue Economy is a marine-based economy based on following factors

1. Provides social and economic benefits for current and future generations by contributing to food security, poverty eradication, livelihoods, income, employment, health, safety, equity, and political stability.
2. Restores, protects, and maintains the diversity, productivity, resilience, core functions, and intrinsic value of marine ecosystems—the natural capital upon which its prosperity depends.
3. Is based on clean technologies, renewable energy, and circular material flows to secure economic and social stability over time, while keeping within the limits of one planet.
4. Is governed by public and private processes that are inclusive, well-informed, precautionary, and adaptive accountable and transparent, holistic, cross-sectoral, and long-term, innovative and proactive

However, to create a sustainable blue economy, the following must be given adequate consideration:

1. Set clear, measurable, and internally consistent goals and targets for a sustainable blue economy and communicate their performance on these goals and targets.
2. Create a level economic and legislative playing field that provides the Blue Economy with adequate incentives and rules.
3. Plan, manage, and effectively govern the use of marine space and resources, applying inclusive methods and the ecosystem approach.
4. Develop and apply standards, guidelines, and best practices that support a Sustainable Blue Economy.
5. Recognize that the maritime and land-based economies are interlinked and that many of the threats facing marine environments originate on land.
6. Actively cooperate, sharing information, knowledge, best practices, lessons learned, perspectives, and ideas, to realize a sustainable and prosperous future for all.

Challenges for Sustainable Development of Blue Economy

The function of marine properties reduction in food productions and securing natural habitat are endless or unrestricted. However, the future may be in danger:

- The absence or severe lack of 'proper policy' and 'marine related resource persons' at higher policy levels and similar national organizations/body in relevant ministry/department is a significant drawback for the implementation of many issues related to the capacity development of different marine sectors in Bangladesh.
- We have to be compelled to guarantee our sovereignty over the entire coastal space & maintaining the safety over the commercial coastal area of the Asian nation.

- The authority should be controlled water level rise and alter in system and temperatures, from coral bleaching.
- Lack of adequate knowledge and expert workforce to benefits from the blue economy, especially for exploiting deep-sea fishes and seabed resources.
- Lack of cordial combination of visionary political leadership, efficient bureaucracy, investors of real entrepreneurial attitude and innovative development thinkers to succeed in that plan.
- Lack of robust master plan that will focus on the whole or complete coastal area and attracting extra-regional players.
- Instituting or setting up a marine friendly infrastructure for marine tourism.
- Promoting an investment-friendly environment in the specific area while managing carbon discharge
- Safeguarding mangrove and ocean grass with economical Utilization of biodiversity
- Prevention of acidification of waters and keeping ocean free from pollution.

Definition and Dimensions of Food Security

Food security exists when all people at all times have physical, social and economic access to sufficient, safe and nutritious food to meet their dietary needs and food preferences for an active and healthy life. The four pillars of food security are: food availability, access to food, utilization and stability. The nutritional dimension is integral to the concept of food security. The nutritional aspect of food and nutrition security is achieved when secure access to food is coupled with a sanitary environment, adequate health services, and knowledgeable care to ensure a healthy and active life (free from malnutrition) for all household members().

Food systems (FS) encompass the entire range of actors and their interlinked value-adding activities involved in the production, aggregation, processing, distribution, consumption and disposal of food products that originate from agriculture, forestry or fisheries, and parts of the broader economic, societal and

The Context of Food Sustainability

The long-term goal of food sustainability is to produce enough food to maintain the human population. The intrinsic factors to guarantee a sustainable food system are a fertile land, water, fertilizers, a stable climate, and energy. However, as the world population grows, the volume of food needed in the future will not depend just on these intrinsic factors, but on human choices. In addition to food directly harvested from the wild, food is mostly produced at farms, and therefore, food sustainability is directly linked to sustainable agriculture. In 1990, the U.S. Congress addressed the issue of sustainable agriculture in the farm bill, which stated that "sustainable agriculture means an integrated system of plant and animal production practices having a site-specific application that will, over the long term:

- provide human food and fiber needs;
- enhance environmental quality and the natural resource base upon which the agricultural economy depends;
- make the most efficient use of nonrenewable resources and on-farm resources and integrate,
- where appropriate, natural biological cycles and controls;
- sustain the economic viability of farm operations; and

- enhance the quality of life for farmers and society as a whole."

Based on the U.S. Congress' definition and the now famous 1997 United Nations' definition about sustainable development, which states that "sustainable development is development that meets the needs of the present without the ability of future generations to meet their own needs," definitions of sustainability have emerged in all sectors of the population. Most businesses have embraced what is called the three dimensions of sustainability, or "triple bottom line," and some variations like "people-planet-profit," "the three pillars," or "the three E's," for economy, equity, and ecology. This idea is based on the premise that for a company to be sustainable it needs to be economically feasible, environmentally dependable, and socially responsible. The concept of the triple bottom line goes even further by allowing interchangeability, which means that if a business falls short in one of the dimensions, it can make up by "investing" in another dimension. For instance, Amining Company is environmentally unsustainable in the long term because it depletes the resource. However, according to the triple bottom line concept, this company could compensate by making social contributions. The general public has their own ideas of food sustainability, which often includes concepts like social justice, animal welfare, fair labor and trade, local farming, organic food production, and the concept of "natural," just to mention the most important ones. There is no official definition of natural. So different people have different ideas of the meaning of "natural". Another idea that most of the time is wrongly attributed to food sustainability by the general public is food miles. Many people believe the biggest impact on the whole environmental impact of food products is transportation and therefore favor local products, which in many cases is not necessarily true. Regardless of definitions and beliefs, food sustainability is about generating food at a productivity level that is enough to maintain the human population. Sustainable food production is fundamentally grounded on the availability of fertile land, water, nutrients, and an adequate climate. In addition, the volume of food needed to feed humans is linked to intended or unintended human behavior. This paper analyzes some population attitudes and choices that have an impact on both the volume of food needed and the environmental impact to produce it.

The Effect of Diet

Different diets have a significant effect on health and severe environmental impacts which is as a result of a change in the global diet which has been attributed to the increased in the consumption of animal protein (Tilman and Clark, 2014). This is due to inefficiency of conversion of feed into animal tissue especially in ruminants which is most inefficient animals to convert feed into muscle. However, ruminants have the advantage of ingesting low-grade feed because they are capable of digesting cellulose while monogastric animals (swine and poultry) are more efficient at converting feed into muscle. In addition to land use, livestock production has an enormous role in soil destruction, water depletion and pollution, impact on biodiversity, and a disturbance of the nitrogen and carbon cycles. Livestock grazing occupies the equivalent of 26 percent of ice-free surface of the planet in addition to 33 percent of arable land dedicated to the production of feed crops (Steinfeld, 2006). Apart from land use, cattle rearing have a profound impact on soil properties such as the constant animal traffic, compacts the soil reducing water infiltration and promotes runoff which leads to soil erosion and bring the nutrients to water surface (Steinfeld, 2006). In addition, ruminants are major producers of green house gases through enteric fermentation leading to the formation of ammonia, carbon dioxide and methane, but methane has a green house potential twelve times higher than carbon dioxide while ammonia is only responsible for alteration of the nitrogen cycle (Morawicki, 2012). With all these problems, the only solution to this environmental impact of animal production is production of diet with more vegetable protein. The only disadvantage however, is that vegetable protein does possess complete amino acid profile which will require the right combination to have all the essential amino acids in the diet. Also, the vegetable proteins are more difficult to be digested by the human. Insects are another source of protein used in many countries around the world and have a significant advantage of reducing environmental impact when compared with traditional livestock. Insects require less water and produce fewer green house gases and ammonia emissions. Green house emission from insects is 1 percent of the emissions of ruminants for the same amount of protein (Oonincx et al., 2010).

Obesity and Over-Consumption

The consumption of more calories than the calories spent in physical activities may result in weight increase and obesity. Most foods can cause weight gain, but the main offenders are calorie dense foods. Reports have shown that out of 1.9 billion adults living in the world, 18 years and above are overweight while 650 million people are obese. Also, about 41 million children under the age of 5, and more than 340 million children and adolescents aged 5 to 19 were reported overweight or obese by the WHO in 2016 (WHO, 2018). Children are getting their calories from calorie dense foods and sweetened beverages made with fats and sugars (Wallinga, 2010). The increase obesity pandemic presents one more challenge for agricultural sustainability, more food will be needed to maintain population's extra weight. Overweight and obesity have shown a significant health and environmental implications as overweight decreases physical activity and personal mobility leading to increased use of motor vehicles (Mann, 2017).

Mann (2017) reported that airlines operator have discovered effect of the increased average weight of passengers on fuel consumption. Other scientific reports have demonstrated the impact of obesity on the environment from direct emissions of CO_2 through respiration which is directly related to body mass. Gryka *et al*., (2010) reported that a 10-kg weight loss of all overweight and obese people would translate into a 0.2 percent reduction in the global CO_2 emissions. This has placed extra burden on the environment to produce and transport additional food for the extra calories required by overweight populations.

Local Versus Transported

It is often believed that locally produced foods have a lower environmental impact than food grown or raised somewhere else and transported; and "food miles" is the indicator commonly used to illustrate how far the food has traveled from production to consumption (Ghoshal, 2014). Nevertheless, does the food produced locally have a lower environmental impact than food produced in other regions and transported? The answer is it depends on the food product and the transportation mode. As a general rule, the faster the transportation mode the higher the environmental impact it produces. Regarding energy used, planes have the highest consumption per ton of food transported followed by trucks, trains, inland barges, and maritime ships (Morawicki, 2012). Because of the perishable nature of foods, not all food products can be transported with all transportation modes. Dry materials, such as grains, can be carried in barges or maritime ships. Fresh produce and fruits, on the other hand, have to rely on faster transportation modes such as trains, trucks, and planes (Morawicki, 2012). On average in the U.S., the energy used to transport foods represents only14 percent of the total energy used to produce, process, distribute, and prepare the food at home, restaurants, and institutions (Heller and Keoleia, 2000). Another factor to consider in the debate of local vs. transported is climate and seasons. Fruits and vegetables cannot be grown in high latitude climates in open agricultural fields during winter. The only alternative is to use greenhouses or to transport the food from temperate climates. If grown in greenhouses, plants need supplement a light and heat with the resulting expenditure of energy and the emission of greenhouse gases. Other foods are more favorable to be produced throughout all the seasons in specific parts of the world. A classic example is lamb meat produced in New Zealand vs. in the UK. Even when grazing is the main source of nutrition for both countries, pastures are more productive in New Zealand due to more solar irradiation and less use of synthetic fertilizers. Therefore, an advantage mayexist in terms of lower environmental impact for lamb produced in New Zealand instead of the UK even when factoring transportation by ship to the UK (Webb et al., 2013). Another consideration is seasonality. In this day and age, especially in developed countries, and as a result of low-cost transportation and logistics, most food products are available all year round. Due to their short shelf life, fruit and vegetables are in most cases transported by plane with the associated environmental impact. On average, the operational energy of a long-haul cargo plane, expressed in MJ/metric ton-km, is around four times more than a truck and 30 times more than a train (Weber and Matthew, 2008)

Food Waste

According to estimates, of the 200 million metric tons of food produced annually in the U.S., 60 million metric tons go to waste. From the analysis of food waste that reaches landfills, 47 percent of the waste comes from the residential sector. Clearly, not all food waste is edible. Food waste can be classified into three main types: avoidable, possibly avoidable, and unavoidable. Avoidable waste is food or drinks that before disposal were perfectly edible or drinkable and for no particular reason were discarded. Potentially avoidable are parts of foods that are eaten by some people and discarded by others. For instance, some fruit peels are edible, but some people prefer not to eat them. The third category, unavoidable food waste, encompasses inedible parts of the food like bones, eggshells, inedible peels, and spent coffee grains.What are the reasons for the food waste generated by the residential sector? There are several, the most important ones being: availability of inexpensive food, poor purchase planning, perishable nature of foods, and confusing shelf life statements. It is fair to say that the main drive to food waste at the household level in the U.S. is that food is inexpensive. According to USDA data, the disposable income to buy food to eat at home has decreased from 10 percent in1970 to around 6 percent in 2009 (USDA,2016). In the same period, food waste increased by 50 percent (Hall et al., 2009). It is important to point out that in the same period, food eaten away from home rose only from 3.5 to 4 percent (USDA, 2016). Another reason food purchased to be consumed at home is often wasted is a combination of lack of purchasing planning and the nature of perishable food, especially fruits and vegetables. Very often, this is exacerbated by packages containing a large volume of food at a reduced price, which is often offered in wholesale clubs. Most foods in the U.S. have some shelf life statement such as "use by," "sell by," or "best by" date. "Use by," mostly used in meat, fish, and cheese, is a firm expiration date that is related to the safety of the food. "Sell by" isa statement aimed at retailers, which informs them when the product has to be pulled from the shelf. Typically, one-third of the product's shelf-life remains after the sell-by date for the consumer to use at home. "Best by" is an indicator to the consumer about when the product will have an optimal quality (Gudners, 2012). Unfortunately, most consumers are not acquainted with the exact meaning of these terms and take them as firm expiration dates. As a consequence, they do not buy the products close to these dates, or they discard the food products once they reach the "sell by" or a "best by" date (Gudners, 2012). Besides being morally questionable, food waste uses resources to produce and transport extra food such as land, energy, water, and fertilizers with the consequent emission of greenhouse gases. At the end of the cycle, wasted food needs to be transported and disposed of with subsequent land use, fuel use, and emission of green house gases from trucks, machinery, and decomposing food (Hall et al., 2009)

Genetically Modified Organisms

Scientists have reported that the world population will increase to 9.2 billion by 2050; a significant increase in agricultural production will be required to provide food for this growing population. Also, Taheri et al., (2017) reported that the agricultural production has to grow at a rate of 1.1 percent annually to cover food demand in 2050. Hence, agricultural biotechnology based on genetically modified organisms (GMOs) provides a new prospects and opportunities to increase agricultural production (food) while reducing the environmental detriment caused by current agricultural practices. Genetically modified organism also called genetically modified food is the process of altering the genetic make-up of crops by the inserting novel genes from other sources or removal of existing genes. James (2010) reported there was an agreement between researchers and farmers that there are many advantages in deploying biotechnology in the food industry in order to solve the world's hunger problem while producing super foods with added vitamins and nutrients and generating economic growth for the farmers. The rapid adoption of the first generation GMO technologies in agriculture has supported their benefits to farmers around the world with no visible benefit to the consumers. The second generation of GMO crops however centered on output traits such as improved nutritional characteristics with no impact on profits made by farmers because the products are indistinguishable from conventional crops. The recent which is the third generation of genetically modified crops are at small scale to generate specialty chemicals, including biodegradable plastics, adhesives, and synthetic proteins. Another group of third generation of GMOs called "Pharmacrops," for vaccines and antibodies production (Buiatti et al., 2013). Some social and environmental implications have recently raised serious concerns about GMOs which include corporate dominance, land concentration, loss of farm jobs, and an increase in income inequality. Environmentalists have expressed their growing concern regarding the possibility of engineered genes exposure to wild populations. Others fear that the use of biotech crops will affect the biodiversity by the persistence of genes after a GMO has been harvested, the susceptibility of non-target organisms, and the instability of new genes. As for human health, the main fear has been the creation of new allergens and the gene transfer from GMO foods to human cells or the intestinal microflora. Another hazard is the transfer of genes from GMO plants into conventional crops, as well as the mixing of GM crops with those derived from conventional seeds, which could have an indirect effect on food safety and food security (Buiatti et al., 2013). The GMOs advocates opined that biotechnology could be an important tool to increase crop productivity, food quality, and the production of vaccines and therapeutic medicines. Also, the GMO crops promoters opined that GMOs are essential for promoting sustainable agriculture because since it can decrease agriculture's environmental footprint by reducing the use of pesticides, saving fossil fuels, lowering CO_2 emissions and conserving soil and moisture James (2010). Hence, GMOs foods could be used to find a solution to the global food security problem. This technology offers the opportunity to generate new crop varieties that would be more resistant to pest or drought, and consequently will increase and enhance productivity yields to ameliorate hunger and the food insecurity problem worldwide.

CONCLUSION

The food system in terms of emission of greenhouse gases has impacts at all stages of the supply chain. However, the agricultural stage is the single largest greenhouse gases emitter with meat and dairy products as the most greenhouse gases-intensive foods. Nevertheless, the role of humans and their consumption patterns have a significant impact on the production of food and the population set of beliefs and attitudes will dictate whether or not the long-term sustainability of the food supply chain can be achieved. Blue Economy provides an opportunity for strengthened partnerships which build on existing maritime and river basin cooperation mechanisms. When fully realized, the partnerships can produce a quantum leap forward in the economic development of individual States and the expansion of progress, peace, and prosperity across the continent. They can also create economies of scale to help address inherent financial, technical, and infrastructure gaps of individual States that prevent the realization of the full potential of their aquatic and marine resources. There is the need to intensify policy attentiveness and to the development of Local, National and International policies, roadmaps and benchmarks for sustainable ocean governance. The blue economy concept therefore generally strives to link the economic opportunities bestowed by the oceans and the urgent demand for improved environmental agent, protection and restoration. If fully exploited and well managed, Africa's Blue Economy can constitute a major source of wealth and catapult the continent's fortunes and play a major role in global structural transformation

RECOMMENDATIONS

The goal must be to improve delivery on growth and development opportunities in the maritime food sector viz-a-viz strategic vision for growth and development which is focused at socioeconomic growth, development and transformation in various areas of maritime food sector

The operation is to encourage the oceans economy through cooperation among government, business and civil society aiming at national development milestone, encouraging economic growth and addressing development challenges like poverty, crime, and unemployment. There is the need to design oceans economy framework, comprising of workshops with key stakeholders from the public and private sectors, academia as well as civil society to cooperate on problem analysis, priority setting, planning and delivery modalities. There is the need to set up ocean economic program that will increase the GDP by job creation through many blue economy activities to consider but focuses fully on the four paramount maritime areas; maritime transport and manufacturing, food/fish processing and preservation, aquaculture and marine protection services and governance. The Nations of the world must be inspired to raise and improve its blue economy by particularly supporting "sustainable industries" in aquaculture and mariculture, food production, sea or ocean transportation, offshore plant engineering, seawater utilization, renewable ocean energy, ecological restoration, and biodiversity conservation. The Nations of the world must come up with strategy that completely overhaul there ocean governance by developing some policies and innovative strategy that will improve the blue economy activities which eventually lead to an in increase the country's GDP

REFERENCES

Bentlage, M., Wiese, A., Brandt, A., Thierstein, A., & Witlox, F. (2014). Revealing relevant proximities knowledge networks in the maritime economy in a spatial, functional, and relational perspective. *Raumforschung und Raumordnung*, *72*(4), 275–291. doi:10.100713147-014-0299-2

Boonstra, W. J., Valman, M., & Bjorkvik, E. (2018). A sea of many colours—How relevant is blue growth for capture fisheries in the Global North, and vice versa? *Marine Policy*, *87*, 340–349. doi:10.1016/j.marpol.2017.09.007

Brookes, G., & Barfoot, P. (2016). Global income and production impacts of using GM crop Technology 1996–2014. *GM Crops and Food: Biotechnology in Agriculture and the Food Chain*, *7*(1), 38–77. doi:10.1080/21645698.2016.1176817 PMID:27116697

Buiatti, M., Christou, P., & Pastore, G. (2013). The application of GMOs in agriculture and in food production for a better nutrition: Two different scientific points of view. *Genes & Nutrition*, *8*(3), 255–270. doi:10.100712263-012-0316-4 PMID:23076994

Burgess, M. G., Clemence, M., McDermott, G. R., Costello, C., & Gaines, S. D. (2018). Five rules for pragmatic blue growth. *Marine Policy*, *87*, 331–339. doi:10.1016/j.marpol.2016.12.005

Caswell, B. A., Klein, E. S., Alleway, H. K., Ball, J. E., Botero, J., Cardinale, M., & Thurstan, R. H. (2020). Something old, something new: Historical perspectives provide lessons for blue growth agendas. *Fish and Fisheries*, *1246*(4), 774–796. Advance online publication. doi:10.1111/faf.12460

Choi, Y. R. (2017). The blue economy as governmentality and the making of new spatial rationalities. *Dialogues in Human Geography*, *7*(1), 37–41. doi:10.1177/2043820617691649

Costa, J. A. V., de Freitas, B. C. B., Lisboa, C. R., Santos, T. D., de Fraga Brusch, L. R., & de Morais, M. G. (2019). Microalgal biorefinery from CO_2 and the effects under the blue economy. *Renewable & Sustainable Energy Reviews*, *99*, 58–65. doi:10.1016/j.rser.2018.08.009

Costanza, R. (1999). The ecological, economic, and social importance of the oceans. *Ecological Economics*, *31*(2), 199–213. doi:10.1016/S0921-8009(99)00079-8

Cristiani, P. (2017). New challenges for materials in the blue economy perspective. *MetallItaliana*, *7–8*, 7–10.

Djavidnia, S., Ott, M., & Seeyave, S. (2014). *Oceans and society: Blue planet.* Cambridge Scholars Publishing.

Edwards, P., & Roberts, I. (2009). Population adiposity and climate change. *International Journal of Epidemiology*, *1*, 1–4. PMID:19377099

European Commission. (2020). *The EU blue economy report.* Publications Office of the European Union., doi:10.2771/073370

Fisher, B., Turner, R. K., & Morling, P. (2009). Defining and classifying ecosystem services for decision making. *Ecological Economics*, *68*(3), 643–653. doi:10.1016/j.ecolecon.2008.09.014

Ghoshal, S. (2014). Understanding food mile: An qualitative study on the concept of food mile. *TSM Business Review.*, *2*(2), 55–70.

Gryka, A., Broom, J., & Rolland, C. (2012). Global warming: Is weight loss a solution? *International Journal of Obesity*, *36*(3), 474–476. doi:10.1038/ijo.2011.151 PMID:21792168

Gudners, D. (2012). *Wasted: How America Is Losing Up to 40 Percent of Its Food from Farm to Fork to Landfill.* NRDC. August iP:12-06-B.

Hall, K. D., Guo, J., Dore, M., & Chow, C. C. (2009). The Progressive Increase of Food Waste in America and Its Environmental Impact. *PLoS One*, *4*(11), e7940. doi:10.1371/journal.pone.0007940 PMID:19946359

Heller, M. C., & Keoleia, G. A. (2000). Life Cycle-Based Sustainability Indicators for Assessment of the U.S. Food System. University of Michigan.

Hoegh-Guldberg, O., Beal, D., Chaudhry, T., Elhaj, H., Abdullat, A., & Etessy, P. (2015). *Reviving the ocean economy: the case for action.* WWF International.

James, C. A. (2010). Global overview of biotech (GM) Crops: Adoption, impact and future prospects. *GM Crops*, *1*(1), 8–12. doi:10.4161/gmcr.1.1.9756 PMID:21912206

Kaczynski, W. (2011). The future of the blue economy: Lessons for the European Union. *Found Manag*, *3*(1), 21–32. doi:10.2478/v10238-012-0033-8

Kathijotes, N. (2013). Keynote: Blue economy-environmental and behavioural aspects towards sustainable coastal development. *Procedia: Social and Behavioral Sciences*, *101*, 7–13. doi:10.1016/j.sbspro.2013.07.173

Klümper, W., & Qaim, M. A. (2014). Meta-Analysis of the impacts of genetically modified crops. *PLoS One*, *9*(11), e111629. doi:10.1371/journal.pone.0111629 PMID:25365303

Mah, A. (2021). Future-proofing capitalism: The paradox of the circular economy for plastics. *Global Environmental Politics*, *21*(2), 121–142. doi:10.1162/glep_a_00594

Mann, R. F. (2017). Controlling the Environmental Costs of Obesity. *Environmental Law (Northwestern School of Law)*, *2007*, 47.

Martinez-Vazquez, R. M., Milan-Garcia, J., & Jaime de Pablo, V. (2021). Challenges of the Blue Economy: Evidence and research trends. *Environmental Sciences Europe*, *33*(1), 61. doi:10.118612302-021-00502-1

Morawicki, R. O. (2012). *Handbook of Sustainability for the Food Sciences.* Wiley-Blackwell. doi:10.1002/9780470963166

Morrissey, K. (2017). It's not just a blue economy moment…. *Dialogues in Human Geography*, *7*(1), 42–44. doi:10.1177/2043820617691651

Oonincx, D. G. A. B., van Itterbeeck, J., Heetkamp, M. J. W., van den Brand, H., van Loon, J. J. A., & van Huis, A. (2010). An Exploration on Greenhouse Gas and Ammonia Production by Insect Species Suitable for Animal or Human Consumption. *PLoS One*, *5*(12), e14445. doi:10.1371/journal.pone.0014445 PMID:21206900

Pelc, R., & Fujita, R. M. (2002). Renewable energy from the ocean. *Marine Policy*, *26*(6), 471–479. doi:10.1016/S0308-597X(02)00045-3

Phelan, A., Ruhanen, L., & Mair, J. (2020). Ecosystem services approach for community-based ecotourism: Towards an equitable and sustainable blue economy. *Journal of Sustainable Tourism*, *28*(10), 1–21. doi:10.1080/09669582.2020.1747475

Potgieter, T. (2018). Oceans economy, blue economy, and security: notes on the South African potential and developments. *J Indian Ocean Region, 14*(1), 49–70. .2018.14109 62 doi:10.1080/19480881

Qi, X., & Xiao, W. (2019). Identifying the evolutionary path of maritime industries from the perspective of super network. *Journal of Coastal Research*, *97*(sp1), 131–135. doi:10.2112/SI97-018.1

Quested, T., & Johnson, H. (2009). *Household Food and Drink Waste in the UK.* Report prepared by WRAP. Banbury.

Schutter, M. S., & Hicks, C. C. (2019). Networking the blue economy in Seychelles: Pioneers, resistance, and the power of influence. *Journal of Political Ecology*, *26*(1), 425–447.

Shojaei, A., Ketabi, R., Razkenari, M., Hakim, H., & Wang, J. (2021). Enabling a circular economy in the built environment sector through blockchain technology. *Journal of Cleaner Production*, *294*, 126352. doi:10.1016/j.jclepro.2021.126352

Steinfeld, H. (2006). *Environment and Development (LEAD) Initiative Livestock, and Food and Agriculture Organization. Animal Production and Health Division. Livestock's Long Shadow: Environmental Issues and Options.* FAO.

Taheri, F., Azadi, H., & D'Haese, M. A. (2017). World without Hunger: Organic or GM Crops? *Sustainability*, *9*(4), 580. doi:10.3390u9040580

Techera, E. J. (2018). Supporting blue economy agenda: Fisheries, food security and climate change in the indian ocean. *Journal of the Indian Ocean Region*, *14*(1), 7–27. doi:10.1080/19480881.2017.1420579

Tilman, D., & Clark, M. (2014). Global diets link environmental sustainability and human health. *Nature*, *515*(7528), 518–522. doi:10.1038/nature13959 PMID:25383533

UNCTAD. (2014). *The state of commodity dependence 2014. United Nations Conference on Trade and Development*, Geneva, Switzerland.

UNCTAD. (2016). *Review of Maritime Transport 2016.* United Nations.

Visbeck, M. (2018). Ocean science research is key for a sustainable future. *Nature Communications*, *9*(1), 690.

Visbeck, M., Kronfeld-Goharani, U., Neumann, B., Rickels, W., Schmidt, J., Van Doorn, E., & Quaas, M. F. (2014). Securing blue wealth: The need for a special sustainable development goal for the ocean and coasts. *Marine Policy*, *48*, 184–191.

Wallinga, D. (2010). Agricultural policy and childhood obesity: A food systems and public health commentary. *Health Affairs (Project Hope)*, *29*, 405–410.

Webb, J., Williams, A. G., Hope, E., Evans, D., & Moorhouse, E. (2013). Do foods imported into the UK have a greater environmental impact than the same foods produced within the UK? *The International Journal of Life Cycle Assessment*, *18*(7), 1325–1343.

Weber, C. L., & Matthew, H. S. (2008). Food-Miles and the Relative Climate Impacts of Food Choices in the United States. *Environmental Science & Technology*, *42*(10), 3508–3513.

Wenwen, X., Bingxin, Z., & Lili, W. (2016). Marine industrial cluster structure and its coupling relationship with urban development: A case pf Shandong Province. *Polish Maritime Research*, *23*(s1), 115–122.

World Bank. (2013). *Fish to 2030—prospects for fisheries and aquaculture.* World Bank Report Number 83177-GLB.

World Bank. (2017). *The potential of the Blue Economy: Increasing long-term benefits of the sustainable use of marine resources for Small Island Developing States and Least Developed Countries.* www.worldbank.org

World Bank and United Nations. (2017). *Blue Economy: Increasing Long-term benefits of the sustainable use of marine resources for small island developing states and coastal least developed countries.* https://documents.worldbank.org/curated/en/523151496389684076/pdf/115545-1-6-2017-14-48-41-BlueEconomyJun.pdf

World Health Organization. (2018). *Obesity and overweight.* Available from: http://www.who.int/mediacentre/factsheets/fs311/en/

Chapter 4
The Threat of Invasive Alien Marine Species to the Blue Economy:
The Mediterranean Case

Seda Yildirim
https://orcid.org/0000-0003-4367-6652
Tekirdag Namık Kemal University, Turkey

Merve Kaplan
https://orcid.org/0000-0001-5096-5546
Canakkale Onsekiz Mart University, Turkey

ABSTRACT

This study aims to explore how invasive alien marine species influence biodiversity and blue economy in the Mediterranean Sea. Thus, this study analyzes the impact of invasive alien marine species on seafood market and marine biodiversity by reviewing the current reports, news, and researches among the Mediterranean region. As a result, this study will determine key points for the rising population of invasive alien marine species in the Mediterranean Sea due to the risk level with alien species. The open access data obtained from Food and Agriculture Organization of the United Nations (FAO) will be used to give main indicators for Seafood Market in the Mediterranean Sea. In addition, recent news and reports will be used to determine the effects of invasive alien marine species on countries from the Mediterranean region. With this study, it is thought to give a brief profile for the link between blue economy and invasive alien marine species in the Mediterranean Sea.

INTRODUCTION

One of the most valuable seas in the world is the Mediterranean basin. The Mediterranean region, which hosts a very rich ecosystem, has an important environment not only ecologically, but also socio-politically

DOI: 10.4018/978-1-6684-3393-5.ch004

and economically. Having higher quality and quantity of seafood, it can be said that the Mediterranean plays a critical role in global food security (Yıldırım and Yıldırım, 2021). On the other side, the Mediterranean countries have suffered from the rapidly increasing invasion of foreign fish species in the seas recently. The Suez Canal has been an important corridor facilitating the entry of alien species into Mediterranean waters. However, Leon Vaillant (French zoologist) who predicted this situation, warned policy makers to investigate the effects of the Suez Canal on the marine ecosystem. Looking at today's picture, we have to face the problem with invasive alien species such as giant jellfish (Galil, 2014). Since last decades, the population of invasive alien marine species has increased and almost the numbers of them has been higher than natural species in the Mediterranean.

A study conducted at the University of Gothenburg in Sweden provides evidence that an invasion of alien marine species in the Mediterranean will disrupt the marine food ecosystem. According to Stefan Kalogirou, one of the study team, although the Mediterranean is the region with the most alien species invasion, the lack of information about animal and plant species makes it difficult to examine the subject (Live Science Staff, 2011). Bella Galil (marine biologist), determined that the increasing sea temperature and the rising numbers of invasive alien marine species were the biggest problem in the Mediterranean Sea. According to Galil, the Suez canal would cause the end of current marine biodiversity and ecosystem in the Mediterranean sea when looking higher numbers of invasive alien marine species (increased higher than doubled in the last 30 years) here. For example, there was almost higher population of invasive alien marine species in Israeli. It can be said that each European countries and others in the EU has this risk of invasion (Heller and Debre, 2020). The sighting of the highly venomous lionfish off the coast of Italy is an important indication that invasive species have spread over large areas in the Mediterranean. The lionfish has continued to spread in the Mediterranean in the following years since it was first seen on the Israeli coast by 1991. According to The International Union for the Conservation of Nature (IUCN), over the past two decades, invasive species have been found mostly in waters near Turkey, Cyprus and Lebanon, and off the Tunisian coast. Since there are no natural predators for species such as the lionfish, the population of these creatures in the local seas is increasing very rapidly and is threatening the extinction of the local species (DW recommends, 2017).

Seafood products play an important role in the global food security. Especially, seafood products are main food sources for people from many developing and least developed countries (Yildirim and Kaplan, 2020; Yıldırım and Yıldırım, 2021). On the other side, fishery industry provides economic and social benefits in the country as employing many people and providing income. Blue economy is an important issue for countries whose economy is mostly based on sources of seas or oceans. Like as green economy, blue economy refers to fight against to climate change other factors which are harmful for the sustainability of oceans and seas when keeping economic growth via sources of oceans/seas (The Commonwealth, n.d). Achieving blue economy is a great challenge for many countries while there are too much problems and threatens in oceans and seas. Climate change, global warming, environmental pollution are all big threatens for achieving blue economy in the long term. In addition, some regions also have troubles to keep natural biodiversity due to the rising population of invasive alien marine species in seas. The Mediterranean Sea has the highest risk of invasion of alien marine species in recent years. Achieving sustainable seafood market in the Mediterranean region is an important issue in the context of 2030 Sustainable Development Goals. While food security is a critical issue in the long term, sustainability of marine biodiversity is also important issue in the context of blue economy. This chapter will review how invasive alien marine species influence marine biodiversity and blue economy in the Mediterranean region. By reviewing prior literature, recent reports and statistics, this chapter will present a conceptual framework for the link between invasive alien species and blue economy in the Mediterranean region.

BLUE ECONOMY IN THE MEDITERRANEAN SEA

The Mediterranean region is a densely populated region with a complex political history that includes many different ethnic groups. Today, 21 countries have a coastline to the Mediterranean. These; Albania, Algeria, Bosnia and Herzegovina, Croatia, Cyprus, Egypt, France, Greece, Israel, Italy, Lebanon, Libya, Malta, Monaco, Montenegro, Morocco, Slovenia, Spain, Syria, Tunisia and Turkey. The Mediterranean Sea is a relatively enclosed sea with a high diversity of sensitive ecosystems with limited contact with ocean basins. (Mediterranean 2017 Quality Status Report, n.d). According to Mappr.co, there are listed countries in the Mediterranean as below (Mappr,n.d):

1. Albania,
2. Bosnia and Herzegovina,
3. Gibraltar,
4. Algeria,
5. Morocco,
6. France,
7. Croatia,
8. Montenegro,
9. Cyprus,
10. North Cyprus Turkish Republic,
11. Libya,
12. Lebanon,
13. Egypt,
14. Malta,
15. Monaco,
16. Slovenia,
17. Syria,
18. Tunisia,
19. Turkey,
20. Vatican city,
21. Greece,
22. Spain,
23. Israel,
24. Italy

The Mediterranean region essentially defines countries with a coastline or cultural similarity. Economic growth in Mediterranean countries is slower than in western and northern Europe and national income is low. Italy is one of the most developed industries in these countries. Although France does not have a coast to the Mediterranean, it is considered a Mediterranean country due to its historical and cultural similarities (Mappr, n.d). The Mediterranean is located within the European region. The dividing zone

Table 1. Countries with population in the Mediterranean Sea

Country	2021 Population
Albania	2.872,933
Algeria	44.616,624
Bosnia And Herzegovina	3.263,466
Croatia	4.081,651
Cyprus	1.215,584
Egypt	104.258,327
France	65.426,179
Gibraltar	33.698
Greece	10.370,744
Israel	8.789,774
Italy	60.367,477
Lebanon	6.769,146
Libya	6.958,532
Malta	442.784
Monaco	39.511
Montenegro	628.053
Morocco	37.344,795
Palestine	5.222,748
Slovenia	2.078,724
Spain	46.745,216
Syria	18.275,702
Tunisia	11.935,766
Turkey	85.042,738

Source: World Population Review, 2021

between the northern border of Africa and the southernmost countries of Europe is the Mediterranean Sea. Table 1 shows the populations of the countries in the Mediterranean region. The Mediterranean Sea has a total length of 2,500 miles. This region is called as the Mediterranean including both of lands and sea (World Population Review, 2021).

As seen by Table 1, there are many countries with different size of population in the Mediterranean Sea. Accordingly, both of big sized and small sized countries are related together and they should keep same purpose of achieving blue economy in Mediterranean Sea.

Based on FishBase data, the list of marine species in the Meditarranean Sea is showed in table 2. It can be seen that there are native, endemic, introduces and questionable species in the Mediterranean Sea.

GFCM (Mediterranean General Fisheries Commission – GFCM) is an important organizing to achieve sustainable blue economy in the Mediterranean region. GFCM recalls that the purpose of the Agreement establishing the Mediterranean General Fisheries Commission (GFCM Agreement) is to provide protection, and to sustain marine biodiversity with social, economic and environmental development (FAO (Food and Agriculture Organization of the United Nations), n.d.a). Mediterranean and Black Sea

Table 2. List of Marine Species in the Mediterranean Sea

Marine species	Name	Status
Acanthurus monroviae	Monrovia doctorfish	native
Acipenser naccarii	Adriatic sturgeon	endemic
Acipenser stellatus	Starry sturgeon	native
Acipenser sturio	Sturgeon	native
Huso huso	Beluga	native
Synagrops japonicus	Blackmouth splitfin	native
Alepisaurus ferox	Long snouted lancetfish	native
Alepocephalus rostratus	Risso's smooth-head	native
Alopias superciliosus	Bigeye thresher	native
Alopias vulpinus	Thresher	native
Ammodytes tobianus	Small sandeel	native
Gymnammodytes cicerelus	Mediterranean sand eel	native
Gymnammodytes semisquamatus	Smooth sandeel	introduced
Anguilla anguilla	European eel	native
Anguilla japonica	Japanese eel	questionable
Apogon imberbis	Cardinal fish	native
Apogonichthyoides nigripinnis	Bullseye	misidentification
Apogonichthyoides pharaonis	Pharaoh cardinalfish	introduced
Apogonichthyoides taeniatus	Twobelt cardinal	misidentification
Jaydia queketti	Spotfin cardinal	introduced
Jaydia smithi	Smith's cardinalfish	introduced
Ostorhinchus fasciatus	Broadbanded cardinalfish	introduced
Argentina sphyraena	Argentine	native
Glossanodon leioglossus	Smalltoothed argentine	native
Carlarius parkii	Guinean sea catfish	introduced
Netuma thalassina	Giant catfish	introduced
Atherina boyeri	Big-scale sand smelt	native
Atherina hepsetus	Mediterranean sand smelt	native
Atherina presbyter	Sand smelt	native
Atherinomorus forskalii	Red Sea hardyhead silverside	introduced
Atherinomorus lacunosus	Wide-banded hardyhead silverside	introduced
Aulopus filamentosus	Royal flagfin	native
Balistes capriscus	Grey triggerfish	native
Bathysaurus mollis	Highfin lizardfish	native
Halobatrachus didactylus	Lusitanian toadfish	native
Belone belone	Garfish	native
Belone svetovidovi		native
Tylosurus acus acus	Agujon needlefish	native
Tylosurus acus imperialis		native
Tylosurus choram	Red Sea houndfish	introduced
Beryx decadactylus	Alfonsino	native
Beryx splendens	Splendid alfonsino	introduced
Aidablennius sphynx		native
Blennius ocellaris	Butterfly blenny	native
Coryphoblennius galerita	Montagu's blenny	native
Hypleurochilus bananensis		native
Lipophrys pholis	Shanny	native
Lipophrys trigloides		native
Microlipophrys adriaticus		native
Microlipophrys canevae		native
Microlipophrys dalmatinus		native
Microlipophrys nigriceps	Black-headed blenny	endemic
Omobranchus punctatus	Muzzled blenny	introduced
Parablennius gattorugine	Tompot blenny	native
Parablennius incognitus		native
Parablennius pilicornis	Ringneck blenny	native
Parablennius rouxi		native
Parablennius sanguinolentus	Rusty blenny	native
Parablennius tentacularis	Tentacled blenny	native
Parablennius thysanius	Tasseled blenny	introduced
Parablennius zvonimiri		native
Petroscirtes ancylodon	Arabian fangblenny	introduced
Salaria basilisca		endemic
Salaria pavo	Peacock blenny	native
Scartella cristata	Molly miller	native
Arnoglossus grohmanni		native

continued on following page

Table 2. Continued

Marine species	Name	Status
Arnoglossus imperialis	Imperial scaldfish	native
Arnoglossus kessleri	Scaldback	native
Arnoglossus laterna	Mediterranean scaldfish	native
Arnoglossus rueppelii	Rüppell's scaldback	native
Arnoglossus thori	Thor's scaldfish	native
Bothus podas	Wide-eyed flounder	native
Brama brama	Atlantic pomfret	native
Bregmaceros atlanticus	Antenna codlet	misidentification
Bregmaceros nectabanus	Smallscale codlet	introduced
Bellottia apoda		native
Cataetyx alleni		native
Cataetyx laticeps		native
Grammonus ater		endemic
Callanthias ruber	Parrot seaperch	native
Callionymus fasciatus	Banded dragonet	native
Callionymus filamentosus	Blotchfin dragonet	introduced
Callionymus lyra	Dragonet	native
Callionymus maculatus		native
Callionymus pusillus	Sailfin dragonet	native
Callionymus reticulatus	Reticulated dragonet	native
Callionymus risso	Risso's dragonet	native
Synchiropus phaeton	Phaeton dragonet	native
Capros aper	Boarfish	native
Alectis alexandrina	Alexandria pompano	native
Alepes djedaba	Shrimp scad	introduced
Campogramma glaycos	Vadigo	native
Caranx crysos	Blue runner	native
Caranx hippos	Crevalle jack	native
Caranx rhonchus	False scad	native
Decapterus macarellus	Mackerel scad	native
Decapterus punctatus	Round scad	native
Decapterus russelli	Indian scad	introduced
Elagatis bipinnulata	Rainbow runner	native
Lichia amia	Leerfish	native
Naucrates ductor	Pilotfish	native
Pseudocaranx dentex	White trevally	native
Seriola carpenteri	Guinean amberjack	introduced
Seriola dumerili	Greater amberjack	native
Seriola fasciata	Lesser amberjack	introduced
Trachinotus ovatus	Pompano	native
Trachurus mediterraneus	Mediterranean horse mackerel	native
Trachurus picturatus	Blue jack mackerel	native
Trachurus trachurus	Atlantic horse mackerel	native
Carapus acus	Pearl fish	native
Echiodon dentatus		native
Echiodon drummondii		native
Carcharhinus altimus	Bignose shark	introduced
Carcharhinus amboinensis	Pigeye shark	native
Carcharhinus brachyurus	Copper shark	native
Carcharhinus brevipinna	Spinner shark	native
Carcharhinus falciformis	Silky shark	introduced
Carcharhinus limbatus	Blacktip shark	native
Carcharhinus longimanus	Oceanic whitetip shark	native
Carcharhinus melanopterus	Blacktip reef shark	questionable
Carcharhinus obscurus	Dusky shark	native
Carcharhinus plumbeus	Sandbar shark	native
Galeocerdo cuvier	Tiger shark	introduced
Prionace glauca	Blue shark	native
Carcharias taurus	Sand tiger shark	native
Macroramphosus scolopax	Longspine snipefish	native
Centrolophus niger	Rudderfish	native
Hyperoglyphe perciformis	Barrelfish	native
Schedophilus medusophagus	Cornish blackfish	native
Schedophilus ovalis	Imperial blackfish	native
Centrophorus granulosus	Gulper shark	native
Centrophorus uyato	Little gulper shark	native
Cepola macrophthalma	Red bandfish	native
Cetorhinus maximus	Basking shark	native

continued on following page

Table 2. Continued

Marine species	Name	Status
Chaetodon hoefleri	Four-banded butterflyfish	questionable
Chaetodon larvatus	Hooded butterflyfish	introduced
Champsodon nudivittis		introduced
Champsodon vorax		introduced
Chanos chanos	Milkfish	introduced
Chaunax suttkusi		introduced
Chimaera monstrosa	Rabbit fish	native
Chlopsis bicolor	Bicolor eel	native
Chlorophthalmus agassizi	Shortnose greeneye	native
Citharus linguatula	Spotted flounder	native
Clinitrachus argentatus	Cline	native
Alosa algeriensis	North African shad	native
Alosa alosa	Allis shad	native
Alosa fallax	Twaite shad	native
Herklotsichthys punctatus	Spotback herring	introduced
Sardina pilchardus	European pilchard	native
Sardinella aurita	Round sardinella	native
Sardinella maderensis	Madeiran sardinella	native
Spratelloides delicatulus	Delicate round herring	introduced
Sprattus sprattus	European sprat	native
Ariosoma balearicum	Bandtooth conger	native
Conger conger	European conger	native
Gnathophis mystax	Thinlip conger	native
Rhynchoconger trewavasae		introduced
Coryphaena equiselis	Pompano dolphinfish	native
Coryphaena hippurus	Common dolphinfish	native
Taurulus bubalis	Longspined bullhead	native
Cynoglossus sinusarabici	Red Sea tonguesole	introduced
Symphurus ligulatus	Elongate tonguesole	native
Symphurus nigrescens	Tonguesole	native
Aphanius dispar	Arabian pupfish	introduced
Aphanius fasciatus	Mediterranean banded killifish	native
Dactylopterus volitans	Flying gurnard	native
Dalatias licha	Kitefin shark	native
Bathytoshia centroura	Roughtail stingray	misidentification
Dasyatis chrysonota	Blue stingray	introduced
Dasyatis marmorata	Marbled stingray	native
Dasyatis pastinaca	Common stingray	native
Dasyatis tortonesei	Tortonese's stingray	endemic
Himantura uarnak	Honeycomb stingray	introduced
Pteroplatytrygon violacea	Pelagic stingray	native
Taeniura grabata	Round stingray	native
Urogymnus asperrimus	Porcupine whipray	questionable
Cyclichthys spilostylus	Spotbase burrfish	introduced
Diodon hystrix	Spot-fin porcupinefish	questionable
Dussumieria acuta	Rainbow sardine	misidentification
Dussumieria elopsoides	Slender rainbow sardine	introduced
Etrumeus golanii		introduced
Etrumeus sadina	Red-eye round herring	misidentification
Echeneis naucrates	Live sharksucker	native
Remora australis	Whalesucker	misidentification
Remora brachyptera	Spearfish remora	native
Remora osteochir	Marlin sucker	native
Remora remora	Shark sucker	native
Echinorhinus brucus	Bramble shark	native
Encrasicholina gloria	Red Sea anchovy	native
Engraulis albidus		endemic
Engraulis encrasicolus	European anchovy	native
Stolephorus insularis	Hardenberg's anchovy	introduced
Platax teira	Longfin batfish	introduced
Epigonus constanciae		native
Epigonus denticulatus	Pencil cardinal	native
Epigonus telescopus	Black cardinal fish	native
Microichthys coccoi		endemic
Microichthys sanzoi		endemic
Etmopterus spinax	Velvet belly	native
Evermannella balbo	Balbo sabretooth	native
Cheilopogon exsiliens	Bandwing flyingfish	native

continued on following page

Table 2. Continued

Marine species	Name	Status
Cheilopogon heterurus	Mediterranean flyingfish	native
Exocoetus obtusirostris	Oceanic two-wing flyingfish	native
Exocoetus volitans	Tropical two-wing flyingfish	native
Hirundichthys rondeletii	Black wing flyingfish	native
Hirundichthys speculiger	Mirrorwing flyingfish	native
Parexocoetus mento	African sailfin flyingfish	introduced
Fistularia commersonii	Bluespotted cornetfish	introduced
Fistularia petimba	Red cornetfish	introduced
Gadiculus argenteus	Silvery pout	native
Gadus morhua	Atlantic cod	introduced
Merlangius merlangus	Whiting	native
Micromesistius poutassou	Blue whiting	native
Trisopterus capelanus		endemic
Trisopterus luscus	Pouting	native
Trisopterus minutus	Poor cod	misidentification
Gasterosteus aculeatus	Three-spined stickleback	native
Ruvettus pretiosus	Oilfish	native
Glaucostegus cemiculus	Blackchin guitarfish	native
Glaucostegus halavi	Halavi ray	native
Apletodon dentatus	Small-headed clingfish	native
Apletodon incognitus		native
Diplecogaster bimaculata	Two-spotted clingfish	native
Diplecogaster umutturali		native
Gouania willdenowi	Blunt-snouted clingfish	native
Lepadogaster candolii	Connemarra clingfish	native
Lepadogaster lepadogaster	Shore clingfish	native
Lepadogaster purpurea	Cornish sucker	native
Opeatogenys gracilis		endemic
Aphia minuta	Transparent goby	native
Bathygobius soporator	Frillfin goby	native
Benthophilus stellatus	Stellate tadpole-goby	native
Buenia affinis	De Buen's goby	endemic
Buenia jeffreysii	Jeffrey's goby	questionable
Buenia lombartei		native
Chromogobius quadrivittatus	Chestnut goby	native
Chromogobius zebratus	Kolombatovic's goby	native
Corcyrogobius liechtensteini	Liechtenstein's goby	endemic
Coryogalops ocheticus		introduced
Crystallogobius linearis	Crystal goby	native
Deltentosteus collonianus	Toothed goby	native
Deltentosteus quadrimaculatus	Four-spotted goby	native
Didogobius bentuvii	Ben-Tuvia's goby	endemic
Didogobius schlieweni		endemic
Didogobius splechtnai		endemic
Favonigobius melanobranchus	Blackthroat goby	native
Gammogobius steinitzi	Steinitz's goby	endemic
Gobius ater	Bellotti's goby	native
Gobius auratus	Golden goby	native
Gobius bucchichi	Bucchich's goby	native
Gobius cobitis	Giant goby	native
Gobius couchi	Couch's goby	native
Gobius cruentatus	Red-mouthed goby	native
Gobius fallax	Sarato's goby	native
Gobius gasteveni	Steven's goby	native
Gobius geniporus	Slender goby	endemic
Gobius incognitus		native
Gobius kolombatovici		native
Gobius niger	Black goby	native
Gobius paganellus	Rock goby	native
Gobius roulei	Roule's goby	native
Gobius strictus	Schmidt's goby	endemic
Gobius vittatus	Striped goby	endemic
Gobius xanthocephalus		native
Gobiusculus flavescens	Two-spotted goby	questionable
Gymnesigobius medits		native
Knipowitschia caucasica	Caucasian dwarf goby	native
Lebetus guilleti	Guillet's goby	native
Lebetus patzneri		native

continued on following page

Table 2. Continued

Marine species	Name	Status
Lesueurigobius friesii	Fries's goby	native
Lesueurigobius sanzi	Sanzo's goby	native
Lesueurigobius suerii	Lesueur's goby	endemic
Millerigobius macrocephalus		endemic
Odondebuenia balearica	Coralline goby	endemic
Oxyurichthys papuensis	Frogface goby	introduced
Oxyurichthys petersii		introduced
Pomatoschistus bathi		endemic
Pomatoschistus knerii	Kner's goby	endemic
Pomatoschistus marmoratus	Marbled goby	native
Pomatoschistus microps	Common goby	native
Pomatoschistus minutus	Sand goby	native
Pomatoschistus norvegicus	Norway goby	questionable
Pomatoschistus pictus	Painted goby	native
Pomatoschistus quagga	Quagga goby	endemic
Pomatoschistus tortonesei	Tortonese's goby	endemic
Pseudaphya ferreri	Ferrer's goby	endemic
Silhouettea aegyptia	Red Sea goby	introduced
Speleogobius trigloides	Grotto goby	endemic
Thorogobius ephippiatus	Leopard-spotted goby	native
Thorogobius macrolepis	Large-scaled goby	endemic
Tridentiger trigonocephalus	Chameleon goby	introduced
Trypauchen vagina		introduced
Vanderhorstia mertensi	Mertens' prawn-goby	introduced
Vanneaugobius dollfusi		native
Vanneaugobius pruvoti		native
Zebrus zebrus		native
Zosterisessor ophiocephalus	Grass goby	native
Cyclothone braueri	Garrick	native
Cyclothone microdon	Veiled anglemouth	native
Cyclothone pygmaea		endemic
Gonostoma denudatum		native
Gymnura altavela	Spiny butterfly ray	native
Parapristipoma humile	Guinean grunt	misidentification
Parapristipoma octolineatum	African striped grunt	native
Plectorhinchus mediterraneus	Rubberlip grunt	native
Pomadasys incisus	Bastard grunt	native
Pomadasys stridens	Striped piggy	introduced
Halosaurus ovenii		introduced
Hemiramphus far	Black-barred halfbeak	introduced
Hyporhamphus affinis	Tropical halfbeak	introduced
Hyporhamphus picarti	African halfbeak	native
Panturichthys fowleri		endemic
Heptranchias perlo	Sharpnose sevengill shark	native
Hexanchus griseus	Bluntnose sixgill shark	native
Hexanchus nakamurai	Bigeyed sixgill shark	native
Sargocentron praslin	Dark-striped squirrelfish	introduced
Sargocentron rubrum	Redcoat	introduced
Kyphosus sectatrix	Bermuda sea chub	native
Acantholabrus palloni	Scale-rayed wrasse	native
Centrolabrus exoletus	Rock cook	introduced
Centrolabrus melanocercus		endemic
Coris julis	Mediterranean rainbow wrasse	native
Ctenolabrus rupestris	Goldsinny-wrasse	native
Iniistius pavo	Peacock wrasse	introduced
Labrus bergylta	Ballan wrasse	questionable
Labrus merula	Brown wrasse	native
Labrus mixtus	Cuckoo wrasse	native
Labrus viridis		native
Lappanella fasciata		native
Pteragogus pelycus	Sideburn wrasse	misidentification
Pteragogus trispilus		introduced
Symphodus bailloni	Baillon's wrasse	native
Symphodus cinereus	Grey wrasse	native
Symphodus doderleini		endemic
Symphodus mediterraneus	Axillary wrasse	native
Symphodus melops	Corkwing wrasse	native
Symphodus ocellatus		native
Symphodus roissali	Five-spotted wrasse	native

continued on following page

Table 2. Continued

Marine species	Name	Status
Symphodus rostratus		native
Symphodus tinca	East Atlantic peacock wrasse	native
Symphodus trutta	Emerald wrasse	native
Thalassoma pavo	Ornate wrasse	native
Xyrichtys novacula	Pearly razorfish	native
Carcharodon carcharias	Great white shark	native
Isurus oxyrinchus	Shortfin mako	native
Lamna nasus	Porbeagle	native
Lampris guttatus	Opah	native
Equulites klunzingeri	Klunzinger's ponyfish	introduced
Equulites popei	Pope's ponyfish	introduced
Monotaxis grandoculis	Humpnose big-eye bream	questionable
Eutelichthys leptochirus		endemic
Paraliparis murieli		endemic
Lobotes surinamensis	Tripletail	native
Lophius budegassa	Blackbellied angler	native
Lophius piscatorius	Angler	native
Lophotus lacepede	Crested oarfish	native
Gaidropsarus biscayensis	Mediterranean bigeye rockling	native
Gaidropsarus granti	Azores rockling	native
Gaidropsarus mediterraneus	Shore rockling	native
Gaidropsarus vulgaris	Three-bearded rockling	native
Molva dypterygia	Blue ling	native
Molva macrophthalma	Spanish ling	native
Molva molva	Ling	native
Lutjanus argentimaculatus	Mangrove red snapper	introduced
Lutjanus jocu	Dog snapper	native
Luvarus imperialis	Luvar	native
Coelorinchus caelorhincus	Hollowsnout grenadier	native
Coelorinchus mediterraneus		native
Coelorinchus occa	Swordsnout grenadier	native
Coryphaenoides guentheri	Günther's grenadier	native
Coryphaenoides mediterraneus	Mediterranean grenadier	native
Hymenocephalus italicus	Glasshead grenadier	native
Nezumia aequalis	Common Atlantic grenadier	native
Nezumia sclerorhynchus	Roughtip grenadier	native
Trachyrincus scabrus	Roughsnout grenadier	native
Merluccius merluccius	European hake	native
Microstoma microstoma	Slender argentine	native
Nansenia iberica		endemic
Nansenia oblita		native
Mobula mobular	Devil fish	native
Mola mola	Ocean sunfish	native
Ranzania laevis	Slender sunfish	native
Aluterus monoceros	Unicorn leatherjacket filefish	introduced
Stephanolepis diaspros	Reticulated leatherjacket	introduced
Eretmophorus kleinenbergi		native
Gadella maraldi	Gadella	native
Guttigadus latifrons		native
Lepidion guentheri		native
Lepidion lepidion	Mediterranean codling	endemic
Mora moro	Common mora	native
Physiculus dalwigki	Black codling	native
Rhynchogadus hepaticus		native
Dicentrarchus labrax	European seabass	native
Dicentrarchus punctatus	Spotted seabass	native
Chelon auratus	Golden grey mullet	native
Chelon caeruleus		native
Chelon labrosus	Thicklip grey mullet	native
Chelon ramada	Thinlip grey mullet	native
Chelon saliens	Leaping mullet	native
Liza carinata	Keeled mullet	introduced
Mugil cephalus	Flathead grey mullet	native
Oedalechilus labeo	Boxlip mullet	native
Planiliza haematocheila	So-iuy mullet	introduced
Mullus barbatus barbatus	Red mullet	native
Mullus surmuletus	Surmullet	native
Parupeneus forsskali	Red Sea goatfish	questionable

continued on following page

Table 2. Continued

Marine species	Name	Status
Pseudupeneus prayensis	West African goatfish	native
Upeneus moluccensis	Goldband goatfish	introduced
Upeneus pori	Por's goatfish	introduced
Cynoponticus ferox	Guinean pike conger	native
Muraenesox cinereus	Daggertooth pike conger	introduced
Anarchias euryurus		native
Enchelycore anatina	Fangtooth moray	introduced
Gymnothorax reticularis		introduced
Gymnothorax unicolor	Brown moray	native
Muraena helena	Mediterranean moray	native
Benthosema glaciale	Glacier lantern fish	native
Ceratoscopelus maderensis	Madeira lantern fish	native
Diaphus holti	Small lantern fish	native
Diaphus metopoclampus	Spothead lantern fish	native
Diaphus rafinesquii	White-spotted lantern fish	native
Diogenichthys atlanticus	Longfin lanternfish	native
Electrona risso	Electric lantern fish	native
Gonichthys cocco	Cocco's lanternfish	native
Hygophum benoiti	Benoit's lanternfish	native
Hygophum hygomii	Bermuda lantern fish	native
Lampanyctus crocodilus	Jewel lanternfish	native
Lampanyctus pusillus	Pygmy lanternfish	native
Lobianchia dofleini	Dofleini's lantern fish	native
Lobianchia gemellarii	Cocco's lantern fish	native
Myctophum punctatum	Spotted lanternfish	native
Notoscopelus bolini		native
Notoscopelus elongatus		endemic
Notoscopelus kroyeri	Lancet fish	native
Symbolophorus veranyi	Large-scale lantern fish	native
Aetomylaeus bovinus	Bull ray	native
Myliobatis aquila	Common eagle ray	native
Myxine glutinosa	Atlantic hagfish	native
Nemichthys scolopaceus	Slender snipe eel	native
Nemipterus japonicus	Japanese threadfin bream	introduced
Nemipterus randalli	Randall's threadfin bream	introduced
Facciolella oxyrhyncha	Facciola's sorcerer	native
Nettastoma melanura	Blackfin sorcerer	native
Saurenchelys cancrivora	Slender sorcerer	native
Cubiceps capensis	Cape fathead	native
Cubiceps gracilis	Driftfish	native
Psenes pellucidus	Bluefin driftfish	introduced
Notacanthus bonaparte	Shortfin spiny eel	native
Polyacanthonotus rissoanus	Smallmouth spiny eel	native
Odontaspis ferox	Smalltooth sand tiger	native
Apterichtus anguiformis	Slender finless eel	native
Apterichtus caecus	European finless eel	native
Dalophis imberbis	Armless snake eel	native
Echelus myrus	Painted eel	native
Mystriophis crosnieri		native
Ophichthus ophis	Spotted snake eel	native
Ophichthus rufus	Rufus snake-eel	endemic
Ophisurus serpens	Serpent eel	native
Benthocometes robustus		native
Ophidion barbatum	Snake blenny	native
Ophidion rochei		native
Parophidion vassali		endemic
Oplegnathus fasciatus	Barred knifejaw	introduced
Acanthostracion notacanthus	Island cowfish	questionable
Acanthostracion quadricornis	Scrawled cowfish	questionable
Lactophrys trigonus	Buffalo trunkfish	questionable
Ostracion cubicus	Yellow boxfish	introduced
Oxynotus centrina	Angular roughshark	native
Arctozenus risso	Spotted barracudina	native
Lestidiops jayakari	Pacific barracudina	native
Lestidiops pseudosphyraenoides		native
Lestidiops sphyrenoides		native
Lestidium atlanticum	Atlantic barracudina	native
Paralepis coregonoides	Sharpchin barracudina	native

continued on following page

Table 2. Continued

Marine species	Name	Status
Paralepis speciosa		endemic
Pempheris mangula	Indian sweeper	introduced
Pempheris rhomboidea		native
Galeus atlanticus	Atlantic sawtail cat shark	native
Galeus melastomus	Blackmouth catshark	native
Peristedion cataphractum	African armoured searobin	native
Lampetra fluviatilis	River lamprey	native
Petromyzon marinus	Sea lamprey	native
Ichthyococcus ovatus	Lightfish	native
Vinciguerria attenuata	Slender lightfish	native
Vinciguerria poweriae	Power's deep-water bristle-mouth fish	native
Phycis blennoides	Greater forkbeard	native
Phycis phycis	Forkbeard	native
Papilloculiceps longiceps	Tentacled flathead	introduced
Platycephalus indicus	Bartail flathead	introduced
Sorsogona prionota	Halfspined flathead	introduced
Platichthys flesus	European flounder	native
Pleuronectes platessa	European plaice	misidentification
Plotosus lineatus	Striped eel catfish	introduced
Galeoides decadactylus	Lesser African threadfin	native
Polyprion americanus	Wreckfish	native
Holacanthus ciliaris	Queen angelfish	introduced
Pomacanthus imperator	Emperor angelfish	introduced
Pomacanthus maculosus	Yellowbar angelfish	introduced
Abudefduf saxatilis	Sergeant-major	introduced
Abudefduf vaigiensis	Indo-Pacific sergeant	introduced
Chromis chromis	Damselfish	native
Chromis viridis	Blue green damselfish	native
Pomatomus saltatrix	Bluefish	native
Priacanthus hamrur	Moontail bullseye	questionable
Priacanthus sagittarius	Arrow bulleye	introduced
Pristis pectinata	Smalltooth sawfish	native
Pristis pristis	Common sawfish	native
Rachycentron canadum	Cobia	introduced
Dipturus batis	Blue skate	native
Dipturus oxyrinchus	Longnosed skate	native
Leucoraja circularis	Sandy ray	native
Leucoraja fullonica	Shagreen ray	native
Leucoraja melitensis	Maltese ray	endemic
Leucoraja naevus	Cuckoo ray	native
Raja africana	African ray	native
Raja asterias	Mediterranean starry ray	native
Raja brachyura	Blonde ray	native
Raja clavata	Thornback ray	native
Raja miraletus	Brown ray	native
Raja montagui	Spotted ray	native
Raja polystigma	Speckled ray	endemic
Raja radula	Rough ray	native
Raja rondeleti	Rondelet's ray	endemic
Raja undulata	Undulate ray	native
Rostroraja alba	White skate	native
Regalecus glesne	King of herrings	native
Rhinobatos rhinobatos	Common guitarfish	native
Rhinoptera marginata	Lusitanian cownose ray	native
Coregonus lavaretus	European whitefish	introduced
Salmo salar	Atlantic salmon	native
Salmo trutta	Sea trout	native
Thymallus thymallus	Grayling	native
Scarus ghobban	Blue-barred parrotfish	introduced
Sparisoma cretense	Parrotfish	native
Scatophagus argus	Spotted scat	introduced
Argyrosomus regius	Meagre	native
Sciaena umbra	Brown meagre	native
Sciaenops ocellatus	Red drum	introduced
Umbrina canariensis	Canary drum	native
Umbrina cirrosa	Shi drum	native
Umbrina ronchus	Fusca drum	native
Scomberesox saurus	Atlantic saury	native

continued on following page

Table 2. Continued

Marine species	Name	Status
Acanthocybium solandri	Wahoo	native
Auxis rochei	Bullet tuna	native
Euthynnus alletteratus	Little tunny	native
Katsuwonus pelamis	Skipjack tuna	native
Orcynopsis unicolor	Plain bonito	native
Rastrelliger kanagurta	Indian mackerel	introduced
Sarda sarda	Atlantic bonito	native
Scomber colias	Atlantic chub mackerel	native
Scomber japonicus	Chub mackerel	misidentification
Scomber scombrus	Atlantic mackerel	native
Scomberomorus commerson	Narrow-barred Spanish mackerel	introduced
Scomberomorus tritor	West African Spanish mackerel	native
Thunnus alalunga	Albacore	native
Thunnus albacares	Yellowfin tuna	misidentification
Thunnus thynnus	Atlantic bluefin tuna	native
Lepidorhombus boscii	Four-spot megrim	native
Lepidorhombus whiffiagonis	Megrim	native
Scophthalmus maeoticus	Black Sea brill	native
Scophthalmus maximus	Turbot	native
Scophthalmus rhombus	Brill	native
Zeugopterus punctatus	Topknot	native
Zeugopterus regius	Eckström's topknot	native
Pontinus kuhlii	Offshore rockfish	native
Pterois miles	Devil firefish	introduced
Scorpaena azorica		questionable
Scorpaena elongata	Slender rockfish	native
Scorpaena loppei	Cadenat's rockfish	native
Scorpaena maderensis	Madeira rockfish	native
Scorpaena notata	Small red scorpionfish	native
Scorpaena porcus	Black scorpionfish	native
Scorpaena scrofa	Red scorpionfish	native
Scorpaena stephanica	Spotted-fin rockfish	native
Scorpaenodes arenai	Messina rockfish	native
Sebastapistes mauritiana	Spineblotch scorpionfish	questionable
Scyliorhinus canicula	Lesser spotted dogfish	native
Scyliorhinus stellaris	Nursehound	native
Helicolenus dactylopterus	Blackbelly rosefish	native
Trachyscorpia cristulata echinata	Spiny scorpionfish	introduced
Anthias anthias	Swallowtail seaperch	native
Cephalopholis taeniops	Bluespotted seabass	introduced
Epinephelus aeneus	White grouper	native
Epinephelus caninus	Dogtooth grouper	native
Epinephelus coioides	Orange-spotted grouper	introduced
Epinephelus costae	Goldblotch grouper	native
Epinephelus malabaricus	Malabar grouper	introduced
Epinephelus marginatus	Dusky grouper	native
Epinephelus tauvina	Greasy grouper	misidentification
Hyporthodus haifensis	Haifa grouper	native
Mycteroperca fusca	Island grouper	native
Mycteroperca rubra	Mottled grouper	native
Serranus atricauda	Blacktail comber	native
Serranus cabrilla	Comber	native
Serranus hepatus	Brown comber	native
Serranus scriba	Painted comber	native
Serrivomer lanceolatoides	Short-tooth sawpalate	native
Siganus luridus	Dusky spinefoot	introduced
Siganus rivulatus	Marbled spinefoot	introduced
Sillago suezensis		introduced
Bathysolea profundicola	Deepwater sole	native
Buglossidium luteum	Solenette	native
Dagetichthys lusitanicus	Portuguese sole	native
Dicologlossa cuneata	Wedge sole	native
Dicologlossa hexophthalma	Ocellated wedge sole	introduced
Microchirus azevia		native
Microchirus boscanion	Lusitanian sole	native
Microchirus ocellatus	Foureyed sole	native
Microchirus variegatus	Thickback sole	native
Monochirus hispidus	Whiskered sole	native

continued on following page

Table 2. Continued

Marine species	Name	Status
Pegusa impar	Adriatic sole	native
Pegusa lascaris	Sand sole	native
Pegusa nasuta	Blackhand sole	native
Solea aegyptiaca	Egyptian sole	native
Solea senegalensis	Senegalese sole	native
Solea solea	Common sole	native
Synapturichthys kleinii	Klein's sole	native
Centroscymnus coelolepis	Portuguese dogfish	native
Somniosus rostratus	Little sleeper shark	native
Acanthopagrus bifasciatus	Twobar seabream	introduced
Boops boops	Bogue	native
Centracanthus cirrus	Curled picarel	native
Crenidens crenidens	Karanteen seabream	introduced
Dentex dentex	Common dentex	native
Dentex gibbosus	Pink dentex	native
Dentex macrophthalmus	Large-eye dentex	native
Dentex maroccanus	Morocco dentex	native
Diplodus annularis	Annular seabream	native
Diplodus bellottii	Senegal seabream	native
Diplodus cervinus	Zebra seabream	native
Diplodus puntazzo	Sharpsnout seabream	native
Diplodus sargus	White seabream	native
Diplodus vulgaris	Common two-banded seabream	native
Evynnis ehrenbergii		native
Lithognathus mormyrus	Sand steenbras	native
Oblada melanura	Saddled seabream	native
Pagellus acarne	Axillary seabream	native
Pagellus bellottii	Red pandora	native
Pagellus bogaraveo	Blackspot seabream	native
Pagellus erythrinus	Common pandora	native
Pagrus auriga	Redbanded seabream	native
Pagrus caeruleostictus	Bluespotted seabream	native
Pagrus major	Red seabream	introduced
Pagrus pagrus	Red porgy	native
Rhabdosargus haffara	Haffara seabream	introduced
Sarpa salpa	Salema	native
Sparus aurata	Gilthead seabream	native
Spicara maena	Blotched picarel	native
Spicara smaris	Picarel	native
Spondyliosoma cantharus	Black seabream	native
Sphyraena chrysotaenia	Yellowstripe barracuda	introduced
Sphyraena flavicauda	Yellowtail barracuda	introduced
Sphyraena obtusata	Obtuse barracuda	introduced
Sphyraena pinguis	Red barracuda	introduced
Sphyraena sphyraena	European barracuda	native
Sphyraena viridensis	Yellowmouth barracuda	native
Sphyrna lewini	Scalloped hammerhead	native
Sphyrna mokarran	Great hammerhead	native
Sphyrna tudes	Smalleye hammerhead	native
Sphyrna zygaena	Smooth hammerhead	native
Squalus acanthias	Picked dogfish	native
Squalus blainville	Longnose spurdog	native
Squalus megalops	Shortnose spurdog	native
Squatina aculeata	Sawback angelshark	native
Squatina oculata	Smoothback angelshark	native
Squatina squatina	Angelshark	native
Argyropelecus hemigymnus	Half-naked hatchetfish	native
Argyropelecus olfersii		native
Maurolicus muelleri	Silvery lightfish	native
Valenciennellus tripunctulatus	Constellationfish	native
Bathophilus nigerrimus	Scaleless dragonfish	native
Bathophilus vaillanti		native
Borostomias antarcticus	Snaggletooth	native
Chauliodus sloani	Sloane's viperfish	native
Stomias boa boa	Boa dragonfish	native
Pampus argenteus	Silver pomfret	native
Stromateus fiatola	Blue butterfish	native
Sudis hyalina		native
Dysomma brevirostre	Pignosed arrowtooth eel	native

continued on following page

Table 2. Continued

Marine species	Name	Status
Entelurus aequoreus	Snake pipefish	native
Hippocampus fuscus	Sea pony	introduced
Hippocampus guttulatus	Long-snouted seahorse	native
Hippocampus hippocampus	Short snouted seahorse	native
Minyichthys sentus		native
Nerophis lumbriciformis	Worm pipefish	native
Nerophis maculatus		native
Nerophis ophidion	Straightnose pipefish	native
Syngnathus abaster	Black-striped pipefish	native
Syngnathus acus	Greater pipefish	native
Syngnathus phlegon		native
Syngnathus rostellatus	Nilsson's pipefish	introduced
Syngnathus taenionotus		endemic
Syngnathus tenuirostris	Narrow-snouted pipefish	native
Syngnathus typhle	Broadnosed pipefish	native
Saurida lessepsianus		native
Saurida undosquamis	Brushtooth lizardfish	questionable
Synodus saurus	Atlantic lizardfish	native
Pelates quadrilineatus	Fourlined terapon	introduced
Terapon jarbua	Jarbua terapon	introduced
Terapon puta	Small-scaled terapon	introduced
Terapon theraps	Largescaled terapon	introduced
Tetragonurus cuvieri	Smalleye squaretail	native
Arothron hispidus	White-spotted puffer	questionable
Ephippion guttifer	Prickly puffer	native
Lagocephalus lagocephalus	Oceanic puffer	native
Lagocephalus sceleratus	Silver-cheeked toadfish	introduced
Lagocephalus spadiceus	Half-smooth golden pufferfish	introduced
Lagocephalus suezensis		introduced
Sphoeroides marmoratus	Guinean puffer	introduced
Sphoeroides pachygaster	Blunthead puffer	introduced
Torquigener flavimaculosus	Yellowspotted puffer	introduced
Tylerius spinosissimus	Spiny blaasop	introduced
Tetronarce nobiliana	Electric ray	native
Torpedo alexandrinsis	Alexandrine torpedo	questionable
Torpedo marmorata	Marbled electric ray	native
Torpedo sinuspersici	Variable torpedo ray	questionable
Torpedo torpedo	Common torpedo	native
Aulotrachichthys sajademalensis	Saya de Malha luminous roughy	native
Gephyroberyx darwinii	Darwin's slimehead	introduced
Hoplostethus mediterraneus	Mediterranean slimehead	native
Echiichthys vipera	Lesser weever	native
Trachinus araneus	Spotted weever	native
Trachinus draco	Greater weever	native
Trachinus radiatus	Starry weever	native
Trachipterus arcticus	Dealfish	native
Trachipterus trachypterus	Mediterranean dealfish	native
Zu cristatus	Scalloped ribbonfish	native
Galeorhinus galeus	Tope shark	native
Mustelus asterias	Starry smooth-hound	native
Mustelus mustelus	Smooth-hound	native
Mustelus punctulatus	Blackspotted smooth-hound	native
Lepidopus caudatus	Silver scabbardfish	native
Trichiurus lepturus	Largehead hairtail	native
Chelidonichthys cuculus	Red gurnard	native
Chelidonichthys lastoviza	Streaked gurnard	native
Chelidonichthys lucerna	Tub gurnard	native
Chelidonichthys obscurus	Longfin gurnard	native
Eutrigla gurnardus	Grey gurnard	native
Lepidotrigla cavillone	Large-scaled gurnard	native
Lepidotrigla dieuzeidei	Spiny gurnard	native
Trigla lyra	Piper gurnard	native
Tripterygion delaisi	Black-faced blenny	native
Tripterygion melanurum		endemic
Tripterygion tripteronotum		native
Uranoscopus scaber	Stargazer	native
Xiphias gladius	Swordfish	native
Zenopsis conchifer	Silvery John dory	introduced
Zeus faber	John dory	native

continued on following page

Table 2. Continued

Marine species	Name	Status
Melanostigma atlanticum	Atlantic soft pout	native
Bathypterois dubius	Spiderfish	native
Bathypterois grallator	Tripodfish	native
Istiompax indica	Black marlin	questionable
Istiophorus albicans	Atlantic sailfish	native
Kajikia albida	Atlantic white marlin	native
Makaira nigricans	Blue marlin	native
Tetrapturus belone	Mediterranean spearfish	endemic
Tetrapturus georgii	Roundscale spearfish	native

Source: FishBase, (2015)

fisheries include an area promoting significant socio-economic development where fishing activities take place on a wide range of scales. The GFCM is involved in taking the necessary measures and developing strategies for sustainable fisheries in the Mediterranean region. At this point, the medium-term strategy for the sustainability of Mediterranean and Black Sea fisheries (2017-2020) is an important contract adopted by the GFCM parties to improve the sustainability of the Mediterranean and Black Seas by 2020 (FAO (Food and Agriculture Organization of the United Nations), n.d.b). It is also known that aquaculture plays an important role for food security, employment and economic development in the Mediterranean and Black Seas. As well as capture production, aquaculture is also an important sector. GFCM has taken responsibility for the sustainable development of aquaculture and marine and other inland aquaculture in the field of application since its first years of operation (FAO (Food and Agriculture Organization of the United Nations), n.d.c). In table 3, captured production quantities of European countries are presented.

According to FAO, GFCM has some subareas with different numbering (see Table 4). Thus, each subareas presents different characteristics of Mediterranean Sea. Table 5 also shows main subareas for GFCM as below:

Between 2015 and 2019, quantities of capture production among each country in Mediterranean Sea can be seen in table 6. It can be said that Turkey had the biggest share in capture production in Mediterranean Sea during the period of 2015-2019. Then, Italy, Algeria, Greece, Ukraine, Croatia, Egypt, Georgia, Russian Federation, Spain and Tunisia had higher share in capture production in a total production.

As mentioned in Table 6, Turkey had the highest share in total capture production among the Mediterranean Sea during the period of 2010-2019. Table 7 shows the rate of capture production for each country in the Mediterranean Sea. Turkey had 27.62% share in total capture production. Then, Italy, Tunisia, Algeria, Spain, Croatia, Greece, Egypt and Russian Federation had higher share in capture production than others in the Mediterranean Sea.

Table 8 shows production rates based on subareas in the Mediterranean Sea. According to FAO's data, Black Sea (Subarea 37.4) had 37.96 share in a total production, Western Mediterranean (Subarea 37.1) had 24.46% share in a total production, Central Mediterranean (Subarea 37.2) had 25.16% share in a total production and Eastern Mediterranean (Subarea 37.3) had 12.42 share in a total production among the Mediterranean Sea.

Table 9 shows top commercial species by value in the Mediterranean Sea and Black sea. It can be said that there were many valuable species in the Mediterranean Sea.

According to The UfM Ministerial on Blue Economy of 2015, the concept of the Blue Economy is understood as "the set of human activities supported by land-sea interactions in the context of maritime and/or sustainable development and involving industry and service sectors, particularly aquaculture". At the Blue Economy Ministerial meeting held in Brussels on 17 November 2015, ministers from 43 UfM countries declared that the Blue Economy should be an approach to support its potential to pro-

Table 3. Captured production by European Countries (2018)

Countries	Ocean Area	Species	2018
Albania	Ionian	Crustaceans	1.811
		Marine fishes	3.916
		Molluscs	386
	Sub-total Ionian		6.113
	Tunas (GFCM area)		107
Total Albania			6.220
Bosnia and Herzegovina	Adriatic	Marine fishes	5F
Bulgaria	Black Sea	Crustaceans	1
		Diadromous fishes	11
		Marine fishes	4.382
		Molluscs	4.128
	Sub-total Black Sea		8.522
	Tunas (GFCM area)	Marine fishes	23
Total Bulgaria			8 545
Croatia	Adriatic	Crustaceans	1.180
		Marine fishes	66.641
		Miscellaneous aquatic animal products	31
		Miscellaneous aquatic animals	138
		Molluscs	1.151
	Sub-total Adriatic		69.141
	Tunas (GFCM area)		881
Total Croatia			70.022
France	Balearic	Marine fishes	1
	Gulf of Lion	Crustaceans	237
		Diadromous fishes	322
		Marine fishes	8.640
		Miscellaneous aquatic animal products	1
		Miscellaneous aquatic animals	107
		Molluscs	2.841F
	Sub-total Gulf of Lion		12 149
	Ionian	Marine fishes	4
	Sardina	Crustaceans	54
		Diadromous fishes	5
		Marine fishes	256
		Miscellaneous aquatic animals	17
		Molluscs	17
	Sub-total Sardina		350
	Tunas (GFCM area)	Marine fishes	4.504F
Total France			17.007
Gibraitar	Balearic	Marine fishes	1F
Greece	Aegean	Crustaceans	6.622
		Diadromous fishes	4
		Marine fishes	52.705
		Miscellaneous aquatic animal products	2F
		Molluscs	6.893
	Sub-total Aegean		66.227
	Ionian	Crustaceans	298
		Diadromous fishes	7
		Marine fishes	6.528
		Molluscs	629
	Sub-total Ionian		7.462
	Tunas (GFCM area)	Marine fishes	2.563F
Total Greece			76.251

continued on following page

mote growth, employment and investment, and reduce poverty. Six years after the first UfM Ministerial

Table 3. Continued

Countries	Ocean Area	Species	2018
Italy	Adriatic	Crustaceans	6.416
		Diadromous fishes	36
		Marine fishes	51.696
		Miscellaneous aquatic animal products	1
		Molluscs	23.846
	Sub-total Adriatic		81.995
	Ionian	Crustaceans	12.668
		Diadromous fishes	33.890
		Marine fishes	78
		Molluscs	10.527F
	Sub-total Ionian		57.164
	Sardina	Crustaceans	4.351
		Diadromous fishes	73
		Marine fishes	32.235
		Molluscs	7.286
	Sub-total Sardina		43.946
	Tunas (GFCM area)	Marine fishes	9.397
Total Italy			192.501
Malta	Ionian	Crustaceans	49
		Diadromous fishes	6
		Marine fishes	1.875
		Molluscs	56
	Sub-total Sardina		1.986
	Tunas (GFCM area)	Marine fishes	747
Total Malta			2.733
Monaco	Gulf of Lion	Marine fishes	1
Montenegro	Adriatic	Crustaceans	50
		Marine fishes	922
		Molluscs	43
	Sub-total Adriatic		1.015
	Tunas (GFCM area)	Marine fishes	132
Total Montenegro			1.147
Portugal	Aegean	Crustaceans	10
	Balearic	Crustaceans	0
	Ionian	Crustaceans	35
	Sardina	Crustaceans	7
Total Portugal			52
Romania	Black Sea	Diadromous fishes	5
		Marine fishes	179
		Molluscs	7.561
	Sub-total Black Sea		7.745
Total Romania			7.745
Russian Federation	Azov Sea	Crustaceans	14
		Diadromous fishes	4.893
		Freshwater fishes	2.117
		Marine fishes	9.260
		Miscellaneous aquatic animal products	476
		Molluscs	1.800
	Sub-total Azov Sea		18.560
	Black Sea	Crustaceans	142
		Diadromous fishes	72
		Marine fishes	54.303
		Molluscs	147
	Sub-total Black Sea		54.664
Total Russian Federation			73.224
Slovenia	Adriatic	Crustaceans	1
		Marine fishes	99
		Miscellaneous aquatic animal products	1
		Molluscs	33
	Sub-total Adriatic		134
	Tunas (GFCM area)	Marine fishes	1

continued on following page

Table 3. Continued

Countries	Ocean Area	Species	2018
Total Slovenia			135
Spain	Balearic	Crustaceans	6.146F
		Diadromous fishes	23
		Marine fishes	67.090
		Miscellaneous aquatic animal products	1
		Miscellaneous aquatic animals	13F
		Molluscs	7.422F
	Sub-total Balearic		80.695
	Gulf of Lion	Crustaceans	102F
		Diadromous fishes	0
		Marine fishes	1.175
		Molluscs	58F
	Sub-total Gulf of Lion		1.335
	Sardina	Marine fishes	24F
		Molluscs	2F
	Sub-total Sardina		26F
	Tunas (GFCM area)	Marine fishes	9.277F
Total Spain			91.333
Ukraine	Azov Sea	Crustaceans	13
		Diadromous fishes	7.935
		Freshwater fishes	117
		Marine fishes	13.107F
		Miscellaneous aquatic animal	314F
	Sub-total Azov Sea		21.487F
	Black Sea	Crustaceans	540
		Diadromous fishes	22F
		Marine fishes	2.649
		Miscellaneous aquatic animal	26F
		Molluscs	5.896
	Sub-total Black Sea		9.133
Total Ukraine			30.620

continued on following page

Declaration, Ministers adopted a new declaration on the Sustainable Blue Economy on 2 February 2021, firmly committed to cooperating closely and addressing common challenges in key blue economy sectors. The Mediterranean region is a fragile ecosystem, subject to different pressures such as overfishing, pollution, illegal fishing, coastal degradation, climate change and marine litter, among other effects. The recent COVID-19 crisis is expected to greatly affect the Mediterranean Blue Economy sectors such as tourism, shipping and fishing. For example, seafood prices in the region have dropped between 20% and 70% during the COVID-19 pandemic, mainly due to the sharp drop in demand in the hotel/restaurant/tourism industry, and limited export ability to international markets (Mediterranean Blue Economy Stakeholder Platform, n.d.).

The State of Mediterranean and Black Sea Fisheries 2020 has shown that Mediterranean and Black Sea fisheries contribute significantly to regional economies. Across the entire region, one in every 1,000 coastal inhabitants is considered a fisherman. In Croatia, Morocco and Tunisia, one out of every 100 coastal inhabitants is a fisherman. However, small-scale fishermen have uncertain livelihoods. This uncertainty has been observed during the Covid-19 pandemic period. A strong social protection program would be beneficial to ensure the Fisheries Sector's resilience to shocks (FAO, 2020:12).

Table 3. Continued

Countries	Ocean Area	Species	2018
Europe	Adriatic	Crustaceans	7.647
		Diadromous fishes	36
		Marine fishes	119.363
		Miscellaneous aquatic animal products	33
		Miscellaneous aquatic animals	138
		Molluscs	25.073
	Sub-total Adriatic		152.290
	Aegean	Crustaceans	6.632
		Diadromous fishes	4
		Marine fishes	52.705
		Miscellaneous aquatic animal products	2F
		Molluscs	6.893
	Sub-total Aegean		66.236
	Azov Sea	Crustaceans	27
		Diadromous fishes	12.828
		Freshwater fishes	2.234
		Marine fishes	22.367F
		Miscellaneous aquatic animal	790
		Molluscs	1.800
	Sub-total Azov Sea		40.047
	Balearic	Crustaceans	6.146F
		Diadromous fishes	23
		Marine fishes	67.092
		Miscellaneous aquatic animal products	1
		Miscellaneous aquatic animal	13F
		Molluscs	7.422F
	Sub-total Balearic		80.697
	Black Sea	Crustaceans	683
		Diadromous fishes	110
		Marine fishes	61.513
		Miscellaneous aquatic animal	26F
		Molluscs	17.732
	Sub-total Black Sea		80.064
	Gulf of Lion	Crustaceans	339
		Diadromous fishes	322
		Marine fishes	9.816
		Miscellaneous aquatic animal products	1
		Miscellaneous aquatic animals	107
		Molluscs	2.899F
	Sub-total Gulf of Lion		13.484
	Ionian	Crustaceans	14.861
		Diadromous fishes	13
		Marine fishes	46.214
		Miscellaneous aquatic animals	78
		Molluscs	11.598
	Sub-total Ionian		72.764
	Sardina	Crustaceans	4.412
		Diadromous fishes	78
		Marine fishes	32.516
		Miscellaneous aquatic animals	17
		Molluscs	7.304
	Sub-total Sardina		44.328
	Tunas (GFCM area)	Marine fishes	27.632F
Total Europe			577.543
Grand total			577.543

Source: FAO (Food and Agriculture Organization of the United Nations), n.d.d

INVASIVE MARINE ALIEN SPECIES In THE MEDITERRANEAN reGION

Invasive alien species (IAS) are considered the second biggest threat to biodiversity globally, after habitat loss, and pose a major threat to many fragile ecosystems (Stille et al., 2021). It is seen that there are different factors in the spread of fish species as invasive alien species. Among these factors can be listed as "man-built canals, dams, shipping, and the degradation of other human-induced ecosystems" (Teletchea and Beisel, 2018). IUCN (2012) categorized the main vectors increasing the spread of invasive alien marine species in MPA (Marine Protected Areas) as: *"Recreational boats, Fishing boats, Use of live bait, Diving, Aquaculture or mariculture, Anchorage and Ports, Commercial boats, Aquariums".* Similarly, there are some factors increasing the introduction of non-native species in to the Mediterranean Sea. The below factors seems as main vectors such as (Öztürk, 2021:31):

- *Suez Canal*
- *Shipping*
- *Connection straits*
- *Intentional or unintentional entry by humans*
- *Small vectors*

The number of alien species detected in European seas between 1949 and 2017 was recorded as approximately 1223 (NIS). It can be said that these species are mostly (63%) invertebrates. It is seen that the highest number of NIS recorded in European seas is in the Mediterranean (European Environment Agency, 2021). Based on EEA (2021)'s data, NIS introduction information for seas in the European region is shown in the Figure. As can be seen in Figure 1, the highest number of NIS (69%; 838) was found in the Mediterranean. Also, the North East Atlantic Sea has the highest number of NIS (21%; 256) among European seas.

An important issue regarding venomous fish species requires extensive research due to public health concerns and threats to fishermen's safety. Foreign invasive fish species are more common in Eastern Mediterranean countries (Öztürk, 2021:45). Table 10 shows poisonous and toxic fish species in the eastern Mediterranean countries as below:

Table 11 shows commercialized non-indigenous crustacean species in the Mediterranean Sea.

Mediterranean and black sea fishing faces some challenges in sustainable fishery stock. The Mediterranean General Fisheries Commission (GFCM) of the United Nations Food and Agriculture Organization (FAO) has developed a programmatic multi-year medium-term strategy (2017 2020) for Mediterranean sustainability to take joint action to improve this situation (Grati et al., 2021).

Recent News and Studies on Invasive Marine Alien Species in the Mediterranean Sea

A rising invasion is taking place among the Mediterranean Sea. According to the 2019 report of the Mediterranean network of climate and environmental change experts (MEDECC), more than 600 invasive species have created populations in their new habitats in the Mediterranean. Built in 1869, the Suez Canal connected the Indo-Pacific to the Mediterranean, stimulating the trade of manufactured goods and grain from Europe south to the Persian Gulf and from the Gulf to Western Europe in the northwest. However, the entry of invasive species into the Mediterranean also accelerated. Bariche (a professor of marine

Table 4. Geographical subareas (GSAs) in the Mediterranean Sea

1	Northern Alboran Sea	16	Southern Sicily
2	Alboran Island	17	Northern Adriatic Sea
3	Southern Alboran Sea	18	Southern Adriatic Sea
4	Algeria	19	Western Ionian Sea
5	Balearic Islands	20	Eastern Ionian Sea
6	Northern Spain	21	Southern Ionian Sea
7	Gulf of Lion	22	Aegean Sea
8	Corsica	23	Crete
9	Ligurian Sea and Northern Tyrrhenian Sea	24	Northern Levant Sea
10	Southern and Central Tyrrhenian Sea	25	Cyprus
11.1	Western Sardinia	26	Southern Levant Sea
11.2	Eastern Sardinia	27	Eastern Levant Sea
12	Northern Tunisia	28	Marmara Sea
13	Gulf of Hammamet	29	Black Sea
14	Gulf of Gabes	30	Azov Sea

Source: FAO (Food and Agriculture Organization of the United Nations), n.d.a

biology at the American University of Beirut (AUB)) studies invasive species in the Mediterranean as one of the world's leading lessepsian experts. The term Lessepsians is used to describe species native to the Indo-Pacific that invaded the Mediterranean via the Suez. Academics state that the negative effects of the Lesseps occupation are greatest in the Levantine Basin, the Far Eastern Mediterranean region bordering Egypt, Palestine, Israel, Lebanon, Syria and Turkey. According to Bella Galil, Levantine Marine Protected Areas (MPAs) are dominated by the invasive ecosystem. Since these species are resistant to containment efforts, their reproduction cannot be stopped. Bariche says that as the Mediterranean warms, "species restricted in the east are gone and are now reaching Italy, Greece, Tunisia, and some to

Table 5. FAO Major Fishing in Mediterranean Sea and Black Sea

Western Mediterranean (Subarea 37.1)	Balearic (Division 37.1.1)
	Gulf of Lions (Division 37.1.2)
	Sardinia (Division 37.1.3)
Central Mediterranean (Subarea 37.2)	Adriatic (Division 37.2.1)
	Ionian (Division 37.2.2)
Eastern Mediterranean (Subarea 37.3)	Aegean (Division 37.3.1)
	Levant (Division 37.3.2)
Black Sea (Subarea 37.4)	Marmara Sea (Division 37.4.1)
	Black Sea (Division 37.4.2)
	Azov Sea (Division 37.4.3)

Source: FAO (Food and Agriculture Organization of the United Nations), n.d.a

Table 6. GFCM capture production (2015-2019)

Countries	2019	2018	2017	2016	2015
Albania	5.938,0	6.220,0	6.516,0	6.179,0	6.209,0
Algeria	100.149,1	115.255,0	104.100,1	100.180,6	95.946,0
Bosnia and Herzegovina	5,0	5,0	5,0	5,0	5,0
Bulgaria	10.270,0	8.545,0	8.507,0	8.562,0	8.743,0
China	0,0	0,0	0,0	0,0	0,0
Croatia	64.020,1	70.022,5	69.566,7	72.867,7	73.484,9
Cyprus	1.476,4	1.470,7	1.737,7	1.470,0	1.470,9
Egypt	48.018,0	56.731,0	58.927,0	53.965,0	57.603,0
France	17.563,3	17.001,1	15.090,3	14.323,3	12.768,5
Georgia	89.921,7	90.056,5	99.608,2	26.680,7	22.500,0
Gibraltar	1,0	1,0	1,0	1,0	1,0
Greece	82.232,0	76.252,5	76.520,5	74.466,5	63.760,7
Israel	1.070,0	1.072,0	1.072,0	1.207,0	1.544,0
Italy	174.690,1	192.500,9	185.068,2	188.783,8	188.927,9
Japan	0,0	0,0	0,0	0,0	0,0
Korea, Republic of	0,1	0,0	0,0	0,0	0,0
Lebanon	2.609,8	2.776,0	3.597,0	4.271,0	3.618,0
Libya	32.450,0	32.266,0	32.000,0	30.002,0	25.787,0
Malta	2.225,7	2.733,0	2.164,0	3.561,0	2.563,0
Monaco	1,0	1,0	1,0	1,0	1,0
Montenegro	1.130,0	1.147,8	934,7	933,0	824,8
Morocco	23.650,9	26.011,0	25.165,0	23.711,0	26.905,0
Other nei	0,0	0,0	0,0	0,0	0,0
Palestine	3.943,0	3.201,0	3.208,0	3.306,0	3.227,0
Panama	0,0	0,0	0,0	0,0	0,0
Portugal	25,5	52,2	58,1	114,8	97,6
Romania	7.148,8	7.745,0	9.553,0	6.840,0	4.843,0
Russian Federation	73.266,0	73.224,0	90.883,0	99.758,0	95.692,0
Serbia and Montenegro	0,0	0,0	0,0	0,0	0,0
Slovenia	135,4	134,7	138,1	165,5	202,4
Spain	75.928,6	91.333,9	86.344,1	78.476,9	77.324,7
Taiwan Province of China	0,0	0,0	0,0	0,0	0,0
Tunisia	107.482,9	105.554,1	108.290,4	111.597,5	116.800,0
Turkey	431.572,1	283.956,0	322.175,4	301.469,9	397.733,1
Ukraine	30.302,7	30.615,0	43.819,0	41.531,0	34.731,0
Un. Sov. Soc. Rep.	0,0	0,0	0,0	0,0	0,0
Yugoslavia SFR	0,0	0,0	0,0	0,0	0,0
Syrian Arab Republic	1.580,0	1.574,0	1.565,0	1.679,0	1.422,0
Grand Total	1.388.807,0	1.297.457,9	1.356.615,5	1.256.109,2	1.324.735,5

Source: FAO (Food and Agriculture Organization of the United Nations), n.d.e

France." Essentially, two factors seem to have accelerated the arrival and spread of the species: a) climate change and b) the expansion of the Suez Canal. A new 35 km of canal was opened in 2015, and the 37 km expansion of existing canals has increased the Suez Canal by 500 million cubic meters (132 billion gallons). For this reason, the effects of the expansion of the Suez Canal should be addressed more deeply (Fitt, 2020) and new policies should be launched to achieve sustainable blue economy

Dr. Baki Yokeş (biologist who provides consultancy in the field of environment) states that puffer fish started to be seen in the Mediterranean in the early 2000s and there was a sudden population explosion

Table 7. The rate of Capture production among countries in the Mediterranean Sea (2010-2019)

Countries	Rate (%)
Turkey	27.62
Italy	14.48
Tunisia	7.90
Algeria	7.87
Spain	6.29
Croatia	5.48
Greece	5.22
Egypt	4.83
Russian Federation	4.80
Ukraine	3.94
Georgia	3.53
Libya	2.45
Morocco	2.10
France	0.99
Bulgaria	0.71
Albania	0.46
Romania	0.33
Lebanon	0.23
Palestine	0.20
Syria	0.14
Malta	0.14
Israel	0.12
Montenegro	0.07
Cyprus	0.07
Slovenia	0.02
Portugal	0.01
Bosina and Herzegovina	0.00
Gibraltar	0.00
Monaco	0.00

FAO (Food and Agriculture Organization of the United Nations), n.d.e

in the Mediterranean. Almost all pufferfish are commonly seen in the Eastern Mediterranean. Dr. Yokeş stated that puffer fish has become a big problem for Turkey and especially for the eastern Mediterranean since the beginning of the 2000s. Since there is no known predator species in the Mediterranean that eats puffer fish and depends entirely on it, there is no element that can suppress pufferfish. In addition to its poisonous meat, puffer fish negatively affects small-scale fishermen. The blowfish has a very strong jaw, it can break fishing rods, hooks, and can break lead lures. It is not possible for people to consume the flesh of puffer fish (Hongur, 2019). It can be said that the fight against puffer fish, which is not only ecologically harmful but also economically unhelpful, must be done in all Mediterranean countries.

Table 8. Production rates among subareas in the Mediterranean Sea (2010-2019)

Subareas	Rate (%)
Western Mediterranean (Subarea 37.1)	24.46%
Central Mediterranean (Subarea 37.2)	25.16%
Eastern Mediterranean (Subarea 37.3)	12.42%
Black Sea (Subarea 37.4)	37.96%

Source: FAO (Food and Agriculture Organization of the United Nations), n.d.e

Table 9. Top commercial species by value: Mediterranean Sea and the Black Sea

Mediterranean Sea		Black Sea	
Species	Value	Species	Value
Sardine	USD 349.375,929	European anchovy	USD 275.784,853
European anchovy	USD 308.438,492	Whiting	USD 19.658,866
European hake	USD 237.433,394	Horse mackerel	USD 19.578,874
Deep-water rose shrimp	USD 218.795,181		
Common cuttlefish	USD 203.874,915		
Common octopus	USD 171.080,261		
Blue and red shrimp	USD 148.740,272		
Red mullet	USD 144.991,024		
Common Pandora	USD 130.492,265		
Surmullets (mainly red mullet and striped mullet)	USD 103.502,345		

Source: FAO, (2020): 13

Figure 1. NIS introduction
Source: adapted from European Environment Agency (EEA), (2021)

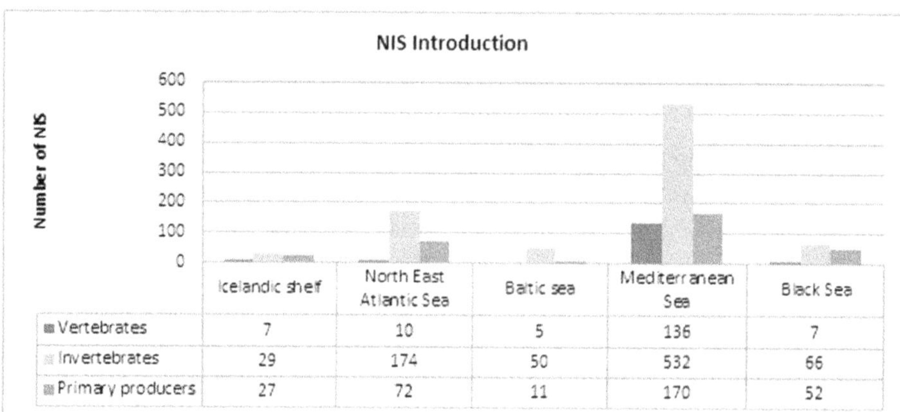

Table 10. Poisonous and toxic fish species in the eastern Mediterranean countries

	Cyprus	Egypt	Greece	Israel	Lebanon	Syrian Arab Republic	Turkey
Poisonous and Toxic fish Species	Lagocephalus Sceleratus	Lagocephalus Sceleratus	Lagocephalus Sceleratus	Lagocephalus Sceleratus	Lagocephalus Sceleratus	Lagocephalus Sceleratus	Lagocephalus Sceleratus
	Lagocephalus Spadiceus	Lagocephalus Spadiceus	Lagocephalus Spadiceus	Lagocephalus Spadiceus	Lagocephalus Spadiceus	Lagocephalus Spadiceus	Lagocephalus Spadiceus
	Lagocephalus Suezensis	Lagocephalus Suezensis	Lagocephalus Suezensis	Lagocephalus Suezensis	Lagocephalus Suezensis	Lagocephalus Suezensis	Lagocephalus Suezensis
	Plotosus Lineatus	Plotosus Lineatus	-	Plotosus Lineatus	Plotosus Lineatus	Plotosus Lineatus	Plotosus Lineatus
	Synanceia Verrucosa	-	-	Synanceia Verrucosa	Synanceia Verrucosa	Synanceia Verrucosa	Synanceia Verrucosa
	Pterois Miles	Pterois Miles	Pterois Miles	Pterois Miles	Pterois Miles	Pterois Miles	Pterois Miles

Source: Öztürk, 2021:45

Table 11. Commercialized non-indigenous crustacean species in the Mediterranean Sea

	Egypt	Greece	Israel	Lebanon	Syrian Arab Republic	Turkey	Tunisia
Species	Callinectes sapidus Portunus segnis Penaeus Japonicus Metapenaeus monoceros	Callinectes sapidus Portunus segnis	Penaeus Japonicus Metapenaeus monoceros Metapenaeus stebbingi Penaeus semisulcatus	Callinectes sapidus Portunus segnis Penaeus Japonicus Trachysalambria palaestinensis	Callinectes sapidus Portunus segnis Penaeus Japonicus Trachysalambria palaestinensis Metapenaeus monoceros Penaeus semisulcatus	Callinectes sapidus Portunus segnis Trachysalambria palaestinensis Metapenaeus monoceros Erugosquilla massavensis Metapenaeus stebbingi Penaeus semisulcatus Penaeus hathor Metapenaeopsis aegyptia	Portunus segnis Penaeus japonicus Trachysalambria palaestinensis Metapenaeus monoceros

Source: Öztürk, 2021:44

Figure 2. A model: Examining threaten of invasive alien species in the Mediterranean Sea
Source: created by the authors

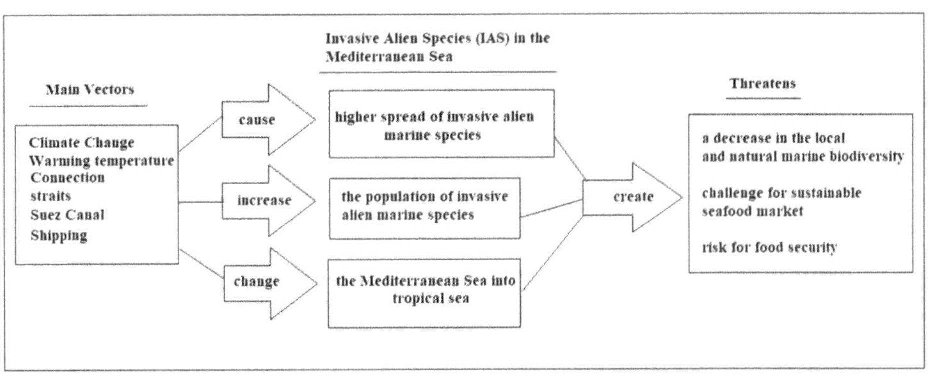

When examining invasive alien marine species in the Mediterranean Sea, Turkey should also be investigated caregully. In Turkey, the recent years have proven that the population of invasive alien marine species has increased (Iklim Haber, 2020; Akgüneş, 2020; Özacar, 2020; Unutmaz, 2021). Çinar et al. (2021) provided some evidences on invasive alien marine species in Turkey. According to their study, a large number of foreign species have entered Turkey with the effect of the Suez Canal. Cinar et al. determined that a decrease in foreign species was detected in the Aegean Sea and the Marmara Sea in Turkey, but an increase in foreign species was detected in the Black Sea between 2010 and 2020. The lack of careful control of alien species is expected to cause serious damage to the country in ecological, economic and sociological aspects. Because, invasive alien marine species are mostly toxic invasive fish or other marine species and these species mostly can't be useable for commercial purpose (Çinar et al., 2021). The number of alien species in the entire Mediterranean exceeded 1000 and the number of alien species in Turkish seas was 263 in 2005 and 429 in 2011, while the number of alien species in 2020 reached 540. Of these alien species, 105 are also invasive alien species. An invasive alien species enters the Suez Canal every 9 days. While the majority of invasive alien species in the Mediterranean come via the Suez Canal, the vast majority of invasive alien species in the Black Sea come from the ballast waters of ships (Özkan, 2021).

Kourantidou et al. (2021) studied on economic costs of invasive alien species among countries in the Mediterranean basin. They also stated that the speed of invasive alien species which were called as Lessepsian IAS increased in the Mediterranean Basin. They categorized countries within two main clusters.The first cluster included France, Italy, Greece, as well as Turkey and several Balkan countries and the second one included Spain and the remaining clusters included Libya, Egypt, Cyprus and Israel based on more specific classification. The study provided new evidences how IAS influenced countries' economic conditions although there were some limitations. According to their study, it was found out inavise aquatic species had lower economic damage than terrestrial species. This result can be caused due to the lack of sufficient reports or data on inavise alien marine species in the Mediterranean Sea (Kourantidou et al., 2021).

Shakman et al. (2019) studies on marine aine species in Libya and they categorized marine aline species in Libya as follow (Shakman et al., 2019:191):

- Recorded 73 alien marine species lived in Libya
- More than 32.88 percent of marine alien species was fishes
- 21.92 percent of them was macrophytes
- 16.44 percent of them was molluscs
- 13.70 of them was crustaceans and
- 9.59 of them was alien parasites.

Zentos et al. (2017) studies on alien species in the Mediterranean region and they gave a list for challenges of recording alien species in this region as below:

1. Single-celled organisms are not included in the list in the current study. The type and number of marine microalgae is not yet known.
2. In the classification of invasive species, it is sometimes difficult to distinguish between local and foreign species in the Mediterranean region. Some species can be considered as local species since they entered the Mediterranean from ancient times.

3. Species currently registered as cryptogenic can also be observed. These species must also be registered as alien species.
4. Among the difficulties encountered in creating an inventory for alien species, it can be said that it is complicated to determine which species are definitive aliens. Suspicious species complicate registration.

SOLUTIONS AND RECOMMENDATIONS

The recent studies and reports all state that the partnerships and collaborations will be an efficient solution for the fight against invasive alien marine species in the Mediterranean Basin. The risk is belonged to all countries in this area and each country should take some efficient measures to reduce the population of invasive alien marine species. Higher population and species of invasive alien fish and others threaten the local and natural biodiversity and so food sources for the humanity. Figure 2 presents a model examining how invasive alien marine species influence the Mediterranean Sea.

FUTURE RESEARCH DIRECTIONS

This study provides a review for the influence of invasive alien marine species in the Mediterranean Sea. In this context, the general impact of invasive alien marine species is evaluated and reviewed based on the available reports and studies in the literature. Based on the current reports and news, it has been seen that the significant increase in the population of invasive alien marine species can't be ignored. On the other side, future studies should examine the effect of invasive alien species in the Mediterranean basin via empirical methods. Limited studies can show some evidences but the real impact can be examined by comprehensive works or projects.

CONCLUSION

The mediterranean sea is turning into a tropical sea due to the warming temperature and climate change. Warming sea temperature welcomes tropical fish and other marine species to live in the mediterranean sea. In addition, suez canal and connection stratits causes higher spread of invasive alien marine species. To sum up, a decrease in natural biodiversity in the mediterranean sea threatens seafood security and seafood market in the area. When considering the importance of seafood products in the global food security (yildirim and kaplan, 2020; yildirim and yildirim, 2021), reducing or ending spread of invasive alien species is an important issue among countries in this area.

NOTE

Turkish sources are translated into English.

REFERENCES

Akgüneş, G. (2020). *We must learn to live with blowfish.* Milliyet.

Çinar, M. E., Bilecenoğlu, M., Yokeş, M. B., Öztürk, B., Taşkin, E., Bakir, K., Doğan, A., & Açik, Ş. (2021). Current status (as of end of 2020) of marine alien species in Turkey. *PLoS One*, *16*(5), e0251086. doi:10.1371/journal.pone.0251086 PMID:33945562

DW Recommends. (2017). *Invasive venomous fish spotted off Italy's coast.* https://www.dw.com/en/invasive-venomous-fish-spotted-off-italys-coast/a-38213006

European Environment Agency (EEA). (2021). *Indicator Assessment, Trends in marine non-indigenous species.* https://www.eea.europa.eu/data-and-maps/indicators/trends-in-marine-alien-species-mas-3/assessment

FAO (Food and Agriculture Organization of the United Nations). (2020). *The State of Mediterranean and Black Sea Fisheries 2020.* General Fisheries Commission for the Mediterranean. doi:10.4060/cb2429en

FAO (Food and Agriculture Organization of the United Nations). (n.d.a). *Geographical subareas (GSAs).* https://www.fao.org/gfcm/data/maps/gsas

FAO (Food and Agriculture Organization of the United Nations). (n.d.b). *General Fisheries Commission for the Mediterranean – GFCM, Fisheries.* https://www.fao.org/gfcm/activities/fisheries

FAO (Food and Agriculture Organization of the United Nations). (n.d.c). *Aquaculture.* https://www.fao.org/gfcm/activities/aquaculture/

FAO (Food and Agriculture Organization of the United Nations). (n.d.d). *Fisheries and Aquaculture.* https://www.fao.org/figis/servlet/SQServlet?file=/usr/local/tomcat/8.5.16/figis/webapps/figis/temp/hqp_4607160407423634 93.xml&outtype=html

FAO (Food and Agriculture Organization of the United Nations). (n.d.e). *GFCM capture production (1970-2019).* https://www.fao.org/gfcm/data/capture-production

FishBase. (2015). *Species in the Mediterranean Sea.* https://www.fishbase.se/TrophicEco/FishEcoList.php?ve_code=13

Fitt, E. (2020). *For the Mediterranean, the Suez is a wormhole bringing in alien invaders.* https://news.mongabay.com/2020/04/for-the-mediterranean-the-suez-is-a-wormhole-bringing-in-alien-invaders/

Galil, B. (2014). *How to stop the Mediterranean's invasive species.* https://www.weforum.org/agenda/2014/12/how-to-stop-the-mediterraneans-invasive-species/

Grati, F., Carlson, A., Carpentieri, P., & Cerri, J. (2021). *Handbook for data collection on recreational fisheries in the Mediterranean and the Black Sea.* FAO Fisheries and Aquaculture Technical Paper No. 669. FAO. doi:10.4060/cb5403enThe

Haber. (2020). *The invasive took its place among 2 species of Mediterranean fish.* News.

Heller, A., & Debre, I. (2020). *Experts say Med Sea altered by Suez Canal's invasive species.* https://apnews.com/article/climate-change-science-invasive-species-mediterranean-sea-europe-bc435ffbf4618b917b1181fb51ad4a8f

Hongur, A. (2019). *The blowfish damaged the ecology and economy of the Mediterranean.* AA.

Kourantidou, M., Cuthbert, R. N., Haubrock, P. J., Novoa, A., Taylor, N. G., Leroy, B., Capinha, C., Renault, D., Angulo, E., Diagne, C., & Courchamp, F. (2021). Economic Costs Of Invasive Alien Species In The Mediterranean Basin. *Neobiota, 67*, 427-458. doi:10.3897/neobiota.67.58926

Live Science Staff. (2011). *Wave Of Alien Species Invade Mediterranean Sea.* https://www.livescience.com/14339-wave-alien-species-invade-mediterranean-sea.html

Mappr. (n.d.). *Mediterranean Map/List of Mediterranean Countries.* https://www.mappr.co/thematic-maps/mediterranean-countries/

Mediterranean 2017 Quality Status Report. (n.d.). *The Mediterranean Marine and Coastal Environment.* https://www.medqsr.org/mediterranean-marine-and-coastal-environment

Mediterranean Blue Economy Stakeholder Platform. (n.d.). *Blue Eonomy.* https://medblueeconomyplatform.org/about/blue-economy/

Özacar, İ.U. (2020). *Climate change is also increasing invasive species in the seas.* TRT News.

Özkan, M. (2021). Invasive species harm ecosystems, human health and the economy. *Tarım ve Orman Dergisi.*

Öztürk, B. (2021). *Non-indigenous species in the Mediterranean and the Black Sea.* Studies and Reviews No. 87 (General Fisheries Commission for the Mediterranean). FAO. doi:10.4060/cb5949en

Shakman, E., Eteayb, K., Taboni, I. & Ben Abdalha, A. (2019). Status of Marine Alien Species Along The Libyan Coast. J. Black Sea/Mediterranean Environment, 25(2), 188-209.

Stille, M., Gasteratos, I., & Stille, B. (2021). Alien and invasive terrestrial vertebrate species on Corfu, Ionian Islands, Greece. *J. of Vertebrate Biology*, *70*(1). doi:10.25225/jvb.20126

Teletchea, F., & Beisel, J. N. (2018). *Alien Fish Species in France with Emphasis on the Recent Invasion of Gobies, Biological Resources of Water, Sajal Ray.* IntechOpen. Available from: https://www.intechopen.com/chapters/59375

The Commonwealth. (n.d.). *Blue Economy.* https://thecommonwealth.org/blue-economy

Unutmaz, Ş. (2021). *14 of the world's 100 worst invasive species are in Turkey.* Hurriyet.

World Population Review. (2021). *Mediterranean Countries 2021.* https://worldpopulationreview.com/country-rankings/mediterranean-countries

Yildirim, S., & Kaplan, M. (2020). Seafood Security and Sustainability Through Sustainable Development: A Review of Turkish Seafood Market. In A. Obayelu & O. Obayelu (Eds.), Developing Sustainable Food Systems, Policies, and Securities (pp. 16–36). IGI Global. https://doi.org/10.4018/978-1-7998-2599-9.ch002

Yıldırım, S., & Yıldırım, D. C. (2021). Achieving Seafood Security in the Mediterranean Region: A Case of Turkey. In R. Castanho & J. Martín Gallardo (Eds.), *Management and Conservation of Mediterranean Environments* (pp. 175–195). IGI Global. doi:10.4018/978-1-7998-7391-4.ch011

Zenetos, A., Çinar, M.E., Crocetta, F., Golani, D., & Rosso, A. (2017). Uncertainties and validation of alien species catalogues: the mediterranean as an example. *Estuarine, Coastal And Shelf Science, 191*, 171-187. .Ffhal-01976050 doi:10.1016/J.Ecss.2017.03.031ff

ADDITIONAL READING

Yildirim, S., & Kaplan, M. (2020). Seafood Security and Sustainability Through Sustainable Development: A Review of Turkish Seafood Market. In A. Obayelu & O. Obayelu (Eds.), *Developing Sustainable Food Systems, Policies, and Securities* (pp. 16–36). IGI Global. doi:10.4018/978-1-7998-2599-9.ch002

Yıldırım, S., & Yıldırım, D. C. (2021). Achieving Seafood Security in the Mediterranean Region: A Case of Turkey. In R. Castanho & J. Martín Gallardo (Eds.), *Management and Conservation of Mediterranean Environments* (pp. 175–195). IGI Global. doi:10.4018/978-1-7998-7391-4.ch011

KEY TERMS AND DEFINITIONS

FAO: Food and Agriculture Organization of the United Nations.

GFCM: General Fisheries Commission for the Mediterranean.

IAS: Invasive alien species.

Marine Alien Species: These marine species spread out of their habitats and threaten the diversity of the ecosystem where they migrated.

Chapter 5
Broad Overview of the Core Aspects and the Dispute Settlement Framework of the Draft High Seas Treaty

Abayomi Al-Ameen
Universiti Brunei Darussalam, Brunei

ABSTRACT

This chapter reviews the draft High Sea Treaty (draft HST) and the on-going deliberations and proposals in the different aspects of the document. With the aim of identifying the potential post-ratification challenges that may be faced in the implementation of the draft HST, this chapter critically reviews the proposals for dispute resolution by various stakeholders. This is done primarily by reviewing the UNCLOS system, which is directly referenced in the Draft HST. As regards the debate on the appropriate forum, the chapter analyses the proposal to adopt the International Tribunal on the Laws of the Sea (ITLOS) and other alternative propositions.

INTRODUCTION

It has been almost two decades since the initiative aimed at establishing a legal regime for the blue economy commenced under the auspices of the United Nations. Over this period, ideas and opinions have congealed into searching questions, deliberations, and draft provisions. Moreover, as the second draft High Sea Treaty (HST) was published in 2019, what might have seemed a mere dream at the inception appears to be gradually taking shape and is likely to come to fruition in the very near future. Moreover, despite the covid hiatus, negotiations got back into full swing in 2021.

The perceived need for a firmer global governance regime for Areas Beyond National Borders (ABNJ) stems from the inadequacies of the United National Convention on Laws of the Sea (UNCLOS) to protect against undue exploitation of the marine commonwealth. For example, though Article 192 of UNCLOS provides that "States have the obligation to protect and preserve the marine environment", this provi-

DOI: 10.4018/978-1-6684-3393-5.ch005

sion does not adequately challenge perceived excesses of others in areas of the sea which are beyond the legally recognised borders of any individual state. Further, Article 194(5) of UNCLOS requires that "measures taken shall include those necessary to protect and preserve rare or fragile ecosystems as well as the habitat of depleted, threatened or endangered species and other forms of marine life." Yet, taking such measures unilaterally and without the support of a global initiative such as the Conference of Parties (COP) would seem too risky.

It is however not uncommon for initiatives to start with such laudable goals but end up with a tamed instrument or create an ineffectual mechanism perhaps due to political compromises. This underscores the importance of analysing the progress of the HST negotiations. This chapter will review draft HST and the on-going deliberations and proposals in the different aspects of the document. A larger section of this review is focused on the proposed dispute resolution mechanism.

The chapter is divided into three parts. Part 1 explains the historical development of the Law of the Sea, particularly the initiatives towards the blue economy. Part 2 addresses the institutional arrangement, 'package deal' as well as providing a review of the dispute settlement system. This is followed by the recommendations and conclusion in part 3.

BACKGROUND

Historical Development of Laws of the Sea and the Initiatives Towards the Blue Economy

Almost two-thirds of the world's ocean lies beyond the authority of any single country (Rochette et al., 2015). These areas beyond national jurisdiction (ABNJs) are home to a diverse range of marine species that have evolved to withstand extreme temperatures, salinity, pressure and darkness. Although very little of these areas have been explored, evidence shows that human activity has severely damaged ecosystems and species in the ABNJs (Census of Marine Life, 2011).

The law of the sea first developed due to conflicts between coastal states who sought to spread their control over marine areas near their coastlines. By the end of the 18 century, states' sovereignty over their territorial seas was beginning to be recognised and respected. At that time, the maximum breadth of a state's territorial sea was generally considered to be three miles or about 5 kilometres; this was the farthest distance that shore-based cannons could fire and that a coastal state could thus control (Kent, 1954). After World War 2, states requested the UN International Law Commission to codify the existing marine laws. The Commission then began this undertaking in 1949 and prepared four draft conventions, which were adopted at the first UN Conference on the Law of the Sea in 1958 (Treves, 2015).

These four conventions are known as the 1958 Geneva Conventions, namely the Convention of the Territorial Sea and Contiguous Zone, the Convention on the High Seas, the Convention on Fishing and Conservation of the Living Resources of the High Seas and the Convention on the Continental Shelf. This was a substantial step forward, nonetheless the conventions failed to address some key matters such as setting a maximum breadth of the territorial sea. The second conference took place in 1960. No new treaties were signed, and the conference again failed to specify a fixed breadth to define territorial waters or establish consensus on sovereign fishing rights. Then in 1973, the third conference began. However, it only ended in 1982. Over 160 nations partook in this 9-year convention, and significant progress was achieved during that time. For one, the third conference finally addressed the issues raised at the previous conferences and for another, the instrument that we now know as the UN Convention on the Law of the Sea was adopted and superseded the previous four conventions adopted in 1958 (Treves, 2015).

Despite being adopted at the Third UN Conference on the Law of the Sea in 1960, it only came into force on 14 November 1994 – a year after ratification by the 60th state. The first 60 states to ratify the Convention were mostly developing states, and now it has been ratified by 168 states.

UNCLOS is composed of 17 parts, 320 articles and nine annexes. Part 1 consists of preliminary provisions, namely definitions of the terms used and the scope of the convention. Parts 2 to 14 provide for matters of marine law, namely the territorial sea and contiguous zone, straits used for international navigation, archipelagic states, exclusive economic zones, continental shelves, high seas, the regime of islands, enclosed or semi-enclosed seas, the right of access of land-locked states to and from the sea and freedom of transit, marine areas beyond national jurisdiction, the protection and preservation of the marine environment, marine scientific research and the development and transfer of marine technology. Part 15, on the other hand, provides for the settlement of dispute while parts 16 and 17 outline the general and final provisions.

Though it is undeniable that UNCLOS made some progress, not even this instrument provided a comprehensive global framework to help conserve and promote the sustainable use of marine ABNJs as well as to stop and prevent further degradation. The shortcoming of the UNCLOS is that though it provides for the protection of areas beyond national borders, the Convention is not far reaching enough (Druel and Gjerde, 2014). While the Convention certainly provides an international legal mechanism for ocean governance and establishes a collective obligation to protect the marine environment, it makes no specific provisions for marine biodiversity conservation in the ABNJs. There are, however, other legal instruments that address parts of the issue, including unsustainable fishing, pollution from ships and the protection of specific geographical areas like the Antarctic. Regardless, they are inadequate to close the existing ABNJ governance gap or to ensure the protection and sustainable use of ABNJ biodiversity (Rochette et al., 2015).

For this reason, in its resolution 69/292 of 19 June 2015, the UN General Assembly decided to develop an international legally binding instrument under UNCLOS on the conservation and sustainable use of ABNJ marine biodiversity. To this end, it decided—before conducting any intergovernmental conference—to form a Preparatory Committee that would be responsible for making recommendations to the General Assembly on the elements of the proposed treaty. The Committee held four sessions over the course of 2016 and 2017. At its fourth session (which took place from 10 to 21 July 2017), the Committee adopted its report to the General Assembly.

Later that year on 24 December 2017, under resolution 72/249 the General Assembly decided to convene an intergovernmental conference (IGC) under the auspices of the UN to consider the recommendations of the Preparatory Committee with a view to developing the instrument as soon as possible. In accordance with the resolution, the IGC held a meeting in New York on 16-18 April 2018 to discuss organisational matters, including the process for preparing the preliminary draft of the instrument. Under the resolution as well, the IGC is mandated to meet for four sessions.

The first session of the IGC to discuss the instrument was convened on 4-17 September 2018 at the UN Headquarters in New York. During the session, the IGC considered a document prepared by the IGC President which identified areas for further discussion not containing a treaty text (IISD IGC-1 Summary Report, 2018). The document was aimed at generating substantive discussions based on the elements of a package agreed in 2011 on marine genetic resources (including questions on benefit-sharing), measures such as environmental impact assessments and area-based management tools (including marine protected areas), and capacity building and marine technology transfer. The IGC made some headway in elucidating the delegates' stances on the package elements and setting out more comprehensive possibilities for a process on area-based management tools. Some of the delegates emphasised the importance of proceeding with a zero draft in order to fully enter negotiation mode at the second session.

The second IGC session was held on 25 March to 5 April 2019. This time around, the IGC discussed on the basis of the IGC President's Aid to Negotiations comprised of options structured along the lines of the four package elements (IISD IGC-2 Summary Report, 2019). In their discussions, the delegates continued to expand their stances on issues previously identified as areas of disagreement, achieving consensus on a few issues. However, by the end the delegates were still unable to agree on major issues including the scope of the instrument, whether benefit-sharing would be executed on a monetary or non-monetary basis as well as the overarching principles governing the future treaty.

The third IGC session was convened later that same year on 19-30 August 2019. During this session, the IGC for the first time entered textual negotiations based on a zero draft containing a treaty text prepared by the IGC President (IISD IGC-3 Summary Report, 2019). The document addressed general provisions, cross-cutting issues as well as the four package elements. It was noted that the deliberations were productive and the spirit of cooperation permeated the session. Significant progress was made on numerous issues along the lines of the package elements. However, by the end there were still many areas of divergence among the delegates and many of the details still need to be worked out. These issues are expected to be deliberated during the next IGC session.

The fourth IGC session, which was postponed twice due to the COVID-19 pandemic, is expected to be convened on 7-18 March 2022. A revised draft of the treaty will be developed prior to this meeting based on discussions during the third session.

The current draft (as at January 2022) is composed of 12 parts, 70 articles and 2 annexes. Part I lays out the general provisions of the treaty, Parts II-V outline substantive provisions concerning the package deal elements, Part VI provides for the institutional arrangements required to enforce the instrument, Part VII addresses questions of financial resources and mechanism, Part VIII pertains to issues of implementation and compliance, Part IX briefly touches on matters regarding dispute settlement, Part X contains a single article enjoining state parties to encourage non-parties to accede to the treaty, Part XI similarly has a single provision directing state parties to always act in good faith and to avoid violating rights, and the final Part XII contains miscellaneous provisions.

Potential Benefits of HST

A preliminary draft of the BBNJ treaty was only presented at the last IGC-3 session in August 2019 and at its conclusion, a number of issues and areas of divergence still remained unresolved (IISD IGC-3 Summary Report, 2019). Therefore, at this point it is premature to assess the exact impact—beneficial or otherwise—that the future agreement will make. However, there is no doubt that a treaty aimed to promote the conservation and sustainable use of marine biodiversity in ABNJs will certainly bring significant benefits to, not only the marine species and ecosystems of those areas, but also affected stakeholders and potentially even the global economy.

Given that the provisions of the BBNJ treaty have not been finalised and the IGC delegates are still in disagreement about many important aspects of the instrument, in assessing the potential benefits of the future treaty, one can only do so based on the perceivable trajectory of the ongoing negotiations as well as the overarching discussion areas of the existing draft treaty, namely the four package elements.

It should also be noted that the existing ABNJ governance gap primarily enriches and protects the more developed nations, especially those that possess a more advanced fishing/naval arsenal, particularly China, Taiwan, Japan, Indonesia, Spain, and South Korea (Sala et al., 2018). The implementation of a fair, equitable BBNJ treaty should help to level out the playing field and render the use of marine resources in the ABNJs more equitable for all.

This section will examine the foreseeable positive impact that the future BBNJ treaty will have along the lines of the four elements of the package agreed on in 2011.

Marine Protected Areas

The BBNJ treaty introduces high seas marine protected areas (Part III, Draft HST). Although many countries have established protected marine areas within their exclusive economic zones, only one per cent of ABNJs is presently protected. This allows greedy industrial fishing fleets from such nations as China, Taiwan, Japan, Indonesia, Spain, and South Korea (Sala et al., 2018) to operate unchecked. Substantial fish stocks—many of which border territorial and international waters—have depleted by 90 per cent in recent decades (Kituyi and Thomson, 2018). As a result, high-seas commercial fishing may become unprofitable by 2050. To conserve healthy ecosystems and help degraded stocks to recover, scientists expostulate that at least 30 per cent of the oceans must be protected. The proposed BBNJ treaty will establish a legal entity authorised to designate such vulnerable areas as protected, thus helping preserve the marine populations and ecosystems of these territories. However, a major hurdle in this undertaking will be overcoming the resistance of major fishing nations which are currently spending substantial amounts in subsidies to keep their fleets operational.

Benefit-Sharing of Marine Genetic Resources

Developing countries are set on profiting off the commercialisation of marine genetic resources, including marine microorganisms (Benkenstein and Maposa, 2017). However, as mentioned previously, the existing ABNJ governance gap primarily enriches more developed nations who possess more resources to spare and more leverage in international politics and commerce (Asimakopoulou and Mohammed, 2019). Presently, firms from ten developed countries own 98 per cent of all patents based on marine species (Blasiak et al., 2018). A single company, BASF of Germany, owns half of all patented genetic sequences. Developing countries insist that resources in ABNJs should be used for the benefit of all mankind. However, nations including the United States, Japan, South Korea and Norway oppose mandatory benefit-sharing. Theoretically, under the BBNJ treaty, the use and commercialisation of these resources should be fairer and more equitable (Part II, Draft HST). However, the rapacious capitalistic attitudes of the developed nations continually impede productive discussion of these issues. After the third IGC session, the delegates had not even agreed on whether to make benefit-sharing mandatory or voluntary. The US, for one, asserts that American corporations should have total liberty to produce and profit from biofuels, chemicals and drugs derived from marine genetic resources

Environmental Impact Assessments

The BBNJ treaty will obligate governments and companies to carry out environmental impact assessments before conducting activities that may potentially harm marine organisms and ecosystems (Part

IV, Draft HST). The treaty will also require monitoring and public reporting of industrial activities and impacts in addition to the designation of vulnerable areas, such as undersea vents, that are off limits to heavy exploitation. It is believed that the BBNJ treaty will impose heavier costs and present fresh strategic considerations for many ocean industries including fishing, shipping, seabed mining, harvesting of genetic resources and surveying (World Ocean Council, 2019).

Capacity-Building and Transfer of Marine Technology

The BBNJ treaty aims to consolidate and expand the scientific and technical capabilities of developing countries to enable them fulfil their obligations under the treaty, partake in the conservation efforts and engage in sustainable use of marine resources (Vierros and Harden-Davies, 2020). The high seas may represent a common global heritage, however access to the resources is not equal. Barriers are exorbitant when it comes to navigating, exploring and utilising the deep ocean. Less developed nations argue that richer counties should share pertinent marine technologies and scientific data so that they may also benefit from the emerging 'blue economy'. The terms and conditions of this undertaking, particularly with regards to matters of financing, have been subject to much rigorous debate and disagreements.

Proponents of the BBNJ treaty envision the instrument to be the 'Paris Accords' for ABNJ governance. It is, however, crucial to remember that the success of the future agreement depends largely on the ability of the global collective to come together and reconcile the conflicting interests of the different constituencies, including the major fishing nations, the Group of 77 bloc comprised of emerging economies and China, small island nations and developed nations such as the US. The fate of the ocean will help determine our own.

MAIN FOCUS OF THE CHAPTER

This chapter focuses on reviewing the review draft HST as negotiations progress in order to identify knotty issues that may impact on the achievement of the potential benefits of the treaty. This is especially in light of the need to find the right balance between the interests of nations and also the need to build a robust dispute settlement system. Analysis here will therefore commence with the package deal and thereafter, on the dispute settlement mechanism.

Institutional Arrangements and the Package Deal

Core parts of the draft HST address the institutional arrangement that will govern the new global ABNJ regime. It also contains the four key areas which provide the substance and content of the draft Treaty. These key areas are broadly referred to as the Package Deal given that all signatories to the treaty have to accept all provisions within this package. Both the institutional arrangement and the package deal are explained in turn:

Institutional Arrangement

Cooperation between State Parties is integral in order to achieve the objectives under the HST. The key to securing such cooperation lies in the development of institutionalised mechanisms which shall operate to ensure the implementation of the Treaty. A robust institutional arrangement is essential for the system of dispute settlement because such institution would limit discord and ultimately prevent chaos that occasions dispute settlements.

Part VI of the Revised Draft provides for institutional arrangements, the primary organs of which consist of a decision-making body called a Conference of the Parties (COP); an advisory body called a Scientific and Technical Body, and a Secretariat. While the establishment of these bodies are generally agreed upon, there are diverging views as to the functions and the extent of their powers, especially regarding the COP and the Scientific and Technical Body. As noted in the introduction of the Draft HST, further difficulties in the negotiation process stems from the fact that drafters have a mandate "not [to] undermine existing relevant legal instruments and frameworks and relevant global, regional and sectoral bodies." It is therefore pertinent to reconcile the institutional arrangements under the HST with existing legal instruments and the regional and sectoral mechanisms.

In light of the foregoing, three main alternative approaches to undergird the institutional arrangements of the HST were discussed. The options are; the regional model, the global model, and the hybrid model. There is no single definition for these three models, and they are best understood as a spectrum of options.

On one end of the spectrum, under the regional model, it has been proposed that the HST should be implemented exclusively within existing sectoral or regional institutions. For example, whenever the establishment of Marine Protected Areas (MPA), would be required, only the relevant competent framework or body would decide whether to establish an MPA and what measures to adopt therein. State parties to the new agreement would only make recommendations to the respective framework or body. Unsurprisingly, this model is mostly advocated by States that prefer freedom of the high seas. However, if this were the outcome of the negotiations, the governance gap would persist.

On the other end, the global model envisions that the decision-making body would be empowered to make decisions that are both specific and binding upon its parties, including on establishing high seas MPAs and approving environmental impact assessments (EIAs), regardless of the existence of relevant regional instruments and bodies. Under this scheme, promoted mainly by developing States, the COP, would be competent to establish a network of MPAs, recognising the existing MPAs under regional bodies.

At the centre is the hybrid approach which offers a model of institutional arrangements that would advance ocean governance. It would however not operate as a centralised global-level decision-making authority. This approach gives a complementary role to the COP who are expected to fill the regulatory gaps when necessary. Whilst this model is the one which has seemed to gain momentum prior to IGC-4, there are still many issues to be settled, particularly concerning MPAs.

Clark (2020) points out that there was a disparity between the delegates as to their understanding of the precise meaning of the terms global, regional, and hybrid. It was observed that delegates were describing the same concepts using two different terms, and different concepts were described by the same term. As such, it may be necessary to dispense with nomenclature and rather focus on the functions of the organs under the institutional arrangement.

Package Deals

The four areas in the package deal are on the Marine Genetic Resources (MGRs), Area-based Management Tool, Environmental Impact Assessment (EIA), and Capacity-Building and Transfer of Marine Technology.

Marine Genetic Resources

Under the Treaty, Marine genetic resources (MGRs) refer to genetic resources derived from the ABNJ. The provisions relating to MGR, and Access and Benefit Sharing (ABS) of such MGRs are found in Part II of the Revised Draft. Many of its provisions are found to be bracketed, and this indicates that negotiations as to this matter are far from over, even at the conclusion of IGC-3.

One of the biggest points of divergence amongst the delegates concerns the legal status of MGRs. There is significant potential in the economic value of MGRs, but research and development in the ABNJ is very costly and only a handful of developed countries, with sufficient funding and technological capabilities, are able to partake in such endeavours. As such, developing countries lose out. Developing countries, including the G-77 and China, are eager to assume the position that the principle of Common Heritage of Mankind (CHM) should underpin the governance of MGRs (Group of 77 and China's Written submission, 2016). In contrast, developed countries, such as Iceland, assume the position that MGRs are subject to the freedom of the high seas. The European Union takes on a wholly different approach, stating that the negotiations do not depend on the legal status of the MGRs.

Wang (2021) underscores the importance of defining the legal status of MGRs in the ABNJ. She advocates for the legal attribute of CHM of MGRs in the Treaty. To this end, she states as follows:

"From the perspective of the principle of CHM, taking the subject, object and content elements of legal relations as the research approach, the legal status of MGRs in ABNJ should be defined as follows: Firstly, an international management body should be established and the scope of actual resource developers should be defined in terms of subject elements. Secondly, the temporal scope, geographical scope and material scope of MGRs in ABNJ should be clarified in the aspect of object elements. Thirdly, the disposition of rights and obligations in the process of development and utilization of MGRs in ABNJ should be defined in terms of content elements."

Leary (2019) sets out the current governance of MGR in respect of the ongoing ABNJ negotiations. In respect of the issue between CHM and freedom of the high seas, he finds that the current protracted discussions on this issue are fruitless and, as a way-forward, suggests that the elements of the common heritage of mankind be incorporated implicitly (i.e., without direct reference to CHM) in the access and benefit sharing regime under the ABNJ. He puts forward the example found in the United Nations Convention on Biological Diversity (CBD) whereupon a "common concern of humankind" was incorporated.

There is also a divergence of opinions between the delegates in the substantive aspects of the Revised Draft. The MGRs may exist in several forms including *in situ, ex situ, in silico*, as well as its derivatives. Reflecting the underpinning tug of war between freedom of the high seas and CHM, developed and developing States have very different ideas about whether all of these three forms, including its derivatives, should be included in the new agreement. The delegates are also at odds as to the stages at which MGRs should be susceptible to access and benefit sharing. To no surprise, developed States prefer the inclusion of only *in situ* MGRs, while developing States call for all three modes as well as derivatives to be included.

Second, as regards to access and benefit-sharing, developing States generally have a preference for stronger rules that would cover both monetary and non-monetary benefit sharing. They also advocate for open access data repositories for *in silico* genetic information obtained in ABNJ. They rely on the 2010 Nagoya Protocol to the CBD an also the International Treaty on Plant Genetic Resources for Food and Agriculture (ITPGRFA) which revolves around a system of facilitated access. On the other hand, the developed States prefer to focus only on free access to *in situ* MGRs. They refer to the UNCLOS provisions on marine scientific research (MSR) on the high seas (IGC 1-4). They therefore insist that benefit sharing should be restricted to non-monetary benefits, including through capacity-building and transfer of marine technology (CB & TT).

Area-Based Management Tools

The concept of Area-Based Management Tools (ABMTs) encapsulates an array of matters including MPAs and sectoral area restrictions (Molenaar, 2007, p. 89; Thiel, 2003). Despite the importance of ABMTs in protecting biodiversity beyond national jurisdiction (BBNJ), there is no central guidance—such as under the UNCLOS—on the use of ABMTs. Rather what exists is a collection of disjointed and sectoral approaches (Freestone, 2019). During the Preparatory Committee meetings as well as the three intergovernmental sessions on ABNJ, the predominant issue concerning ABMTs was whether to grant primary authority over designating ABMTs to regional and sectoral bodies or to the institutions established under the HST. Underlying this rudimentary issue is the bigger issue concerning the polarity between freedom of the seas and the common heritage of mankind (CHM), and thus addressing this question is crucial to the future regulation of ABMTs under the HST.

According to the revised draft text, ABMT proposals are to be submitted individually or collectively by States to the Secretariat based on indicative criteria on the identification of areas. Such proposals must contain, among others, the spatial or geographical identification of the area, a description of the specific conservation and sustainable use objectives, and the relevant measures to be applied to the area. There should also be a consultation period and the decision-making would be left to the COP whereby they would decide whether to make ABMTs complementary to and/or independent from the relevant regional instruments or bodies as well as whether to recommend those regional bodies to adopt such measures (Articles 17-19, Draft HST).

The international community has made numerous efforts to establish a network of MPAs, including targets that cover a substantial portion of the ocean. However, currently no global mechanism exists to institute MPAs in ABNJ or to coordinate the use of existing ABMTs with management organisations. Under the draft treaty, matters relating to ABMTs are covered in Part III which comprises eight draft Articles (14-21) that aim to resolve this governance gap. For instance, draft Article 14 provides a number of options for the objectives, including enhancing cooperation and coordination in order to establish a comprehensive system of ABMTs and MPAs. Draft Article 15, on the other hand, addresses international cooperation and coordination and requires State parties to promote coherence and complementarity in the establishment of ABMTs, such as through applicable legal instruments, framework and bodies. Draft Article 16 provides for a list of indicative criteria (draft Annex I) to identify areas needing protection through ABMTs/MPAs with the use of the best available science, the precautionary approach/principle and the ecosystem approach. Furthermore, per draft Article 17, proposals to establish ABMTs/MPAs shall be submitted by State parties individually or collectively to the secretariat while draft Article 18 states that consultations on such proposals are to be inclusive, transparent, and open to all relevant stakeholders. Draft Article 19 grants the COP authority over the decision-making process. Lastly, draft Articles 20 and 21 focus on the implementation, monitoring and review of these provisions and measures.

Environmental Impact Assessment

In general, Environmental Impact Assessment (EIA) refers to the procedure where the potential impacts of a proposed project on the environment is evaluated and subsequently prevented or mitigated. EIA can be defined as "a study of the effects of a proposed project, plan or program on the environment" (Ogola, 2007). However, it should be noted that a comprehensive definition of the EIA under the Treaty is yet to be agreed upon. The Revised Draft devotes a total of 21 articles under Part IV to EIA issues. Much of its provisions remain in bracketed form. In the latest version, the Revised Draft features Article 21bis concerning the proposed objectives of the Part.

The following Article 22 sets out that State Parties shall assess the potential effects of planned activities under their jurisdiction or control [on the marine environment] [in accordance with their obligations under articles 204 to 206 of the Convention]. To that end, it is set out herein that Article 204 of the UNCLOS provides that States shall endeavour to observe, measure, evaluate and analyse the risks or effects of pollution of the marine environment, and at Article 205, States are obligated to publish reports of the results obtained through such observation, measure, evaluation, or analysis and make them available to all States. Of particular importance to the ongoing negotiations is Article 206, which sets out the trigger for when an EIA shall be conducted. Under Article 206, the threshold is set at when States have reasonable grounds to believe that planned activities under their jurisdiction or control may cause "substantial pollution of or significant and harmful changes to the marine environment."

Identification of the threshold of EIA is important in the ongoing negotiations. Article 24 of the Draft HST sets out the threshold and criteria for EIAs. However, parties are yet to reach an agreement on this threshold. There are presently two alternatives, both with similar provisions whereby planned activities will go through EIA if such activity is likely to have "more than minor or transitory" effect on the marine environment. The term purports to be wider than the word "significant", which is based on the Madrid Protocol. As per Article 25 and 26, an EIA would need to consider the cumulative impacts and any possible transboundary impacts of the project undertaken. As indicated by Article 29, there was some convergence amongst the delegates as to the inclusion of an indicative, non-exhaustive list of activities that would require, or otherwise do not require, an EIA in an annex or in the form of a guidance prepared by the COP. However, it was averred that such lists can be inadequate, as the impact of an activity depends on its scope and the area where it was undertaken and can also be difficult to negotiate and amend (Oral Plenary Report, 2018).

Article 32 provides that if it is determined that a project requires an EIA, a State Party shall ensure that such EIA is conducted using the best available scientific information and relevant traditional knowledge of indigenous peoples and local communities. As per Article 34, State Parties shall also ensure early notifications to stakeholders about projects under their jurisdiction or control, and ensure effective, time-bound opportunities for stakeholder participation throughout the EIA process. At this juncture, some delegates including the G-77 and China, CARICOM, Switzerland, Norway and PSIDS called for provisions specifying the stakeholders. On the other hand, other delegates, including the Russian Federation, China, US and Republic of Korea, on the other hand, proposed that the paragraph be deleted as it is too broad (Oral Plenary Report, 2018).

It has been proposed under Article 37 that the EIA reports shall be considered and reviewed, but there is a divergence of views as to who shall consider and review the reports. The African Group, Indonesia, Seychelles, Senegal and the High Seas Alliance (HSA) proposed that the reports be considered and reviewed by scientific and technical bodies. It was also proposed that the review be done by State Parties instead, as advanced by like-minded Latin American countries, Norway and New Zealand.

This divergence of views on decision-making reflects the fundamental dichotomy between parties. For instance, the default freedom of the individual State to ultimately decide on its activities on the high seas, and the CHM, which dictates that the relevant decisions should only be made through a collective entity, as for example, the International Seabed Authority in the Area.

In the 2021 High Seas Treaty Dialogue focused on the EIA, parties deliberated two core questions. First, they discussed on how the "benefits" from the sharing of scientific research and knowledge derived from MGRs can be distinguished from the duty to promote scientific research, its publication and dissemination (Articles 242, 244 of UNCLOS). Secondly, parties deliberated on the objectives and function of pre-cruise and post-cruise notification in relation to the Agreement. For instance, they considered whether the requirements for pre and post-cruise notification should be detailed within the Agreement or developed afterwards by scientific expert body under the Agreement. They also discussed how notifications should be monitored.

Capacity-Building and Transfer of Marine Technology (CB&TT)

Part XIV of the UN Convention on the Law of the Sea (UNCLOS) already obliges States to cooperate on matters pertaining CB & TT either directly or through international organisations (Boczek, 1982; González, 2007, p. 345). Particularly, Article 268 of the Convention highlights the key issues underlying this element which are pertinent to the new agreement, including the promotion of the acquisition, assessment and distribution of marine technological knowledge, ease of access to such data and information as well as the development of the required technological infrastructures to enable the transfer of marine technology (Bartenstein, 2017).

However, there would be no need to include this element in the package deal if Article 268 of the Convention functioned properly. Currently, it is important to find ways to consolidate the obligations under article 268 in order to achieve conservation and sustainable use of marine resources in ABNJ. To accomplish this goal, the new agreement should develop and strengthen the capacity of those States (i.e. developing States) that require assistance in this area to request and obtain such assistance. This would enable these States to protect their rights and execute their obligations under the new agreement. That said, the negotiations so far have not specifically focused on this matter. Instead, those discussions mainly revolved around whether States' participation in the capacity-building measures should be mandatory or voluntary (Oral Plenary Report, 2018). This issue is still under negotiation as evidenced by the bracketed language of draft Article 44(2): '[c]apacity-building and the transfer of marine technology [shall] [may] be provided on a [mandatory and voluntary] [voluntary] [bilateral, regional, subregional and multilateral] basis'.

Although CB & TT is its own element of the package deal, nonetheless it seems to be more of a cross-cutting issue. For many States, it was also one of the more important elements of the package deal. As a matter of fact, during the IGCs, CB & TT pervaded discussions of the other package deal elements including the debates about access and benefit-sharing pertaining to MGRs and the implementation of requirements related to marine conservation and impact assessments. This was reflected in the discussions on a clearing-house mechanism being one of the institutional machineries of the new agreement. Such mechanism would comprise an open-access web-based platform that will serve as a centralised hub enabling States to access and disseminate information relating to MGRs activities, EIA Reports, and other relevant technological information (Article 51, Draft HST).

Under the draft text, CB & TT is addressed in Part V which contains six draft Articles (42-47) intended to facilitate capacity-building and technology transfer efforts. As stated previously, the objective of this part is to ensure that developing State parties are capable of developing, implementing, monitoring, managing and enforcing relevant measures (Article 42(f)(v)-(vi), Draft HST). The text on cooperation provides that this goal shall be promoted and executed through 'enhanced cooperation at all levels and in all forms, including partnerships with and involving all relevant stakeholders'. Draft Article 46 introduces Annex II which provides a non-exhaustive list of types of capacity-building and transfer of marine technology. In order to future-proof the list, the COP is empowered to review, assess and amend the list so as to 'reflect technological progress and innovation and to respond and adapt to the evolving needs of States, subregions and regions' (Article 46(3), Draft HST). However, there is still not consensus on modalities with draft Article 44 suggesting that CB & TT could be voluntary and/or mandatory and provided on a bilateral, regional, subregional and multilateral basis.

Dispute Settlement

Matters related to the settlement of disputes are addressed under Part IX of the draft treaty. The current position which are still up for debate are in Articles 54 and 55. Article 54 obligates state parties to settle any dispute by peaceful means such as negotiations, inquiry, mediation, conciliation, arbitration, judicial settlement or seeking recourse to regional agencies or arrangements. Article 55, on the other hand, outlines the basic procedures for dispute settlement and comprises only three paragraphs. Its first paragraph stipulates that the provisions on dispute settlement under Part XV of the Convention apply *mutatis mutandis* to any dispute between state parties to the treaty, and the other two paragraphs essentially provide that parties to a dispute under the treaty are free to adopt their own preferred means of resolution (Article 55(1)-(3) Draft HST).

Mossop (2019) outlines how the dispute settlement provisions of the draft Treaty were modelled after, those of the UN Fish Stocks Agreement (UNFSA). She also evaluates whether other articles in the UNFSA could be applied to the draft treaty. Mossop is of the view that many provisions from the UNFSA on dispute settlement (i.e. Articles 27-32) could have been included in the draft treaty but were instead omitted.

Compliance and dispute resolution issues have been addressed at different points in the negotiation process. Of note are some of the issues raised at the Third Intergovernmental conference and the recently concluded dialogue in October 2021.

At the Third Session of the Intergovernmental Conference (IGC) on the Conservation and Sustainable Use of Marine Biodiversity of Areas Beyond National Jurisdiction held in 2019, it was proposed that the default dispute settlement forum should be changed from just any suitable arbitral tribunal (per article 287 of UNCLOS) to specifically the International Tribunal for the Law of the Sea (ITLOS). The other proposal was that ITLOS should be authorised to provide an advisory opinion at the request of the COPs.

At the Informal Intersession of the High Sea Treaty Dialogue which was held in October 2021, questions that were deliberated upon include; the role of COP in promoting compliance and addressing cases of noncompliance. Deliberators also discussed the kind of measures that can be envisaged in cases of non-compliance. Specifically on dispute settlement, the stakeholders discussed the available mechanisms for settling disputes that can be subsumed under the phrase "by other peaceful means of their own choice" as stated in Article 54. There was also discussion on whether a dispute prevention mechanism should be included in the agreement and how such a mechanism should work

The potential for jurisdictional conflict is already evident from this negotiation phase as there are some disagreements on the application of external law and procedures. El Savador and Colombia or example, argue that reference to ITLOS would not reflect the spirit of a universal instrument. They contend that to apply a provision of another agreement to which a State is not a party would contravene an international principle of Treaty Law. Therefore, they argue for a wider spectrum of options to solving disputes (3rd IGC, 2019).[1] Turkey also objects to any reference to UNCLOS in the dispute settlement provisions. Mossop foresees future disagreements as she cites the cases of the *Southern Bluefin Tuna* and the *South China Sea* which show that these kinds of concerns are far from resolved and can disrupt the efficacy of future dispute settlement processes (Mossop, 2019).

Nevertheless, as the content of the present draft HST suggests, UNCLOS is directly referenced and perhaps ITLOS may end up being the default forum. It is therefore pertinent to analyse ITLOS as a forum and UNCLOS provisions in order to predict the nature of dispute settlement under the HST.

ITLOS as Default Forum

A number of states and groups including the African Group, Pacific Small Island States and Sri Lanka had put forward the proposal for ITLOS as the default forum under the Treaty. The primary rationale behind this proposal was that the cost of arbitration is very high compared to resolving a dispute before an existing court or tribunal. Thus, for developing nations, this would make dispute settlement under the HST more accessible.

Questions need to be raised as to whether states are willing to adopt the approach. States already have the option, through declaration, to select ITLOS as their default forum, and some countries have already done so. Mossop argues therefore that as the number of states choosing ITLOS has been increasing over the years, it may reflect a growing preference for ITLOS as states' default forum to resolve ABNJ disputes.

Mossop (2019) also addresses whether having a different default forum under the HST compared to UNCLOS would lead to other problems. In a situation where two disputing states have made no declarations under either UNCLOS or the HST, there may be confusion as to whether the dispute shall be brought to an arbitral tribunal or ITLOS. She suggests that the HST could include provisions to the effect that where such a situation occurs, ITLOS would be the default forum. However, she feels that such step may only invite further confusion and disagreement.

ITLOS Advisory Opinion

It as also been proposed to allow the COP to request an advisory opinion from ITLOS. The key issue here is whether this proposal is consistent with UNCLOS. Parties may challenge the authority of ITLOS in providing such advisory opinion as it happened when ten States challenged the jurisdiction of ITLOS in providing advisory opinion that was requested by the Sub-Regional Fisheries Commission. It is noteworthy though that in that case, the ITLOS decided that it did have jurisdiction (Tanaka, 2015) even though not all States and commentators agreed with that decision (Ruys and Soete, 2016). Regardless, it is conceivable that ITLOS's jurisdiction to provide advisory opinions when authorised under a treaty is now a *fait accompli*. That said, opposition to such authority may prevent agreement to include this proposal in the HST.

Overview of the Dispute Settlement Mechanism under UNCLOS

The United Nations Convention on the Law of the Sea (UNCLOS) incorporates comprehensive procedures for the settlement of law of the sea disputes. Under Part XV of the Convention, States are obliged to resolve their disputes through peaceful, voluntary means of their own choice, including negotiation and conciliation. Should that fail, then they may consider compulsory procedures that will entail binding decisions, namely litigation or arbitration.

This paper will discuss these procedures as well as the provisions under Part XV before proceeding to assess whether the dispute settlement machinery under UNCLOS is effective as well as providing recommendations to ameliorate the current shortcomings of the mechanism.

Consensual and Compulsory Settlement Procedures

The dispute settlement mechanism under UNCLOS consists of two kinds of settlement procedures, namely 'consensual' procedures under section 1 of Part XV of the Convention and compulsory procedures under section 2 of the same part.

Section 1 of Part XV outlines the foundational principles of dispute settlement. Firstly, States are obliged to endeavour to settle their disputes by peaceful means of their own choice (Arts. 279-280, UNCLOS). That said, if parties have pre-existing dispute settlement obligations under other general, regional or bilateral agreements, then they are obliged to respect them (Art. 282, UNCLOS). Otherwise, parties are obliged to proceed expeditiously to an exchange of views to settle their dispute by negotiation or other peaceful means. If the parties fail to reach a settlement through the agreed procedure, one of them may invite the other to conciliation, which is expanded upon in Annex V (Arts. 283-284, UNCLOS). The outcome of conciliation is non-binding in nature and parties are expected to come to a resolution by themselves based on the conciliation report. This may prove to be a problem to State parties particularly where the opposing party is not willing to negotiate based on the conciliation result. For this reason, the Convention has provided for multiple dispute settlement options. If these preliminary efforts fail, parties may then resort to compulsory settlement procedures, the outcome of which is binding on the parties. The Convention empowers disputing parties to choose any one or more of the four different litigious or arbitral procedures under article 287. This paper will elaborate further on all these procedures below.

Conciliation

If the parties to a dispute have agreed to submit it to conciliation, either of the parties may institute the proceedings by written notification addressed to the other party (Art. 1, Annex V, UNCLOS). If the invitation is not accepted or the parties cannot agree on the procedure, the conciliation proceedings shall be considered terminated (Art. 284(3), UNCLOS). Moreover, a list of conciliators shall be created and maintained by the UN Secretary-General and each State party shall be entitled to nominate four conciliators whose names shall constitute the list (Art. 2, Annex V, UNCLOS). Ultimately, the conciliation commission shall consist of five members: each party shall appoint two conciliators to be chosen ideally from the list, one of whom may be the State party's national. Within 30 days after all four conciliators have been appointed, the parties shall then appoint a fifth conciliator from the list to serve as the chairman. If the parties fail to do so, the responsibility shall then fall on the UN Secretary-General (Art. 3, Annex V, UNCLOS). After the conciliation commission has been constituted, they shall then determine its own procedure, unless the parties agree otherwise. The commission may, with the parties' consent, invite either party to submit its views orally or in writing. The Commission's decisions regarding procedural matters, the report and recommendations shall be made by a majority vote (Art. 4, Annex V, UNCLOS).

Compulsory Procedures

Under UNCLOS, disputing parties have considerable freedom to choose their preferred compulsory procedure to find resolution to their disputes. As stated previously, the primary difference between consensual and compulsory settlement procedures is that while consensual procedures are voluntary and lead to non-binding decisions, compulsory procedures result in binding decisions that parties must comply with. Furthermore, the main benefit of this freedom is to allow parties to choose the most suitable procedure given their means, needs and goals, thus making dispute settlement more accessible to developing States. The Convention empowers parties to choose, by a written declaration, one or more of the following compulsory procedures: 1. International Tribunal for the Law of the Sea; 2. International Court of Justice; 3. Arbitral tribunal; 4. Special arbitral tribunal. These procedures will be looked at in more detail later.

According to Article 287 of UNCLOS, such a declaration by a state shall not affect or be affected by a State party's obligation to accept the jurisdiction of the Seabed Disputes Chamber of the International Tribunal for the Law of the Sea. Seabed disputes shall exclusively be submitted to the Chamber. Moreover, a State party to a dispute not covered by a declaration in force shall be deemed to have accepted the arbitration procedure according to Annex VII or Annex VIII of the Convention. Also, a new declaration, a notice of revocation, or the expiry of a declaration shall not in any way affect proceedings pending before a court or tribunal of competent jurisdiction unless the parties agree otherwise. Unless they agree otherwise, where the parties to a dispute have accepted the same procedure, it must be adopted in resolving their dispute. If they have not agreed on the same procedure, then the dispute may be submitted only to arbitration—again, unless the parties agree otherwise (Art. 287, UNCLOS).

However, there are limitations and exceptions to these procedures, such as in cases where States have agreed to settle their disputes in different forums, for example, the European Court of Justice to which European Union member States may bring their fisheries disputes. Moreover, certain substantive matters may also be excluded—even by the Convention itself, such as certain disputes concerning coastal States' sovereign rights in the exclusive economic zone, marine scientific research and, more notably, issues pertaining to 'allowable catch' and certain exclusive economic Zone fisheries disputes (Art. 297, UNCLOS). That said, these disputes may be submitted to compulsory conciliation. The purpose of these exceptions is to protect the vital interests of States. Additionally, Article 298 of the Convention stipulates that, without prejudicing obligations to settle disputes by peaceful means, a State may declare in writing that it refuses any one or more of the compulsory procedures involving boundary delimitations, military activities, law enforcement activities or disputes on which the UN Security Council is already exercising its functions.

Another noteworthy optional exception is disputes pertaining to the interpretation or application of Articles 15, 74 and 83 on sea boundary delimitations or historic bays or titles. This exception applies provided that: the disputing parties have not come to an agreement during negotiations; the State having made such a declaration agrees to submit the matter to conciliation under Annex V. After the conciliation commission has presented its report (which shall state the reasons on which the report is based), the parties shall negotiate an agreement based on that report. If these negotiations fail to result in an agreement, the parties shall by mutual consent submit the matter to one of the compulsory procedures—unless they agree otherwise (Art. 298(a)(i)-(ii), UNCLOS).

To add, in any dispute involving scientific or technical matters, a court or tribunal may, at the request of a party or *proprio motu* (by its own motion), consult with the parties to select no fewer than two experts chosen ideally from the appropriate list to sit with the court or tribunal but without voting rights (Art. 289, UNCLOS). Additionally, if a dispute has been duly submitted to litigation, the court or tribunal may prescribe any provisional measures which it considers appropriate under the circumstances to preserve the respective rights of the parties or to prevent serious harm to marine environment, pending the final decision (Art. 290, UNCLOS). Such measures may be modified or revoked as soon as the circumstances justifying them have changed or passed. Provisional measures, however, may only be prescribed, modified or revoked only at the request of a party and after the parties have had the opportunity to be heard.

Litigation

As stated previously, the compulsory procedures entailing binding decisions for law of the sea dispute settlement refer in part to recourse to the International Tribunal for the Law of the Sea (ITLOS) and the International Court of Justice (ICJ) (Art. 287(1), UNCLOS).

To begin, ITLOS was established under Annex VI of the Convention. It consists of 21 members who are recognised for their expertise in the law of the sea and elected by parties to the Convention so as to ensure equitable representation in this particular component of the international justice system. However, not every member will necessarily be present at every adjudication. The tribunal possesses compulsory jurisdiction in cases concerning provisional measures or the prompt release of vessels. Additionally, the tribunal is empowered to exercise its advisory jurisdiction in instances where a non-UNCLOS agreement stipulates that the parties may request an advisory opinion from the tribunal (ITLOS Case No. 21 of 2013) Furthermore, ITLOS has adopted its own set of rules called the Rules of the Tribunal, which are recognised to be cost-effective and user-friendly. As stated under Article 49 of the Rules: 'proceedings before the Tribunal shall be conducted without unnecessary delay or expense.' This appears to be true. For example, with cases concerning the prompt release of vessels under Article 292 of the Convention, the entire litigation process cannot last for more than 30 days. Oral submissions may only last one day and must begin 15 days after application while the tribunal's decision must be delivered 14 days after the end of the oral submissions. It should also be noted that a large portion of ITLOS's caseload consists of cases involving the prompt release of vessels. All in all, the tribunal is relatively efficient in processing cases.

The ICJ, located in the Hague, Netherlands, was established in June 1945 upon the signing of the UN Charter which sets up the ICJ as 'the principal judicial organ of the United Nations (Art. 92, UN Charter).' As for its structure, the ICJ is made up of 15 judges from different nations who are elected to nine-year terms of office by the UN General Assembly and Security Council. The Court serves a dual role: firstly, to resolve legal disputes brought by States according to international law; and secondly, to dispense advisory opinions on legal enquiries from duly authorised international organs and agencies. Therefore, the Court possesses two distinct kinds of jurisdiction, namely contentious and advisory jurisdictions. The ICJ is largely viewed as the primary avenue of dispute settlement between sovereign States, and the Court is recognised for its key role in the development of international law. At the same time however, the ICJ has been repeatedly criticised for being ineffective in achieving international peace and security (Llamzon, 2007). Furthermore, the Court's jurisdiction is inherently limited. This is because only States—and not individuals—have standing to bring a claim against another State, and then only with the consent of the respondent State.

Arbitration

As an alternative to recourse to ITLOS or ICJ, any State party to a dispute may submit the matter to arbitration according to Annex VII of the Convention (Art. 287(1)(c), UNCLOS). Although the Convention uses the term 'arbitral tribunal', it is not actually a standing legal body. Such a tribunal only keeps a list of arbitrators and arbitrations are conducted on an ad hoc basis (Lyou, 1997). When a dispute has been submitted to arbitration, each State party is entitled to nominate four arbitrators. Per Annex VII of UNCLOS, the UN Secretary-General is responsible for preparing and maintaining a list of arbitrators (Art. 2(1) UNCLOS). The arbitral tribunal shall consist of five members: each party shall appoint one arbitrator to the tribunal—ideally from their list—and the other three arbitrators shall be appointed by consensus of the parties (Art. 3 UNCLOS). The parties shall then appoint the president of the tribunal from among those three arbitrators. If the parties cannot agree on the appointment of the three arbitrators or the president, then it shall fall on the ITLOS President to make those appointments. If the ITLOS President is a national of either State party or is otherwise unable to make the appointments, then this duty will shift to the next senior member of ITLOS who is available and not a national of either State party. After the tribunal is constituted, it shall determine its own procedure unless the State parties agree otherwise (Art. 5 UNCLOS). At the conclusion of the proceedings, the final decision shall be made by a majority vote. Where the votes are split, the President shall make the casting vote (Art. 8 UNCLOS). As for the arbitral award, it shall be confined to the subject-matter of the dispute and the tribunal shall explain its rationale. The award shall be final and cannot be appealed so the parties must comply with it . Any disagreement from either party as to the interpretation of the award or how it is implemented may be submitted to the tribunal that granted the award (Art 10 – 12 UNCLOS.

Special Arbitration

Where a dispute involves specialised scientific or technical knowledge and experience, the matter may be submitted to a special arbitral tribunal according to Annex VIII of the Convention. According to Annex VIII of UNCLOS, a dispute may be brought to special arbitration if it relates to fisheries, the protection and preservation of the marine environment, marine scientific research or navigation, including pollution from vessels and by dumping (Art. 1 UNCLOS). Lists of experts shall be created and maintained in various fields (Art. 2(2) UNCLOS). As for the arbitral proceedings, each State party shall be entitled to nominate two arbitrators (Art. 2(3) UNCLOS). They may be scientific or technical, rather than legal, experts. The special arbitral tribunal shall consist of five members: each party shall appoint two members to be picked ideally from the appropriate lists and one of them may be a national of the State party. Moreover, the parties shall also by agreement appoint the president of the tribunal, ideally chosen from the applicable list, who shall not be a national of either State party—unless the parties agree otherwise. The rest of the special arbitration procedure is similar to the rules of regular arbitral tribunal, including the rule that if the parties are unable to agree on the appointment of the tribunal president, the UN Secretary-General shall assume the undertaking (Art. 3 UNCLOS).

Critical Analysis of the Effectiveness of the UNCLOS Dispute Settlement Mechanism

It must be stated that the potential of the dispute settlement machinery under UNCLOS has not been adequately developed, especially when assessing the successes and limitations of ITLOS. These limitations can be attributed to several factors including the fact that States are reluctant to utilise international dispute settlement mechanisms as well as the exceptions and limitations to the UNCLOS compulsory procedures.

Unrealised Potential of UNCLOS Dispute Settlement

The LOSC dispute settlement machinery has significant potential to contribute to oceans governance, extending to a number of areas including the enforcement and implementation of the Convention, maintenance of the integrity of UNCLOS principles, unification of the substantive legal provisions, regulation and allocation of resources, interpretation and development of the law, maintenance of peace, etc. However, much of this potential has not been realised. For one, certain elements of the jurisprudence thus far have not had a constructive influence on oceans governance, especially with regards to prompt release. Bonds have been discounted which led to uncertainties among coastal states as to what constitutes a 'reasonable' bond and ITLOS has been unable to provide clear guidance on this issue. ITLOS has also been unable to support coastal states in their efforts against Illegal, Unreported, and Unregulated (IUU) fishing. Moreover, there are inconsistencies as to the Tribunal's prompt release jurisprudence, particularly concerning the consideration of the proceeds of catch to determine a reasonable bond. Additionally, by 2006 while the overall influence of dispute settlement on oceans governance has been mostly constructive, the real impact of cases was less significant. This was because a good portion of the cases disputed were interlocutory in nature and only sought interim relief.

Critical Assessment of ITLOS

Dolliver Nelson (2002), the former President of ITLOS once stated that the Tribunal had not fully developed and utilised its potentials as a veritable judicial organ for the settlement of LOSC disputes. In addition to streamlining its emergent jurisprudence, the Tribunal also needs to ensure that its decisions are more in line with present day global developments and to focus more on the environmental aspect of effective oceans governance. To this day, the Tribunal remains under-utilised and by 2019 only around 37 States had declared their preference for ITLOS as their default LOSC dispute settlement forum; that is a small portion of the 168 State parties (Mossop, 2019). While there have been predictions that the Tribunal will be seeing a progressively increasingly caseload, it is also worth noting that if States are not seeing ITLOS as a body that is capable of propounding the law by giving balanced, well-reasoned decisions, then it will never attain the level of utilisation that it aspires to. Additionally, while ITLOS seems to mostly be interested specifically in maritime boundary delimitation cases (Nelson, 2005), fulfilling this goal is not easy for the Tribunal given that it has stiff competition in other, perhaps more established, dispute settlement avenues such as the ICJ which has decades of experience in international adjudication over ITLOS. As pointed out before, the Tribunal is 'unseasoned' and 'seemingly divorced from the settled jurisprudence of the International Court' which 'may be a deterrent to its selection by State Parties.' (Highet, 1991)

States' Reluctance to Use Formal Dispute Settlement

It has been asserted that the current problem with international dispute settlement in general and certainly in the law of the sea is a general reluctance on the part of States to utilise it (Sohn, 1983). To use ITLOS as an example, it should be noted that since its establishment, although its Registry has received numerous requests for information on instituting prompt release cases, disputes often do not proceed to the Tribunal on the grounds that 'negotiations between parties had proved successful.' (Nelson, 2005) It has also been suggested that 'NGO pressure and diplomatic considerations' may explain why certain prompt release cases are not brought to the Tribunal (Treves, 2004). Furthermore, arbitration is at times more appealing to States and is thus often utilised to deal with non-legal political or technical disputes. That said, States' reluctance to make use of formal dispute settlement even extends to arbitration as there may be confusion as to whether the role of arbitration is negotiatory or adjudicatory (Simpson, 1959). In any case, this continued reluctance is affecting the potential of dispute settlement in facilitating oceans governance.

Limitations and Exceptions to Compulsory Procedures

There are certain limitations and exceptions to the compulsory settlement procedures under the Convention. During the Third UN Conference on the Law of the Sea that took place from 1973 until 1982, the acceptance of the dispute settlement provisions by many States was conditional on the inclusion of these limitations and exceptions (Rosenne and Sohn, 1989). They are thus not only significant because they played a crucial role in the universal acceptability of the 'package deal' that the Convention represents, but also they limit the scope of the dispute settlement mechanisms and therefore restrict the mechanisms' potential to contribute to oceans governance (Klein, 2005).

RECOMMENDATIONS AND CONCLUSION

The draft HST aims to herald a new global order in the blue economy. To achieve this, much attention need be paid to the on-going deliberative process in terms of the institutional arrangement, the package deal, and the dispute settlement.

Though the content of the final HST is still up in the air as parties still disagree about some vital issues, there is cause for optimism given the steady progress being made. Moreover, there is significant political motivation for many states to ensure that the discussion is not truncated as the vast benefit of the ocean is mainly harnessed by a few developed countries. This governance gap primarily enriches the Western nations and also those that possess a more advanced fishing/naval arsenal, particularly China, Taiwan, Japan, Indonesia, Spain, and South Korea (Sala et al., 2018). The implementation of a fair, equitable BBNJ treaty should help to level out the playing field and render the use of marine resources in the ABNJs more equitable for all. It is therefore expected that the proposed HST will establish a legal entity authorised to designate such vulnerable areas as protected, thus helping preserve the marine populations and ecosystems of these territories. It is also expected that the proposed HST will impose heavier costs on unsustainable practices and present fresh strategic considerations for many ocean industries including fishing, shipping, seabed mining, harvesting of genetic resources and surveying (World Ocean Council, 2019). It is further expected that the HST will consolidate and expand the scientific and technical capabilities of developing countries to enable them fulfil their obligations under the treaty, partake in the conservation efforts and engage in sustainable use of marine resources (Vierros and Harden-Davies, 2020).

The aims and potential achievements of the proposed HST stated in the preceding paragraph are truly laudable. However, it must be noted that its success is very much dependent on the available mechanisms. Whilst genuine political will goes a long way to achieve the stated goals, there must also be a robust mechanism that will help resolve issues where the political solution fails. Hence, it is imperative to pay adequate attention to the dispute settlement system adopted in the proposed HST.

With regards to the dispute settlement, it is pertinent built on the strength of the present settlement system of the UNCLOS whilst also improving on weak areas. Formal dispute settlement at the international level as always been tricky because all states often give priority to their strategic and immediate national interest. The effectiveness of such dispute settlement system is therefore dependent on the extent to which it aligns with the interest of member states. It is therefore inevitable that the final provision on dispute settlement in the HST will entail significant political compromise. However, to make up for the expected weakness in the dispute settlement provisions, deliberators must take seriously the infusion of dispute prevention mechanisms. To this end, the most potent dispute prevention mechanism would be to ensure that provisions concerning the institutional arrangements and the package deals are as clear as possible. Further, potential lacuna should be blocked.

REFERENCES

Asimakopoulou, E., & Mohammed, E. Y. (2019). *Marine genetic resources in areas beyond national jurisdiction: a 'common heritage of mankind.'* IIED Briefing Papers. Retrieved January 14, 2022, from https://pubs.iied.org/17498iied

Bartenstein, K. (2017). Article 268. In United Nations Convention on the Law of the Sea: A Commentary. C.H. Beck/Hart/Nomos.

Benkenstein, A., & Maposa, S. (2017). Governing the High Seas: Marine Genetic Resources in Areas Beyond National Jurisdiction. South African Institute of International Affairs Policy Insights, (51).

Blasiak, R., Jouffray, J.-B., Wabnitz, C. C., Sundström, E., & Österblom, H. (2018). Corporate control and global governance of Marine Genetic Resources. *Science Advances*, *4*(6). https://doi.org/10.1126/sciadv.aar5237

Boczek, B. A. (1982). The Transfer of Marine Technology to Developing Nations in International Law. The Law of the Sea Institute, University of Hawaii.

Census of Marine Life. (2011). *Scientific Results to Support the Sustainable Use and Conservation of Marine Life*. Author.

Charter of the United Nations (UN Charter). (1945). Available from https://www.un.org/en/about-us/un-charter/full-text

Clark, N. A. (2020). Institutional arrangements for the new BBNJ agreement: Moving beyond global, regional, and hybrid. *Marine Policy*, *122*, 104–143. https://doi.org/10.1016/j.marpol.2020.104143

Druel, E., & Gjerde, K. M. (2014). Sustaining marine life beyond boundaries: Options for an implementing agreement for Marine Biodiversity Beyond National Jurisdiction under the United Nations Convention on the law of the sea. *Marine Policy*, *49*, 90–97. https://doi.org/10.1016/j.marpol.2013.11.023

Freestone, D. (2019). The UN process to develop an international legally binding instrument under the 1982 law of the Sea Convention: Issues and Challenges. *Conserving Biodiversity in Areas beyond National Jurisdiction*, 3–46. doi:10.1163/9789004391703_002

González, A. W. (2007). Cutting a gordian knot? Towards a practical and realistic scheme for the transfer of Marine Technology. *Law, Science & Ocean Management*, 345–380. doi:10.1163/ej.9789004162556.i-850.100

"Group of 77 and China's Written submission" in response to the General Assembly Resolution 69/292. (2016). Available from https://www.un.org/depts/los/biodiversity/prepcom_files/rolling_comp/Group_of_77_and_China.pdf

High Sea Alliance, Guiding Questions: Environmental Impact Assessments (EIAs) with a focus on Strategic Environmental Assessments (SEAs). (2021). UN.

Highet, K. (1997). Maritime Boundary Disputes and Settlement. In Sustainable Development and Preservation of the Oceans: The Challenges of UNCLOS and Agenda 21 (p. 775). The Law of the Sea Institute, University of Hawaii.

IISD. (2018). *IGC-1 Summary report, 4–17 September 2018.* Retrieved January 14, 2022, from https://enb.iisd.org/events/1st-session-intergovernmental-conference-igc-international-legally-binding-instrument-12

IISD. (2019). *IGC-2 Summary report, 25 March – 5 April 2019.* Retrieved January 14, 2022, from https://enb.iisd.org/events/2nd-session-intergovernmental-conference-igc-conservation-and-sustainable-use-marine/summary

IISD. (2019). *IGC-3 Summary report, 19–30 August 2019* [web log]. Retrieved January 14, 2022, from https://enb.iisd.org/events/3rd-session-intergovernmental-conference-igc-conservation-and-sustainable-use-marine/summary

Inclusive and Sustainable Industrial Development (ISID) Reporting Service. (2019a, September 2). Third Session: Summary and Analysis. *Earth Negotiations Bulletin*, *25*(218), 1–2. https://enb.iisd.org/download/pdf/enb25218e.pdf

ISID Reporting Service. (2019b, September 2). Summary of the Third Session of the Intergovernmental Conference (IGC) on the Conservation and Sustainable Use of Marine Biodiversity of Areas Beyond National Jurisdiction: 19-30 August 2019. *Earth Negotiations Bulletin*, *25*(218). https://enb.iisd.org/download/pdf/enb25218e.pdf

Kent, H. (1954). The Historical Origins of the Three-Mile Limit. *The American Journal of International Law*, *48*(4), 537–553.

Kituyi, M., & Thomson, P. (2018, July 13). *90% of fish stocks are used up – fisheries subsidies must stop* [web log]. Retrieved January 14, 2022, from https://unctad.org/news/90-fish-stocks-are-used-fisheries-subsidies-must-stop

Klein, N. (2009). *Dispute settlement in the UN Convention on the law of the sea*. Cambridge University Press.

Leary, D. (2019). Agreeing to disagree on what we have or have not agreed on: The current state of play of the BBNJ negotiations on the status of Marine Genetic Resources in areas beyond national jurisdiction. *Marine Policy*, *99*, 21–29. https://doi.org/10.1016/j.marpol.2018.10.031

Llamzon, A. P. (2007). Jurisdiction and compliance in recent decisions of the International Court of Justice. *European Journal of International Law*, *18*(5), 815–852. https://doi.org/10.1093/ejil/chm047

Lyou, B.-H. (1997). *International Law Ii*. CUPL Press.

Molenaar, E. (2007). Managing biodiversity in areas beyond National Jurisdiction. *International Journal of Marine and Coastal Law*, *22*(1), 89–124. https://doi.org/10.1163/157180807781475263

Mossop, J. (2019). Dispute settlement in the New Treaty on marine biodiversity in areas beyond national jurisdiction. *SSRN Electronic Journal*. doi:10.2139/ssrn.3508734

Nelson, D. (2002). *Statement on the Commemoration of the 20th Anniversary of the Opening for Signature of the 1982 United Nations Convention on the Law of the Sea at the Plenary of the fifty-seventh Session of the United Nations General Assembly*. https://www.itlos.org/fileadmin/itlos/documents/statements_of_president/nelson/ga_091202_eng.pdf

Nelson, D. (2005). *Statement on the occasion of the presentation of the Report of the Tribunal at the fifteenth Meeting of States Parties*. https://www.itlos.org/fileadmin/itlos/documents/statements_of_president/nelson/msp_160605_eng.pdf

Nordquist, M. H., Rosenne, S., & Sohn, L. B. (Eds.). (1989). *United Nations Convention on the Law of the Sea, 1982: A Commentary* (Vol. 5). Nijhoff.

Ogola, P. (2007). *Environmental Impact Assessment General Procedures*. Paper presented at Short Course II on Surface Exploration for Geothermal Resources, organized by UNU-GTP and KenGen, at Lake Naivasha, Kenya.

"Oral report of the Facilitator to the plenary" submitted during the BBNJ IGC1. (2018). Available from https://www.un.org/bbnj/sites/www.un.org.bbnj/files/final_oral_report_facilitator_abmts_mpas_final.pdf

Request for an advisory opinion submitted by the Sub-Regional Fisheries Commission (SRFC), Advisory Opinion, ITLOS Case No 21. Available from https://www.itlos.org/index.php?id=252

Revised draft text of an agreement under the United Nations Convention on the Law of the Sea on the conservation and sustainable use of marine biological diversity of areas beyond national jurisdiction ("Draft HST"). (2019). Available from https://www.un.org/bbnj/sites/www.un.org.bbnj/files/revised_draft_text_a.conf_.232.2020.11_advance_unedited_version.pdf

Rochette, J., Wright, G., Chabason, L., Unger, S., Ardron, J., & Houghton, K. (2015). *Advancing governance of marine areas beyond national jurisdiction* (Brief for Global Sustainable Development Report 2015). Retrieved January 14, 2022, from https://sustainabledevelopment.un.org/content/documents/5774Brief%20ABNJ%20GSDR_rev.pdf

Ruys, T., & Soete, A. (2015). 'Creeping' Advisory Jurisdiction of International Courts and Tribunals? The Troublesome Case of the International Tribunal for the Law of the Sea. *Leiden Journal of International Law*. doi:10.2139/ssrn.2645895

Sala, E., Mayorga, J., Costello, C., Kroodsma, D., Palomares, M. L., Pauly, D., Sumaila, U. R., & Zeller, D. (2018). The economics of fishing the High Seas. *Science Advances, 4*(6). https://doi.org/10.1126/sciadv.aat2504

Simpson, J. L., & Fox, H. (1959). International Arbitration: Law and Practice. *The American Journal of International Law, 54*(2), 433–435. https://doi.org/10.2307/2195272

Sohn, L. B. (1983). The Future of Dispute Resolution. In The Structure and Process of International Law: Essays in Legal Philosophy, Doctrine and Theory (Vol. 6, p. 1131). Martinus Nijhoff Publishers.

South China Sea Arbitration, *Philippines v China*, Award, PCA Case No 2013-19

Southern Bluefin Tuna Cases (*New Zealand v Japan; Australia v Japan*), Provisional Measures, ITLOS Case Nos 3 and 4, (1999) 38 ILM 1624

Tanaka, Y. (2015). Reflections on the advisory jurisdiction of ITLOS as a full court: The Itlos Advisory Opinion of 2015. *The Law and Practice of International Courts and Tribunals, 14*(2), 318–339. doi:10.1163/15718034-12341296

Thiel, H. (2003). *Approaches to the Establishment of Protected Areas on the High Seas*. Kluwer Law International.

Treves, T. (2004). Flags of Convenience before the Law of the Sea Tribunal. *San Diego International Law Journal, 6*(1). doi:https://doi.org/https://digital.sandiego.edu/ilj/vol6/iss1/9/

Treves, T. (2015). Historical Development of the Law of the Sea. In D. Rothwell, A. Oude Elferink, K. Scott, & T. Stephen (Eds.), *The Oxford Handbook of the Law of the Sea*. OUP.

UN General Assembly Resolution 72/249, *International legally binding instrument under the United Nations Convention on the Law of the Sea on the conservation and sustainable use of marine biological diversity of areas beyond national jurisdiction.* (2017). Available from https://undocs.org/A/RES/72/249

United Nations Convention on the Law of the Sea (UNCLOS). (1982). Available from https://www.un.org/depts/los/convention_agreements/texts/unclos/unclos_e.pdf

Vierros, M. K., & Harden-Davies, H. (2020). Capacity building and technology transfer for improving governance of marine areas both beyond and within National Jurisdiction. *Marine Policy, 122*. doi:10.1016/j.marpol.2020.104158

Wang, C. (2021). On the Legal Status of Marine Genetic Resources in Areas beyond National Jurisdiction. *Sustainability, 13*(14), 7993. https://doi.org/10.3390/su13147993

World Ocean Council. (2019). *The Law of the Sea "BBNJ Agreement" and Ocean Business Activities.* World Ocean Council. Retrieved January 14, 2022, from https://www.oceancouncil.org/resources/the-law-of-the-sea-bbnj-agreement-and-ocean-business-activities/

Chapter 6
Blue Economy of the Arctic:
China's Involvement in Establishing the International Agenda

Gao Tianming
Harbin Engineering University, China

Vasilii Erokhin
https://orcid.org/0000-0002-3745-5469
Harbin Engineering University, China

ABSTRACT

With the emergence of economic globalization, the concept of the blue economy has evolved from fisheries to a wider context that comprised all kinds of biological and mineral resources, maritime trade, shipping, energy, and tourism. Intensive economic exploration of water areas is changing ecosystems, affecting biodiversity, and threatening sustainability. The transformations are felt globally in a form of climate change and environmental degradation, but the Arctic has appeared to be particularly vulnerable. Using the case of China, this chapter attempts to contribute to the convergence of economic benefits of exploring the Arctic with the urgent need for the protection of a fragile Arctic environment. The authors discuss how China's involvement in the Arctic-related activities can benefit the sustainable development of the blue economy in the region.

INTRODUCTION

The blue economy concept has been increasingly gaining attention in both the international agenda and the national development strategies. It has emerged from the broader understanding of the green economy to address contemporary challenges and the development prospects of various kinds of marine activities (Kolesnikova, 2018). On the international level, the principles of the green economy were first defined at the United Nations Conference on Sustainable Development in Rio de Janeiro in 2012. The green growth approach (defined as the mainstream development of the modern world) aims to spur economic development and eliminate poverty and social equity while maintaining ecological balance (Steblyan-

DOI: 10.4018/978-1-6684-3393-5.ch006

skaya et al., 2021). Being an integral part of the green growth model, the blue economy acts as a basis for sustainable development by conceptualizing the oceans as "development spaces" (World Bank & United Nations Department of Economic and Social Affairs, 2017). It provides economic activities that are in balance with the long-term ability of ocean ecosystems to sustain these activities. Thus, the blue economy concept assumes the creation of conditions for economic growth and improving the quality of life of people while preserving the environment.

The evolution and contemporary development of the blue economy concept (further detailed in the Background section) reflect the recognition of the exceptional role of oceans, seas, rivers, and water-related industries in general in the global economy. The World Wildlife Fund (WWF) (2021) estimates the global value of oceans at $24 trillion – a combined value of fishing, cargo and passenger traffic, offshore and deep-sea drilling and mining, jobs created in coastal communities, etc. The market value of marine and coastal resources is estimated at 5% of global GDP, while marine-related activities employ hundreds of millions of people around the world (United Nations, 2021a). Oceans provide people with enormous opportunities and abundant resources for green (or blue, in this case) development, including renewable energy (wave energy, tidal energy, offshore wind energy, marine solar energy, marine bioenergy) and marine biotechnologies (new pharmaceuticals, medicines, cosmetics, feed additives for agricultural animals) that allow for reducing methane and carbon dioxide emissions into the atmosphere. Also, oceans generate oxygen, absorb greenhouse gases, and determine weather patterns and temperatures (United Nations Conference on Trade and Development [UNCTAD], 2021), which all relate to one of the most urgent problems the world is facing today – climate change.

On the one hand, oceans and seas play a fundamental role in mitigating climate change by capturing carbon and extra heat (The Ocean Foundation, 2021). On the other hand, in recent decades, the changes in oceans have been contributing to climate warming through increases in sea temperatures, salinity, and upwelling of surface and deeper waters (Lewis-Brown et al., 2008). According to Poloczanska et al. (2013), since the early 2000s, there have been widespread systemic shifts in marine ecosystems. 57% of the fish stocks of the world's oceans are exhausted, while another 30% are being depleted. 80% of the sea and coastal areas' pollution comes from land. The waters are polluted by untreated sewage, plastic waste, pesticides, and agricultural runoff. Annually, up to 12 million tons of plastic enter the oceans. 89% of the plastic garbage found in the ocean is made up of disposable plastic items, primarily plastic bags. Thus, being one of the most powerful tools to combat climate change, the global ocean is experiencing the increasing burden of climate change effects in such forms as species migration, lower levels of oxygen in water, increases in water temperatures and frequency of marine heatwaves, coral bleaching, and overall loss of marine biodiversity (McCauley et al., 2015; Breitburg et al., 2018; Hughes et al., 2018; Pinsky et al., 2019; Schartup et al., 2019; Smale et al., 2019).

Remarkably rapid changes are taking place in the Arctic, where progressing sea ice loss and activations of both sea ice motion and sea water circulation are exacerbating warming and accelerating climate change effects (Lewis-Brown et al., 2008). However, few studies have touched upon the blue economy issues concerning the Arctic, primarily focusing on the conservation of biodiversity and prevention of pollution in the Arctic Ocean (Erokhin et al., 2018; Zvorykina & Teteryatnikov, 2019). The economy-related works mainly focus on studying the economic perspectives and challenges of trans-Arctic shipping routes and analyzing transcontinental cargo traffic going through the Northeast and the Northwest polar passages (Stephenson et al., 2013; Meng et al., 2017; Guy & Lasserre, 2016). Farre et al. (2014) and Zalyvsky (2015) investigated the perspectives of exploration of mineral and hydrocarbon resources in the Arctic, including in offshore water areas, Lasserre (2014) and Zhao et al. (2016) studied perspectives of bulk and container transport in the Arctic Ocean and the Northern Atlantic, while Xu et al. (2011) and Cao et al. (2021) modeled transit and cabotage cargo flows in the Arctic with account for climate change.

Amid rapid degradation of ocean ecosystems due to increased extraction of various kinds of mineral resources in the Arctic (both onshore and offshore), impacts on natural habitats, and pollution of the marine environment, transition to sustainable management practices in the Arctic has been gaining relevance and importance. Many scholars (Gao et al., 2021a; Erokhin et al., 2019) emphasize the need to accelerate the development of national approaches to sustainable and integrated management of the blue economy in the Arctic based on such tools as integrated coastal zone management, marine spatial planning, and the creation of protected marine areas. Many countries include the blue economy agenda in their development strategies. Contemporary global challenges in the sphere of blue growth call for establishing international approaches to address them. New formats of international cooperation in the field of blue economy are emerging, an international legal framework for the development of ocean resources is being developed, new financing mechanisms for blue economy projects are being launched, etc. (Nagy & Nene, 2021). Nevertheless, the country-specific research in possible responses to the blue economy challenges in the Arctic and their potential effects on the sustainable development of circumpolar territories remains insufficient. It has been particularly scarce in relation to non-Arctic actors, who have been upscaling their economic activities in the region over the past decade. One of such countries is China. Being one of the largest economies in the world, China has been blamed for being the largest CO_2 emitter (about 30% of global emissions) (Zheng et al., 2020; Turnbull et al. 2016), i.e., the major contributor to climate change. Among non-Arctic states, China has been the most active actor in the Arctic in various areas, including exploration of natural resources, shipping, and tourism (Gao & Erokhin, 2020a, 2020b, 2021).

Notwithstanding the fact that the international community generally recognizes the vulnerability of the Arctic environment and the need to balance economic development with environmental problems, economic arguments still overpower environmental ones. In the sphere of the blue economy, there is a lack of developing solutions and priorities for the use of the Arctic Ocean shelf areas, waste disposal, increasing populations of marine organisms, and control over industrial fishing and overfishing. The participation of Chinese companies in addressing the blue economy challenges in the Arctic is studied predominantly from the point of view of navigation along the Northern Sea Route (NSR) without paying due attention to the integrated development of adjacent coastal territories and water areas. Significant gaps in the China-related studies in the sphere of sustainable development of Arctic's blue economy include inadequate coverage of individual interactions between China and the Arctic states in particular sectors of the blue economy, poor comparative analysis of the national development programs of Arctic countries in view of potential collaboration with China, and the lack of practically-oriented studies of the impact of climate change or spatial factors on China's interaction with Arctic countries. In an attempt to bridge these gaps, this chapter aims to review China's regulations related to the sustainable development of natural resources and ecosystems and analyze the country's contribution to the establishment of the international agenda in the sphere of the blue economy of the Arctic.

The remainder of the chapter is organized as follows. In the Background, the authors summarize the contemporary blue economy narrative and outline spheres and elements of the blue economy. The chapter's main focus is to review major blue economy sectors in the Arctic, such as fisheries, aquaculture, extraction of non-living marine resources, renewable energy, shipping and marine engineering, and marine tourism. In this section, the authors discuss China's approaches to defining national priorities and interests in the Arctic, China's collaboration with Arctic and non-Arctic states in the region, and China's role in establishing sustainable development of water areas and coastal territories in the High North. The Solutions and Recommendations section summarizes the authors' vision of actions needed to promote academic and practical cooperation between China and other stakeholders in the Arctic in the field of the blue economy. Most relevant, promising, and challenging areas of advanced research in the spheres of climate change and environmental, technological, and social consequences of developing Arctic's blue economy are outlined in Future Research Directions. The Conclusion summarizes key challenges that the transition to the blue economic growth model in the Arctic poses to the world community and blueprints promising areas for cooperation between China and other countries in the region.

BACKGROUND

Over the past two decades, the blue economy has slowly but steadily evolved as a term and a concept encompassing a variety of ocean-related economic opportunities while recognizing, accounting for, and addressing the related threats of climate change, overfishing, pollution, or habitat destruction (Voyer et al., 2018). As in the case of the green economy, which is not limited to green ecosystems, the blue economy is not limited to the marine ecosystem. It leads to a new way of building a business, using the resources available in systems where the waste of one product becomes a raw material that provides a new cash flow. Thus, in a narrow sense, while green economy refers to terrestrial ecosystems, blue one refers to marine ecosystems. In a broader sense, the blue economy is a business model that provides opportunities for business development and investments that are more profitable from an economic and environmental point of view. Thus, the blue economy is a tool that can be used to improve economic conditions and create a sustainable development model (Komarova et al., 2015). In 2015, this understanding of the blue economy concept was used when establishing the basis for the definition of the UN Sustainable Development Goals (SDGs) (United Nations, 2021b), particularly, Goal 14 "Conserve and Sustainably Use the Oceans, Seas and Marine Resources for Sustainable Development" (United Nations, 2021a). The blue economy concept is aimed at the systematic and sustainable development of industries (sectors) related to the use of oceans. It reflects the desire of the world community to find a balance between economic growth, preservation of the marine environment, and ensuring the well-being of the population.

The contemporary blue economy narrative emphasizes the systematic and sustainable development of industries related to using various kinds of marine resources. However, despite a certain unification of the blue economy concept within the SDGs, there remain differences in understanding individual blue economy elements. This complicates international comparisons. Even the term "blue economy" is interpreted in different ways. In this study, the authors use the World Bank's comprehensive interpretation of blue economy as a concept that "seeks to promote economic growth, social inclusion, and the preservation or improvement of livelihoods while at the same time ensuring environmental sustainability of the oceans and coastal areas" (World Bank & United Nations Department of Economic and Social Affairs, 2017). This approach is commonly employed in many studies worldwide, since it effectively captures the range of economic sectors and related policies that together determine whether the use of marine resources is sustainable.

The range of services and properties of marine and coastal ecosystems is wide. It includes habitats of marine organisms, resources for aquaculture, protection of coastal areas from erosion and extreme weather events, tourism and recreation, development of shipping, mining and exploration of offshore resources, development of local industries, and many more (Figure 1). Irrational use of one habitat

Figure 1. Spheres and elements of the blue economy
Source: authors' development based on World Bank & United Nations Department of Economic and Social Affairs (2017)

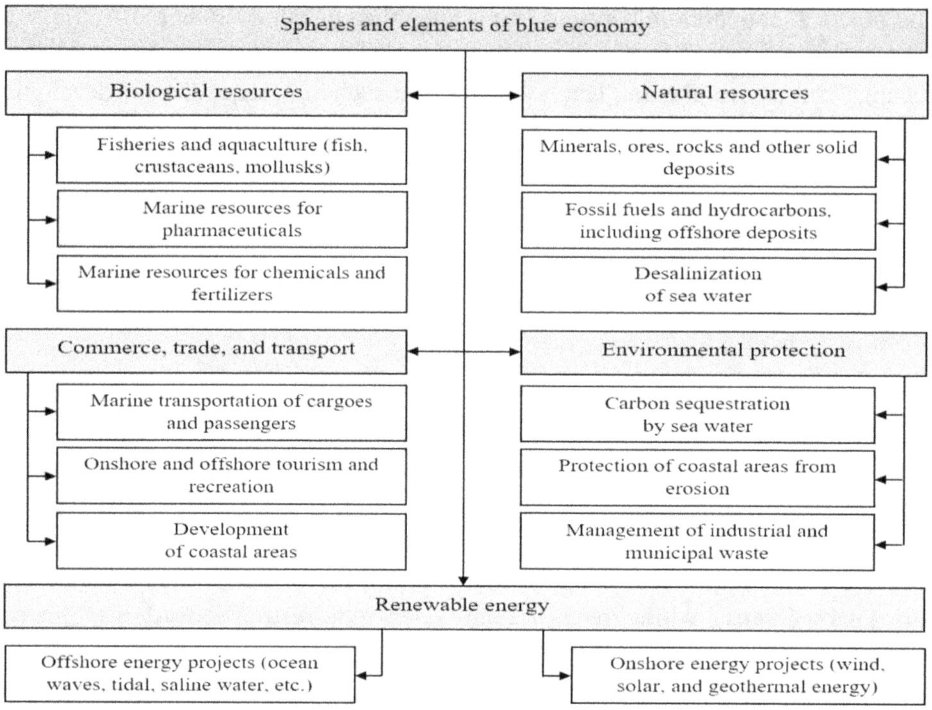

inevitably leads to the loss of other services and valuable resources. Understanding and tracking the interrelationships between ecosystems, economic activities, anthropogenic impacts, and climate change is crucial to ensure the sustainable use of coastal and marine resources.

The Organization for Economic Cooperation and Development identifies eleven basic and six emerging branches of the blue economy. The former include conventional areas such as fishing, seafood processing, shipping, port infrastructure, shipbuilding and ship repair, offshore gas and oil production, marine engineering and construction, marine tourism, marine business services, marine scientific research and education, and dredging. Emerging sectors include innovative and high-tech maritime industries, such as wind and offshore energy, other types of renewable energy, marine biotechnologies, high-tech marine products and services, oil and gas production in deep-sea zones, and aquaculture. The range of emerging sectors can be widened. For example, Simionov et al. (2021) emphasized the importance of reduction in coastal air and water emissions, Bhattacharya and Dash (2021) and Kabil et al. (2021) – tourism in coastal areas, Gao et al. (2021b) – food security, Funk et al. (2021) – algae production, Zheng et al. (2021) and Gao et al. (2021a) – integrated coastal and marine area management. Other potential sectors could include decarbonizing onshore energy projects, developing energy-saving technologies, waste disposal management in water and coastal areas, and health-related aspects of the blue economy. Seas and oceans are a vast field for innovation and experimentation with new technologies. According to the World Bank and the United Nations Department of Economic and Social Affairs (2017), 10% of food in the world can be obtained from seaweed. Seawater is an almost unlimited source of lithium (about 230 billion tons). Antiviral medicines derived from marine organisms are already being tested. The most advanced companies and even countries are working on the development of blue energy projects that would substantially reduce the carbon footprint of the energy sector and the cost of energy.

MAIN FOCUS OF THE CHAPTER

Blue Economy of the Arctic: An Overview

The Arctic has been receiving increasing attention from the perspective of the development of the blue economy. Until recently, the blue economy of the Arctic was considered from the point of view of fisheries and aquaculture (Snyder & Erbaugh, 2020; Fauchald et al., 2021), but over the past years, the scope of the blue economy issues has been substantially expanded.

Fisheries

Water areas in the High North are covered with floating annual and perennial ice throughout the year, which significantly complicates fishing in the Arctic seas. However, since the 2000s, many studies and observations (Cavalieri & Parkinson, 2012; Intergovernmental Panel on Climate Change, 2013; National Snow and Ice Data Center, 2016) have been demonstrating that progressing climate change in the Arctic result in the substantial loss of ice cover in both the Arctic Ocean and the inland circumpolar territories (for instance, glaciers in Greenland and Iceland or permafrost in Russia and Canada). This extends the fishing window, contributes to the expansion of the geography of fishing, diversifies the forms of use of fish resources, and allows for the development of Arctic fish resources (Tortsev, 2018).

The Arctic is home to many species of fish and cyclostomes, which are integral elements of Arctic ecosystems. In quantitative terms, the Barents Sea and the adjacent waters of the Norwegian and Greenland Seas are the richest in commercial biological resources (cod, haddock, pollack, capelin, whiting, herring, sea bass, and mackerel) (Shuvalova & Glubokov, 2015). The number of fish species in the Barents Sea (222 species) almost equals that in the Northern Atlantic (the Norwegian Sea and the North Sea) and exceeds that in neighboring Arctic waters. Thus, there are 70 species (ten freshwater species) in the Kara Sea, 67 species (fifteen freshwater species) in the White Sea, and about 40 species in the Laptev Sea. Almost 70 species have been identified in the basin of the East Siberian Sea, including 36 freshwater species. The Eastern section of the Arctic Ocean is richer in terms of the quantitative composition of the fish fauna compared to the western and central sections. Thus, due to the northward migration of Arctic-boreal and boreal fish through the Bering Strait, the number of species discovered in the Chukchi Sea exceeds 110. The southwestern sector of the Chukchi Sea between Wrangel Island and the Bering Strait is characterized by the greatest biological productivity. Thirty species have been identified during trawl surveys (pollack population being the largest). Also, capelin, herring, and some salmon species (chum salmon, sockeye salmon, chinook salmon) are found in commercial quantities in the Chukchi Sea. Currently, the number of these fish is relatively low, but it is expected to grow due to climate warming. In addition to fish, crustaceans and mollusks could be promising for fishing in the Chukchi Sea. In general, with the increase in water temperature, there have been more Arctic-boreal and boreal fish migrating from the Bering Sea to the Arctic Ocean. Thus, the biological resources of the Arctic make it possible to develop the large-scale fishing of many kinds of aquatic organisms, rather than meeting the needs of the local population.

Nevertheless, experts note the low resistance of Arctic ecosystems to anthropogenic impact. Thus, the destruction of a particular species or a reduction in its populations in the Arctic entails a significant transformation of the entire food chain and the ecosystem as a whole. In addition, it takes a long time for the ecosystem to get restored. In recent years, habitats have been increasingly affected by the exploration and exploitation of mineral deposits in the Arctic, including offshore, the construction of industrial facilities, highways, seaports, pipelines, etc. For example, the construction of industrial and infrastructure facilities in the Russian Arctic has caused damage to fish resources equivalent to more than eight thousand tons of fish. To compensate this loss, Russia should artificially grow and release into the rivers nine million sturgeons, 25 million muksuns, and 700 million pelyads (Tortsev, 2018). Overfishing also negatively affects fish resources. Thus, overfishing of cod off the coast of Newfoundland and in adjacent waters led to a significant reduction in the cod population, which resulted in a decrease in catch and the moratorium on fishing (Cochrane, 2000; Dolan et al., 2005).

Aquaculture

To some extent, the damage caused by the economic activity to fish resources and habitats can be compensated through aquaculture development. The prospects for the development of aquaculture in the Arctic are determined by the diversity of aquatic ecosystems, a variety of potential sites for the location of aquaculture facilities, the possibility of directed formation and improvement of coastal biological communities, relative cleanness of water, availability of natural biotopes suitable for the placement of aquafarms (fjords, bays, and coves isolated from wave action), and high market value of artificially farmed fish species (Atlantic salmon, rainbow trout, Kamchatka crab, sugar wrack, etc.) (Nikandrov et al., 2018; Sterligova et al., 2019). The cage cultivation of coldwater species is the most promising aquaculture sector in the region (Lukin et al., 2016). Aquaculture farms are mainly focused on cultivating rainbow trout and Atlantic salmon. The aquaculture-related potential of the Arctic is evidenced by the success of Norway, where the output of Atlantic salmon first exceeded one million tons in 2017. Among Arctic countries, Norway is the leader in the development of aquaculture. Intensive farming of Atlantic salmon accounts for 80% of the total aquaculture production in this country. Other important species are rainbow trout, marine finfish (cod, halibut), and shellfish (blue mussel, oysters). Denmark has been developing its aquaculture by increasing the production of rainbow trout from freshwater ponds and mariculture units and eel in recirculated freshwater tank systems. Iceland specializes in Atlantic salmon, Arctic char, and Atlantic cod, Sweden – rainbow, sea trout, Arctic char, and salmon, Finland – rainbow trout, crayfish, fry, and salmon, Canada – Atlantic salmon. In the USA and Russia, aquaculture facilities are concentrated outside the Arctic in the southern seas (southeastern states around the Mexican Gulf and the Atlantic Ocean shore in the USA and Russia's Black and Caspian Seas and the Far East). However, new farms have been established in Alaska and the Russian Arctic. The mainstay of US aquaculture is the production of channel catfish. Russia farms many fish species, crustaceans, and mollusks, including domesticated forms of carp, salmon, sturgeon, coregonid, and cichlid fish (Arctic Portal, 2012).

The contribution of aquaculture into establishing a more stable and predictable production of fish (and therefore the solution of the food security problem or creation of opportunities for the development of circumpolar territories) is hardly disputable. However, since the ecosystem of Arctic waters is exceptionally fragile, it can be disrupted or destroyed by the uncontrolled growth of the aquaculture population. According to the Arctic Portal (2012), the development of aquaculture in the Arctic gives rise to two critical concerns: the intrusion of fish farms into vulnerable marine and coastal areas and the overall sustainability of an industry that depends on large catches of wild fish to feed farmed fish. Therefore, fish farmers need to consider the self-purification capacity of water areas and reservoirs with an increase in the fish population.

Extraction of Marine Non-Living Resources

The Arctic is rich not only in unique ecosystems and biological resources of the Arctic seas, but also in significant reserves of various types of mineral and other non-living resources in offshore areas (Gautier et al., 2009). Despite certain doubts regarding the economic, social, political, logistical, and technological feasibility of extracting hydrocarbons and other resources in the Arctic Ocean (Kondratiev, 2020), significant investments in the exploration and development of resources have been intensively carried out in recent years, including with the participation of China. According to the United States Geological Survey (2021), there could be up to 22% of undiscovered technically recoverable oil and gas resources in the Arctic (412 billion barrels of oil equivalent), 84% of which are located offshore. Among them, there are about 90 billion barrels of oil (13 billion tons) and 47.3 trillion m^3 of natural gas. Oil reserves are concentrated in offshore areas in Russia and the USA (43% and 33%, respectively), while most of the gas reserves are accounted for by Russia (92%).

Russia was the first country to discover hydrocarbon deposits in the Arctic Ocean in 1962. Currently, Russia's section of the Arctic Ocean shelf accounts for about 60% of the Arctic's total oil and gas resources and more than 90% of its proven reserves (of which natural gas accounts for 90%). The deposits are concentrated in the Barents, Kara, East Siberian, Chukchi, Pechora, and Laptev seas. To date, more than twenty large promising oil and gas basins have been identified on Russia's Arctic shelf, 36 fields have been discovered, including unique gas fields (Shtokmanovskoye, Rusanovskoye, Leningradskoye) in the Western Arctic and several oil fields on the northeastern shelf of Sakhalin Island. While Russia was the first to discover hydrocarbons, Canada became the first to start exploratory drilling in the Arctic Ocean shelf. Canada's offshore fields are concentrated in the Beaufort Sea (over thirty, most of which are oil and gas). The recoverable hydrocarbon reserves of the Beaufort Sea are located in shallow areas (up to 100 m depth). The estimated volume of the Amauligak deposit is 68.5 million tons of oil and 56 billion m^3 of natural gas. The USA has been developing offshore fields in the Arctic for more than forty years, since the discovery of the Prudhoe Bay field in 1968 (recoverable reserves of about 25 billion barrels of oil and 730 billion m^3 of gas, about 20% of the US total oil production). Offshore deposits are located in the Beaufort Sea and the Chukchi Sea. The deposits in the Beaufort Sea are better studied and developed. The sea is relatively shallow. Also, it is located closer to the existing infrastructure (the Trans-Alaska oil pipeline). In 1990, the Burger gas field, one of the largest on the Alaska shelf, was discovered in the Chukchi Sea. The Barents Sea shelf is being explored and developed by Norway. The deposits in the Arctic zone of Norway are estimated at 1.9 billion barrels of oil equivalent.

Due to a considerable amount of undiscovered oil and gas reserves, the Arctic shelf attracts increasing attention of both Arctic and non-Arctic countries amid depletion of on-land deposits. The Beaufort Sea (USA's and Canada's shelf), the Chukchi Sea (USA), the Barents Sea (Norway and Russia), the Pechora, and the Kara seas (Russia) have been well studied by seismic exploration. Still, Russia's shelf, the biggest among the Arctic states, remains scantily explored (Russia's sections of the Chukchi Sea, the East Siberian Sea, and the Laptev Sea). Having the most significant resource potential in the Arctic, Russia's continental shelf is less studied compared to those in other countries. The Barents Sea in Russia has been studied twenty times less than in Norway, and the Chukchi Sea is ten times less than in the USA.

Renewable Energy

The portion of hydrocarbons produced in the Arctic in the world's total energy mix is growing, but extracting fossil fuels from the Arctic shelf is not the only solution to the global energy problem. Over the past few years, the primary trend in the energy sector has been a sharp increase in the share of renewable energy in the global energy mix. In 2019, renewable sources first-ever overtook nuclear power plants in terms of energy output (GoArctic, 2020). The use of renewable energy sources is essential for the Arctic both because of the lower cost compared to conventional types of energy and the significantly less negative impact on the environment. Due to the very cold climate, low population density, and remoteness of settlements from each other, it is costly to build new energy facilities. In many remote territories in Russia and Canada, it is almost impossible. The use of renewable energy sources will help reduce the cost of construction and maintenance of municipal infrastructure, as well as improve the environmental situation in the region. Currently, power supply systems in the High North run on imported coal, oil, and diesel, harmful emissions from which pollute the environment and contribute to climate change.

Regarding the blue economy, the key renewable energy sectors in the Arctic are wind energy and sea energy (waves and tidal). Long winters (up to 300 days a year) with frosts reaching -35-50°C produce strong and steady winds. In the coastal areas of the White Sea and the Barents Sea, as well as in the Novaya Zemlya Archipelago and the Franz Josef Land Archipelago, the wind speed reaches 5-8 m/s. As the Arctic warms, there is an increase in the frequency and strength of winds. Cold air is of higher density than hot one. Therefore, at the same wind speed, the energy efficiency of wind turbines in the High North is higher than that in the middle latitudes. These features create favorable conditions for the development of the wind energy sector in the Arctic, as well as the integration of disparate wind farms into a single energy generation grid (Zmieva, 2020). The USA and the EU have accumulated a lot of experience in this matter. According to Deloitte Center for Energy Solutions (Motyka et al., 2018), previously, it was not possible to ensure the stability of the united grid system with the use of wind turbines. Now the problem has been solved. The increase in the share of wind energy and other renewables in the energy mix is accompanied by an increase in the reliability and stability of power systems. Renewable energy sources either do not affect the operation of the energy system, or require minor changes to the operation and use of existing energy resources (International Energy Agency, 2018).

Tidal power plants are being built in coastal areas. The Kislogubskaya tidal power plant (1,7 MW) operates in Russia. The Northern power plant (12 MW, annual energy output of 23.8 million kWh) is being built on the Kola Peninsula. This will be the first tidal power plant in Russia to reach the industrial level of energy generation. Also, Russia plans to build a power plant in the Mezen Bay of the White Sea (8 GW, annual energy output of 38.9 billion kWh). However, most tides' characteristics important for stable energy generation (intensity, frequency, constancy, water elevation, ice situation, wind-driven inertial currents, etc.) remain poorly studied across the Arctic (Baumann et al., 2020). Moreover, due to technical issues, both tidal and wave power generation are limited to ice-free areas or far offshore in open water (Hemsath, 2010).

Shipping and Marine Engineering

The development of new deposits of mineral resources in the Arctic shelf results in the rise in the intensity of shipping, which, in turn, increases the risks to fragile marine ecosystems. In many territories, especially in Russia's sector of the Arctic as the most industrially developed, negative environmental processes have led to the transformation of the natural geochemical background, atmospheric pollution, degradation of vegetation and soil, the introduction of harmful substances into food chains, and increased morbidity of the population. Polar nights, storms, and unstable ice and weather conditions increase the risk of accidents and decrease the possibilities for eliminating the consequences. Even a minor leakage of hydrocarbons into ice-covered water could lead to significant environmental damage on the shelf. Vessels in the Arctic mainly use heavy fuel oil (up to 75% of all fuel), damaging the environment (Pierre & Olivier, 2015). It is a leftover product of the refining process and is a viscous type of fuel. The burning of heavy fuel oil releases soot, which then settles on ice and snow, contributing to greater absorption of solar heat and, as a result, melting of ice. Due to the decrease in the sea surface albedo, water absorbs more solar energy, which contributes to the aggravation of the greenhouse effect and spurs climate change. Fuel oil spills cause critical damage to marine ecosystems. Due to its dense consistency, heavy fuel oil does not dissolve in water. It forms a chocolate mousse-type paste in the sea water that is difficult to recover. Therefore, its impact on birds and marine mammals is hugely destroying. In the Arctic, eliminating oil spills is difficult due to ice conditions, poor visibility and weather, and long distances. The self-purification of the environment in the cold waters is slow. Since the 2010s, there has been a search for ways to limit or even ban the use of heavy fuel oil in the Arctic. The Arctic Council conducted a comprehensive assessment of the impact of shipping on Arctic ecosystems and the threat of accidental oil spills. It resulted in a proposal to ban heavy fuel oil in the Arctic by the International Maritime Organization. It is expected that the ban will come into force in 2024. However, some vessels, primarily those with a double hull, will be able to continue using heavy fuel oil until 2029. In addition, coastal Arctic states will be allowed to issue special permits for individual vessels also until 2029.

Marine Tourism

The attractiveness of the Arctic as a tourist destination has been growing in recent years due to the significant competitive advantages of the region in the eyes of tourists from around the world (untouched nature, environment, exotic and unusual travel, etc.) (Brouder, 2013). The marine tourism sector includes ocean waters, island territories, and coastal zones. It is characterized by such features as the prevalence of marine vehicles (including icebreakers), compliance with stereotypical ideas about the Arctic (shelf glaciers, icebergs), specific fauna commonly associated with Arctic territories (marine mammals, polar bears), and indigenous peoples whose way of life is linked with the sea. However, like other types of economic activity in the Arctic discussed above, the intensification of tourism in territories in the High North threatens the unique and fragile Arctic ecosystems (Dawson et al., 2007). Negative impacts of tourism on nature include environmental pollution due to the presence of people and the construction of tourist infrastructure in areas previously not affected by anthropogenic influence; depletion of biological resources due to the nature-oriented types of tourism (hunting and fishing); disturbance of ecological balance due to intensive fishing or catching marine species (carried out by tourists themselves or organized by a travel agency); and increase in the likelihood of environmental disasters (fuel leakages and garbage from cruise ships). Despite the high environmental risks that the development of tourism creates for the Arctic, tourism is one of the few activities to diversify the economy of circumpolar communities. However, the economic prospects for this sector face objective difficulties, since most of the destinations in the Arctic are hardly accessible for mass tourism (Sevastiyanov et al., 2014). The lack of regular rail and road connections with the outside world, as well as the complexity of sea navigation and air travel in high latitudes, have become constraining factors in the development of mass tourism in the High North. Due to the underdeveloped on-land communications, tourism is serviced by sea and river transport, where there is a high level of ship wear and outdated infrastructure of ports and berths.

China and the Blue Economy Narrative in the Arctic

Sustainable integrated management of the blue economy sectors related to marine and coastal ecosystems is at the center of the national agenda of Arctic countries and, since recently, some of non-Arctic (or near-Arctic) states. Despite all the differences in approaches to regulating certain blue sectors, coordination mechanisms, statistics, and measurements, there is unity in terms of goal-setting (sustainable development, decarbonization, biodiversity, food security, social well-being), descriptions of key policy approaches (spatial development, assessment and monitoring of SDGs, selection of target sectors, investments in research), priority areas of development (employment, skills, innovation, emerging markets and technologies, clusters and coastal territories), and regulation (shadow sector, over-exploitation of biological and mineral resources, illegal trade). The focus on the blue transition, along with appropriate actions, contributes to the transformation in managing marine resources and spaces (for example, international governance of the oceans). Among the key actors in this area is China, one of the world's biggest maritime powers and shipping nations and the leader in most of the sectors of the blue economy discussed above.

In 2013, China joined the Arctic Council and thus demonstrated its will to get equally involved in shaping the Arctic-related international agenda. In 2017, the development of potential transport routes in the Arctic Ocean (Northwest and Northeast passages, Northern Sea Route, and the central areas of the Arctic Ocean) was incorporated into the Belt and Road (BRI) network. In the Vision for Maritime Cooperation under the Belt and Road Initiative (Xinhua, 2017), China expressed its continuing readiness to collaborate with Arctic countries to improve sea transit conditions and survey for new resources in the High North. China's Arctic Policy adopted in 2018 (State Council of the People's Republic of China, 2018) underscored the intention of the country to participate in the governance of the Arctic and promotion of sustainable development. According to Lanteigne (2019) and Górski (2019), the Arctic Policy stressed China's support for the peaceful use of the Arctic and cooperation in various non-military areas, but also noted that China as a non-Arctic state still had the rights to economic, trade, shipping, and investment activities in the High North in accordance with international law including the United Nations Convention on the Law of the Sea (UNCLOS).

Comparative studies of the national environmental regulations of circumpolar territories in the Arctic states (including the regulation of marine ecosystems and blue economy sectors) show that in some areas, economic arguments overpower environmental ones (Heininen et al., 2020; Gao & Erokhin, 2020b). All countries recognize the vulnerability of the Arctic environment and the need to balance economic development with environmental problems. But at the same time, there is a lack of developing solutions and priorities. Among the main topics of international cooperation in the Arctic are the development of a special regime for the use of natural resources, monitoring of pollution of ecosystems, restoration of landscapes, creation of nature reserves, waste disposal, increasing populations of marine organisms, animals, and birds, and control over industrial fishing and overfishing. Therefore, international efforts are focused on searching for ways to smooth out the contradictions between the national interests of coastal states and the requirements of the ecosystem approach. This problem will become one of the central topics of scientific and political discussions within the Arctic Council for the next decade. Many scholars (Nuttall & Callaghan, 2019; Conde & Sánchez, 2016) agree that the most relevant topics would include the following: how to avoid the situation so that ecosystem approaches and ecosystem management do not create ecological borders in the Arctic in addition to the existing borders of national jurisdiction; how should the gradual transformation of the convention regime and its adaptation to new international political and economic conditions take place; how to take into account the solution of these problems in the development of national policies of the Arctic Council member states and observer countries.

In the light of this vision of the environmental agenda in the Arctic, China's participation in the formation of internationally agreed responses to contemporary challenges in the sphere of the blue economy is essential. In 2017, China's President Xi Jinping underscored the commitment of the country to "the principles of prioritizing resource conservation and environmental protection" (Xi, 2017: 45) by promoting low-carbon development, preventing and controlling pollution of air, water, and soils, restoring ecosystems, and developing biodiversity protection networks (Xi, 2017: 45-46). China "embraces the vision of a global community of shared future and accelerates its transformation towards green and low-carbon development in economy and society" (State Council Information Office of the People's Republic of China, 2020) and aims to "speed up the building of … an industrial system for green, circular, and low-carbon development" (Xi, 2017: 429). China is also an active participant in global energy governance, exploring a path of worldwide sustainable energy and sustainable development in general. At the 75th United Nations General Assembly in September 2020, President Xi Jinping pledged that China would scale up its Intended Nationally Determined Contributions by "adopting more vigorous policies and measures, striving to have carbon dioxide emissions peak before 2030 and to achieve carbon neutrality before 2060" (State Council Information Office of the People's Republic of China, 2020). Such a vision of China's role in building an "ecological civilization" (Xi, 2017: 47) is enshrined in China's Arctic Policy 2018, which states that "the Arctic situation now goes beyond its … regional nature, having a vital bearing on … the survival, the development, and the shared future for mankind" (State Council of the People's Republic of China, 2018: Foreword).

With regard to the blue economy of the Arctic, it seems possible to identify five priority areas for China in which cooperation with the Arctic Council countries and the international community in general could be promising (Figure 2).

China's policy in the Arctic is based on the interconnection of the three principles: respect for partners, cooperation, and mutual benefit for all parties involved. China respects the rights of the Arctic countries (members of the Arctic Council) and indigenous peoples living in the High North, enshrined in international law, and stands for the peaceful resolution of disputes over the claims of different countries to the Arctic shelf and commercial shipping regimes in the Arctic Ocean. The cooperation principle declares China's intention to participate in the development and implementation of the international cooperation agenda in certain blue economy sectors, in particular through the convergence of the BRI activities into the paradigm of Arctic cooperation, coordination of national economic strategies of China and the Arctic countries, the interconnection of infrastructure systems based on the establishment of transport and economic corridors in the High North, and the development of trade and investment, financial cooperation, and humanitarian ties. The mutual benefit principle is about offering investment and technology in exchange for participation in developing resources and accessing transport routes. One of the main tasks is to diversify routes connecting China with deposits of natural resources and the markets in Europe and North America. Despite the BRI's strategic orientation to the southern routes of the Maritime Silk Road, China's commercial shipping critically depends on the bottlenecks of the corridors. The initial vision of BRI's maritime corridors was expanded in 2017 by including the Polar Silk Road (PSR) as the blue economic passage in the Arctic (State Council of the People's Republic of

Figure 2. China's priorities in the development of the blue economy of the Arctic
Source: authors' development based on State Council of the People's Republic of China (2018)

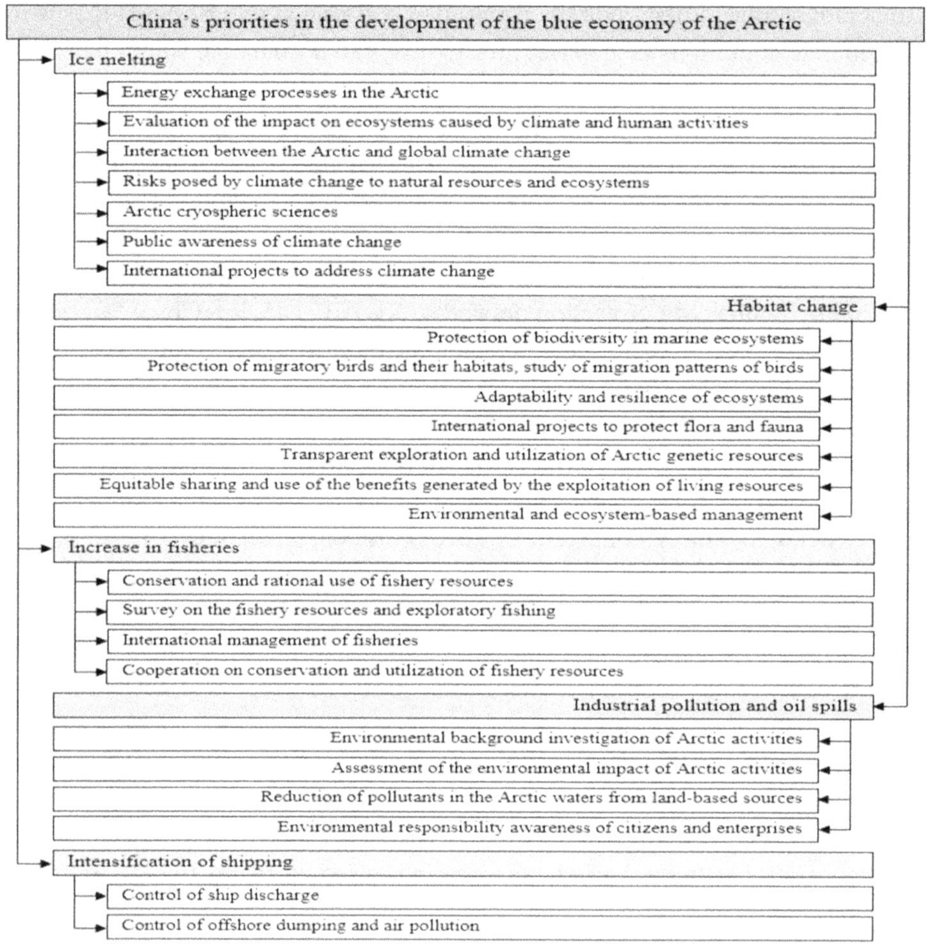

China, 2017). However, among other BRI's blue passages, the PSR remains poorly explored in terms of its potential impact on changing the landscape of maritime trade (Gao et al., 2021b; Wiederer, 2018). China's Arctic Policy states that the PSR "facilitates connectivity and sustainable economic and social development of the Arctic" (State Council of the People's Republic of China, 2018) by opening up an economic passage between China and Europe through Russia's Northern Sea Route (NSR) (Tillman et al., 2018; Gao, 2019). That is why China is actively involved in the Arctic agenda and is aimed at directly participating in the development of the Arctic territories.

China's Role in Establishing Sustainable Development of Coastal Territories

The economy of circumpolar territories is commonly considered the economy of extremes (Pelyasov et al., 2017; Tortsev, 2018), which is characterized by geographical remoteness of economic activity from the main markets, isolation of resources and factors and production, and small size of local markets. Conley et al. (2013) emphasize the need for Arctic countries to take into account a variety of natural (harsh climate, vulnerable ecosystems) and spatial (remoteness, long distances) factors that affect the blue economy. Thus, in the USA, the regulation of fish resources in Alaska considers a harsh climate, ice cover, low biological productivity of the Arctic seas, vulnerable ecosystems, and climate change (North Pacific Fishery Management Council, 2009).

Even though China is not an Arctic country, China is increasingly becoming involved in international cooperation on the development of Arctic territories. Climate change in the region affects the ecology of the entire planet, including China. The progressing reduction of ice cover opens up new opportunities for China to participate in developing natural resources and intercontinental transport corridors in the Arctic (Lanteigne, 2014). As discussed in the above section of the chapter, China is interested in interacting with Arctic countries and near-Arctic states to protect and promote peace, stability, and sustainable socio-economic and environmental development of the Arctic (Erokhin, 2018). China's Arctic Policy emphasizes that the use of sea routes and energy resources of the Arctic has a direct impact on the economic and energy strategy of China (State Council of the People's Republic of China, 2018), one of the world's largest economies and consumers of energy and other resources.

Many scholars, including Peng and Wegge (2015) and Su and Lanteigne (2015), study the aspects of China's political interaction with Arctic countries only in the format of the Arctic Council, without due attention to the geopolitical, spatial, and economic factors that affect the interests of China and other countries. Other researchers agree that economic issues establish the basis of China-Nordic and China-Russia collaboration in the Arctic (Moe & Oystein, 2010; Melia et al., 2017), but focus on institutional policy and governance in the Arctic by the community of countries, rather than on regional aspects of development and deployment of productive forces with China's involvement. Despite the actualization of the PSR initiative, participation of Chinese companies in the development of economic and transport corridors in the Arctic is studied from the point of view of navigation along the NSR without paying due attention to the integrated development of territories adjacent to the NSR and other potential sea routes in the Arctic Ocean and the North Atlantic (Bertelsen & Gallucci, 2016; Flake, 2013). Among Chinese sources, the adaptation of cooperation mechanisms to the changing conditions of spatial, industrial, and socio-economic development of the Arctic is poorly addressed compared to the studies in the spheres of political science, exploration of resources and transport routes, and climate change (Liu et al., 2016; Xu, 2016; Zhu et al., 2018; Yang & Zhao, 2019). The existing gaps in the sustainability-related studies in the sphere of the blue economy of the Arctic could be summarized as follows:

- studies focus on the multilateral format of China's interaction with the Arctic Council, where the implementation of China's interests is primarily affected (sometimes even blocked) by the unified position of the member countries, to the detriment of the study of individual interactions between China and the Arctic states in individual sectors of the blue economy;
- comparative analysis of the national development programs of Arctic countries in view of potential collaboration with China is poor, which makes it challenging to implement joint projects in the sphere of the blue economy;
- most of the studies address geopolitical and macro-regional issues, while practically-oriented studies of the impact of climate change or spatial factors on China's interaction with Arctic countries remain scarce;
- when analyzing the state and development trends of the Arctic territories, China's role is viewed in the narrow sense (participation of Chinese companies in focal resource mega-projects in Russia and Northern Europe and navigation on the NSR), while environmental aspects of the blue econo-

my agenda in combination with the solution of social and economic issues of sustainable development in the High North are not taken into account.

China is now one of the most valuable partners for Arctic countries, but few of the joint projects result in any decisive contribution to the development of the blue economy of the region and protection of the marine environment and ecosystems. Major investment projects with the involvement of Chinese enterprises include Yamal LNG and Arctic LNG 2 in Russia; Boreal Bioref Ltd. (bio-refinery), Kaidi (biofuels), and Arctic tourism in Finland; ChemChina (energy sector and chemical industry), CNOOC (energy), and Grand China Logistics (transportation) in Norway; Geely (methane production), Huawei (5G networks), and China-Iceland Joint Arctic Science Observatory in Iceland; exploration of uranium and rare earth metals in Kvanefjeld site, Greenland. Russia (the so far biggest recipient of Chinese investment in the Arctic) prioritizes sustainable development, including those related to the blue economy concept (establishment of land-based natural reserves and marine protected areas; cleaning up the environmental mess both on the coastline and archipelagos; creation of a state ecological monitoring system) (President of the Russian Federation, 2020). However, apart from a skyrocketing development of the LNG industry in the Russian Arctic, other investment projects where Chinese enterprises were expected to participate have not been that successful (Gao & Erokhin, 2020a, 2021). Some countries (for instance, the USA) express a hostile and suspicious attitude towards China's activities in the region.

SOLUTIONS AND RECOMMENDATIONS

The degradation of marine ecosystems in the Arctic, along with the depletion of resources of the Arctic Ocean due to an increase in environmental and economic burden, inevitably affect the well-being and health of people in circumpolar territories and beyond. The development of the blue economy of the Artic faces a number of challenges. Climate challenges include the oxidation and warming of water, ice cover loss, rising sea levels, and increased frequency and intensity of natural disasters in coastal areas. The negative anthropogenic impact on marine ecosystems is aggravating. It is manifested in the pollution of the Arctic Ocean, ship accidents, discharge of untreated wastewater from on-land industrial and municipal facilities, as well as waste from vessels into the sea. Overexploitation of the biological resources of the Arctic Ocean leads to the destruction of the habitat of fish and marine animals and the destruction of fragile ecosystems as a result of urbanization, industrialization of coastal territories, and the development of mass coastal and marine tourism.

China's presence in the Arctic is growing, but a number of countries (as well as a significant part of the research community) do not consider China as a full-fledged actor in international regulation of the Arctic. Nevertheless, both China's willingness to cooperate and the country's economic and academic resources can be used to improve the sustainable development of the entire region. The soonest possible blue transition in the Article is the task of the entire world community, the solution of which is difficult to imagine without China. In the light of the identified shortcomings in both research and practices of cooperation in the field of blue economy, the following recommendations could be made:

- summarization of trends in the industrial, infrastructural, and socio-economic development of the blue economy of the Arctic and their effects for spatial changes in territories along potential PSR corridors (the Russian Arctic, Nordic countries, Alaska, and Canada's North)

- understanding and modeling the interdependencies between changes in individual sectors of the blue economy (Figures 1 and 2 above) and the content of China's geopolitical and economic relations with individual countries of the Arctic Council and in the Arctic macro-region as a whole;
- adaptation of economically justified and practically feasible options for China's presence in the Arctic to the processes of permanent changes in the blue economy sectors and the multi-vector interests of the international community in the region.

To increase the effectiveness of cooperation, the overall commitment to the blue economy should be narrowed down to specific economic sectors and ecosystems, on which attention will be focused. For example, the aquaculture strategy should provide for the expansion of pasture fish farming to increase the catch in offshore areas, as well as the development of inland water reservoirs. The solution of these tasks is based on the use of innovative biotechnologies of reproduction to restore, preserve, and increase the number of valuable and vulnerable aquatic species. The advancements in the spheres of shipbuilding and marine engineering should focus on reducing emissions and the carbon footprint of vessels used in the Arctic (icebreakers, tankers, cruise ships). China's competencies in renewable energy technologies could be particularly valuable in developing the wind energy sector in the High North and launching new tidal and wave power facilities. When planning cooperation between China and the Arctic countries, it is necessary to highlight such sectors as fishing, minerals, transport, tourism, energy, as well as the specific context of coastal regions. Such a planning process should focus on identifying ways in which economic activities and ecosystems interact with each other both positively and negatively, and what joint actions of Chinese, European, Russian, and North American companies can contribute to expanding positive effects for the blue economy and reducing negative ones.

FUTURE RESEARCH DIRECTIONS

As the marine ecosystems of the Arctic will be experiencing changes at an increasingly rapid pace, the scale of exploitation of biological and mineral resources of the region will also grow. Identifying and analyzing the complexities, challenges, and best practices of managing the emerging blue economy in regional and national contexts and sectors will remain the main line of research in the future. The critical task is to ensure the sustainable development of the Arctic based on the principles of blue economic growth. In this light, the research agenda in the sphere of the blue economy should capture three dimensions: environmental risks, technological risks, and social risks.

Most of the climate changes in the Arctic are associated with global warming. It causes the reduction in the area and thickness of sea ice, melting of permafrost, transformation of ecosystems, migration of fish and animals. Among the most dangerous risks that should be addressed in future studies are methane emissions and contamination of marine ecosystems with persistent organic pollutants. Methane is emitted from seabed wells, accumulated in marine sediments, as well as captured from the atmosphere. The release of methane during the development of new oil and gas fields in the Arctic will accelerate the warming process, which, in turn, will release new volumes of methane. Oceanic methane production and causes of methane release in climatic conditions of the Arctic should be better studied and understood. Warming and permafrost degradation will increase the likelihood of toxic substances from chemical and radioactive waste disposal sites entering marine ecosystems. These effects have been poorly studied so far, but they definitely must be modeled to prevent adverse effects of organic pollution.

Among the future technogenic risks, the following should be particularly addressed in future studies: accidental oil spills, emissions of pollutants into the atmosphere and marine environment, burning of associated petroleum gas, greenhouse gas emissions, seismological danger due to drilling and excavation in offshore and coastal areas, and spills during loading, unloading, and bunkering at ports.

Social consequences of climate change and anthropogenic activities are most noticeable in indigenous communities. The integrity of landscapes and the maintenance of biological diversity are prerequisites for maintaining an established lifestyle of the indigenous population. Climate change along with increasing industrial exploration of the Arctic will undermine the ability of indigenous peoples to adapt to the changes and threaten their traditional way of life. Although social aspects have not been widely addressed in the blue economy studies, the importance of these issues for establishing sustainable development of the blue economy will grow in the future.

CONCLUSION

In recent years, China has become an increasingly important actor in the Arctic, even an indispensable actor in some areas. It is evident that the solution of such global problems as climate change control, reduction of greenhouse gas emissions, decarbonization of the economy, protection of fragile marine and terrestrial ecosystems, and ensuring sustainable development of the northern territories is impossible without the participation of one of the world's largest economies and one of the leading maritime powers. This study examined the main challenges that the transition to the blue economic growth model in the Arctic poses to the world community: sustainable development of fisheries and aquaculture, protection of biodiversity in marine ecosystems, environmentally responsible development of mineral resources in shelf areas, reducing the carbon footprint of economic activities in the Arctic through the development of renewable energy, waste management and improvement of the ecological safety of marine transport, as well as the development of practices of marine and coastal tourism, which would not threaten Arctic ecosystems. The study concludes that the strategic guidelines of the Arctic countries and China regarding the development of the Arctic overlap in many ways. This creates a basis for cooperation. Thus, promising areas for cooperation are joint counteraction to climate change, protection of marine habitats, fisheries control, the introduction of environmentally friendly technologies for the production and transportation of oil, gas, and other natural resources, as well as the use of China's experience and competencies in shipbuilding, marine engineering, and energy. However, for a qualitative transition from focal investment projects to the implementation of comprehensive cooperation in all blue economy sectors, some Arctic countries (primarily, the USA) should change their attitude towards China. China expresses its openness to equal and mutually beneficial cooperation in the Arctic, therefore, China should be considered a full partner for solving global problems, not a threat.

ACKNOWLEDGMENT

This research was supported by the Sino-Russian Cooperation Fund of Harbin Engineering University (project no. 2021HEUCRF007) and the Grant of Central Universities of the Ministry of Education of the People's Republic of China (project no. 3072021CFP0904).

REFERENCES

Arctic Portal. (2012). *Aquaculture in the Arctic*. Retrieved October 22, 2021, from https://arcticportal.org/ap-library/yar-features/625-aquaculture-in-the-arctic

Baumann, T., Polyakov, I., Padman, L., Danielson, S., Fer, I., Janout, M., Williams, W., & Pnyushkov, A. (2020). Arctic Tidal Current Atlas. *Scientific Data*, *7*(1), 275. doi:10.103841597-020-00578-z PMID:32826909

Bertelsen, R. G., & Gallucci, V. (2016). The Return of China, Post-Cold War Russia, and the Arctic: Changes on Land and at Sea. *Marine Policy*, *72*, 240–245. doi:10.1016/j.marpol.2016.04.034

Bhattacharya, P., & Dash, A. K. (2021). Determinants of Blue Economy in Asia-Pacific Island Countries: A Study of Tourism and Fisheries Sectors. *Ocean and Coastal Management*, *211*, 105774. doi:10.1016/j.ocecoaman.2021.105774

Breitburg, D., Levin, L., Oschlies, A., Grégoire, M., Chavez, F., Conley, D., Garçon, V., Gilbert, D., Gutiérrez, D., Isensee, K., Jacinto, G. S., Limburg, K. E., Montes, I., Naqvi, S. W. A., Pitcher, G. C., Rabalais, N. N., Roman, M. R., Rose, K. A., Seibel, B. A., ... Zhang, J. (2018). Declining Oxygen in the Global Ocean and Coastal Waters. *Science*, *359*(6371), eaam7240. Advance online publication. doi:10.1126cience.aam7240 PMID:29301986

Brouder, P. (2013). *Tourism Development in Peripheral Areas: Processes of Local Innovation and Change in Northern Sweden*. Mid Sweden University.

Cao, Y., Yu, M., Hui, F., Zhang, J., & Cheng, X. (2021). Review of Navigability Changes in Trans-Arctic Routes. *Chinese Science Bulletin*, *66*(1), 21–33. doi:10.1360/TB-2020-0596

Cavalieri, D. J., & Parkinson, P. (2012). Arctic Sea Ice Variability and Trends, 1979-2010. *The Cryosphere*, *6*(4), 881–889. doi:10.5194/tc-6-881-2012

Cochrane, K. (2000). Reconciling Sustainability, Economic Efficiency and Equity in Fisheries: The One That Got Away? *Fish and Fisheries*, *1*(1), 3–21. doi:10.1046/j.1467-2979.2000.00003.x

Conde, E., & Sanchez, S. I. (2016). *Global Challenges in the Arctic Region: Sovereignty, Environment and Geopolitical Balance*. Routledge., doi:10.4324/9781315584768

Conley, H., Pumphrey, D., Toland, T., & David, M. (2013). *Arctic Economics in the 21st Century. The Benefits and Costs of Cold. A Report of the CSIS Europe Program*. Center for Strategic and International Studies.

Dawson, J., Maher, P., & Scott, S. (2007). Climate Change, Marine Tourism, and Sustainability in the Canadian Arctic: Contributions from Systems and Complexity Approaches. *Tourism in Marine Environments*, *4*(2-3), 69–83. doi:10.3727/154427307784772057

Dolan, A. H., Taylor, M., Neis, B., Ommer, R., Eyles, J., Schneider, D., & Montevecchi, B. (2005). Restructuring and Health in Canadian Coastal Communities. *EcoHealth*, *2*(3), 195–208. doi:10.100710393-005-6333-7

Erokhin, V. (2018). Northern Sea Route as an Infrastructure Framework of the Russia-China Arctic Blue Economic Corridor. *Marketing and Logistics, 15*(1), 12–29.

Erokhin, V., Gao, T., & Zhang, X. (2018). Arctic Blue Economic Corridor: China's Role in the Development of a New Connectivity Paradigm in the North. In L. Heininen & H. Exner-Pirot (Eds.), *Arctic Yearbook 2018* (pp. 456–474). Northern Research Forum.

Erokhin, V., Gao, T., & Zhang, X. (Eds.). (2019). *Handbook of Research on International Collaboration, Economic Development, and Sustainability in the Arctic*. IGI Global., doi:10.4018/978-1-5225-6954-1

Farre, A. B., Stephenson, S. R., Chen, L., Czub, M., Dai, Y., Demchev, D., ... Wighting, J. (2014). Commercial Arctic Shipping through the Northeast Passage: Routes, Resources, Governance, Technology, and Infrastructure. *Polar Geography, 37*(4), 298–324. doi:10.1080/1088937X.2014.965769

Fauchald, P., Arneberg, P., Debernard, J. B., Lind, S., Olsen, E., & Hausne, V. H. (2021). Poleward Shifts in Marine Fisheries under Arctic Warming. *Environmental Research Letters, 16*(7), 074057. doi:10.1088/1748-9326/ac1010

Flake, L. E. (2013). Russia and China in the Arctic: A Team of Rivals. *Strategic Analysis, 37*(6), 681–687. doi:10.1080/09700161.2013.847048

Funk, C., Jensen, P. E., & Skjermo, J. (2021). Blue Economy in the North: Scandinavian Algal Biotechnology to the Rescue. *Physiologia Plantarum, 173*(2), 479–482. doi:10.1111/ppl.13534 PMID:34528273

Gao, T. (2019). Going North: China's Role in the Arctic Blue Economic Corridor. In V. Erokhin, T. Gao, & X. Zhang (Eds.), *Handbook of Research on International Collaboration, Economic Development, and Sustainability in the Arctic* (pp. 133–161). IGI Global. doi:10.4018/978-1-5225-6954-1.ch007

Gao, T., Bobylev, N., Gadal, S., Lagutina, M., Sergunin, A., & Erokhin, V. (2021a). Planning for Sustainability: An Emerging Blue Economy in Russia's Coastal Arctic? *Sustainability, 13*(9), 4957. doi:10.3390u13094957

Gao, T., & Erokhin, V. (2020a). China-Russia Collaboration in Arctic Shipping and Maritime Engineering. *The Polar Journal, 10*(2), 353–374. doi:10.1080/2154896X.2020.1799612

Gao, T., & Erokhin, V. (2020b). Widening the Scope of Responses to Environmental Concerns in the High North: Arctic Countries' Policies and the Role of China. In L. Heininen, H. Exner-Pirot, & J. Barnes (Eds.), *Climate Change and the Arctic: Global Origins, Regional Responsibilities? Arctic Yearbook 2020* (pp. 357–397). Arctic Portal.

Gao, T., & Erokhin, V. (2021). China-Russia Research and Education Collaboration in the Arctic: Opportunities, Challenges, and Gaps. *The Polar Journal, 11*(1), 188–207. doi:10.1080/2154896X.2021.1889837

Gao, T., Erokhin, V., Arskiy, A., & Khudzhatov, M. (2021b). Has the COVID-19 Pandemic Affected Maritime Connectivity? An Estimation for China and the Polar Silk Road Countries. *Sustainability, 13*(6), 3521. doi:10.3390u13063521

Gautier, D., Bird, K., Charpentier, R., Grantz, A., Houseknecht, D., Klett, T., Moore, T. E., Pitman, J. K., Schenk, C. J., Schuenemeyer, J. H., Sørensen, K., Tennyson, M. E., Valin, Z. C., & Wandrey, C. (2009). Assessment of Undiscovered Oil and Gas in the Arctic. *Science*, *324*(5931), 1175–1179. doi:10.1126cience.1169467 PMID:19478178

GoArctic. (2020). *Alternative Energy in the Arctic*. Retrieved October 22, 2021, from https://goarctic.ru/work/alternativnaya-energetika-v-arktike/

Górski, J. (2019). Northern Sea Route: International Law Perspectives. In V. Erokhin, T. Gao, & X. Zhang (Eds.), *Handbook of Research on International Collaboration, Economic Development, and Sustainability in the Arctic* (pp. 292–313). IGI Global. doi:10.4018/978-1-5225-6954-1.ch014

Guy, E., & Lasserre, F. (2016). Commercial Shipping in the Arctic: New Perspectives, Challenges, and Regulations. *The Polar Record*, *52*(3), 294–304. doi:10.1017/S0032247415001011

Heininen, L., Everett, K., Padrtova, B., & Reissell, A. (2020). *Arctic Policies and Strategies – Analysis, Synthesis, and Trends*. International Institute for Applied Systems Analysis.

Hemsath, J. (2010). *The Arctic Energy Summit: The Arctic as an Emerging Energy Province*. The Institute of the North.

Hughes, T., Kerry, J., Baird, A., Connolly, S., Dietzel, A., Eakin, M., Heron, S. F., Hoey, A. S., Hoogenboom, M. O., Liu, G., McWilliam, M. J., Pears, R. J., Pratchett, M. S., Skirving, W. J., Stella, J. S., & Torda, G. (2018). Global Warming Transforms Coral Reef Assemblages. *Nature*, *556*(7702), 492–496. doi:10.103841586-018-0041-2 PMID:29670282

Intergovernmental Panel on Climate Change. (2013). Summary for Policymakers. In T. F. Stocker, D. Qin, G.-K. Plattner, M. Tignor, S. K. Allen, & J. Boschung (Eds.), *Climate Change 2013: The Physical Science Basis. Contribution of Working Group I to the Fifth Assessment Report of the Intergovernmental Panel on Climate Change*. Cambridge University Press.

International Energy Agency. (2018). *Status of Power System Transformation 2018: Advanced Power Plant Flexibility*. International Energy Agency. doi:10.1787/9789264302006-

Kabil, M., Priatmoko, S., Magda, R., & Dávid, L. D. (2021). Blue Economy and Coastal Tourism: A Comprehensive Visualization Bibliometric Analysis. *Sustainability*, *13*(7), 3650. doi:10.3390u13073650

Kolesnikova, M. (2018). Promoting the Blue Economy in the Mediterranean Region. *Scientific and Analytical Herald of the Institute of Europe of the Russian Academy of Sciences*, *5*(5), 121–127. doi:10.15211/vestnikieran52018121127

Komarova, I., Kopteva, E., & Kondakov, A. (2015). Marine Clusters as a Management Tool of Blue Economy. *Modern Production Forces*, *2*, 145–354.

Kondratiev, V. (2020). Mineral Resources and Future of the Arctic. *Russian Mining Industry*, *1*(1/2020), 87–96. doi:10.30686/1609-9192-2020-1-87-96

Lanteigne, M. (2014). *China's Emerging Arctic Strategies: Economics and Institutions*. University of Iceland Press.

Lanteigne, M. (2019). *China's Emerging Strategies in the Arctic.* Retrieved October 23, 2021, from https://www.highnorthnews.com/en/chinas-emerging-strategies-arctic

Lasserre, F. (2014). Case Studies of Shipping along Arctic Routes. Analysis and Profitability Perspectives for the Container Sector. *Transportation Research Part A, Policy and Practice*, *66*, 144–161. doi:10.1016/j.tra.2014.05.005

Lewis-Brown, E., Reid, P., Andersson, A., Arthurton, R., Bates, N., Barange, M., … Wood, R. (2008). The Impacts of the Oceans on Climate Change. *IEEE*, 29-32. . doi:10.1109/ESTC.2008.4684318

Liu, N., Lin, L., Kong, B., Wang, Y., Zhang, Z., & Chen, H. (2016). Association between Arctic Autumn Sea Ice Concentration and Early Winter Precipitation in China. *Acta Oceanologica Sinica*, *35*(5), 73–78. doi:10.100713131-016-0860-7

Lukin, A., Bogdanova, V., Kostyunichev, V., & Korolev, A. (2016). Prospects for Development of Aquaculture in the Western Part of the Russian Arctic. *Arctic: Ecology and Economy*, *24*(4), 100–108.

McCauley, D., Pinsky, M., Palumbi, S., Estes, J., Joyce, F., & Warner, R. (2015). Marine Defaunation: Animal Loss in the Global Ocean. *Science*, *347*(6219), 6219. doi:10.1126cience.1255641 PMID:25593191

Melia, N., Haines, K., & Hawkins, E. (2017). *Future of the Sea: Implications from Opening Arctic Sea Routes*. Government Office for Science.

Meng, Q., Zhang, Y., & Xu, M. (2017). Viability of Transarctic Shipping Routes: A Literature Review from the Navigational and Commercial Perspectives. *Maritime Policy & Management*, *44*(1), 16–41. doi:10.1080/03088839.2016.1231428

Moe, A., & Oystein, J. (2010). *Opening of New Arctic Shipping Routes. Standard Briefing*. Directorate-General for External Policies of the Union / European Parliament.

Motyka, M., Slaughter, A., & Amon, C. (2018). *Global Renewable Energy Trends. Solar and Wind Move from Mainstream to Preferred.* Retrieved October 22, 2021, from https://www2.deloitte.com/us/en/insights/industry/power-and-utilities/global-renewable-energy-trends.html?id=gx:2el:3dc:4direnenergy:5awa:6di:09132018

Nagy, H., & Nene, S. (2021). Blue Gold: Advancing Blue Economy Governance in Africa. *Sustainability*, *13*(13), 7153. doi:10.3390u13137153

National Snow and Ice Data Center. (2016). *Arctic Sea Ice News and Analysis*. Retrieved October 21, 2021, from https://nsidc.org/arcticseaicenews/2016/10/

Nikandrov, V., Pavlisov, A., Schindavina, N., Lukin, A., Golod, V., & Lipatova, M. (2018). Arctic Char (Salvelinus alpinus L.) – A Perspective Aquaculture Object for the North of Russia. *Arctic: Ecology and Economy*, *31*(3), 137–143. doi:10.25283/2223-4594-2018-3-137-143

North Pacific Fishery Management Council. (2009). *Fishery Management Plan for Fish Resources of the Arctic Management Area*. North Pacific Fishery Management Council.

Nuttall, M., & Callaghan, T. (Eds.). (2019). *The Arctic: Environment, People, Policy*. Routledge., doi:10.4324/9780429340475

Pelyasov, A., Galtseva, N., & Atamanova, E. (2017). Economy of the Arctic "Islands": The Case of Nenets and Chukotka Autonomous Okrugs. *Economy of Region*, *13*(1), 114–125. doi:10.17059/2017-1-11

Peng, J., & Wegge, N. (2015). China's Bilateral Diplomacy in the Arctic. *Polar Geography*, *38*(3), 233–249. doi:10.1080/1088937X.2015.1086445

Pierre, C., & Olivier, F. (2015). Relevance of the Northern Sea Route (NSR) for Bulk Shipping. *Transportation Research*, *78*, 337–346. doi:10.1016/j.tra.2015.05.020

Pinsky, M., Eikeset, A., McCauley, D., Payne, J., & Sunday, J. (2019). Greater Vulnerability to Warming of Marine versus Terrestrial Ectotherms. *Nature*, *569*(7754), 108–111. doi:10.103841586-019-1132-4 PMID:31019302

Poloczanska, E., Brown, C., Sydeman, W., Kiessling, W., Schoeman, D., Moore, P., Brander, K., Bruno, J. F., Buckley, L. B., Burrows, M. T., Duarte, C. M., Halpern, B. S., Holding, J., Kappel, C. V., O'Connor, M. I., Pandolfi, J. M., Parmesan, C., Schwing, F., Thompson, S. A., & Richardson, A. (2013). Global Imprint of Climate Change on Marine Life. *Nature Climate Change*, *3*(10), 919–925. doi:10.1038/nclimate1958

President of the Russian Federation. (2020). *Decree #645 from October 26, 2020, "On the Strategy for the Development of the Arctic Zone of the Russian Federation and Ensuring National Security up to 2035"*. Retrieved October 18, 2021, from http://static.kremlin.ru/media/events/files/ru/J8FhckYOPAQQfxN6Xlt6ti6XzpTVAvQy.pdf

Schartup, A., Thackray, C., Quershi, A., Dassuncao, C., Gillespie, K., Hanke, A., & Sunderland, E. (2019). Climate Change and Overfishing Increase Neurotoxicant in Marine Predators. *Nature*, *572*(7771), 648–650. doi:10.103841586-019-1468-9 PMID:31391584

Sevastiyanov, D., Colpaert, A., Korostelyov, E., Mulyava, O., & Shitova, L. (2014). Management of Tourism and Recreation Possibilities for the Sustainable Development of the North-Western Border Region in Russia. *Nordia Geographical Publications*, *43*(1), 27–38.

Shuvalova, T., & Glubokov, A. (2015). Aquatic Bioresources Development in the Arctic Zone: Problems and Prospects. *Fisheries (Bethesda, Md.)*, *4*, 11–13.

Simionov, I.-A., Cristea, D. S., Petrea, Ş.-M., Mogodan, A., Jijie, R., Ciornea, E., Nicoară, M., Turek Rahoveanu, M. M., & Cristea, V. (2021). Predictive Innovative Methods for Aquatic Heavy Metals Pollution Based on Bioindicators in Support of Blue Economy in the Danube River Basin. *Sustainability*, *13*(16), 8936. doi:10.3390u13168936

Smale, D., Wernberg, T., Oliver, E., Thomsen, M., Harvey, B., Straub, S., Burrows, M. T., Alexander, L. V., Benthuysen, J. A., Donat, M. G., Feng, M., Hobday, A. J., Holbrook, N. J., Perkins-Kirkpatrick, S. E., Scannell, H. A., Sen Gupta, A., Payne, B. L., & Moore, P. (2019). Marine Heatwaves Threaten Global Biodiversity and the Provision of Ecosystem Services. *Nature Climate Change*, *9*(4), 306–312. doi:10.103841558-019-0412-1

Snyder, H., & Erbaugh, J. (2020). Fishery Observers Address Arctic Fishery Discards. *Environmental Research Letters, 15*, 0940c4. . doi:10.1088/1748-9326/aba57d

State Council Information Office of the People's Republic of China. (2020). *Energy in China's New Era*. The State Council of the People's Republic of China.

State Council of the People's Republic of China. (2017). *Vision for Maritime Cooperation under the Belt and Road Initiative*. Retrieved October 18, 2021, from http://english.www.gov.cn/archive/publications/2017/06/20/content_281475691873460.htm

State Council of the People's Republic of China. (2018). *China's Arctic Policy*. The State Council of the People's Republic of China.

Steblyanskaya, A., Ai, M., Bocharnikov, V., & Denisov, A. (2021). Strategies for Green Economy in China. *Foresight and STI Governance*, *15*(1), 74–85. doi:10.17323/2500-2597.2021.1.74.85

Stephenson, S. R., Brigham, L., & Smith, L. C. (2013). Marine Accessibility along Russia's Northern Sea Route. *Polar Geography*, *37*(2), 111–133. doi:10.1080/1088937X.2013.845859

Sterligova, O., Kuchko, Y., Savosin, E., & Ilmast, N. (2019). Prospects of Cultivation of Aquaculture Objects in the Lakes of Karelia. *Problems of Fisheries*, *20*(2), 216–224. doi:10.36038/0234-2774-2019-20-2-216-224

Su, P., & Lanteigne, M. (2015). China's Developing Arctic Policies: Myths and Misconceptions. *Journal of China and International Relations*, *3*(1), 2. doi:10.5278/ojs.jcir.v3i1.1144

The Ocean Foundation. (2021). *Ocean and Climate Change*. Retrieved October 20, 2021, from https://oceanfdn.org/ocean-and-climate-change/

Tillman, H., Yang, J., & Nielsson, E. T. (2018). The Polar Silk Road: China's New Frontier of International Cooperation. *China Quarterly of International Strategic Studies*, *4*(3), 345–362. doi:10.1142/S2377740018500215

Tortsev, A. (2018). Efficiency of Management of Fishery Resources in the Arctic Zone of the Russian Federation: Features of Assessment. *Arctic: Ecology and Economy*, *30*(2), 131–141. doi:10.25283/2223-4594-2018-2-131-141

Turnbull, J., Keller, E., Norris, M., & Wiltshire, R. (2016). Independent Evaluation of Point Source Fossil Fuel CO_2 Emissions to Better than 10%. *Proceedings of the National Academy of Sciences of the United States of America*, *113*(37), 10287–10291. doi:10.1073/pnas.1602824113 PMID:27573818

United Nations. (2021a). *Goal 14. Conserve and Sustainably Use the Oceans, Seas and Marine Resources for Sustainable Development*. Retrieved October 18, 2021, from https://sdgs.un.org/goals

United Nations. (2021b). *The 17 Goals*. Retrieved October 18, 2021, from https://sdgs.un.org/goals

United Nations Conference on Trade and Development. (2021). *Oceans Economy and Fisheries*. Retrieved October 23, 2021, from https://unctad.org/topic/trade-and-environment/oceans-economy

United States Geological Survey. (2021). *Data and Tools*. Retrieved October 22, 2021, from https://www.usgs.gov/products/data-and-tools/data-and-tools-topics

Voyer, M., Quirk, G., McIlgorm, A., & Azmi, K. (2018). Shades of Blue: What Do Competing Interpretations of the Blue Economy Mean for Oceans Governance? *Journal of Environmental Policy and Planning*, *20*(5), 595–616. . doi:10.1080/1523908X.2018.1473153

Wiederer, C. K. (2018). *Logistics Infrastructure Along the Belt and Road Initiative Economies*. World Bank Group.

World Bank & United Nations Department of Economic and Social Affairs. (2017). *The Potential of the Blue Economy: Increasing Long-term Benefits of the Sustainable Use of Marine Resources for Small Island Developing States and Coastal Least Developed Countries*. Washington, DC: World Bank.

World Wildlife Fund. (2021). *Oceans*. Retrieved October 20, 2021, from https://www.wwf.org.uk/where-we-work/oceans

Xi, J. (2017). *The Governance of China II*. Foreign Languages Press.

Xinhua. (2017). *Vision for Maritime Cooperation under the Belt and Road Initiative*. Retrieved October 23, 2021, from http://news.xinhuanet.com/english/2017-06/20/c_136380414.htm

Xu, G. (2016). China's Arctic Interests and Policy: History, Legal Ground and Implementation. *World Economy and International Relations*, *60*(2), 52–62. doi:10.20542/0131-2227-2016-60-2-52-62

Xu, H., Yin, Z., Jia, D., Jin, F., & Ouyang, H. (2011). The Potential Seasonal Alternative of Asia-Europe Container Service via Northern Sea Route under the Arctic Sea Ice Retreat. *Maritime Policy & Management*, *38*(5), 541–560. doi:10.1080/03088839.2011.597449

Yang, J., & Zhao, L. (2019). Opportunities and Challenges of Jointly Building of the Polar Silk Road: China's Perspective. *Outlines of Global Transformations: Politics, Economics, Law*, *12*(5), 130–144. doi:10.23932/2542-0240-2019-12-5-130-144

Zalyvsky, N. (2015). The Northern Sea Route: The Potential of Expectations and the Real Functioning Problems. *Arctic and North*, *20*, 37–57. doi:10.17238/issn2221-2698.2015.20.37

Zhao, H., Hu, H., & Lin, Y. (2016). Study on China-EU Container Shipping Network in the Context of Northern Sea Route. *Journal of Transport Geography*, *53*, 50–60. doi:10.1016/j.jtrangeo.2016.01.013

Zheng, H., Liu, X., Xu, Y., & Mu, H. (2021). Economic Spillover Effects of Industrial Structure Upgrading in China's Coastal Economic Rims. *Sustainability*, *13*(7), 3855. doi:10.3390u13073855

Zheng, X., Lu, Y., Yuan, J., Baninla, Y., Zhang, S., Stenseth, N., Hessen, D. O., Tian, H., Obersteiner, M., & Chen, D. (2020). Drivers of Change in China's Energy-Related CO_2 Emissions. *Proceedings of the National Academy of Sciences of the United States of America*, *117*(1), 29–36. doi:10.1073/pnas.1908513117 PMID:31871172

Zhu, S., Fu, X., Ng, A., Luo, M., & Ge, Y.-E. (2018). The Environmental Costs and Economic Implications of Container Shipping on the Northern Sea Route. *Maritime Policy & Management*, *45*(4), 456–477. doi:10.1080/03088839.2018.1443228

Zmieva, K. (2020). Problems of Energy Supply in the Arctic Regions. *Russian Arctic*, *8*, 5–14. doi:10.24411/2658-4255-2020-00001

Zvorykina, J., & Teteryatnikov, K. (2019). The Northern Sea Route as a Tool of Arctic Development. *Russian Economic Journal*, *4*(4), 21–44. doi:10.33983/0130-9757-2019-4-21-44

ADDITIONAL READING

Blunden, M. (2012). Geopolitics and the Northern Sea Route. *International Affairs*, *88*(1), 115–129. doi:10.1111/j.1468-2346.2012.01060.x

Coates, K. S., & Holroyd, C. (Eds.). (2020). *The Palgrave Handbook of Arctic Policy and Politics*. Palgrave Macmillan. doi:10.1007/978-3-030-20557-7

Daly, J., Knott, C., Keogh, P., & Singh, G. (2021). Changing Climates in a Blue Economy: Assessing the Climate-Responsiveness of Canadian Fisheries and Oceans Policy. *Marine Policy*, *131*, 104623. doi:10.1016/j.marpol.2021.104623

Erokhin, V., & Gao, T. (2021). Better Connectivity for Greater Eurasia: China-Russia Cooperation on the Development of the Economic Corridor in the High North. In A. Aseeva & J. Gorski (Eds.), *The Law and Policy of New Eurasian Regionalization: Economic Integration, Trade, and Investment in the Post-Soviet and Greater Eurasian Space* (pp. 32–47). Brill Nijhoff. doi:10.1163/9789004447875_004

Erokhin, V., Gao, T., & Andrei, J. V. (Eds.). (2020). *Sustainable Economic Development: Challenges, Policies, and Reforms*. MDPI.

Erokhin, V., Gao, T., & Ivolga, A. (2021). Cross-Country Potentials and Advantages in Trade in Fish and Seafood Products in the RCEP Member States. *Sustainability*, *13*(7), 3668. doi:10.3390u13073668

Fairhall, D. (2011). *Cold Front: Conflict Ahead in Arctic Waters*. I.B. Tauris.

Finger, M., & Heininen, L. (Eds.). (2019). *The Global Arctic Handbook*. Springer. doi:10.1007/978-3-319-91995-9

Fratila, A., Gavril, I. A., Nita, S. C., & Hrebenciuc, A. (2021). The Importance of Maritime Transport for Economic Growth in the European Union: A Panel Data Analysis. *Sustainability*, *13*, 7961. doi:10.3390u13147961

Gao, T., & Erokhin, V. (2020). Widening the Scope of Responses to Environmental Concerns in the High North: Arctic Countries' Policies and the Role of China. In L. Heininen, H. Exner-Pirot, & J. Barnes (Eds.), *Climate Change and the Arctic: Global Origins, Regional Responsibilities? Arctic Yearbook 2020* (pp. 357–397). Arctic Portal.

Gao, T., & Erokhin, V. (2021). China-Russia Collaboration in Shipping and Marine Engineering as One of the Key Factors of Secure Navigation Along the NSR. In J. Barnes, H. Exner-Pirot, L. Heininen, & P. W. Lackenbauer (Eds.), *China's Arctic Engagement: Following the Polar Silk Road to Greenland and Russia* (pp. 234–263). North American and Arctic Defence and Security Network.

Garcia, A. A. (2021). Relationship between Blue Economy, Cruise Tourism, and Urban Regeneration: Case Study of Olbia, Sardinia. *Journal of Urban Planning and Development, 147*(3), 05021029. doi:10.1061/(ASCE)UP.1943-5444.0000712

Guerreiro, J. (2021). The Blue Growth Challenge to Maritime Governance. *Frontiers in Marine Science, 8*, 681546. doi:10.3389/fmars.2021.681546

Heininen, L. (2014). Northern Geopolitics: Actors, Interests and Processes in the Circumpolar Arctic. In R. C. Powell & K. Dodds (Eds.), *Polar Geopolitics: Knowledges, Resources and Legal Regimes* (pp. 241–258). Edward Elgar. doi:10.4337/9781781009413.00023

Hong, N. (2018). *China's Interests in the Arctic: Opportunities and Challenges.* Institute for China-America Studies.

Keil, K., & Knecht, S. (Eds.). (2017). *Governing Arctic Change: Global Perspectives.* Palgrave Macmillan. doi:10.1057/978-1-137-50884-3

Nikčević, J., & Škurić, M. (2021). A Contribution to the Sustainable Development of Maritime Transport in the Context of Blue Economy: The Case of Montenegro. *Sustainability, 13*(6), 3079. doi:10.3390u13063079

Queiros, A., Talbot, E., Beaumont, N., Somerfield, P., Kay, S., Pascoe, C., ... Aonghusa, C. (2021). Bright Spots as Climate-Smart Marine Spatial Planning Tools for Conservation and Blue Growth. *Global Change Biology, 27*(21), 5514–5531. doi:10.1111/gcb.15827 PMID:34486773

Raspotnik, A., Rottem, S. V., & Østhagen, A. (2021). The Blue Economy in the Arctic Ocean: Governing Aquaculture in Alaska and North Norway. *Arctic and North, 42*(42), 122–144. doi:10.37482/issn2221-2698.2021.42.122

Rovný, P., Moroz, S., Palkovič, J., & Horská, E. (2021). Impact of Demographic Structure on Economic Development of Ukrainian Coastal Regions. *Sustainability, 13*(4), 1798. doi:10.3390u13041798

Sauve, S., Lamontagne, S., Dupras, J., & Stahel, W. (2021). Circular Economy of Water: Tackling Quantity, Quality and Footprint of Water. *Environmental Development, 39*, 100651. doi:10.1016/j.envdev.2021.100651

Wiber, M., Mather, C., Knott, C., & Gomez, M. A. L. (2021). Regulating the Blue Economy? Challenges to an Effective Canadian Aquaculture Act. *Marine Policy, 131*, 104700. doi:10.1016/j.marpol.2021.104700

Zaikov, K., Saburov, A., Tamitskiy, A., & Nikiforov, A. (2021). Online Education in the Russian Arctic: Employers' Confidence and Educational Institutions' Readiness. *Sustainability, 13*(12), 6798. doi:10.3390u13126798

Zeng, W., He, J., Qiu, Y., & Cao, X. (2021). Unravelling the Temporal-Spatial Distribution of the Agricultural Water Footprint in the Yangtze River Basin (YRB) of China. *Water (Basel), 13*(18), 2562. doi:10.3390/w13182562

KEY TERMS AND DEFINITIONS

Aquaculture: Breeding and cultivation of aquatic organisms (fish, crustaceans, mollusks, algae) in natural and artificial reservoirs, as well as on specially created marine plantations.

Arctic Countries: Eight member countries of the Arctic Council (Canada, Denmark, Finland, Iceland, Norway, Russia, Sweden, and the United States) which possess territories in the High North within the Arctic Circle, have strategic interests in the Arctic, and elaborated strategies for the development of the region.

Belt and Road Initiative: A development strategy proposed by the Chinese government in 2013 and focused on improving connectivity and collaboration among the countries of Eurasia through the increase of China's role in global affairs.

Blue Economy: The economy of the world ocean, the socio-economic development of coastal territories, and the conservation of water territories.

Climate Change: Observed and predicted long-term changes in average climatic indicators caused by human activity, as well as climate variability, including such anomalies as droughts, severe storms, and floods.

Fishing: Activities related to the extraction (catch) of aquatic biological resources and processing, transshipment, and transportation of fish.

Non-Arctic Countries: The countries geographically located apart from the Arctic region, but those that consider the Arctic as a region of their strategic interests and assert that their participation in international cooperation in the Arctic is as useful as it is warranted and legitimate. Most of them are now observers in the Arctic Council.

Chapter 7
Blue Economy and Foreign Direct Investment to Maritime Nations

Taoreed Alaba Amodu
Arab Academy for Science, Technology, and Maritime Transport, Egypt

ABSTRACT

For policy enrichment, this chapter discusses the opportunities available to maritime nations in the blue economy and explicates the roles of policymakers in achieving an improved economy by encouraging and attracting foreign investors and grants, which is a catalyst to achieving a blue economy. First, the author argues that the transition to the blue economy has encouraged maritime nations to look inward and diversify their economies by harnessing ocean resources and other economic potentials. Second, the proximity to the seas and oceans has made maritime nations realize the possibility of converting ocean resources to boost their national GDPs. However, this opportunity comes with enormous responsibilities. Third, policymakers must ensure proper conservation and management measures so that living creatures in the exclusive economic zones (EEZ) are not endangered. Finally, maritime nations need to exercise their jurisdiction for the protection and preservation of the marine environment.

INTRODUCTION

Globally, nations are faced with the challenges of improving their economies to maintain their sovereignty and provide a good livelihood for citizens. In the past, military power and navigational strengths were used as metrics to prove national superiority among the comity of nations. Currently, however, countries engage in economic warfare to prove their national strengths, as evident in the trade war and diplomatic relations between the United States of America and the Republic of China. The "blue economy" seeks to promote economic growth, social inclusion, and the preservation or improvement of livelihoods while at the same time ensuring the environmental sustainability of the oceans and coastal areas. At its core, it refers to the decoupling of socioeconomic development through ocean-related sectors and activities from environmental and ecosystem degradation. It draws from scientific findings that ocean resources

DOI: 10.4018/978-1-6684-3393-5.ch007

are limited and that the health of the oceans has drastically declined due to anthropogenic activities. The consequences of climate change are already being profoundly felt, affecting human well-being and societies, and the impacts are likely to be amplified in the future, especially in view of projected population growth (United Nation, 2006).

More recently, the United Nations Human Settlements Program produced a background paper on cities that proposed an expanded definition of the blue economy to encompass all water bodies, including the world's oceans, lakes, rivers and wetlands, with the increased prevalence of drought set to be an extreme emerging issue globally. It also recognized that 'cities are at the forefront since most urban centres (70%) are located along coasts and waterfronts around the world' (UN, 2018). Scholars opined that the blue economy is geared towards the sustainable use of ocean resources for economic advancement while also preserving the ocean ecosystem. They also explicated that the blue economy phenomenon is a new development agenda designed to expose maritime nations and coastal states to the wealth of research and potentials that are untapped and to encourage harnessing them for optimal socioeconomic benefits through investments (Secretariat, 2018; Madiraju, 2019; Clegg et al., 2020). Investments of course proceed from interest, which is an essential factor in the business environment. Most times, these interests are exhibited by willing participants who do not ordinarily have access to these resources, as stated in Ocean resource use: building the coastal blue economy (Bax et al., 2021.). Hence, the option of a Foreign Direct Investment (FDI). FDI helps provide these littoral states with not only the required capital but also the expertise, technology and management that usually lead to economic growth. The blue economy aims to move beyond business as usual and to consider economic development and ocean health as compatible propositions. It is generally understood to be a long-term strategy aimed at supporting sustainable and equitable economic growth through ocean-related sectors and activities. One of the prospects of the blue ocean is access by people and organizations to fisheries and marine resources on the high seas. However, the threats posed by climate change, if not well managed, would exacerbate inequalities, as marine resources may not be shared equally among developing countries where many people depend on fish for food security, livelihoods and well-being. (Cheung et al., 2019).

To make the blue economy a reality in developing countries, high seas fisheries governance is required to aid the process of redistributing ocean benefits and reducing climate risks in developing countries. While the blue economy, both as a concept and in practice, is relevant to all countries, in this chapter, the author focuses on the prospects of maritime nations in achieving a blue economy through foreign direct investments (FDI).

To the best of the author's knowledge, there are no papers that have linked the relationship of the blue economy and FDI specifically to Maritime Nations. This study attempts to fill this gap by estimating the impact of FDI on the Blue Economy Project. The main aim of the study was to establish the reality of a blue economy through the attraction of foreign investment by maritime nations. The study has the originality of taking a closer look at the determinants of FDI. The findings of the study will help individuals, managers, professionals, academia and decision-makers determine the factors used by foreign investors when developing their investment strategy.

From the foregoing, the blue economy is relevant to all countries and can be applied on various scales, from local to regional to global. To become actionable, the blue economy concept must be supported by a trusted and diversified knowledge base and complemented with management and development resources that not only help inspire and support innovation but also encourage investment. The entire chapter is structured into five sections. Section 1 provides an introduction to the paper. Section 2 explains the methods and approach. Section 3 focuses on the literature review. Section 4 discusses the link between the blue economy and FDI. Section 5 focuses on the prospects and challenges of BE and solutions. Section 6 concludes with policy recommendations.

METHODS AND APPROACH

This chapter follows the desk-research strategy. Specifically, relevant information on the blue economy and foreign direct investment (FDI) was extracted from scholarly articles, texts, policy documents, working papers, and online resources. The valuable insights from over 20 articles were synthesised and critically discussed. The thoughts from the reviewed literature provided a basis for the informed analysis.

Background

In recent years, efforts have been made to use colours to define various challenges confronting the world today. Colours such as WHITE, BLACK, GREY, GREEN, BROWN, PURPLE and BLUE have all been used to conceptualize different types of economies (Buheji & Ahmed, 2021). While white depicts the health industry, black for any illegal activity, gray for informal or underground economy, green refers to plants and agricultural resources, brown for fossil fuels, purple for care activities and services, the blue economy describes activities related to water resources such as Marine Biotechnology, Fisheries and aquaculture (Paulli, 2010). Marine nations and coastal countries must make the blue economy a reality by leveraging the right strategies to join leading economies soon. China strategically pulled it human and material resources together to emerge as world's second leading destination for foreign direct investment behind the United States of America (Enright, 2002). Therefore, firms in the blue economy operating around the same ecology and facing the same challenges can emerge as very strong players by developing strategies and business models to serve the majority of humanity today excluded from world trade (Ricart et al., 2004). The last half century has seen concerns escalating over the impacts of human activities on marine ecosystems, giving rise to various initiatives seeking to incorporate the concept of sustainability into policy (Stojanovic & Farmer 2013). This has meant that recent initiatives, collectively called the blue economy, comprise a range of economic sectors and related policies that together determine whether the use of oceanic resources is sustainable. An important challenge is thus to understand and better manage the many aspects of oceanic sustainability, ranging from sustainable resource exploitation to ecosystem health to pollution (The World Bank, 2017). This vision's origins sit within the 'Green Economy' (Pearce et al., 1989).

The concept of the 'Blue Economy' came to the fore when, during preparations for the Rio+20 or Earth Summit (UN, 2012)), many coastal nations (particularly island states) expressed concern that the green economy primarily addressed land-based resources but neglected the role of the oceans in the economic and cultural lives of hundreds of millions of the world's poorest and most vulnerable coastal and island nations. Approximately 97 percent of the world's fishers, for example, live in developing countries, fishing for their major source of food and income (Kelleher et al., 2012). The blue economy is an extension of sustainable development because it is directly related to economic growth through the process of responsible sustainable utilization and management of ocean resources with technological inputs to improve people's livelihoods (Sarker et al., 2019). Additionally, the fact that oceans and seas matter for sustainable development is undeniable. Oceans and seas cover over two-thirds of Earth's surface, contribute to poverty eradication by creating sustainable livelihoods and decent work, provide food and minerals, generate oxygen, absorb greenhouse gases and mitigate the impacts of climate change, determine weather patterns and temperatures, and serve as highways for seaborne international trade. With an estimated 80 percent of the volume of world trade carried by the sea, international shipping and ports provide crucial linkages in global supply chains and are essential for the ability of all countries to gain access to global markets (Unite Nation Conference on Trade and Development [UNCTAD], 2016).

Threats to oceans that have escalated climate change have the potential to engender widespread suffering, displacement and unrest. Consequently, the UN was urged to incorporate the 'Blue Economy' into discussions. As a result, member states pledged to protect and restore the health, productivity and resilience of oceans and marine ecosystems to maintain their diversity, enabling their conservation and sustainable use for present and future generations (United Nations Conference on Sustainable Development [UNCSD], 2012).

Global ocean economic activities are estimated to be worth US$1.5 trillion per annum, with blue growth expected to continue at a faster rate than terrestrial activities for at least the next few decades, US$3–5 trillion by 2030 (Organisation for Economic Co-operation and Development [OECD] 2016, 2019). This growth, however, is affected by the inherent contest within coastal spaces that current policy and management strategies struggle to fully address (Alexander, 2019). Another factor that has the propensity to influence the growth of the blue economy is infrastructural funding and investment. Ocean states that are the beneficiaries of the blue ocean have all proactively ratified the key international environmental treaties and framework for ocean governance that create obligations required to make the ideal a reality. These ocean states play a prominent and legally embedded role in the field of sustainable ocean governance (Roy, 2019). Arguably, foreign investments have a potential influence on regional technological advancement, local market growth and skill upgrading. FDI does not come without preconditions, however, and its benefits will not be automatically reaped by the host country/region (Sun et al., 2002). This is where the domestic regulatory framework of host countries comes into play and where the role of national policy makers becomes crucial. Territorial capital is determined by critical factors, including geographical location, size, quality of life or the agglomeration economies provided by its cities and particular for maritime nations, their proximity to the seas or oceans. The nexus between ideas around sustainability and what constitutes blue growth remains contentious (Jouffray et al., 2020), but a blue economy emphasizes three themes of sustainability: environmental, economic, and social sustainability.

LITERATURE REVIEW

Over the years, sufficient data and statistics have not been available due to low marine scientific research. Under "business as usual," the costs of marine ecosystem degradation from human uses should be high, but they are not quantified or accounted for. At the same time, the economic contribution of the ocean to humankind has been significantly undervalued (Economist Intelligence Unit [EIU], 2015). These details are necessary to aid policy making, identify loopholes and, in some cases, reveal the gains that might boost confidence in investors. Many variables have been identified in the literature as determinants of FDI. Events across the globe affirm that foreign direct investment (FDI) is an influential channel through which foreign capital comes into a country. The factors that play a significant role in the inflow of FDI are sociocultural, bilateral investment treaties, regional integration agreements, gross domestic product growth, language, and culture (Chakrabarti et al., 2014).

In addition, there exists a two-way relationship between FDI and the level of economic development (Anuchitworawong & Thampanishvong, 2015). For Eastern European countries, there is a coexistence of horizontal FDI and vertical FDI patterns. The differences in location advantages represent an important determinant of FDI among potential host countries, as will be X-rayed subsequently in this chapter. The development of the market economy and institutions, particularly the private sector, has the greatest influence on the dynamics of FDI inflows into the Serbian economy (Marija et al., 2013). In Vietnam, market size, availability of international standard infrastructure, availability of human capital, and level of openness are the major determinants of FDI. The other determinants of FDI include the GDP growth rate, macroeconomic stability and domestic investment per capita (Anwar & Nguyen, 2010). The analysis of the potential interaction between FDI and the host country's infrastructure base (employing a panel dataset involving 46 countries, using the size of three types of infrastructure capital: telecommunication, power generation, and network of roads or highways) shows that the size of the host country's infrastructure base assists in increasing the effect of FDI on real income (Nourzad et al., 2014).

Globalization and internationalization are 2 factors that make FDI possible. FDI is one of the most crucial channels of direct investments between countries. Unlike foreign portfolio investment (FPI), an investor in one country can hold a controlling stake of any business or organization in a foreign country that receives the investment. For instance, ships may be owned in one country, managed from another, registered in a third country and crewed by seafarers from many more. However, the celebrated Canadian economist Stephen Hymer, considered the 'Father of International Business', theorised in the 1960s that foreign investments would continue growing rapidly because it provided control over companies in a foreign land. It helped certain business sectors overthrow monopolistic practices, and most importantly, since market imperfections will always exist, such investments provide companies with a cushioning effect if there was a sharp and unpredictable decline in business activity.

BLUE ECONOMY AND FOREIGN DIRECT INVESTMENT (FDI)

Defining Blue Economy

Economists have helped in coding the problems facing the world. The blue economy particularly discusses exploring the oceans for economic growth through investments while also preserving the natural habitat around these oceans. In particular, the blue economy gained traction as a novel concept in the era of sustainability to stem marine biodiversity loss on the one hand and stimulate economic development on the other (Schutter & Hicks, 2019). To achieve an effective shift in the use of ocean resources, all hands must be on deck in maritime nations. Moreover, the blue economy is relevant to all coastal states and can be applied on various scales and sectors. Thus, there is a need for synergy among willing countries via financial, technical and capacity building support. The mix of oceanic activities varies in each country, depending on their unique national circumstances and the national vision adopted to reflect its own conception of a blue economy. The report of the United Nations on the potential of the blue economy underscored the need for responsible utilization of ocean resources for social and economic benefits for current and future generations. Second, the blue economic model must restore, protect, and maintain the diversity, productivity, resilience, core functions, and intrinsic value of marine ecosystems. Third, the blue economy must embrace clean technologies, renewable energy, and circular material flows that will reduce waste and promote recycling of materials.

There is an urgent need for broad and resilient partnerships for the coordination and collaboration of blue economy projects and initiatives. According to an analysis of case studies by the United Nations Environment Programme (2015), the blue economy makes its strongest gains when leveraging existing institutional relationships to address strategic gaps that affect multiple sectors and players and that catalyse visible benefits for them in the long term. A shift to a blue economy requires dedicated short- and long-term efforts, which can seize existing opportunities to bring together stakeholders. In addition, the blue economy requires the building of inclusive processes, including a concerted effort to identify and involve Innovative financing to direct investments into economic activities that can enhance ocean health. However, many public and private economic activities that could serve to restore ocean health will carry higher upfront costs and returns that will not immediately accrue to investors (EIU, 2015). This suggests the need for new and innovative financing mechanisms, more capital than is currently being deployed, and a greater degree of collaboration between the public and private sectors (EIU, 2015). The private sector can play a key role in the blue economy. Business is the engine for trade, economic growth, and jobs, which are critical to poverty reduction. Indicators used to track progress toward social and ecological sustainability are largely ignored in standard economic metrics such as gross domestic product (GDP) and will be needed to measure key transformation changes in different sectors of the blue economy (UNEP, 2015). Thus, in countries such as Mauritius, an important step in developing a blue economy has been the exploration of alternative economic indicators based on the recognition that well-being is supported by a variety of economic, social, cultural, and natural assets and processes. Such initiatives are fundamental to developing more diversified, country-specific goals and progress indicators (UNEP, 2015). These, in turn, are crucial to formulating policies that can halt ecosystem losses and thereby provide clearer pathways to sustained blue economy prosperity in the long term. Where prosperity is sustained and progress assured, investment will be encouraged. Sector-specific monitoring is also necessary to fully understand the economic, environmental, and social impacts of each sector on local and national levels. For example, the International Network of Sustainable Tourism Observatories of the United Nations World Tourism Organization (UNWTO) monitors these impacts.

Foreign Direct Investment

FDI is defined as a category of investment that reflects the objective of establishing a lasting interest by a resident company or individual in one country having business interests in another country, such as ownership or controlling interest in a foreign company (OECD, 2008). FDI is considered one of the main levers on which countries expect to rely for sustainable economic development. The development of FDI in any country increases domestic production and allows a better use of resources and easy access to technology and new products. FDI can act as a mechanism to accumulate physical capital and transfer human capital to the receiving country, which can increase the economic growth rate. Technology transfer increases the efficiency of production factors, which in turn reduces the technological gap between national and international enterprises (Anwar & Nguyen, 2010). FDI is an important source of development financing, particularly for developing and less developed economies, as it contributes to productivity gains by bringing in new investment, better technology, and management expertise and by opening up export markets (Sahoo et al., 2014). FDI usually represents a long-term commitment to the host country and contributes significantly to gross fixed capital formation in developing countries (Kaur & Dhillon, 2017). The analysis of FDI should be viewed as a necessity in the context of contemporary trends of investment liberalization. The literature on FDI determinants shows that there exists a relationship between FDI and several macroeconomic variables, such as the gross domestic product (GDP), the exchange rate, the host country's market, sociocultural stability, economic stability, bilateral investment treaties, the degree of openness, regional integration agreements, language, and culture. Although the literature on FDI determinants is quite rich, there are other variables that could influence FDI, such as performance logistics and shipping connectivity.

FDI is a key element in international economic integration because it creates stable and long-lasting links between economies. FDI is an important channel for the transfer of technology between countries, promotes international trade through access to foreign markets, and can be an important vehicle for economic development.

Determinants of FDI

Companies considering a foreign direct investment generally look only at companies in open economies that offer a skilled workforce and above-average growth prospects for the investor. Light government regulation also tends to be prized. FDI is also a significant and insightful indicator of a certain country's political and socioeconomic stability. This essentially implies that a country that receives large amounts of investments from foreign entities on a regular basis is more likely to have a dynamic and vibrant economy. Sun et al. (2002) identify several components that make up an enabling environment for FDI. First, FDI requires a stable political and macroeconomic environment. Second, and closely related, is the importance of a sound policy and regulatory framework and efficient institutions to support its enforcement and uphold the relevant laws and regulations. Creating and maintaining a regulatory and administrative climate conducive to investment can have a huge impact on an investor's location choices as well as predicting the extent to which FDI inflow will benefit the host country. Third, a good policy and regulatory framework should be complemented by adequate physical and social infrastructure. One of the largest examples of foreign direct investment (FDI) in the world today is the Chinese initiative known as One Belt One Road (OBOR). This program sometimes referred to as the Belt and Road initiative, involves a commitment by China to substantial FDI in a range of infrastructure programs throughout Africa, Asia, and even parts of Europe. It is observed that the determinants here are the fact that China's outward FDI is attracted to countries with high volumes of exports from China, large GDP per capital and rapid GDP growth. Additionally, China's foreign investments are promoted by natural resource-rich countries and open economic regimes (Zhang & Daly, 2011). In developing and emerging economies such as India and other parts of Southeast Asia, FDIs offer a much-needed fillip to businesses that may be in poor financial shape. Since foreign direct investment is a non-debt financial resource, it has the potential to become a major driver of economic development.

Types of Foreign Direct Investment

Foreign direct investments are commonly categorized as horizontal, vertical, or conglomerate.

- With a **horizontal direct investment**, a company establishes the same type of business operation in a foreign country as it operates in its home country. A U.S.-based cell phone provider buying a chain of phone stores in China is an example.

- In a **vertical investment**, a business acquires a complementary business in another country. For example, a U.S. manufacturer might acquire an interest in a foreign company that supplies it with the raw materials it needs.
- In a **conglomerate** type of foreign direct investment, a company invests in a foreign business that is unrelated to its core business. Since the investing company has no prior experience in the foreign company's area of expertise, this often takes the form of a joint venture.

While maritime nations can allow vertical and/or horizontal FDIs, conglomerate and platform investments must be discouraged if national economic growth is prioritized. Furthermore, foreign investments can be either 'organic' or 'inorganic'. With organic investments, a foreign investor will pump in funds to expand and accelerate growth in established businesses. Inorganic investments are instances when an investing entity buys out a business in its target country.

Impacts of FDI on National Economic – China Ocean Nation

The impacts of FDI on the emerging blue ocean cannot be undermined. The ocean economy, with reference to China, has resulted in infrastructure improvements, led to job creation and increased exports and has helped the formal sector to a great extent. Foreign direct investments may involve mergers, acquisitions, or partnerships in retail, services, logistics or manufacturing. They indicate a multinational strategy for economic growth. Using China as a case study, foreign direct investment (FDI) has contributed 33% to China's GDP and 27% to its employment in recent years. For instance, Maersk had approximately 26,000 employees in China and registered USD 11 billion in China-related revenues. The Group estimates that its direct investment and procurement of ships and other items in China exceeded USD 15 billion from 1996 to 2014 (Maersk, 2014).

Procurement in China alone was estimated at USD 2.24 billion in 2013 and USD 2.6 billion in 2014 (Maersk, 2015). In 2014, the Maersk China Limited shipping arm had branches in 28 Chinese cities, and its logistics arm had branches in 17 cities. Maersk has been a significant player in port operations in China, with its activities in 2015 in Qingdao, Dalian, Guangzhou, Shanghai, and Tianjin, as well as Hong Kong. The impact of Maersk on China, however, has gone well beyond its employment and investment amounts. It has been an earlier investor in Chinese ports, a major customer providing substantial technology transfer to Chinese shipyards, a force for improving logistics in China, and a major enabler of China's development into a leading trading nation (Hinrich Foundation, 2017). FDI can foster and maintain economic growth, both in the recipient country and in the country making the investment. Developing countries have encouraged FDI as a means of financing the construction of new infrastructure and the creation of jobs for their local workers. Thus, for maritime nations that receive foreign funds, some benefits include greater employment opportunities, a stimulus to their domestic economy and access to some of the latest technologies and modern management methods (Hinrich Foundation, 2017).

PROSPECTS, CHALLENGES OF BE AND SOLUTIONS

Blue Economy Prospects

The blue economy stimulates economic growth through the sustainable utilization of ocean resources with technological inputs to improve livelihoods and meet the growing demands for jobs without hampering the health of the ocean ecosystem (Sarker et al., 2018). The blue economy supports food security, manages and protects the ocean environment, creates new jobs and has diversification to add new resources for energy, drugs, chemicals, food and minerals for human welfare (Ninawe, 2017). In addition, the blue economy also builds resilience to climate change. It is estimated that ocean-based businesses contribute more than 500 billion USD to the world's economy. It is reported that the economic value of the ocean outputs in 2010 was 1.5 trillion USD, which is equivalent to approximately 2.5% of the world's gross economic value. The blue economy also contributed approximately 31 million direct full-time jobs in 2010, which is approximately 1% of the global workforce (OECD, 2016; Sarker et al., 2018). Oceans contribute approximately 81.5 MT of global fisheries production annually (Food and Agriculture Organization [(FAO], 2016). The marine fisheries sector directly or indirectly supports the livelihood of 8% of the world's population and contributes 230 billion USD to the global economy (Sarker et al., 2018). The oceans also provide convenient transportation routes for approximately 80% of global trade i.e. goods are transported by sea routes (Corbet & Winebrake, 2017). Approximately 161 billion USD in revenue comes annually from global marine and coastal tourism (FAO, 2016). Ocean energy, including aquatic biofuels and renewable energies, could be an important way to meet the world's energy demands. However, this sector is still in its early stage of development. There are a number of new and potentially valuable industrial products derived from the ocean. These include pharmaceuticals, antibiotics, antifreeze and antifouling paints (FAO, 2016). By the mid-century, enough food, jobs, energy, raw materials and economic growth will be required to sustain a likely world population level of between 9 and 10 billion people (Sarker et al., 2018). However, the importance of oceans for sustainable development is widely recognized by the international community and was embodied in, among others, Agenda 21, the Johannesburg Plan of Implementation, various decisions made by the Commission on Sustainable Development, the Rio+20 outcome document The Future We Want, and the 2030 Agenda for Sustainable Development. The 1982 United Nations Convention on the Law of the Sea (UNCLOS), together with its implementing agreements—the 1994 Agreement relating to the implementation of Part XI of UNCLOS and the 1995 United Nations Fish Stocks Agreement—sets out the legal framework within which all activities in the oceans and seas must be carried out and is of strategic importance as the basis for national, regional, and global action and cooperation in the marine sector. This includes the conservation and sustainable use of all areas of the oceans and their resources.

Blue Economy Challenges and Solutions

Despite all its promises, the potential to develop a blue economy is limited by a series of challenges. First and foremost is the need to overcome current economic trends that are rapidly degrading ocean resources through unsustainable extraction of marine resources, physical alterations and destruction of marine and coastal habitats and landscapes, climate change, and marine pollution. The second set of challenges is the need to invest in the human capital required to harness the employment and development benefits of investing in innovative blue economy sectors. Low participation in careers related to the maritime industry is another problem faced by maritime nations. They are a shortage of seafarers, oceanographers, hydrographers, marine biologists and environmentalists.

The third set of challenges relates to strengthening the concept and overcoming inadequate valuation of marine resources and ecosystem services provided by the oceans; isolated sectorial management of activities in the oceans, which makes it difficult to address cumulative impacts; inadequate human, institutional, and technical capacity; underdeveloped and often inadequate planning tools; and lack of full implementation of the 1982 United Nations Convention on the Law of the Sea (UNCLOS) and relevant conventions and instruments. While stimulating growth in individual oceanic sectors is comparatively straightforward, it is not always clear what a sustainable blue economy should look like and the conditions under which it is most likely to develop.

Therefore, an important challenge of the blue economy is aptly captured in the executive summary of the report-World Bank and United Nations Department of Economic and Social Affairs. 2017. The Potential of the Blue Economy: Increasing Long-term Benefits of the Sustainable Use of Marine Resources for Small Island Developing States and Coastal Least Developed Countries-is thus to understand and better manage the many aspects of oceanic sustainability, ranging from sustainable fisheries to ecosystem health to pollution. A second significant issue is the realization that the sustainable management of ocean resources requires collaboration across nation-states and across the public–private sectors and on a scale that has not been previously achieved.

Blue Economy Sustainability

Development implies that economic development is both inclusive and environmentally sound and to be undertaken in a manner that does not deplete the natural resources that societies depend on in the long term. The need to balance the economic, social, and environmental dimensions of sustainable development in relation to oceans is a key component of the blue economy. It is also a difficult balance to reach in practice, given that ocean resources are limited and the health of the oceans has drastically declined due to human activities—ranging from damage caused by carbon dioxide emissions to nutrient, chemical, and plastic pollution, unsustainable fishing, habitat degradation and destruction, and the spread of invasive species. The scientists and experts who prepared the First Global Integrated Marine Assessment (also known as the World Ocean Assessment) warned that the world's oceans face major pressures simultaneously with such great impacts that the limits of their carrying capacity are being reached—or in some cases have been reached—and that delays in implementing solutions to the problems that have already been identified as threatening to degrade the world's oceans will unnecessarily lead to greater environmental, social, and economic costs (United Nations, 2016). Additionally, they are issues bothering the jurisdiction of boundaries among maritime nations, which often results in legal conflicts. This has actually seen some countries enter into bilateral and multilateral agreements, such as the 1818 US-Great Britain fisheries convention and the 1882 North Sea Fisheries Convention.

Finally, the blue economy has diverse components, including established traditional ocean industries, such as fisheries, tourism, and maritime transport, as well as new and emerging activities, such as offshore renewable energy, aquaculture, seabed extractive activities, marine biotechnology and bioprospecting. A number of services provided by ocean ecosystems, for which markets do not exist, also contribute significantly to economic and other human activities, such as carbon sequestration, coastal protection, waste disposal and the existence of biodiversity.

Government Roles

All the aforementioned problems rely upon the governments of maritime nations. Some specific institutional frameworks should be put in place to support the attraction of FDI and some form of investment promotion agencies (IPAs). The organization of these agencies varied from 100 percent state operated (e.g., Catalonia) to semistate (e.g., IDA Ireland) to collaboration between state institutions and private entities (e.g., Invest in Wrocław). Maritime business can only operate effectively if the regulations and standards are adopted and implemented on an international basis. Hence, if the government can encourage maritime education and research and provide infrastructure that would guarantee return on investments, the resultant effect will be evident in the economy.

Policy for FDI attraction

In the absence of a common language through which to debate FDI attraction, policy discussions often become confused, resulting in different conceptualizations of what constitutes a strategy for FDI promotion, FDI incentives, policy competition and the like. The aim of policies for attracting FDI is to create an enabling environment for foreign investors using different incentives. UNCTAD (2003) defines incentives as 'any measurable advantage accorded to specific enterprises or categories of enterprises by (or in the direction of) government'. However, the use of different incentives is not necessarily a substitute for the pursuit of appropriate general policy measures. In certain cases, incentives may 'serve either as a supplement to an already attractive enabling environment for investment or as a compensation for proven market imperfections that cannot be otherwise addressed'.

The OECD (2003) identifies the following broad categories of FDI incentives:

- **Broadly based FDI incentives** A simple strategy that uses FDI incentives to increase the attractiveness of the host economy beyond what can be achieved through an enabling environment. Within this framework, two distinct categories are identified: proactive policies that aim to attract foreign investors by building on the advantages of the host economy's enabling environment. For example, providing financial support for relocation or covering the initial lossmaking period of an investment. - Defensive strategies that aim to match investment incentives on offer elsewhere.
- **Targeted strategies** most incentive-based FDI strategies are limited in scope and focus on specific aspects of the host economy. The following four strategies appear to be prevalent: Regionally oriented strategies. These strategies aim to attract foreign enterprises to economically depressed areas, often in response to the closure of another plant. They may be crafted by national authorities, or subnational authorities may have sufficient freedom to pursue them on their own. -Developing prioritized activities. One of the main examples of such strategies is the establishment of export processing zones, which aim to integrate the host economy more closely into international trade flows. -Building on particular advantages. A classic example of this type of strategy is countries with an abundant workforce that benefit from labour-intensive industries. - Nurturing selected sectors. Some countries and regions attempt to use FDI as an instrument to lay the foundations for completely new sectors in which they have no history or for developing "priority industries" in sectors where they were not previously regarded as having particular leverage. This strategy has, for example, been used in the case of high-tech industries, high-value segments of the service sectors and high added-value sound projects (e.g., machine tool-making, precision engineering).

- **Improvisation** Not all FDI incentives are granted as part of specific or targeted programmes. In fact, in some of the most heavily publicised examples of incentivised FDI, a large degree of improvisation from the host area authorities has been observed. The generosity of the incentives used in these cases was largely due to the sheer magnitude of the investment projects.

The effect, appropriateness and attractiveness of FDI incentives will depend on at least two aspects: (a) whether incentive schemes are operated by national or subnational jurisdictions;

(b) The territorial setting in which the policy objective is being pursued. This implies a need for host governments to provide 'institutional preconditions in order to promote outward FDI because the institutional content and form might affect the cognition, behaviour and motivation of firms in their decision on whether or not to go abroad'. FDI incentives are often divided into three major groups of tools that the government uses to attract and sustain FDI inflows (Yu & Li, 2020).

Regulatory FDI incentives offer foreign companies derogation from national or subnational rules or regulations, thus easing the environmental, social and labour market requirements placed on investors. Barbour (2005) defines these as nonfiscal incentives, for example, fast-track approval processes or exemptions from certain regulations. Generally, these policies promote investment and subsidies to grow certain sectors. However, as argued by Nicoletti (2001), regulatory incentives have different impacts according to the type of firm and the sector of operations. For instance, regulatory concessions on labour or the environment will not affect the cost base of large international firms whose investment is based on technological leadership in a sector (such as telecommunications, banking or aerospace). However, these firms may rely on patents and brand names and thus depend upon intellectual property rules. The protection of unskilled labour does not present a problem to large international firms that require a skilled labour force, and high labour standards may be a positive attraction to the extent that these are associated with public human capital investment.

- Financial FDI incentives consist of direct contributions to the foreign company from the government and include grants, subsidised loans, loan guarantees, the participation of publicly funded venture capital in investments involving high commercial risks and government insurance at preferential rates. Thomas (2007) argues that there are two reasons why authorities compete for FDI using location subsidies: 'their need for investment and the fact that capital is mobile'. To meet the first need, the government negotiates the conditions of investment with foreign investors, while the second need 'creates the competitive aspect of this relationship in thus far as a given investment potentially could be located in more than one jurisdiction'.
- Fiscal FDI incentives are designed to reduce a firm's tax burden and include a reduced corporate income tax rate, tax holidays, accelerated depreciation allowances on capital taxes, exemption from import duties and duty drawbacks on exports. Barbour (2005) defines fiscal incentives as direct 'cash' grants or tax breaks and identifies two types: direct and indirect incentives. Direct incentives comprised cash payments and payments-in-kind (e.g., the provision of land/infrastructure to international companies). Indirect incentives comprised reductions in the rate of direct taxation (e.g., tax holidays with reduced Corporate Income Tax (CIT) rates or investment tax credits).

In improving the living condition of people using the human and material resources with which the country is endowed, maritime nations' government should be willing to play the following three major roles: *(a)* Participant, *(b)* Facilitator and *(c)* Regulator.

1. **As a participant:** As part of the political environment, which is related to regulations and government agencies and their activities that affect all business matters, the government functions as a participant to enable it to protect the interest of all and sundry in the business environment: business owners, workers, consumers, suppliers, distributors, public and local communities, as well as ensuring the achievement of predetermined social or national goals.
2. **As a facilitator:** In this case, government roles in promoting enterprise by creating an enabling environment on which business can thrive. This is usually done by enhancing economic expansion and growth through policies discussed earlier in the chapter, which are provision of assistance, grants, incentives, tax reliefs, needed infrastructure, supporting research, and maintaining political stability, law and order.
3. **A regulator:** One of the primary functions of the government in economic development is regulatory. The government controls or influences business activities by means of laws, rules, policies, conventions and regulations to ensure that business is carried out legally and according to best practices. This also ensures that workers, consumers, communities and even the government are protected from the actions and decisions of business managers.

Collective Roles in the Blue Economy

Generally, the different pathways toward the blue economy depend on national and local priorities and goals. Nevertheless, there are common steps that are required by all countries aiming to adopt this approach to managing their oceans. These include:

The countries within the blue economy must accurately value the contribution of natural oceanic capital to welfare to make the right policy decisions, including with regard to trade-offs amongst different sectors of the blue economy. Investment in and use of the best available science, data, and technology is critical to underpinning governance reforms and shaping management decisions to enact long-term change as proposed in MARLOG 5 - THE INTERNATIONAL MARITIME TRANSPORT & LOGISTICS CONFERENCE TOWARDS SMART PORTS (MARCH, 2016).

Furthermore, each country should weigh the relative importance of each sector of the blue economy and decide, based on its own priorities and circumstances, which ones to prioritize. This prioritization can be carried out through appropriate investments and should be based on accurate valuation of its national capital, natural, human and productive. The urgent need to anticipate and adapt to the impacts of climate change is an essential component of a blue economy approach. National investments to that end must be complemented by regional and global cooperation around shared priorities and objectives - the 'Ukrainian ports are going green' Project and EU's climate Change Agenda case study.

Moreover, the blue economy must boost ocean health with new investment through targeted financial instruments that include blue bonds, insurance and debt-for-adaptation swaps, which can help leverage this investment to ensure that it maximizes a triple bottom line in terms of financial, social, and environmental returns.

More importantly, effective implementation of the Law of the Sea by the United Nations Convention is a necessary condition for promoting the blue economy concept worldwide. That convention sets out the legal framework within which all activities in the oceans and seas must be carried out, including the conservation and sustainable use of the oceans and their resources. The effective implementation of the Convention, its implementing agreements and other relevant instruments is essential to build robust legal and institutional frameworks, including for investment and business innovation. These frameworks will help achieve Sustainable Development Goal (SDG) and Nationally Determined Contribution (NDC) commitments, especially economic diversification, job creation, food security, poverty reduction, and economic development.

Related to the point above is the need to develop coastal and marine spatial plans (CMSPs), which is an important step to guide decision-making for the blue economy and to resolve conflicts over ocean space. CMSP brings a spatial dimension to the regulation of marine activities by helping to establish geographical patterns of sea uses within a given area. Private sector investment and interventions are critical because private sector organizations play a key role in the blue economy. Private-sector businesses are the engines for trade, economic growth and jobs and poverty reduction across the globe.

Considering the challenges facing coastal states, partnerships can be considered a way to enhance capacity building. Such partnerships already exist in more established sectors, such as fisheries, maritime transport, and tourism, but they are less evident in newer and emerging sectors. There is thus an opportunity to develop additional partnerships to support national, regional, and international efforts in emerging industries, such as deep-sea mining, marine biotechnology, and renewable ocean energy. The goal of such partnerships is to agree on common goals, build government and workforce capacity in coastal states and leverage actions beyond the scope of individual national governments and companies.

CONCLUSION

This policy-focused chapter discusses the opportunities available to maritime nations in the blue economy and explicates the roles of policymakers in achieving an improved economy by encouraging and attracting FDI, which is a catalyst to achieving a blue economy. Despite the qualitative and exploratory focus of the chapter, it is unique and distinct, as it opens the space for further studies on this topic.

REFERENCES

Anuchitworawong, C., & Thampanishvong, K. (2015). Determinants of foreign direct investment in Thailand: Does natural disaster matter? *International Journal of Disaster Risk Reduction*, *14*, 312–321. doi:10.1016/j.ijdrr.2014.09.001

Barbour, P. (2005*). An assessment of South Africa's investment incentive regime with a focus on the manufacturing sector.* Economic and Statistics Analysis Unit (ESAU), ESAU Working Paper 14. Overseas Development Institute.

Bax, N., Novaglio, C., Maxwell, K. H., Meyers, K., McCann, J., Jennings, S., Frusher, S., Fulton, E. A., Nursey-Bray, M., Fischer, M., Anderson, K., Layton, C., Emad, G. R., Alexander, K. A., Rousseau, Y., Lunn, Z., & Carter, C. G. (2021). Ocean resource use: Building the coastal blue economy. *Reviews in Fish Biology and Fisheries*, 1–19. doi:10.100711160-021-09636-0 PMID:33679009

Buheji, M., & Ahmed, D. (2021). Forward: The Pandemic Calls for More Colours Economies. *Forward: The Pandemic Calls for More Colours Economies*, *5*(1), 1–3. doi:10.5923/j.ijire.20210501.01

Chakrabarti, S., Paul, A., & Ghosh, I. (2014). FDI and Retail Regulation in India. *From the Editors Desk*, 111.

Cheung, W. W., Lam, V. W., & Wabnitz, C. C. (2019). *Future scenarios and projections for fisheries on the high seas under a changing climate.* IIED Working Paper. IIED. https://pubs.iied.org/16653IIED

Clegg, P., Mahon, R., McConney, P., & Oxenford, H. A. (Eds.). (2020). *The Caribbean blue economy.* Routledge. doi:10.4324/9780429342233

Corbett, J. J., & Winebrake, J. (2008, November). The impacts of globalization on international maritime transport activity. In *Global forum on transport and environment in a globalizing world* (Vol. 31). Academic Press.

Economist Intelligence Unit. (2015). *The blue economy: Growth, opportunity and a sustainable ocean economy.* https://www. eiuperspectives. economist. com/sustainability/blue-economy/white-paper/blue-economy

Enright, M. J. (2002). Trends in multinational strategies and organizations in the Asia-Pacific. In *Japanese foreign direct investment and the East Asian industrial system* (pp. 41–68). Springer. doi:10.1007/978-4-431-66990-6_3

Enright, M. J. (2016). *Developing China: The remarkable impact of foreign direct investment.* Routledge. doi:10.4324/9781315393346

FAO. (2016). The state of world fisheries and aquaculture 2016. *Contributing to food security and nutrition for all, 200.*

Franckx, E., Gustafson Juras, K., & Noyes, J. (2010). *Law of the Sea in a Nutshell.* West Publishing Company.

Groww. (2022). *Foreign Direct Investment (FDI).* https://groww.in/p/foreign-direct-investment

Habitat, U. N. (2018). *Tracking progress towards inclusive, safe, resilient and sustainable cities and human settlements.* https://apo.org.au/node/182836

Hinrich Foundation Case Study. (2017). *Maersk's contribution to China through FDI.* https://www.hinrichfoundation.com/media/snfhzwm3/hinrich-foundation-fdi-in-china-maersk-case-study-9-8-17.pdf

Investopedia. (2021). *Foreign Direct Investment (FDI).* https://www.investopedia.com/terms/f/fdi.asp

Jouffray, J. B., Blasiak, R., Norström, A. V., Österblom, H., & Nyström, M. (2020). The blue acceleration: The trajectory of human expansion into the ocean. *One Earth*, *2*(1), 43–54. doi:10.1016/j.oneear.2019.12.016

Jouili, T. (2018). Determinants of foreign investment in maritime nations. *International Journal of Advanced and Applied Sciences*, *5*(5), 43–47. doi:10.21833/ijaas.2018.05.006

Kaur, M., & Dhillon, S. S. (2017). Determinants of foreign direct investment in India: An empirical analysis. *Asian Journal of Research in Business Economics and Management*, *7*(8), 244–260. doi:10.5958/2249-7307.2017.00142.6

Madiraju, K. S. (2019). Contemplating a Domestic Regulatory and Enforcement Framework for Deep Seabed Mining. *Natural Resources and Environment*, *34*(2), 17–21.

Maersk. (2014). *Exploring Maersk in China*. Sustainability Report.

Maersk. (2015). *Maersk Line orders seven ice-class container vessels*. http://www.maerskline.com/ro-ro/countries/int/news/news-articles/2015/03/seven-iceclass-container-vessels

Maersk. (2015a). *Maersk to move China office from HK to Beijing*. Maersk Press Release.

Nicoletti, G. (2001). *Regulation in services: OECD patterns and economic implications*. OECD.

Ninawe, A. S. (2017). Blue economy is the economic activities that directly or indirectly take place in the ocean and seas, use outputs, goods and services into ocean and land based activities. *Examines in Marine Biology & Oceanography*, 1-3.

Nourzad, F., Greenwold, D. N., & Yang, R. (2014). The interaction between FDI and infrastructure capital in the development process. *International Advances in Economic Research*, *20*(2), 203–212. doi:10.100711294-013-9457-5

OECD. (2016). *The ocean economy in 2030*. OECD. https://www.oecd.org/ocean/data/

OEDDiLibrary. (2022). *Foreign direct investment (FDI)*. https://www.oecd-ilibrary.org/finance-and-investment/foreign-direct-investment-fdi/indicator-group/english_9a523b18-en

Pauli, G. A. (2010). *The blue economy: 10 years, 100 innovations, 100 million jobs*. Paradigm publications.

Ricart, J. E., Enright, M. J., Ghemawat, P., Hart, S. L., & Khanna, T. (2004). New frontiers in international strategy. *Journal of International Business Studies*, *35*(3), 175–200. doi:10.1057/palgrave.jibs.8400080

Roy, A. (2019). *Blue economy in the Indian Ocean: Governance perspectives for sustainable development in the region*. ORF Occasional Paper, 181.

Sarker, S., Ara Hussain, F., Assaduzzaman, M., & Failler, P. (2019). Blue economy and climate change: Bangladesh perspective. *Journal of Ocean and Coastal Economics*, *6*(2), 6. doi:10.15351/2373-8456.1105

Sarker, S., Bhuyan, M. A. H., Rahman, M. M., Islam, M. A., Hossain, M. S., Basak, S. C., & Islam, M. M. (2018). From science to action: Exploring the potentials of Blue Economy for enhancing economic sustainability in Bangladesh. *Ocean and Coastal Management*, *157*, 180–192. doi:10.1016/j.ocecoaman.2018.03.001

Schutter, M. S., & Hicks, C. C. (2019). Networking the Blue Economy in Seychelles: Pioneers, resistance, and the power of influence. *Journal of Political Ecology*, *26*(1), 425–447.

Secretariat, C. (2018). *Commonwealth Blue Charter*. Shared Values, Shared Ocean. A Commonwealth Commitment to Work Together to Protect and Manage Our Ocean.

Sunesen, E. R., Jeppesen, T., Henriksen, J. J., & Grunfelder, J. (2018). *The World in Europe, global FDI flows towards Europe. Intra-European FDI*. ESPON EGTC.

Thomas, K. P. (2009). *Subnational FDI competition in developing countries: The case of Viet Nam*. APSA 2009 Toronto Meeting Paper. https://papers.ssrn.com/sol3/papers.cfm?abstract_id=1450115

UNCTAD. (2016). World Investment Report 2016: Investor Nationality: Policy Challenges. New York: United Nations Conference on Trade and Development, United Nations United Nations Blue Economy Concept Paper. *Conference on Sustainable Development.*

United Nations Blue Economy Concept Paper. (2014). Available at https://sustainabledevelopment.un.org/concent/documents/2978BEconcept.pdf

United Nations Environment Programme. (2015). *Blue Economy: Sharing Success Stories Inspire Change*. UNEP Regional Seas Report.

World Bank and United Nations Department of Economic and Social Affairs. (2017). *The Potential of the Blue Economy: Increasing Long-term Benefits of the Sustainable Use of Marine Resources for Small Island Developing States and Coastal Least Developed Countries.* World Bank.

Yu, X., & Li, Y. (2020). Effect of environmental regulation policy tools on the quality of foreign direct investment: An empirical study of China. *Journal of Cleaner Production*, *270*, 122346. doi:10.1016/j.jclepro.2020.122346

Zhang, X., & Daly, K. (2011). The determinants of China's outward foreign direct investment. *Emerging Markets Review*, *12*(4), 389–398. doi:10.1016/j.ememar.2011.06.001

Chapter 8
Blue Economy and Foreign Direct Investment to Maritime Nations:
Lessons for Nigeria

Moshood Abiola Sanni
University of Ibadan, Nigeria

ABSTRACT

The blue economy provides a unique opportunity to policymakers in Nigeria to diversify the economy by exploiting ocean resources to attract foreign direct investment and generate foreign exchange. The chapter adds to the existing body of knowledge by discussing the nexus between the blue economy and foreign direct investment (FDI). Three key issues were articulated in the chapter. First, the blue economy has the potential to provide an opportunity for Nigeria to develop and exploit the diverse ocean resources while protecting and conserving endangered marine resources. Secondly, the transition to a blue economy presents some challenges; hence, the policymakers need to develop ocean governance and policies for strengthening its realisation. LastlySecond, the blue economy enhances wealth creation and youth employment in different ocean-related industrial activities such as shipping, shipbuilding and repair, fisheries, ocean mining, sustainable energy development, biomedical, innovative industries shipbuilding, and repair and port services, amongst others.

INTRODUCTION

Nigeria preference of oil sector over agriculture in the 70`s has done worse than good. Relentless efforts by policy maker in diversifying to other sectors as most preferable source of generating foreign currency are daunting. Blue Economy has played and continued to play significant role in developed maritime nations which gave hope to other developing nations Nigeria inclusive. One of the things BE capable of bringing to the table is ensuring youth employments and thus proffering solutions to youthful exorbitance. It enables youth to be gainfully employed in different ocean-related activities which further aid in ensur-

DOI: 10.4018/978-1-6684-3393-5.ch008

ing food availability and securing enough food thus putting end to hunger. Other vital role played by BE are employment opportunities in sustainable energy, natural resources and innovative industries such as ship owning and operating, supply of trained sea personnel, ship recycling opportunity, shipbuilding and repair and port services, among others. The coastline of our dear country is estimated approximately 870 km with over 3,100 kilometres of inland waterways well-endowed with natural resources like petroleum, natural gas, tin, columbite, coal, zinc, limestone, iron ore, lead to mention but little. Aside agriculture which was perceived as the current means of livelihood, BE possessed greater opportunities to change the narrative of Nigeria economy overnight. According to Abdullahel (2017), BE relevance not only to the food chains as a means of sustainability but also render ecosystem and biodiversity, and assist in climate regulation for Nigeria population earmarked to be 400million by 2050. According to the United Nations Environment Programme (2015), some of the key benefits that Blue oceans provided include: ensuring food security and food abundance, natural oxygen and means of sustainability. The BE still encountered series of challenges despite its economic value. Challenges such as compartmentalization of ocean, activities of the coastal and marine industries, i.e., emission and pollution of the ocean, to the harmonization of traditional economic activities.

This chapter is significant for several reasons. Human economic activities and development approaches put at risk the ability to maintain the marine environment for the purpose of providing jobs opportunities and nutrition in the long-run. Blue economy presents several opportunities to the maritime nations (developed and developing) few of these include integrating sustainable development and growth that benefits local communities, coastal states, and the global economy. Blue Economy is devoted to delivering services and values that benefit local communities, coastal states, and the world economy at large. In a bid to benefit the wellbeing of all citizens and mankind, a country must achieve long-term prosperity while preserving the environment, most importantly the oceans. It is indisputable that oceans and seas are vital for sustainable development because the earth's surface is covered by water. The key goal of this paper is to analyse the concept of Blue Economy and how it can be harnessed to benefit the society and ensure sustainable development. The chapter examines the importance and principles of blue economy and offers recommendations, it suggested possible solutions to Blue Economy bottlenecks. The recommendations from this paper will be of immense benefits to policy makers in changing their perception about BE and its underlying benefits.

There are obvious research gaps in Literature that this chapter intends to bridge. In 2012, the United Nations provided a platform that promoted the idea of a Blue Economy, also known as "Blue Growth" or "Ocean Economy" which prompt nations to key into BE and take advantage of the opportunities in unlocking their golden potentials. There are lots of journals, articles and paper on Blue Economy as compared to Green Economy. Albeit, there is a perceived gap which this paper seeks to address by adding to existing knowledge on BE and suggest likely solutions to factors militating against BE in Nigeria. The chapter lays emphasis on creating awareness on human capacity development and tailoring youth mindset towards BE. This chapter seeks to add to existing knowledge on Blue Economy and suggest solutions to augment perceived gap based on literature on the implementation of Blue Economy to the betterment of Nigeria economy through the development and protection of marine resources. It seeks to address the challenges, economy opportunities and policies that will strengthen the Blue Economy of Nigeria and to analyse benefits accrued to the implementation of Blue Economy, challenges acting as bottlenecks to the progress of Blue Economy and suggest ways on how the Blue Economy can boost Nigeria`s economy. From the foregoing, the chapter attempts to ascertain if there is a direct link between BE and Youth Development (YD) in Nigeria. In the course of this study, some of the major bottle neck will revealed and attempts will be made as to how it can be addressed. Finally, the study will be an eye opener to policy makers and suggest ways on how the Blue Economy can boost Nigeria economy.

BACKGROUND

The possible links between the Blue Economy (BE) and Foreign Direct Investment (FDI) have been recognized as sustainable economic activities of the Maritime Nations which have been confirmed in a number of symposiums. BE presents huge opportunities to maritime nations as the oceans and seas are perceived as the agents of global development. It presents full capacity for the potential for growth and innovation and its commercial active activities functioned as a collaborator as it synergies with other economic sectors, including tourism, transport, energy, aquaculture, etc. The relationship between the blue economy and foreign direct investment has been recognized as sustainable economic activities relatively confirm in many international forums and documents. New discoveries in technology include: marine bio technologies, ocean energy, desalination, etc. preservation of the ocean to retain its utmost nature and its usability to the beneficiaries of humanity such as conversion of waste-to-energy, waste-water management and insidious species management. Nigeria economy as maritime nations has been accelerated by the sea as it opens door for innovative business opportunities in aquaculture territory, carbon emission and seashore protection.

Despite the economy challenge, different business innovation surfaces as blue economy presents greater opportunity and sustainable growth to the maritime economy. Perceiving seas as a golden chance, it changes business narrative in the ever dynamic business environment thus presenting potential for generating residual income from different sources including aqua-farming, energy, transport and tourism. The innovations and emerging markets opportunities open business for investments for the betterment of blue economy nation. Ecotourism, Eco-ships and Eco-ports provide industries more environmentally sound. BE as a new economic paradigm has the propensity to enhance standard of living and boosts output which has positive effects on the total Gross Domestic Product (GDP). Since BE promote economic growth, foreign direct investment plays great role in Nigeria local markets and contribute significantly as source of generating foreign currency. Existing study claims BE is gradually changing the phase of doing business compare to the 80`s where the oil was perceived as the solely means of generating income in Nigeria. BE promote economic growth, improve living standards and ensure social inclusion without jeopardizing ocean`s ecological sustainability. Direct human activities often play significant role in the coastal regions while foreign direct investment plays growing role in the global markets as it represents an integral part of developing nations.

It's a renowned fact that ocean occupies over 70% of the earth surface which pave way for business opportunity to the maritime world (European Commission, 2012). In the next decade, the ocean will record high rate of environmental pressure due to the influence of sociocultural, tech-innovation and governmental policies leveraging more on the outputs from coastal industry, agro-related, and aquaculture. More so, Sustainable Development Goals (SGDs) emphasis the need to balance the inclusive and environmental-friendliness of the ocean world, thereby reducing activities that can affect the wet animals such as carbon emissions, recycling and disposal of chemicals, etc in the Ocean, thus the need to address effective ways of curtailing negative consequences of human activities that can tamper with oceans inhabitants (Griggs et al., 2013). In Hoegh-Guldberg (2015) opinion the ocean will fail to sustain the ever increasing population if not properly managed due to the huge large dependence. The sustainable development goals focuses on enhancing the economic activities of the Small Island Developing States (SIDS), water enclosed areas and Less Developed Countries (LDCs) as well as ensuring sustainable management of fisheries, cultivation, tourism and business enterprise (UNCTAD, 2014). BE integrates a novel approach to the effective utilization of the ocean-related resources in ensuring better living standards by providing jobs opportunities to the teeming population while protecting environmental sustainability. In 2015, the United Nations General Assembly adopted a Resolution 70/226 to "convene the high-level United Nations conference to support the implementation of Sustainable Development Goal 14; Conserve and sustainably use the oceans, seas and marine resources for sustainable Development Goal (SDG-14).

LITERATURE REVIEW

Definition of the Subject Matter 'BE'

The term BE being used in different ways and manners which "ocean economy" or "marine economy "are used without clear definitions." Spamer J (2015) also observes literature most often ascribed that ocean economy (OE), marine economy (ME), and blue growth (BG) were used interchangeably to describe Blue Economy. Various attempt in defining BE has led to the following definitions: The sustainable use of ocean resources for economic growth, the improvement of livelihoods and jobs, and the health of ocean ecosystems (World Bank, 2013). The concept of rethinking industrial processes and searching for a viable biological solution that reduces contamination (Costa et al. 2019). It has become synonymous with generating wealth from activities related to the oceans while protecting and supporting marine ecosystems (Phelan et al, 2020). According to Graziano et al., (2019), the definition of BE arises from the growing worldwide interest in the growth of water-based activities. Schutter and Hicks (2019) defines BE as economy activities aimed at curbing biodiversity loss while stimulating economic development, thereby integrating environmental and economic interests.

Kathijotes (2012) defines BE as the mainstream of national development and can integrate land and sea-based socioeconomic sustainable development and Kaczynski (2011) refers to BE as the commercially sustainable development of the oceans. Blue Economy is defined as a marine-based economy that provides social and economic benefits for current and future generations, restores, protects and maintains the diversity, productivity and resilience of marine ecosystems and is based on clean technologies, renewal energy and circular material flows. According to European Commission, Blue economy encompasses all economic activities related to oceans, seas and coasts. It covers a wide range of inter linked established and emerging sectors. The Commonwealth of Nations defined Blue Economy as an emerging concept which encourages better stewardship of our ocean or blue resources. In line with this study, BE can be define as an investment opportunity which opens sea space for amassing of untapped benefits that can positively influence foreign direct investment.

BLUE ECONOMY VERSUS GREEN ECONOMY

The distinction in the use of color reference when describing the ecosystems is that "Blue" refers to the marine ecosystem, while "Green" refers to the terrestrial ecosystem. The Green Economy was first initiated in 2012 at the Rio+20 world summit, where the United Nations described the Green Economy as the type of economy beyond terrestrial that "should contribute to eradicating poverty, sustain economic growth, enhance social inclusion, improve human welfare and create new opportunities for employment and decent work for all, while maintaining the healthy functioning of the earth's ecosystems". The Green Economy refers to renewable energy, clean transportation, water management, waste management, natural resource management and sustainability. Blue economy is the sustainable use of ocean resources for economic growth, improve livelihoods and preserve the health of ocean ecosystem. On the one hand, Green economy aims at reducing environmental risk, ecological scarcities and sustainable development without degrading the environment. While the Green Economy is more about renewable energy, the Blue Economy focuses more on ocean and its products on the other hand. According to the United Nations Environment Program (UNEP), the Green Economy is one that results in "improved human wellbeing and social equity, while significantly reducing environmental risks". The UNEP and other international organizations extract blue economy from green economy. They encourage the tackling of climate change through low-carbon and resource-efficient shipping, fishing, marine tourism, and marine renewable energy industries. Blue economy is seen as an integration of sustainable development and green growth.

Brief History on Nigeria's Economy

The Federal Republic of Nigeria lies at the extreme innermost corner of the Gulf of Guinea in West Africa (Coleman, 1958) (see Figure 1). Nigeria shares land borders with the Republic of Niger and Chad to the North, with the Republic of Benin to the West, with the Republic of Cameroon to the east and with the Atlantic Ocean to the South (Nwilo and Badejo, 2006a). Nigeria has multiple potential maritime boundaries including lateral maritime boundaries with Benin, as well as potentially Ghana, to the west, Cameroon to the east as well as with Equatorial Guinea and Sao Tome and Principe to the south Nigeria has a total land surface area of approximately 923,768 square kilometres (km2). Nigeria also has a coastline area of approximately 853 kilometres (km) directly facing the Atlantic Ocean which lies between the latitude of 4° 10' to 6° 20'N and longitude of 2° 45' to 8° 35E (Nwilo & Badejo, 2006b). The country Nigeria declared her independence from the United Kingdom (UK) on the 1st of October 1960. The country currently has 36 states and its Federal Capital Territory (FCT) known as Abuja.

There are about two hundred million nine hundred and seventy-seven thousand five hundred and thirty-three (200,977,533) people in the country, with a population density of nearly 200 individuals per square kilometre. The whole population of Nigeria accounts for approximately 2.35% of the entire world's population, this expresses that one (1) out of every 43 people in the world is a Nigerian (World Population Review, 2019). The country Nigeria has over five hundred (500) different ethnic groups and different languages. Among the ethnic groups in the country, the Hausa-Fulani ethnicity provides the majority. Indeed, the Hausa-Fulani accounts up to two-thirds of the whole country's total population.

A long-standing objective for successive Nigerian governments has been affecting change in the structure of production and consumption patterns, diversification of the economic base and reducing dependence on oil, with the focus of supporting the economy in a position of sustainability for the benefit of the future. Nigeria's economy shows a rapid growth as measured by the real gross domestic product (GDP), even though, the transformation of the various sectors of the economy are even more critical, that is a lack of the will to transform and or improve various country's economic sectors (Sanusi, 2010) Successive governments in Nigeria have, since independence in 1960, chased the goal of structural changes without much success. The dynamic growth of Nigeria's economy has been largely driven by the existence and exploitation of natural resources and primary products. Initially, the agricultural sector, driven by the demand for food and cash crops production was at the centre of the growth process contributing 54.7% to the country's GDP during the 1960s.

The second decade of independence experiences the emergence of the oil industry as the main driver of growth to Nigeria's economy in which almost all or most of the government expenditure rely on it. Since then, the economy has mainly revolved with the boom bust cycles of the oil industry. The Nigerian economy has flagrantly underperformed comparative to her tremendous resource endowment and her peer nations. Nigeria is the 6th largest gas reserves nation and the 8th largest crude oil reserve nation in the world. Nigeria with her current population has almost over 37 solid mineral types in commercial quantities including tin, iron ore, coal, limestone, niobium, lead and zinc (Chircop, Dzidzornu, and Oguamanam, 2016), but still the economic performance has been feeble or puny which does not display the economic development progress that might be expected for a country with these endowments. Given Nigeria's abundant natural resources, economic performance has been weedy and as a result, has not delivered expected increases in the citizen's wellbeing which is the causal effect of poverty in the blessed land.

Nigeria's poor economic performance is demonstrated when compared with other emerging economy countries like Asian countries, particularly Thailand, Malaysia, China, India, and Indonesia. Although these countries were far behind Nigeria in terms of Gross Domestic Product (GDP) per capita in 1970, they have now transformed their economies and are now not only far ahead of Nigeria in GDP terms, but are also major players in the world economic sectors. Unfortunately, this situation shows little sign of changing and Nigeria remains in the state of poor economic performance. Nigeria's limited economic gains are also brought into stark relief when comparing Nigeria's economy with that of China. China is now the second (2nd) largest economy in the world, whereas back in 1970, Nigeria's GDP per capita of US$ 233.35 placing it 88th in the world while China was ranked 114th with a GDP per capita of US$ 111.82. Noticeably, political instability has been perceived as the primary reason for Nigeria's economic woes, coupled with poor leadership that is leaders with limited focus and vision towards economic development. Economic mismanagement also remains a significant contributing factor as well as endemic corruption impacting almost all government functionaries (Rose-Ackerman, 1997).

Oil remains the major sources of revenue to Nigerian economy, generating two-thirds of Nigeria's total income. The oil contributes almost 85% to the country's GDP (Ite et al., 2013). Nigeria supplies approximately 2.7% oil to the worlds market when compared with Saudi Arabia, Russia and the United States of America which contribute 12.9%, 12.7%, and 8.6%, respectively (OPEC, 2018). The Nigerian economy has different major sectors as; Primary - (Agriculture, Oil and Gas, Mining and Forestry), Secondary - (Light and Heavy Industries) and Tertiary - (Service) (FMF, 2018). As all these sectors solidly depend on import and export through maritime transportation, they greatly impact the blue economy as almost 100% of Nigeria's crude oil and refined product are both been exported and imported, respectively through the ocean

Relevancy of Blue Economy to Developing Nations

Blue economy is an emerging concept which encourages sustainability of ocean, natural resources at sea and a healthy climate. It is an initiative fast developing around the world. It was pioneered by SIDS and has since become relevant to all coastal states and countries with an interest in waters beyond national jurisdiction. The blue economy ensures efficient management and sustainable exploitation of resources in oceans, seas, rivers and lakes. It entails the sustainable use of ocean resources for economic growth, improved livelihoods and a healthy ocean ecosystem growth. It encompasses many activities such as

Figure 1. Map of Nigeria. Sourced from Geology.com (2022).

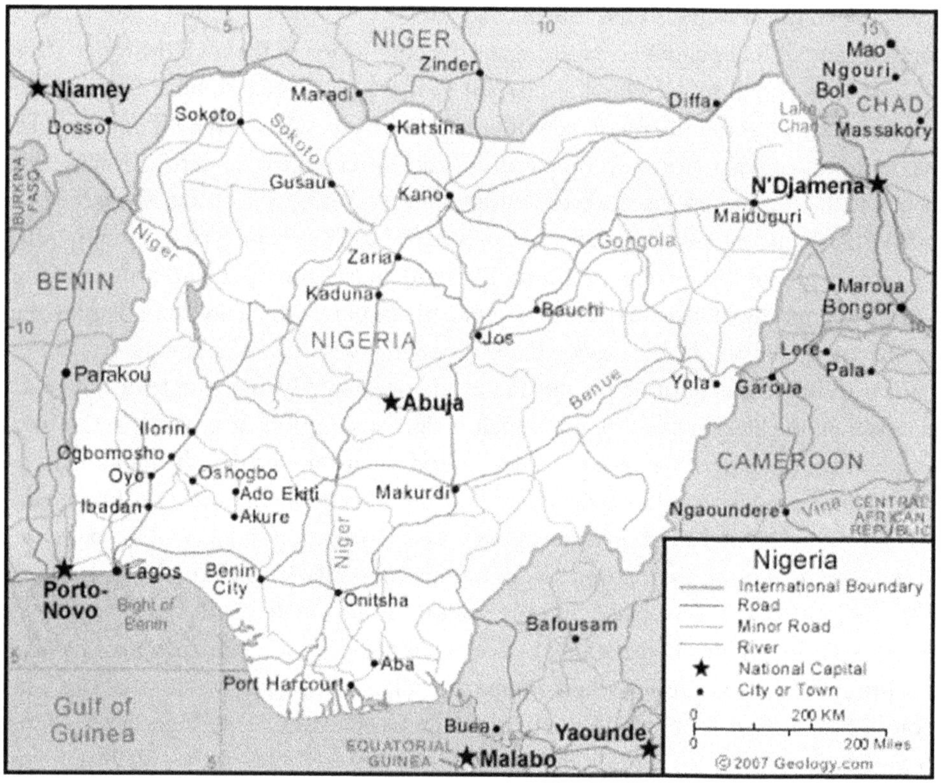

Renewable Energy, fisheries, Maritime Transport, Waste Management, Tourism and Climate change. The main advocates and frontlines of the Blue Economy has always been the Coastal and Island developing countries who recognize that the oceans have a major role to play in humanity's future and that the Blue Economy offers an approach to sustainable development better suited to their circumstances, constraints and challenges.

The BE as a concept surfaces in year 2009 at the congress of the Senate Committee on Commerce, Science and Transportation of the United States. In the opinion of Cantwell M (2009), BE directly impact the economy of the US in all totalities, as it comes with new business opportunities in form of blue jobs in the renewable energy. The congress was succeeded by the international symposiums on Blue Economy held in Korea in the same year, the outcomes of the events present scalable businesses ideas emanating from the ocean which also highlight the sustainability of the ocean resources by instituting policies that ensures its protection of the oceans and its habitants (Joroff M, 2009).

Following the trend, the UN conference on Sustainable Development held In Rio de Janeiro in 2012 reported the significant Impact of the BE in enhancing sustainable consumption and production patterns, ensuring food security and sustainability, sustainable energy, and risk reduction and resilience. This new concept, i.e., "Blue Economy" has gained ground as evidenced by the endorsement of international bodies such as: The Organization for Economic Co-operation and Development (OECD), United Nations (UN) and World Bank. In recent years, Blue Economy (BE) has been perceived as a concept closely related to maritime resources and developed economies in the oceans. The BE aims to promote economic growth, improve life and social inclusion without compromising the oceans' environmental sustainability and coastal areas since the sea's resources are limited and their physical conditions have been harmed by human actions most especially in the developing nations (European Commission, 2020). Indisputably, ocean resources generate plentiful benefits to the world economy and offer essential opportunities for transportation, food production, energy, mineral resources extraction, biotechnology, renewable energy, human settlement in coastal areas, tourism and recreation, and scientific research (Kaczynski W, 2011).

The ocean also provides humans with the basics, necessary for their needs such as food, raw materials, energy, and transportation. Furthermore, ocean provides seascape for recreational and or religious practices. Currently, there are more than 40% of the world population living in the areas within 200 km of the global ocean and out of the 15 megacities in the world, 12 are coastal cities (Visbeck, 2018a). Human depends largely on the activities of the Oceans for sustainability which by implication infers that activities which affects the ocean has direct effects on man. The oceans assist man in the provision of Oxygen for breathing, and thus absorb the excess of heat and carbon dioxide generated, recycle the water drink and provide protein all these for our sustainability (Djavidnia, Ott, and Seeyave, 2014).

Costanza et al., (1999) argued that oceans and society are intricately and inextricably interconnected. The oceans regulate climate and control atmospheric gases. These claims were further corroborated by Fisher, Turner, and Morling study, (2009), which claims that ecosystem services rendered by the ocean played pivotal role in aiding waste recycling thus, sustaining human existence. With the aid the Ocean, transportation has been redefined by networking cities and countries around the globe. According to UNCTAD, maritime transport offer significant benefits as it accounts for over 82% of the world trade thus aiding international trade. Pelc and Fujita, (2002), research shows that ocean possessed the capacity to provide renewable energy via Offshore Wind Farm (OWF) reconstructed as alternative sources of power generation purposes. To harness this opportunity presented by ocean, there were lots of human activities that post as danger to the ocean, which is having negative impacts on the ocean (McIntyre, 1995). The pressure on the ocean was further exacerbated by various activities ranging from persistent rise in the world population, industrial development, and growing human wealth, non-sustainable resources extraction from the sea, pollution as a result of industrial activities, climate change, amongst other factors contribute to degradation of ocean-health in the developing nations (Visbeck, 2018). Oceans are increasingly gaining in importance in terms of enabling International trade by linking sellers and buyers. The behavior patterns of such linking enablers on the oceans are receiving more attention from a regulatory and economic perspective as the relationship between land and ocean evolves in its role and importance. The "Blue Economy" as a concept finds its origin against this background.

Blue economy promotes sustainable usages of ocean resources for economic growth and development including preservation of the health of ocean ecosystem, has become a crucial element of the broader ecosystem of sustainable and inclusive development. The desire to sustainably harness the potential of ocean and marine resources has been amply visible at the national and global level. Technological innovations, investment and multilateral cooperation have further been facilitating progress in the sectors of blue economy. Placed in a central position in the Indian Ocean and with a vast exclusive economic zone (EEZ), India has substantial potential for tapping marine resources and blue economy could emerge as the paradigm of development in the future. New Delhi has taken many initiatives to promote blue economy activities and development of modern infrastructure for greater connectivity, international collaboration and trade facilitation. Furthermore, it is seeking wider multilateral cooperation in areas of financing, technology transfer, capacity building and knowledge sharing. This paper underlines the importance of blue economy in a broader framework of sustainable development and analyses Nigeria`s policy orientation and implementation towards blue economy. Finally, it also addresses inter-allies' cooperation between Nigeria and other developing maritime nations.

Blue Economy as a New Form of Globalization and FDI Opportunity in Nigeria

Globalization acts as catalyst and agent of development as it boosts productivity and increase the standard of living. It gives rooms for specialization where developed nations focus more on a particular trade that enhance its economic status (Guillermo et.al., 2006). Blue economy is the new trends of business opportunity and it's more connected to generating consistent income from marine amusement to aquaculture and resources mining. Investments in the blue economy unlock golden opportunities including capacity to boost energy supply, seafood, and other natural minerals endowed in the ocean and other untapped business opportunities. Ocean helps in proffering solution to transportation problems as it acts of avenue of moving people and goods from one geographical location to another. FDI constitutes essential components of the Nigeria ecosystems by contributing to production growth through employment opportunity for youth and export trade promotion.

Challenges and Opportunities Accrued to Blue Economy in Nigeria

To better understand the role of oceans in the Nigeria economy system we must first consider increasing convergence of environmental, economic, social, and technical factors that are bringing greater opportunities that are offered by the world's oceans: in transportation, food production, energy generation, mineral extraction, biotech, human settlement in the coastal zones, tourism and recreation, and the scientific research. Giving special consideration to these factors, it enables policy makers to identify a number of opportunities that ocean resources create for the benefit of our dear nation. These include:

Transition from Fossil Fuel to Renewable Energy

As the worlds transit from fossil fuel to renewable energy, the ocean present huge benefits as it possessed wind, thermal, kinetic and other forms of renewable energy. Nigeria as a riverside area yet to take full advantage in transforming her economy situation. In the few decades, the patronage for oil and natural gas will be automatically replaced with renewable energy which comes with loads of promissory to the betterment of our nation.

Development of bioscience

Synthetic biology helps us to create new microorganisms to accomplish specific tasks, such as cleaning toxic waste, producing biofuels, and healing our bodies. In the world of biology, genetic data is like gold, and the oceans contain the vast bulk of the earth's genetic diversity. Survey conducted by Biotechnology Pioneer Craig Venter and other studies on marine genetics has helped in understanding and exploiting economic advantages of the genetic treasury of the sea.

A New Source of Protein

Human activity is often answerable as a major contributor to the global environmental hazards. Nonetheless, in the absence of these activities, agricultural production would take charge and continue to warm the planet. The urgent need to reduce carbon emission to the barest minimum and raising demands for animal protein, meanwhile protein production through meat is highly inefficient; thus, the dire need to develop new sources of protein from the most efficient means capable of satisfying ever increasing Nigeria population gave rise to fish farming which is foresaw to overtake beef consumption globally.

Mineral wealth

The oceans present golden opportunity with bounties of natural resources such as gold, diamonds, tin and magnesium. Extracting these resources requires innovative technology that will ensure clean water without causing harms to ocean habitats. Although it requires huge capital in accessing these tools and other possible constraints like transportation, accessing depth of ocean, etc. To satisfy the increasing population might requires digging dip into the bottom of the oceans to take advantage of its full potentials.

Marine transportation

Apart from mineral wealth, the marine transportation has humongous opportunities. Ships as a means of transportation provides ease conveying of persons and good from one point to another. However, piracy and other bandits in the watersides still affect the progress of marine transportation. Niger Delta part of Nigeria often suffers the threat of piracy and armed robbery thus causing hullabaloos to seafarers which further affect foreign trade and globalization. The expected positive outcome of marine transportation might be futile thus causing havoc to the economic activities and hindering interdependence and export trade promotion.

Contribution of FDI Nigeria economy

One of the common yet understandable misconceptions about foreign direct investment, FDI, is that most of it flows from rich, developed nations to poor, developing ones. Nothing could be further from the truth. FDI is in fact an activity conducted primarily between rich countries. Trends about FDI in the developing world shows that very little of FDI originates from or goes to developing countries. Of the small amount that goes to the developing countries, about two-thirds go to just ten countries in Latin America and Asia (primarily Brazil, Mexico, Singapore, Malaysia, Hong Kong, and China). These countries have very large internal markets or have developed quite a sophisticated infrastructure (e.g., ports, banking, education, etc.) to be able to attract FDI, (Grunberg, 1996). It is also from among these countries that we see the development of a small but growing number of multinational corporations that are today referred to as Third World multinationals, (Kumar, 1982).

IMPORTANCE OF BLUE ECONOMY

The concept of Blue Economy is an independent concept, not in competition with green economy, although similar to the 'Green Economy' with the aim of improving human wellbeing and social equity while also reducing environmental risk and ecological scarcities. It has the potential to create both economic growth and development.

For proper understanding of the Blue Economy, some economic forms such as marine economy development, economy coping with global water crisis, and economy to develop innovations must be put into consideration. It is a model to develop and sustain marine economic with the aim of developing marine economy, protecting marine ecosystem and sustaining utilization of resources. The desirability and achievement of the blue economy is hinged on three (3) pillars – the economic sustainability, the environmental sustainability and the social sustainability.

Oceans protect biodiversity, drive economic growth, provide jobs, keep the planet cool and absorb approximately 30% of global carbon dioxide emission. Approximately 3-5% of global Gross Domestic Product (GDP) is derived from oceans.

Due to the importance of Blue Economy, the World Bank established a Multi-Donor Trust Fund (MDTF) called PROBLUE to support implementation of sustainable and increasing income and welfare of the people in a sustainable way. The focus of PROBLUE is on four key themes;

1. The management of fisheries and aquaculture
2. The threats posed to ocean health by marine pollution including litter and plastics
3. The sustainable development of key ocean sectors such as tourism, maritime transport and offshore renewal energy.
4. Building the capacity of government to management their marine and coastal resources in an integrated fashion to deliver more and long lasting benefits to countries and communities including the role of nature-based solutions to climate charge

PROBLUE was established for better understanding of current trends and emerging threats to oceans; identify appropriate solutions for action, and due to client demand. PROBLUE is a key instrument for raising awareness and promoting investment.

The first global conference of the Blue Economy was held in Nairobi, Kenya with the theme "Blue Economy and the 2030 Agenda for Sustainable Development", new technologies and innovation for oceans, seas, lakes and rivers well discussed, as well as challenges, potential opportunities, priorities and partnerships. Therefore, to build a blue economy, there is need to put sustainability at its center and ensure that policies do not undermine each other and that interlinkages are leveraged for the benefit of people, planet, and prosperity.

The Nairobi Blue Economy Conference has two main goals:

1. To harness the potential of the World's Oceans, Seas, lakes and rivers to improve the lives of all, particularly people in developing countries, women, youth and indigenous people.
2. To leverage the latest innovations, scientific advances and best policies to build prosperity, while conserving the earth's waters for future generations.

The world's attention is focused on the outcome of the Blue Economy conference in Nairobi due to the importance of the oceans and inland waters. Over 80 percent of World trade merchandise is moved by water and thus maritime transport is major international trade facilitation Offshore Technology (2018).

The Blue Economy strengthens partnerships built on existing maritime, riparian, lacustrine, and river basin cooperation mechanisms which has a high possibility to produce growth in the economic development of individual States and the expansion of progress, peace, and prosperity across the continent.

Blue Economy also addresses inherent financial, technical, and infrastructure gaps of individual States by creating economies of scales that prevent the realization of the full potential of their aquatic and marine resources. To realize the full advantages and importance of the Blue Economy, there has to be delimitation of maritime boundaries. There has to be joint development, regional co-operation and states are encouraged to resolve their disputes by using existing instruments, including third-party dispute settlement procedures, such as international courts or tribunals.

On the issue of co-operation and balanced approach to the Blue Economy, some options must be considered by States such as:

- Ensure the existence of interdependence between security and development as vital keys to achieving sustainable peace.
- Create opportunities to enhance livelihood and well-being of coastal, lacustrine, and riparian populations.
- Ratify and implement relevant international and regional instruments related to maritime safety and security, as well as illegal practices, and harmonize national legislation with their provisions.
- Foster social inclusion such as local communities, youths, women and minority groups.
- Strengthen continental, sub-regional, and transnational cooperation mechanisms for preventive diplomacy and mediation, for the maintenance of international peace and security, conflict resolution, and the sharing of relevant information.

Legal and Institutional Framework of Blue Economy

Under International Law, state parties have rights, jurisdictions and responsibilities on issues relating to the peaceful use of oceans as stated under the United Nations Convention on the Law of the Sea (UNCLOS, 1982). A Blue Economy policy articulates the policy direction of littoral states, although landlocked states can also emplace Blue Economy Policies subject to the provisions of UNCLOS for the attainment of sustainable development from the ocean.

UNCLOS answers critical legal questions on the delineation of maritime zones and the extent of the territorial boundaries of adjoining coastal states. It also highlights other provisions of nonliving resources within the seafloor, the obligation for the protection and preservation of the marine environment, provisions on the transfer of marine technology, marine scientific research among others. UNCLOS established the ocean governance framework which provides for cooperation amongst states and the promotion of peace, socioeconomic progress and sustainable development of the oceans and seas.

The Blue Economy legal framework connotes legislative enactments for the establishment of Blue Economy under 3 balanced dimensions (economy, environment and society). To this end, South Africa established the Ocean Act and the Integrated Ocean Governance Regime to give Operation Phakisa the force of law as a blue economy component of South Africa's national development plan 2030. Similarly, the United States of America Magnuson – Stevens Fisheries Conservation and Management Act (MSA)

1976 was amended in 2007 to achieve long term sustainability in Fisheries. In Nigeria, shipping and fisheries sectors are the two developed maritime economy with no single Comprehensive Policy bridging these two sectors. There is no fusion of policies between key maritime stakeholders in Nigeria and this does not allow for synergized ocean economy development and accountability.

Some of Nigeria's shipping and fisheries laws have generated areas of operational conflict and duplication of statutory functions while others are simply obsolete.

BLUE ECONOMY AS A STRUCTURE FOR SUSTAINABLE DEVELOPMENT

Sustainable development implies that economic development is both inclusive and environmentally sound, and to be undertaken in a manner that does not deplete the natural resources that societies depend on in the long term. The key component of the blue economy lies in the balance of economic, social, and environmental dimensions of sustainable development. The Blue Economy since pioneered by SIDS has become relevant to all coastal states and countries with an interest in waters beyond national jurisdiction and more. The concept of Blue Economy constitutes a sustainable development structure for developing countries to address equity in access, development and the sharing of benefits from marine resources; also offers scope for human development reinvestment and the alleviation of national debt burdens. An effective and sustainable Blue Economy will entail preserving socioeconomic development from environmental degradation; efficient and optimized use of resources; regards for environmental and ecological parameters; sustainable use of biodiversity; advancement of the narrow resource base; environmentally sound, and socially inclusive economic growth.

The World Bank identified four (4) major points in ensuring sustainable Blue Economy and improving the growth potential of the Blue Economy.

1. Investment in good governance – According to the World Bank, a good investment in governance will protect resources for future growth and create numerous opportunities to grow the blue economy for the benefits of both national economies and local communities. It will promote sustainable management of aquatic resources, ensure resilience of biodiversity and ecosystem, empower local communities, reduce risk and provide incentives for innovation by private sector investors. Effective governance will also enhance the contribution of fisheries, aquaculture and mariculture to the macroeconomy.
2. Technology – The World Bank states that the vital use of science, data and technology is critical to influence decision making, reform governance and discern the impact of any management changes. A credible information and data base will foster effective and defensible fisheries conservation and management measures. In addition, to sustain aquaculture, its environmental impacts must be measured, understood and limited.
3. Market – The improvement of market infrastructure and access will benefit the poor and create more sustainable outcomes. There will be creation of incentives for good practices and drive for new investment opportunities if there is heavy investment in market demand for sustainable seafood. Another critical step is to coordinate among investors, public funding agencies, and philanthropic donors to develop new deal structures that sequence or layer investments so that those with greater risk tolerance can begin to engage with fisheries.

4. Finance - To reduce risk and ensure the development of bankable investments, there must be improved governance and incentives that align natural capital with investment capital, and secure returnable finance that will contribute significantly to the growth of blue economy. For more sustainable fisheries, especially at the global level, there is need to increase the number of potential investors that will support social and environmental impacts.

PRINCIPLES OF A SUSTAINABLE BLUE ECONOMY

1. A Sustainable Blue economy is a marine-based economy that provides social and economic benefits for current and future generations. It seeks to restores, protect and maintain the diversity, productivity, resilience, core functions and intrinsic value of marine ecosystem leveraging clean technologies, renewable energy and circular material flows.
2. A Sustainable Blue economy is governed by public and private processes that are inclusive well-informed, precautionary and adaptive. It is also accountable and transparent; holistic, cross-sectorial and long term, innovative and proactive.
3. To create a Sustainable Blue economy, public and private actors must set clear, measurable and internally consistent goals and target for a sustainable Blue economy. Assess and communicate their performance on these goals and targets. Besides, it creates a level economic and legislative playing field that provides the Blue economy with adequate incentives and rules. Additionally, it plans, manages and effectively governs the use of marine space and resources, applying inclusive methods and ecosystem approach based on standards, guidelines and best practices. The principle recognize that the maritime and land-based economies are interlinked and that many of the threats facing marine environments originate on land. Moreover, the principle encourages active cooperate in sharing information, knowledge, best practices, lessons learned, perspective and ideas to realize a sustainable and prosperous future for all.

SOLUTIONS AND RECOMMENDATIONS

It is obvious from the critical discourse that BE presents lots of opportunities that are yet to be accomplished or fully harnessed. Activities that hindered BE are so numerous and has to be properly taken care. There should proper monitoring to all economics aspect of the ocean and all form of corruptions must be combated. Unemployment and underemployment is very prevalent in Nigeria and Youth should be encourage to take full advantage of the ocean by engaging in legit businesses that will further enhance the economy of the nation. Evidence from advanced economy shows that BE employs over 275 million youth. Efforts should be geared towards investing heavily in tourism, biotech and biodiversity, renewable energy and acquaculture and other sustainable businesses by the policymakers at the levels of government in Nigeria. Additionally, there should partnership with foreign investors with local, multinationals and private investors that will aid the implementation of favorable policies that will support their growth. It is pertinent to mention the need for strong support for a diversified sustainable blue economy and the integration of traditional and emerging sectors in the Blue Economy through the support of policy makers on flexible maritime policy, secured and protected maritime areas and maritime spatial planning.

FUTURE RESEARCH DIRECTIONS

Future research should focus more on the local sea ports and upgrading it to standard as compare to other developing nations like Ghana and all forms of atrocities happening in the ocean arena should be well research.

CONCLUSION

The overall objective of this study was to explore Nigeria's Blue Economy potential with particular reference to Foreign Direct Investment as best investment option. This study also highlight the potential threats to Nigeria oceans and coasts which jeopardize its full effectiveness to local, national and foreign polices roadmaps for sustainable ocean governance. Nigeria policy makers recognizes the significant impact of the ocean which calls for enactment of policies in favor of BE, but unfortunately, it lacks gratification.

The study also shows there is strong link between economic advancement that demands for youth participation int the ocean-related activities as entrepreneur with lots promising futures promises as compared to green-economy. Nigeria is recognized as rightly blesses among other developing countries oceanwise but still needs better insights from countries like China and South Africa. The potential opportunity for sustainable blue economy activities will include the application of Integrated Coastal Management (ICM), Ecosystem-based Management (EBM) and the establishment of special forces that protect the maritime areas, i.e., Maritime officers.

REFERENCES

Abdullahel, B. (2017). Our Oceans and the blue economy: opportunities and challenges. *10th International Conference on Marine Technology*.

Cantwell, M. (2009). *The blue economy: the role of the Oceans in our Nation's Economic Future*. U.S. Committee on Commerce, Science, and Transportation United States Senate One Hundred Eleventh Congress. Government Printing Office.

Chang. (2015). *A Preliminary Assessment of the Blue Economy in South Korea*. Powerpoint presented in the Inception Workshop on Blue Economy Assessment, Manila.

Chircop, A., Dzidzornu, D., & Oguamanam, C. (2016). Ocean law reform: A multilevel comparative law analysis of nigerian maritime zone legislation. *Marine Policy*, *67*, 60–75.

Concepcion, G. P. (2008). *Marine Biodiversity and Marine Biotechnology: A Philippine Competitive Advantage. In Selected Essays on Science and Technology for Securing a Better Philippines*. Department of Science and Technology.

Costa, J. A. V., de Freitas, B. C. B., Lisboa, C. R., Santos, T. D., de Fraga Brusch, L. R., & de Morais, M. G. (2019). Microalgal biorefinery from CO2 and the effects under the blue economy. *Renewable & Sustainable Energy Reviews*, *99*, 58–65.

European Commission. (2020). *The EU blue economy report*. Publications Office of the European Union. .2771/073370 doi:https://doi.org/10

Fahrudin, A. (2015). *Indonesian Ocean Economy and Ocean Health*. Powerpoint presented in the Inception Workshop on Blue Economy Assessment, Manila.

Geissdoerfer, M., Savaget, P., Bocken, N. M., & Hultink, E. J. (2017). The circular economy—A new sustainability paradigm? *Journal of Cleaner Production, 143*, 757–768.

Geology.com. (2022). *Nigeria Map and Satellite Image*. https://geology.com/world/nigeria-satellite-image.shtml

Graziano, M., Alexander, K. A., Liesch, M., Lema, E., & Torres, J. A. (2019). Understanding an emerging economic discourse through regional analysis: Blue economy clusters in the US Great Lakes basin. *Applied Geography (Sevenoaks, England), 105*, 111–123.

Grunberg, L. (1991). The Changing International Political Economy of Multinational Corporations. In *Introduction to International Political Economy*. Prentice Hall.

Hoegh-Guldberg, O. (2015). *Reviving the Ocean Economy: the Case for Action – 2015*. Academic Press.

Ite, A. E., Ibok, U. J., Ite, M. U., & Petters, S. W. (2013). Petroleum exploration and production: Past and present environmental issues in the Nigeria's Niger delta. *American Journal of Environmental Protection*, *1*(4), 78–90.

Joroff, M. (2009). The Blue Economy: Sustainable industrialization of the oceans. *International Symposium on Blue Economy Initiative for Green Growth,* 173–181.

Kaczynski, W. (2011). The future of the blue economy: Lessons for the European Union. *Found Manag*, *3*(1), 21–32.

Kumar, K. (1982). Third World Multinationals. International Studies Quarterly, 26(3), 397 – 424.

Lee, K., Noh, J., & Khim, J. S. (2020). The blue economy and the United Nations' sustainable development goals: challenges and opportunities. *Environ Int*. .1016/j.envint.2020.105528 doi:https://doi.org/10

Nwilo, P. C., & Badejo, O. T. (2006a). *Impacts and management of oil spill pollution along the Nigerian coastal areas*. Academic Press.

Offshore Technology. (2018). *Nigeria tops countries with largest remaining deepwater oil reserves*. Offshore Technology. Available at https://www.offshore-technology.com/comment/nigeria-tops-countries-largestremaining-\deepwater-oil-reserves/

Phelan, A., Ruhanen, L., & Mair, J. (2020). Ecosystem services approach for community-based ecotourism: Towards an equitable and sustainable blue economy. *Journal of Sustainable Tourism*, *28*, 1–21.

Rose-Ackerman, S. (1997). The political economy of corruption. *Corruption and the Global Economy*, *31*, 60.

Sanusi, L. S. (2010). Growth prospects for the Nigerian economy. Eighth Convocation Lecture of the Igbinedion University, Okada, Nigeria.

Schutter, M. S., & Hicks, C. C. (2019). Networking the blue economy in Seychelles: Pioneers, resistance, and the power of influence. *J Political Eco*, *26*(1), 425–447.

Spamer, J. (2015). Riding the African blue economy wave: a South African perspective. In *2015 4th international conference on advanced logistics and transport (ICALT)*. IEEE. .1109/ICAdLT. 2015.7136591 doi:https://doi.org/10

United Nations Environment Programme. (2015). *Blue Economy: Sharing Success Stories Inspire Change*. UNEP Regional Seas Report.

World Bank. (2013). *Fish to 2030—prospects for fisheries and aquaculture*. World Bank Report Number 83177-GLB.

World Population Review. (2019). *Nigeria Population 2019*. World Population.

KEY TERMS AND DEFINITIONS

GDP: Gross domestic product.

Marine Environment (ME): Can be described as the oceans, seas, bays, estuaries, and other major water bodies, including their surface interface and interaction with the atmosphere and with the land seaward of the mean high-water mark.

OWF: Offshore Wind Farm

Sustainable Development: Sustainable development is development that meets the needs of the present, without compromising the ability of future generations to meet their own needs.

Chapter 9
Women's Blue Entrepreneurship Economic Empowerment Strategy

Shefiu Raheem
Yaba College of Technology, Nigeria

ABSTRACT

There is a growing attestation from development scholars and policymakers across the globe that blue entrepreneurship is a powerful tool for furthering economic empowerment, poverty alleviation, employment creation, sustainable development, among others. To enrich the discourse of blue entrepreneurship beyond conjecture, this chapter discusses the phenomenon of women blue entrepreneurship as a novel economic empowerment strategy in the developing context. It explicates that abundant oceanic resources in coastal countries have for long been used sustainably by women entrepreneurs for augmenting Earth's future prosperity, promoting welfare enhancement and tackling growing gender inequalities. Overall, the chapter outlines the contributions of women in onshore fisheries, aquaculture, processing of marine products, managing plastic on the sea through waste recycling, eco-tourism, conservation, and disaster-risk reduction initiatives in marine and coastal areas.

INTRODUCTION

In the development literature, the blue economy, otherwise called the ocean economy, is receiving serious attention. Blue economy refers to "a subset of, and complement to, the evolving development paradigm emphasising greener and more sustainable and inclusive economic paths. Practically, the emphasis on the blue economy is a proactive attempt to expand the economic frontiers of coastal countries beyond their land territories. Ocean health is important; hence, the United Nations' sustainable development goal (SDG) agenda designated SDG 14 as *life below water to* protect the planet for future generations. The ocean economy encompasses a sustainable economy based on marine environment, related biodiversity, ecosystems, species and genetic resources including marine living organisms (from fish and

DOI: 10.4018/978-1-6684-3393-5.ch009

algae to microorganisms) and natural resources in the seabed, while ensuring their sustainable use and hence conservation."

The contribution of the ocean economy to global GDP has rarely been measured, although a number of recent estimates have been made generally on the order of some US$1.5 to 3 trillion annually, or approximately 3 to 5 percent (see Global Ocean Commission 2014a; Hoegh-Guldberg et al. 2015). Subsequent to these estimates, the most extensive effort to date has been the development of an Ocean Economy Database by the OECD, conservatively a contribution in 2010 on the order of US$1.5 trillion in value added (or 2.5 percent of world gross value added) (OECD 2016). The relative contribution of the ocean economy is much higher in a number of coastal and island states with large ocean areas, for example, providing an estimated 10 percent of China's GDP in 2014.

Blue entrepreneurship evolves from the concept of blue economy. The World Bank defines the blue economy as 'comprising the range of economic sectors and related policies that together determine whether the use of oceanic resources is sustainable. There is now increasing recognition that sustainable and integrated marine and coastal ecosystem management requires gender-sensitive and gender-responsive planning, implementation, monitoring and evaluation at the project, policy and grassroots levels. This recognition is evident in the Call for Action issued by Member States at the UN Conference to Support the Implementation of Sustainable Development Goal 14 (UN Ocean Conference) held in June 2017, which highlighted the crucial role of women in the implementation of Sustainable Development Goal 14, "Conserve and sustainably use the oceans, seas and marine resources for sustainable development".

The participation of women in maritime activity has been encouraged and well endorsed by the African Union (AU). Inspired by calls made by the Chairperson of the African Union, Dr Nkosazana Dlamini Zuma, to maritime associations for women, the Women in Maritime Association – Angola hosted the first seminar for women in African Maritime in Luanda, Angola. The theme 'African Maritime Women: Towards Africa's Blue Economy 2050 AIM strategy and Agenda 2063' was in line with the focus of the 2015 ordinary sessions of the AU assembly. Based on the foregoing, this chapter discusses the phenomenon of women blue entrepreneurship as a novel economic empowerment strategy in the developing context. In specific terms, the chapter seeks to outline the contributions of women in marine and coastal areas. The abundant resources and new economic opportunities inherent in the blue economy are depicted in Figure 1 below.

BACKGROUND ON WOMEN IN MARITIME ACTIVITIES TODAY

For ages, women have been very active in coastal countries. Unfortunately, the contributions of women in onshore fisheries, aquaculture, processing and trading of marine products, in managing plastic and other waste from urban and tourist growth, and their important role in conservation and disaster-risk reduction initiatives in marine and coastal areas have been routinely ignored or underestimated in research, management and policy. Women have maintained close relationship with ocean and sea for ages as shown Figure 2 below. They fish, trade and conserve ocean resources for existential purposes.

The African Union (AU) has done well to draw attention to the need for more women in the African maritime sector by facilitating spaces of dialogue and information sharing and promoting a blue economy that is based on gender equitable human capital. However, in reality, only two percent of the world's maritime workforce is composed of women.

Figure 1.
Source: World Bank 2016)

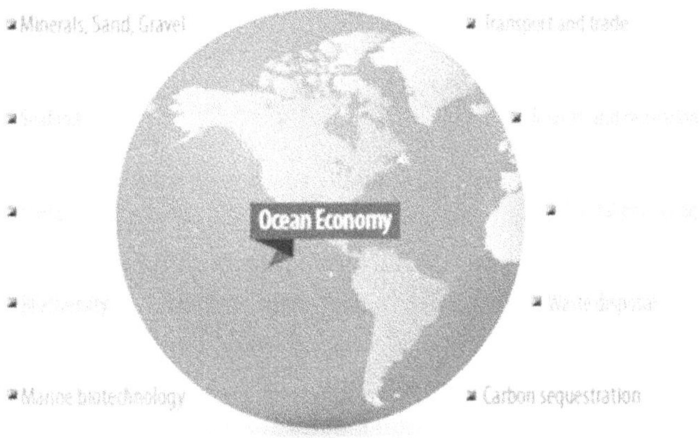

The protection of women's rights in the maritime sector needs more exposure in both regional maritime frameworks and the AIMS 2050. The regional maritime frameworks present a largely securitized approach that places the state as the referent object of security and therefore lacks an important 'people-to-people' component that advocates for more of a human security element.

RESEARCH METHODOLOGY

This chapter adopted a qualitative research design that entailed a critical review of the literature on women's blue entrepreneurship's economic empowerment strategy and how the blue economy could be deployed effectively to emancipate the womenfolk from excruciating poverty. The study adopted a

Figure 2.
Source: World Bank (2016)

conceptual approach. The use of systematic literature reviews as adopted in this chapter is consistent with the best practice social and management research (Bryman & Bell, 2007; Bryman, 2008).

OCEANS AND SEAS AND THE CONCEPT OF GENDER MAINSTREAMING

For centuries, oceans, seas and marine and coastal resources have sustained our world and life on it. Forming the largest ecosystem on the planet, they play a major role in providing food, livelihoods, income and recreation for people, as well as transport, telecommunication and energy. Oceans generate approximately 16% of animal protein for the human diet worldwide, and in many countries, the figure is 50%. Over 3 billion people across the world depend on coastal and marine resources for income and livelihood3. Increasingly, they are being valued for the essential ecosystem functions they fulfil by regulating temperatures, producing oxygen, acting as natural sinks for carbon dioxide from the atmosphere and protecting coastal areas from flooding and erosion. Oceans and seas absorb approximately 30 percent of the carbon dioxide produced by humans and contribute an estimated $24 trillion to the global economy each year through ecosystem services. Marine and coastal resources are scarce and deteriorate at an alarming rate under increasing pressure from population growth, overfishing, industrial and urban expansion, tourism and climate change, causing irreversible damage to marine and coastal biodiversity and ecosystems. Thirty percent of the world's fish stock is being overexploited, and there has been a 26 percent rise in ocean acidification since the beginning of the industrial revolution. Marine pollution is reaching alarming levels, with 4.8 to 12.7 million tonnes of plastic waste entering the ocean in 2010, numbers that are predicted to double by 2025. Mainstreaming gender in coastal and marine ecosystem management has two major components:

- First, women and men have common but also different needs, interests, knowledge, skills, and responsibilities in relation to the use and management of coastal and marine resources. Unequal valuation of women's work and skills and lack of consideration of their needs and interests, at macro and microlevels, has historically undermined women's power, income, decision-making and enjoyment of benefits and status in marine and coastal development.
- The second component involves working with this recognition to devise ***practical strategies*** that make women's as well as men's concerns and experiences an integral part of coastal and marine policy and project formulation, implementation, monitoring and evaluation. This is so that women and men benefit from and contribute equally to sustainable coastal and marine ecosystem management that women are supported in their empowerment, and gender and social inequality are not perpetuated.

On the one hand, women and marginal groups will benefit from improved marine development if the two mentioned components are taken into account, and on the other hand, oceans and seas will deteriorate less or even recover if women and vulnerable groups are more involved in marine development.

Figure 3.
Source: World Bank 2016)

GENDER AND OCEANS IN THE 2030 AGENDA SDGS

Both the sustainable management of oceans, seas and marine resources as well as gender equality and women's empowerment are central to the five pillars that underpin the 2030 Sustainable Development Agenda as depicted in Figure 3.

However, while this is explicitly recognised through a dedicated goal for gender equality and empowerment of women and girls – SDG 5 – and another one for the conservation and sustainable management of oceans, seas and marine resources – SDG 14 – the two goals are distinct even though their synergetic implementation is needed to holistically achieve sustainable development. The need for this was signaled at the UN Ocean Conference, where Member states underlined the "crucial role of women in the conservation and sustainable use of oceans, seas and marine resources for sustainable development" in the Call for Action.

THE CONCEPT OF A 'BLUE ECONOMY'

With the simultaneous growth of (a) the ocean economy and (b) the current rate of change to the ocean's ecological systems, the concept emerging worldwide over the last decade for a 'green economy' and 'green growth' has become a more widely used lens for viewing the risks and opportunities in the ocean. The term was featured prominently, for example, in the outcome statement by countries at the Rio+20 Earth Summit in 2012, as a tool for policymaking that provides a lens for looking at economic and environmental policy together—focusing on economic growth without a reduction in aggregate natural capital and the link between poverty reduction and conservation of ecological commons.

Women are hence increasingly present in several spheres of maritime trade, whether as top management administrators in the maritime or port administration, as top executives in ship owning or ship management companies or involved at high levels of management in other ancillary maritime activities. It can even be said that women are now playing a preponderant role in the development of the maritime sector, and an increasing number of them gather knowledge and experience in this different segment of shipping.

The change in the culture and mindset of local communities has helped bring women into this new business environment. More efforts are needed, however, to ensure sustained support and incentives to encourage women to join this sector, which includes attracting women to opt for maritime-focused education and training, as the careers that may be embraced within the maritime industry are varied. The journey is still long before we reach the point where men and women will be equally represented in the shipping sector, but to achieve an inclusive shipping sector and an inclusive blue economy, this is what we need to strive for.

The slogan for the Sustainable Development Goals (SDGs) – *leave no one behind* – draws attention to marginalized and excluded groups in society, one of which is women. Their active participation in the maritime sector is low, and they remain a male-dominated space.

Women are continually hindered by discrimination, legal barriers and harassment at their workplace that restrict their ability to meaningfully participate within maritime industries, leading to their marginalisation or exclusion. Another reason for gender inequality within the maritime sector is the numerous assumptions made about the roles, responsibilities and identities of men and women. These assumptions stem from a complex combination of historical and traditional cultural traits, pervasive work culture and societal barriers.

The maritime environment is male-dominated, and women's inclusion into the maritime sector remains a challenge. There are a number of cultural, structural and workplace barriers that render the maritime environment unattractive to many women. Comprehensive changes need to take place, not only within the maritime sector but also within societies, to create conditions conducive to women's inclusion and meaningful participation.

Women currently make up approximately 2% of the world's seafarer workforce, and their experiences are seldom considered in the design, development, or implementation of maritime programmes and policies.

Even when a government enacts laws against discrimination based on sex or gender, such as the South African National Policy Framework for Women's Empowerment and Gender Equality, this rarely extends into the maritime space. Women's contributions often go unacknowledged, which results in a low policy prioritisation for addressing gender inequality issues. Evidence suggests that utilising women's potential as leaders, economic actors and consumers will result in higher levels of industrialization and sustained growth. If more women are allowed to participate in the same roles as men in the markets, global GDP could increase by 25% by 2025.There have been some notable achievements recently. The underrepresentation of women in the maritime industry has not changed greatly over the past decade. Within maritime and related industries such as seafarers, port operators and government officials, there is a gender gap, and most senior positions remain male-dominated. The issue of women's representation and inclusion is not unique to the maritime sector.

Women and men use and manage marine and coastal ecosystems differently, have specific knowledge, capabilities and needs related to this and are differently impacted by changes in their environment due to climate change, pollution, and globalisation. Historically, the contributions of women in onshore fisheries, aquaculture, processing and trading of marine products, in managing plastic and other waste from urban and tourist growth, and their important role in conservation and disaster-risk reduction initiatives in marine and coastal areas have been routinely ignored or underestimated in research, management and policy.

There is now increasing recognition that sustainable and integrated marine and coastal ecosystem management requires gender-sensitive and gender-responsive planning, implementation, monitoring and evaluation at the project, policy and grassroots levels. This recognition is evident in the Call for Action1 issued by Member States at the UN Conference to Support the Implementation of Sustainable Development Goal 14 (UN Ocean Conference) held in June 2017, which highlighted the crucial role of women in the implementation of Sustainable Development Goal 14: "Conserve and sustainably use the oceans, seas and marine resources for sustainable development".

THE POTENTIAL OF BLUE ECONOMY FOR GENDER EQUALITY

The potential of the blue economy to benefit the human population is far more than what has been realised. The diverse varieties of jobs and sources of income that the blue economy offers can promote gender equality. Economies of the scale of US$ 3–6 trillion/year, as mentioned above, and where strong economic sectors are emerging outside the traditional domain of shipping and fishing that have been dominated by men, offer immense opportunities for gender equality. The OECD (2016a) report contains facts and figures that suggest the enormous potential of ocean-based industries in terms of value added and employment. The projections presented indicate that between 2010 and 2030 on a "business-as-usual" scenario basis, the ocean economy could more than double its contribution to global value added.

Undoubtedly, women accounting for almost half of the world's population stand to gain from the growth of the blue economy. There are strong driving forces in many ocean-related services and industrial sectors that have shaped up as engines of blue growth and created enormous opportunities. These vital sectors of economy and community welfare are likely to continue their development trajectories and offer gender-inclusive opportunities.

The two great sectors of the blue economy, namely, fisheries and aquaculture, are well established. Data collection in these sectors has been fairly comprehensive because of its importance to the general public, the diverse nature of the enterprises, the gender policies of international agencies such as the Food and Agriculture Organisation of the United Nations, and the national policies of many countries aimed at social welfare. The most recent statistics provided by FAO (2018) indicate that the primary sector of capture fisheries and aquaculture provided jobs to 59.6 million people in 2016. Of this total number, 40.3 million people were engaged in fisheries and 19.3 million in aquaculture.

Analysis of employment trends in these sectors suggests that the proportion of people employed in capture fisheries declined from 83% in 1990 to 68% in 2016. On the other hand, the proportions of those working in aquaculture correspondingly increased from 17% to 32%. This is because the contribution of aquaculture to global production by capture fisheries and aquaculture has increased steadily, reaching 46.8% in 2016, up from 25.7% of its value in 2000 (FAO 2018).

GENDER ROLES IN INCLUSIVE BLUE ECONOMY

The male and female population have very important roles to play in the emerging blue economy. The role includes working collaboratively toward developing an enduring blue economy; utilising and exploiting the oceans and their abundant resources for human development; preserving and conserving the oceans and their resources for the present and future generation; and working at ensuring strong governance in the blue economy. Table 1 below explains the components of the blue economy.

BENEFITS OF BLUE OCEAN FOR WOMEN, YOUTH, INDIGENOUS GROUPS AND MIGRANTS

Blue growth promotes the sustainable development of aquatic resources for the benefit of communities that rely on them for their livelihoods and food security. It seeks to maximise economic and social benefits while minimising environmental degradation from activities within the fisheries and aquaculture sector.

Table 1. Components of the blue economy

Type of activity	Ocean service	Industry	Drivers of growth
Harvesting of living resources	Seafood	Fisheries	Food security
		Aquaculture	Demand for protein
	Marine biotechnology	Pharmaceuticals, chemicals	Research and development for healthcare and industry
Extraction of nonliving resources, generation of new resources	Minerals	Seabed mining	Demand for minerals
	Energy	Oil and gas	Demand for alternative energy sources
		Renewables	
	Freshwater	Desalination	Demand for freshwater
Commerce and trade in and around the oceans	Transport and trade	Shipping	Growth in seaborne trade; international regulations
		Port infrastructure and services	
	Tourism and recreation	Tourism	Growth of global tourism
		Coastal development	Coastal urbanization
			Domestic regulations
Response to ocean health challenges	Ocean monitoring and surveillance	Technology research and industry	Research and industry in ocean technologies
	Carbon sequestration	Blue carbon	Growth in coastal and ocean protection and conservation activities
	Coastal protection	Habitat protection and restoration	
	Waste disposal	Assimilation of nutrients and wastes	

Source: World Bank 2016

These goals are closely aligned with the three pillars of the 2030 Agenda for Sustainable Development and its Sustainable Development Goals (SDGs), which pay special attention to traditionally marginalized groups. Analysing the needs and interests of women, youth, indigenous peoples and migrants is central to the Blue Growth approach.

Women play a key role in the fisheries and aquaculture value chain, and yet their contribution is often overlooked or undervalued. As a result, many women working in the sector have limited access to natural resources, credit, + technology and training, mobility and bargaining power. They also face discrimination in rights to land or fishing grounds. Existing power structures combined with financial and social capital constraints often limit women's ability to obtain fish and sell the products of their labour at a fair price. This inequality of access to fisheries resources greatly undermines women's productivity and results in substantial postharvest losses with negative implications for food security and nutrition.

THE BLUE ECONOMY AND WOMEN'S ECONOMIC EMPOWERMENT

The blue economy is a concept that looks to advance economic development and social inclusion and to enhance livelihoods while working to ensure the environmental sustainability of the oceans and coastal territories (World Bank, 2017: . At its core lies the commitment "to decouple socioeconomic development from environmental degradation, by the incorporation of the real value of the natural capital (ocean values and services) into all aspects of economic activity" (World Bank, 2017: vi). A key component of

Figure 4.
SOURCE: Foreign and Commonwealth office: A Blue Economy for Women's Economic Empowerment, nd

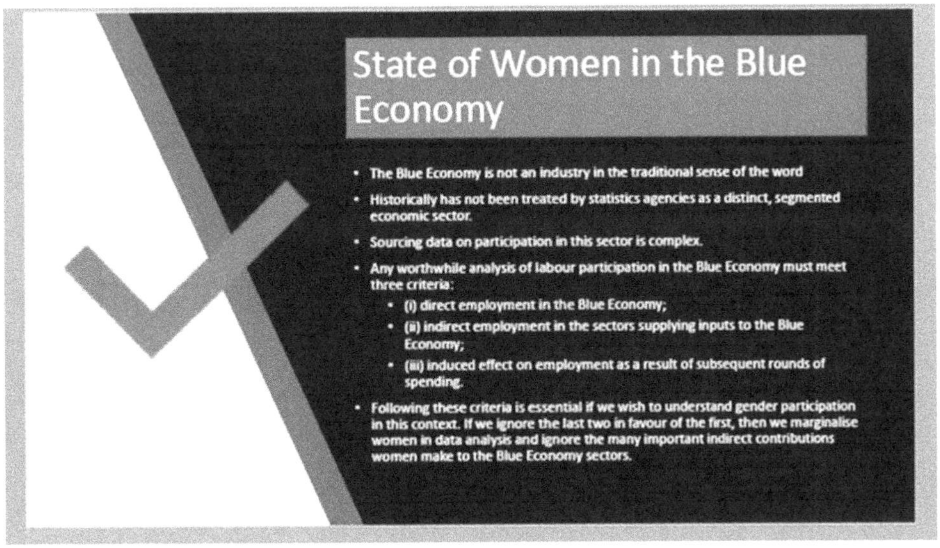

the blue economy is its emphasis on recognising that the ecosystem services provided by the ocean are essential global priorities and have both intrinsic and fiscal qualities that support well-being and development. This is a considerable shift from the "traditional 'brown – high energy, low employment and industrialized development' model, which considers seas and oceans as a free resource extraction and waste dumping, where environmental costs are externalized from economic calculations" (Blue Economy Project, 2016: However, it has also been noted that there is a need to ensure "equitable access to marine resources even as we put in place measures to better manage that access to reduce unsustainable use. As an alternative model of development – what has been termed a "paradigm shift" by some economists – the idea that the blue economy may generate employment and facilitate inclusive and sustainable growth dominates international policy discourse. Africa has a coastline of approximately 26 000 nautical miles, with 90% of its trade conducted at sea. The importance of the oceans allows Africa to sustainably use its marine resources to shift the paradigms of power in an increasingly unequal global sphere. In viewing the ocean as a historical space of exchange, diplomacy and development, the importance of human rights is relevant here, as this is fundamental to ensuring the success of the abovementioned activities. Central to this is the protection of society's most vulnerable – women and children.

In 2015, the African Union (AU) paid special tribute to this by supporting the first ever conference for women in Africa's maritime sector in Angola in keeping with the theme of the 25th AU summit, *'Women's Empowerment and Development Towards Agenda 2063'*. This piece considers the progress that the AU has made in protecting and promoting the rights of women in the maritime sector and blue economy while also paying close attention to how this translates into positive developmental outcomes that are in line with Agenda 2063.

THE CONCEPT OF THE BLUE ECONOMY WOMEN'S EMPOWERMENT

Figure 5.
SOURCE: Foreign and Commonwealth office: A Blue Economy for Women's Economic Empowerment, nd

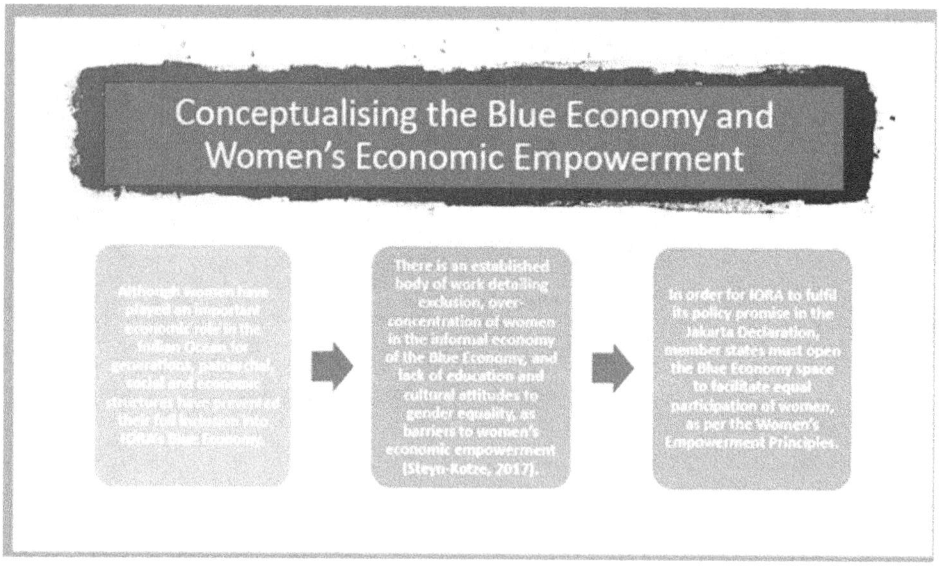

HISTORICAL LINKS OF WOMEN TO THE SEA: WEST AFRICA PERSPECTIVE

African women and maritime is an age-old theme in African history, although it has recently been invigorated through talks on the blue economy and overcoming what some refer to as 'sea blindness'. Zoning in on a specific case of the West African experience that exemplifies this, women were socialised to understand their environments and eco-systems through their own systems of indigenous knowledge. This meant that they knew how to address the challenges and sustainability of the ocean. In fact, sometimes referred to as the people of the riverine, women were already employing "rich harvesting techniques of the marine resources". Here, women were not only linked to the ocean in terms of survival but also displayed a strong spiritual connection to the ocean. If a woman was considered 'unstable' in society, she was thought to be troubled by a "marine spirit". The rights of African women in maritime therefore need to be understood in their historical context, which represented a deep rooted connection to the ocean. Unfortunately, there is a major gap in the scholarship and knowledge on African women and their historical experience and engagement in maritime. This historical experience needs to be invoked in the memory of Africans to merge historical experience and ownership with the current context and landscape to formulate a relevant and rights-based maritime policy framework.

Women in Nigeria play a key and vital role in the fisheries value chain in Nigeria, especially when we look at their involvement in the marine, artisanal and aquaculture subsector of the fisheries sector. The women who constitute the greater percentage of the fish mongers/processors represent the first segment of the fish market chain, buying fresh fish directly from the fishermen. The fish is either sold fresh by the women or processed by smoking. In the aquaculture sector, women also play key roles in buying and processing. The women in the fisheries value chain are grouped into Cooperatives Societies, although few that go solo. However, women's activities in the value chain are characterised by low capital and technology input. Women's work in the fish value chain has not been optimised/linked to value chain finance in Nigeria; thus, they are limited to various financial services being put up by the commercial banks for the Agricultural Sector in the country. This lack of corporate finance has in essence debared the women from upgrading their fisheries activities and businesses in the various steps along the fisheries value chain, and they have thus not been able to build sustainable and viable fish trade, especially in regard to the export of their fish and other fishery products.

Fish provide high quality, easily absorbable protein and a wide variety of vitamins and minerals, and even a small amount of fish is an important dietary protein supplement for poor people who cannot easily afford animal protein and who rely mainly on starch diets. "Fish is an important part of daily diet in many countries and provide nearly one quarter of world's supply of animal protein and in many countries fisheries are important sources of employments, income and foreign exchange" (FAO, 1984).

Fish trade, like any traded commodity, enhances living standards and sustainable development and contributes to the food security of a country. International fish trade (imports) has a positive impact on Nigeria's food security since Nigeria's fish demand cannot meet supplies; currently, from the Federal Department of Fisheries 2007 statistical data collation, the total fish demand for the country is 2.5 million metric tones per annum, while the total fish supply (domestic and imports) is 1.34 metric tones per annum. The overall assessment of both the export and import aspects of Nigeria's fish trade has shown a very positive outlook on outcomes related to the national impact of fisherfolks, fish workers, fish consumers, fish sellers and fisheries resources.

NIGERIAN FISHERIES SECTOR

Nigeria is located on the West Coast of Africa (West Africa); it is among the countries in the Gulf of Guinea and a key member of the Economic Community of West Africa (ECOWAS).

Nigeria has a continental shelf area of 37,934 km2 and a coastline length of 853 km. Aside from its marine waters, the country is also endowed with large numbers of bodies of waters – lakes and lagoons, dams, etc.; the Nigeria fisheries sector is thus made up of the following:

- Artisanal fisheries- consisting of coastal and brackish waters; inland rivers and lakes.
- Aquaculture (Fish Farm)
- Industrial (Commercial Trawlers) – this involves inshore fishing and shrimping, i.e., fishing between 5-20 nautical miles of our territorial waters. We also have an EEZ of 200 nautical miles where fishing also takes place, and
- Distant Waters – this involves Reefer vessels bringing in fish into Nigeria from other countries; termed imports.

FISH VALUE CHAIN PROCESSES AND ORGANIZATION OF WOMEN IN NIGERIA

Women in the Nigerian fisheries sector play a key and vital role in the fisheries value chain in Nigeria, especially when we look at their involvement in the fisheries sector. The women who constitute the greater percentage of the fish mongers/processors represent the first segment of the fish market chain; buying fresh fish directly from the producers as they land the fish at shores.

In the case of aquaculture production, women often buy fish directly at the farm gate. There are also a few women in aquaculture production in Nigeria. The fish bought by the women are either sold in fresh form, chilled, packed in ice, and as live fish as in aquaculture production. Often, the fish undergoes further processing by smoking before it is sold. In aquaculture, women play key roles in buying, processing and marketing.

On the whole, the women are involved from when the fish is landed at shore; farm gate in Aquaculture; thereafter the fish undergoes some basic or extensive processing, after which the first set of wholesaler women sell to other women/men retailers who in turn sell to consumers. The women wholesalers have more funds for the business than the retailers; however, their challenges are similar but to various degrees. Generally, the women have little capital or net worth to put up as collateral for financial institutions, and the financial institutions thus see them as too high a risk to be given a loan even at high interest rates.

Over the years, the Nigerian women in the fisheries value chain have been organised into fisheries cooperative society, although we have a very few that do not belong to any union but operate solo (alone) with their operation. Being members of cooperative societies has enabled the women to upgrade their status (to an extent), as members are able to get government and private sector assistance in terms of loans (though often this funds are not enough): subsidized inputs, capacity building, etc.

Additionally, these cooperative societies are often used to protect the interest of the members as well as to facilitate equitable dealings with their fish suppliers (especially in the industrial and Aquaculture Sector); for often the members of the cooperative societies are able to argue and stick to a certain price regime with the supplier rather than the other way round (for example, if their leaders insist that no members should buy the fish at a price above a certain margin, you can be sure none of their members will) – this in essence shows their power as being part of a cooperative society.

ROLES OF WOMEN IN FISHERIES

Women are less involved in fish trawling at sea and even artisanal fisheries in lakes because of its inherent dangers, long period of fishing voyage and their dominant role in household activities. Research findings have indicated that women have traditionally been occupied in pre- and postharvest processing of fish products, distribution and marketing of fish and other income-generating non-fisheries activities. Nwabeze (2010) explained that women perform the functions of auctioneers, retailers, fish vendors and dealers in export as explained below.

- **Feed Formulators**: Women are more involved in feed formulation and daily maintenance in homestead ponds. In Nigeria, many women (most of whom are members of the Lagos State Catfish Farmers Association and Fisheries Society of Nigeria) are involved in homestead fish rearing of African catfish (*Clarias gariepinus*).
- **Fish preservation, storage, marketing and packaging**: Smoking in artisanal fisheries is predominantly performed by women, as confirmed by various workers apart from postharvest ice storage, distribution, packaging and marketing.
- **Direct fishing**: The involvement of women in direct fishing using small-scale fishing gear such as pots, baskets, traps, fences, barriers and shelter, hooks and lines.

- **Sorting and transportation**: Fish are transported to market centres through open systems using open carriers with or without artificial aeration.

CONSTRAINTS FACED BY WOMEN IN FISHERY BUSINESS IN NIGERIA

Women face a number of challenges in fisheries business in Nigeria. Key challenges facing women include the following:

Low Participation in Decision Making due to Gender Inequality

In most patrilineal societies such as Nigeria, women are only to be seen and not heard; they are therefore not usually consulted before making decisions. Because of gender inequality in some communities in Nigeria, the efforts of women in fisheries are not recognised, no matter how hard they try because they are regarded as minorities. There is therefore a need for attitudinal changes.

Lack of Basic Education

This apathy towards women as equal partners in progress also contributed to the higher illiteracy level among female fisher folks. The age-old belief that women are weaker and meant only for procreation and culinary function should stop in the new millennium.

Lack of Land Ownership

Nigeria is a patrilineal society unlike Ghana and Rwanda, and rural women are often disadvantaged in terms of land accessibility. Only in very few states can women own land. The land tenure system does not favour women. Changing the land tenure system could greatly affect the status of women, thus making them go into fish farming.

Dearth of Social and Infrastructural Facilities

The presence of infrastructural facilities such as power, municipal water, good roads, and health centres in rural fishing communities could stimulate rural income and reduce fishing efforts and subsequently sustainability and development.

Restricted Access to Credit

This is a major barrier to the effective participation of women in fisheries. Generally, fisheries is considered a 'no go area' by most formal agric lending institutions in Nigeria, as confirmed by many workers. The low literacy level of women has always been a constraint on accessing funds from formalized sources. They have to depend on credit from friends and thrift to purchase fish inputs such as nets, boats, fertilisers, and feeds at subsidized rates. Cooperative society formation was recommended to facilitate better access to inputs. Bureaucratic bottlenecks such as collateral securities have further aggravated the situation and hence the need to train women. Past workers have confirmed women as being better managers of funds than their male counterparts. Women repay loans faster than their male counterparts (most of whom divert loans to ostentatious transactions).

BARRIERS OF WOMEN PARTICIPATION IN BLUE ECONOMY

The first set of barriers and opportunities is structural. The current blue growth narrative is framed in the context of the maximal exploitation of vastly untapped common goods via large investments with the assumption that this will create jobs for locals, small-scale fishers and women. However, most of the jobs created are low skilled, including cleaning and maintenance work. Big capital prevents, in fact, innovation from reaching small-scale fisheries and especially women who provide more than 85% of the landed catches, ensure food security and nutrition, and secure livelihoods and intraregional trade in Africa. Moreover, the market for licenses in the fisheries sector facilitates unregulated access to foreign fleets in a number of African countries' territorial waters or exclusive economic zones, with negative impacts on local catches and livelihoods. Finally, ecosystem degradation through large-scale activities has not been sufficiently addressed despite growing research evidence of impacts. A human rights approach to the governance of tenure, small-scale fisheries, the right to food and ecosystem conservation, and which explores its trade-off consistently is urgently needed. This requires the use of a political economy lens to dismantle the unequal distribution of wealth and resources and allow the modernization of small-scale economic activities.

The second set is social and cultural. Discriminatory gender and social norms prohibit women from participating in certain aspects of the blue economy and create an additional labour burden on them. Social attitudes frown on and punish women for being in certain spaces. For women to catalyse transformative chance, investments and innovations, we must think beyond just participation: in Malawi and Zambia, researchers have used processes designed to surface awareness of gender dynamics in the context and in relation to fish processing and spark local ideas for constructive shifts in cultural and social norms that marginalise women. The findings *challenge the 'business as usual' idea* that it is sufficient for projects to *include* women in order for research or development to be empowering and transform gender dynamics.

A third set of barriers is around capacity. Women engaged in the blue economy continue to face a lack of investments and access to capital and equipment to grow their businesses. In Kenya, in 2016, 80.9% of women-to-women business partnerships were denied loans, including by microfinance institutions. Women *are* building their capacity: now financial institutions need to start viewing their businesses as bankable and develop suitable products. In some countries, this has worked. The Bolivian Financial Institute for Development (CIDRE) developed innovative financial services, including equipment leasing for indigenous women and women's cooperatives working in the fisheries sector. CIDRE built two new agencies in the project area and placed two women in charge. Women are bankable, and in most cases, it is financial institutions that need to change become 'womenable' to address the priorities and needs of women.

Finally, there is a lack of women's voices in decision making. Women's movements are and will continue to play a key role in building women's voices to participate in development and planning processes and demanding accountability from governments. There are successful examples of organisations in Africa mobilising women to amplify their voices, including the Grassroots Organisations Operating Together in Sisterhood -GROOTS Kenya and the Katosi Women Development Trust in Uganda. While global threats, including climate change, will continue to threaten women's livelihoods, they also provide opportunities for the adoption of climate-resilient innovations while also opening up new roles for women. Research in the Volta Delta in Ghana has, for example, shown that as men migrate to look of off-farm seasonal opportunities, women become more empowered to make decisions and to engage in activities in fisheries that they would not otherwise engage in. The women's activities in the value chain are characterised by low capital and technology input. Most of their fish handling operations are without appropriate capacity to meet national and international sanitary and technical standards and hence possess low substantial benefit in fish trade.

Women's work in the fish value chain has not been optimised or linked to value chain finance in Nigeria; thus, they are limited to various financial services being put up by the commercial banks for the agricultural sector in the country. This lack of cooperative finance has in essence debared the women from upgrading their fisheries activities and businesses in the various steps along the fisheries value chain; therefore, they have not been able to build sustainable and viable fish trade, especially with regard to the export of fish and other fishery products.

SOLUTIONS AND RECOMMENDATIONS

The following recommendations are suggested in alignment with the Women's Empowerment Principles (WEPs) adopted in 2018 (inclusivity, equal opportunities, fairness, education, nondiscrimination, the creation of structures that are gender sensitive and other issues):

- *Generate evidence-based knowledge on the blue economy and women.*

Women are not a homogenous group. Efforts to differentiate the lived experiences of rural and urban women, among others, are crucial in bringing about inclusive policy development for sustainable development. Second, information regarding the involvement of women in the blue economy is not well documented. A scan of literature on the subject does not disaggregate data by gender. Where available, the data characterise women as a homogenous group. There is a need for governments to invest in research specifically focused on women and their contributions to real value. This would be a great starting point for understanding both the extent of their plight and their potential – and actual – contribution to sustainable socioeconomic development.

- *Enable the participation of women in blue economy policy-making processes.*

The objective of the blue economy is to 'promote economic growth, social inclusion, and the preservation or improvement of livelihoods while at the same time ensuring environmental sustainability of the oceans and coastal areas.

Breathing life into economic development opportunities at sea cannot happen without bringing women into the blue. Policymaking processes that seek to take advantage of economic opportunities offered by the blue economy should include the voices of all women, urban and rural – the latter being less vocal owing to higher levels of poverty, inequality and unemployment, which by default creates conditions for marginalisation.

Rural women should be well informed about participatory processes and their role through formal and/or informal consultative policy dialogues. Such participation should not only reflect the interests of upper-class and/or elite urban women but should also involve vulnerable and marginalized women from rural areas who are involved in the ocean space.

- *Create gender-sensitive institutions and transnational gender networks.*

Women'sparticipation in the blue economy is invisible, and where it is visible, it is confined to the 'nonmonetised core economy'. This has led to most women being pushed to the low levels of the value chain, with little or no social protection. The creation of gender-sensitive policies could assist in bringing women to the forefront of both the narrative and practice of the blue economy.

Gender barriers to women in the maritime sector in Africa need to be addressed urgently if women are to play a meaningful role in harnessing the potential of the blue economy

The conference also focused on attracting and targeting investments inclusive of poor and rural coastal women in the sectors of the blue economy to ensure equal access to resources and opportunities. It seems that a more collaborative approach, building on discursive practice and enabling transnational women's networks to engage in dialogue and interact, may be a viable gender justice option to consider.

- *Change the narrative of women as passive participants in development to women having agency to influence development in the blue economy*

The policy narrative on gender and development has the potential to shape women as passive recipients of development rather than active agents in advancing their own development through the opportunities presented by the Indian Ocean's blue economy.

- Other recommendations include: Prioritise capacity-building initiatives for officials and policy-makers on Women's Economic Empowerment through the Blue Economy; Awareness campaign for women to understand blue economy and roles to play in its development; Support and facilitate research collaboration on key sectors of the Blue Economy and women's participation rates in those sectors; Encourage academic collaborations and engage Ministries of Higher Education in member states to invest in research and academic mobility; Map and engage NGOs advancing women's issues within key Blue Economy sectors; Facilitate and increase women's representation at all IORA conferences, seminars, training programmes, and workshops and develop a matrix to capture relevant data on Women's Economic Empowerment through the Blue Economy

CONCLUSION

The rights of women in the maritime sector ultimately start with the rights of women on land, as maritime activity is essentially an extension of land-based activity. The sustained attention of the AU collaborating with the regional economic communities (RECS) and global maritime structures will go a long way to protect the rights of women at sea. African women have a historically organic and important link to the ocean, the memory of which needs to be invoked when harnessing the potential prospects and marine endowments of the African blue economy. The AU has done well to profile the importance of women in the blue economy and the realisation of Agenda 2063. However, this will only be effective if women's rights are protected in this space.

A global effort to protect ocean and ocean ecosystems is needed. There needs to be an improvement in engagement mechanisms, which includes all relevant actors to ensure proper stewardship of the ocean. The Blue Economy discourse at the moment excludes the very people who depend on coastal areas and marine resources for their livelihoods – indigenous peoples and local communities. They who live close to and have long depended on the ocean have spiritual, cultural and traditional links to the ocean, and their understanding and leadership must guide future ocean governance.

High-time women are considered equal partners in sustainable fisheries development in Nigeria. Women should never be seen as invincible but should be recognised as partners in progress towards sustainable fisheries development. They should be more involved in direct production, especially in the area of culture fisheries, which are more environmentally friendly and less risky than capture fisheries. Women should be encouraged through the introduction of specially designed programmes. Fishing inputs should be made available to all irrespective of sex. They should be encouraged to form cooperative associations that would facilitate cheaper and better access to credit and inputs at concessionary rates.

Policy makers should adopt the 'Bottom-Up approach', which is tailored to the needs of rural women/ fisher folks. They should be consulted during policy formulation because they are the stake holders. There is a need for gender-sensitiveness in Nigeria's move to sustainable fisheries development

The government should create a conducive enabling environment, such as the provision of social amenities in fishing communities. Despite being the major contributor to the domestic fish output, coastal communities lack basic infrastructural facilities such as power, postharvest storage structures, health centres, municipal waters and so on.

REFERENCES

Balogun, A. M. (2015). *The Fisheries subsector in a declining Oil-based Economy: Paradigm shift for Economic Diversification and Employment generation*. Keynote address at the 30th Annual Conference of Fisheries Society of Nigeria, Nigeria.

Blue Economy Department. (2018). *Seychelles Blue Economy, strategic policy framework and roadmap: charting the future*. Blue Economy Department.

Bolarinwa, J. B. (2014). Role of Extension Services and Public Relations in Nigerian Fisheries Industry. *International Journal of Agricultural Research*, *9*(7), 325–330. doi:10.3923/ijar.2014.325.330

Bolarinwa, J. B. (2015). *The ichthyofauna Resources of The Coastal waters of Ondo State, Nigeria* (PhD Thesis). Federal University of Technology, Akure, Nigeria.

Brown, C. J., Smith, S. J., Lawton, P., & Anderson, J. T. (2011). Benthic habitat mapping: A review of progress towards improved understanding of the spatial ecology of the seafloor using acoustic techniques. *Estuarine, Coastal and Shelf Science*, *92*(3), 502–520. doi:10.1016/j.ecss.2011.02.007

Bryman, A. (2008). *Social Research Methods* (Vol. 3). Oxford University Press Inc.

Bryman, A., & Bell, E. (2007). *Business research methods* (Vol. 2). Oxford University Press Inc.

Buhl-Mortensen, L., Olsen, E., Røttingen, I., Buhl-Mortensen, P., Hoel, A. H., Ringheim, L., & Cheke, A. O. (2012). Establishment of model Fish Market For Women. Fish handling and processing methods in Nigeria. NAFDAC Workshop on Fish Imports and Exports Procedures.

Cliffe, P. T., & Akinrotimi, O. A. (2015). The Role of Women in Fisheries activities in Some Coastal communities of Rivers State. *International Journal of Agricultural Research*, *10*(1), 24–32. doi:10.3923/ijar.2015.24.32

Dankelman, I. (2002). Climate change: Learning from gender analysis and women's experiences of organising for sustainable development. *Gender and Development*, *10*(2), 21–29. doi:10.1080/13552070215899

Elliot, M. (2002). *The role of women on fisheries*. Internet.

FAO. (2012). Strategies for Sustainable Animal Agriculture in Developing countries. *Proceedings of the FAO Expert Consultation, Animal Production and Health.*

FAO. (2018). *Blue Economy Project*. FAO.

FDF. (2010). *Fisheries Statistics of Nigeria* (5th ed.). Federal Department of Fisheries.

Federal Department of Fisheries. (n.d.). *Fisheries statistics of Nigeria; 1995 – 2007.* Author.

Gorman, G., & Clayton, P. (2005). Qualitative Research for the Information Professional, a practical handbook (2nd ed.). London: Facet Publishing.

Gulseven, O. (2020). Measuring achievements towards SDG 14, life below water, in the United Arab Emirates. *Marine Policy*, *117*, 103972. doi:10.1016/j.marpol.2020.103972

Gustafsson, B., Hermerén, G., & Petterson, B. (2011). *God Forskningssed.* Bromma: Vetenskapsrådet.

Hsieh, H.-F., & Shannon, S. E. (2005). Three Approaches to Qualitative Content Analysis. *Qualitative Health Research*, *15*(9), 1277–1288. doi:10.1177/1049732305276687 PMID:16204405

Huo, J. (2015). *How nations innovate* (Vol. 1). Oxford University Press. doi:10.1093/acprof:oso/9780198735847.001.0001

Jensen, R. (2012). Do labor market opportunities affect young women's work and family decisions? Experimental Evidence from India. *The Quarterly Journal of Economics*, *127*(2), 753.

Kathijotes, N. (2013). Keynote: Blue economy-environmental and behavioural aspects towards sustainable coastal development. *Procedia: Social and Behavioral Sciences*, *101*, 7–13.

Knol, M. (2010). Scientific advice in integrated ocean management: The process towards the Barents Sea plan. *Marine Policy*, *34*, 252–260.

Leech, B. L. (2002). Asking questions: Techniques for semistructured interviews. *PS, Political Science & Politics*, *35*(4), 665–668.

Leedy, P. D., & Ormrod, J. E. (2010). *Practical Research: Planning and Design* (Vol. 9). Pearson Education, Inc.

Ministry of Family Affairs. (2018). *The National Gender Policy, Republic of Seychelles*. Gender Equality Department.

Ministry of Foreign Affairs. (2010). *Seychelles Millennium Development Goals, status report 2010.* Ministry of Foreign Affairs.

Ministry of Foreign Affairs. (2014). The Blue Economy. Ministry of the Environment.

Momsen, J. (2010). *Gender and Development* (Vol. 2). Routledge.

Mortensen, D. T., & Pissarides, C. A. (1998). Technological progress, job creation, and job destruction. *Review of Economic Dynamics, 1*(4), 733–753.

Nation. (2013). *Seychelles ranks second in Africa for gender equality.* Retrieved 10 28, 2017, from Nation: https://www.nation.sc/article.html?id=239473

Nature Seychelles. (2014). *Blue Economy, nature inspired technologies to drive the economy forwards.* Retrieved 04 02, 2018, from Nature Seychelles: http://natureseychelles.org/what-we-do/blue-economy

Nwabueze, Eric, Ifejika, Ayanda, & Tafida. (2007). Strengthening Fisheries extension under a unified Agricultural Extension System. *UAES Proceeding of Fisheries Society of Nigeria.*

Nwabueze, A. A. (2010). The role of women in sustainable aquacultural development in Delta state. *Journal of Sustainable Development in Africa, 12*(5), 23–25.

Odili, O. E., Nwabeze, G. O., & Tafida, A. A. (2012). Contribution of women to Fisheries Development in Nigeria: A review. *27th Annual Conference of Fisheries Society of Nigeria Proceedings*, 435-437.

OECD. (2016). *Blue Economy*. OECD.

The Commonwealth. (2018). *Seychelles Blue Economy Strategic Roadmap and Implementation*. Retrieved 02 09, 2018, from The Commonwealth: https://thecommonwealth.org/project/seychelles-blue-economy-strategic-roadmap-and-implementation

The World Bank. (2016a). *Blue Economy Project.* Author.

The World Bank. (2016b). *The Components of The Blue Economy*. Author.

The World Bank. (2013). *Shared prosperity; a new goal for a changing world.* Retrieved 05 29, 2018, from World Bank: https://www.worldbank.org/en/news/feature/2013/05/08/shared-prosperity-goal-for-changing-world

Tirole, J. (2017). *Economics for the Common Good.* Princeton University Press.

United Nations. (2017). Goal 14: Conserve and sustainably use the oceans, seas and marine resources. United Nations.

United Nations. (n.d.b). *Goal 5: Achieve gender equality and empower all women and girls.* Retrieved 04 02, 2018, from United Nations: https://www.un.org/sustainabledevelopment/gender-equality/

United Nations. (n.d.a). *Sustainable Development Goals.* Retrieved 10 28, 2017, from United Nations: https://www.un.org/sustainabledevelopment/sustainable-development-

United Nations Development Program (UNDP). (1998). Baseline Survey of Agriculture. Rural Development, Health and Mass Literacy of States of Nigeria. conducted by Gothards-IHLS Consortium.

United Nations Development Programme. (2018). *Millennium Development Goals*. Retrieved 05 26, 2018, from UNDP: http://www.undp.org/content/undp/en/home/sdgoverview/mdg_goals.html

United Nations Environment Programme and Gender and Water Alliance (2019). *Gender Mainstreaming in the Management of Marine and Coastal Ecosystems*. Author.

Chapter 10
The Blue Economy's Entrepreneurial Potential and Its Poverty Mitigative Powers in Nigeria

Shefiu Raheem
Yaba College of Technology, Nigeria

ABSTRACT

The chapter critically reviews the extant literature on the blue economy and advances a number of managerial and policy issues. First, the chapter argues that the blue economy is an evolving concept with varying definitions and perspectives based on stakeholders' visions and priorities. Second, despite different understandings, there exists a broad consensus that with diminishing land resources, there is greater pressure on ocean resources to feed the growing global population. Equally, there is also a compelling need for policymakers in marine nations to account for "eco-system services" and initiate sustainable policies for the healthy exploitation, usage, management, protection, and conservation of ocean and ocean resources. Finally, to diversify the economy of Nigeria, the chapter canvases the adoption of a new paradigm called the "blue economy" as an antidote for unpredictable and harsh implications of overdependence on oil. Future ocean-based productivity has been forecasted to exceed land-based production both in value and employment generation by 2030.

INTRODUCTION

The Blue Economy concept was first articulated by the Small Island Developing States (SIDS) at the Rio+20 Summit on Sustainable Development in 2012. This new approach essentially sought to transform the traditional ocean economy into an ecosystem-driven harnessing of oceanic resources for better conservation of the marine environment. The BE concept is still evolving and different stakeholders have adopted its varying definitions based on their own visions and priorities. However, there exists a broad consensus that with the diminishing land resources, there will be a much greater pressure on the

DOI: 10.4018/978-1-6684-3393-5.ch010

oceans for more resources to feed faster growth to meet the demands of a growing population. Equally, there is also a compelling realisation of the dangers of unsustainable approaches.

According to the World Bank (2016), the blue economy is the sustainable use of ocean resources for economic growth, improved livelihoods, and jobs whereas protecting the health of ocean scheme. European Commission defines the blue economy as all economic activities associated with oceans, seas, and coasts. It covers a large vary of interlinked established and rising sectors. The Commonwealth of Nations considers it, as an arising idea that inspires a higher situation of our ocean or 'blue' resources. Conservation International in Bertazzo (2008) added that the blue economy additionally includes economic edges that will not be marketed, like carbon storage, coastal protection, cultural values, and diversity.

The Center for the Blue Economy says, the concept is currently a widely used term around the world with 3 connected however distinct meanings the general contribution of the oceans to economies, the necessity to deal with the environmental and ecological property of the oceans, and therefore the ocean economy as a growth chance for each developed and developing countries.

According to OECD (2012) projections, by 2030, the Blue Economy will stand out as an economic sectors that have an on the spot or indirect link to the ocean that would outmatch the expansion of the global economy entirely, in terms of its usefulness and employment within the coming decade. The marine energy, marine biotechnology, coastal business enterprise, transport,

and food production sectors might provide unexampled development and investment opportunities. The East Asian Seas (EAS) Congress (2012, 23) outlined the blue economy as: "a resource ocean primarily based economic model that's for the most parts mitten by coastal and marine ecosystems and resources, however one that employs environmentally sound and innovative infrastructure, technologies and practices, as well as institutional and funding arrangements, for meeting the goals of:

A. property and inclusive development;
B. protective the coasts and oceans, and reducing environmental risks and ecological scarcities; (c) addressing water, energy and food security;
C. protective the health, livelihoods and welfare of the folks within the coastal zone; and
D. fostering an ecosystem-based global climate change mitigation and adaptation measures."

It seeks to harness the ocean resources for sustainable development. The major Blue Economy resources include fish, other living organisms, genetic resources, minerals and other non-living substances, offshore energy and a host of marine services, namely, transport, tourism and communications. Oceans have historically supported humanity for meeting their many essential needs and if harnessed in keeping with their carrying capacity, they would continue to do so forever.

The oceans are the foremost climate stabilizers as they directly absorb a lot of heat and recycle an overwhelming share of the greenhouse gases. They also provide significant support to the humanity through food, energy, transport, recreation, and many more intangible benefits. Unfortunately, in the rush for higher and faster growth, we have long ignored their health resulting in dangerous levels of pollution, acidification and warming with extremely serious consequences.

The rising sea levels could submerge valuable land, extreme weather and rising temperature could disrupt water cycle and hurt agriculture, fisheries, rich marine biodiversity and further to aggravate tropical diseases. This could cause unimaginable suffering and economic loss. The good news, though, is that the world community has realised this impending danger and has been working hard to find mitigating solutions. A fast-growing public opinion is clearly demanding the future economic growth and development to be more sustainable. Caring for the oceans' health would always be central to any meaningful solutions.

Some estimates suggest that in many sectors, the ocean-based productivity will exceed the corresponding land-based production both in value and employment generation by 2030. However, these benefits would accrue only if the oceans remain healthy. This realisation over time has culminated in the emergence of a whole new paradigm called the "Blue Economy".

Policy makers, civil society and scientists have been extensively engaged with the evolving Blue Economy dialogue for many years now. Ironically, the business community, which would eventually implement these measures, has not been fully involved.

THE ORIGIN AND CONCEPTUALIZATION OF THE BLUE ECONOMY

The emergence and the recent evolution of the concept of the blue economy in several fora bear testimony to its importance as an alternative economic model for sustainable development that acknowledges nations' dependency on the oceans (UNECA, 2016). It also reflects a modern view that further development can also be feasible while maintaining sustainability and social justice, including intergenerational equity as the main guiding principles.

The concept Blue Economy as an economic philosophy was first introduced by Professor Gunter Pauli in 1994 when asked by the United Nations to reflect on the business models of the future in preparation for COP3 in Japan where the Kyoto Protocol was decided (Pauli, 2010).

The idea 'blue economy' was propounded within the urban center Summit of 2012 that is additionally acquainted as 'Rio+20', by the world organization setting Program. Practically, the planned idea is an application of each 'green economy' in cycle with inexperienced growth and ideas to the ocean realm, up human eudemonia and social equity in parallel with less environmental hurt and economical resource utilization were the very important causes behind underpinning the blue economy idea within the Rio+20 summit (UNEP, 2013). Blue economy acknowledges the ocean realm because of the new inducted platform of ocean development still as ocean governance.

The idea mirrors the dragging line between socioeconomic development and reckless environmental degradation. The term blue economy has been utilized in various ways. However, it's understood to comprise of a variety of economic sectors and connected policies that along confirm whether or not the utilization of oceanic resources is property. The blue economy idea seeks to market economic process, social inclusion, and therefore the preservation or improvement of livelihoods whereas at identical time guaranteeing the environmental property of the oceans and coastal areas. It's considered the decoupling of socio-economic activities and development from environmental degradation and optimizing the advantages which can be derived from marine resources (Wairimu & Khainga, 2017).

At the core of the Blue (ocean), the economy idea is the de-coupling of socioeconomic development from environmental degradation. To attain this, the Blue Economy approach is supported upon the assessment and incorporation of the Billion Dollars' worth of the natural (blue) capital into all aspects of economic activity (conceptualization, planning, infrastructure development, trade, travel, natural resources exploitation, energy production/consumption).

Potency and optimization of resource use square measure preponderating while respecting environmental and ecological parameters. This includes wherever sustain sourcing and usage of natural raw materials and utilizing wherever possible "blue" low energy choices to grasp efficiencies and edges as

Table 1. General characteristics of the ocean

Contains 80% of Earth's life
Carries more than 90% of internationally traded goods
Produces more than half of the oxygen we breathe and provides a livelihood for an estimated three billion people who depend on marine and coastal areas, including for fishing, tourism, trade, transport and energy (UN Conference on Sustainable Development 2012 Fact Sheet).
Moderates the planet's climate by absorbing about 90% of the heat trapped in the ever-thickening atmosphere.
Provides the primary source of protein for more than 3.5 billion people.
Fisheries alone contribute $100 billion per year to the global economy (Food and Agriculture Organization of the United Nations 2014)
13 of the world's 20 megacities are coastal

against the business as was common "brown" situation of high energy, low employment, and industrial development models (UNEP, FAO, IMO, UNDP, IUCN, GRID

GENERAL CHARACTERISTICS OF THE OCEAN

In reality, these statistics act only as a backdrop to the need for an economy classification specifically related to the ocean and its myriad of goods and services. Half of the world's people live within 100 kilometers of the coast (Small and Nicholls 2003). According to a National Ocean Economics Program study, "In 2010 the ocean economy comprised over 2.7 million jobs and contributed over $258 billion to the GDP of the United States" (Kildow et al. 2014, 8). Some argue that global ocean economic activity is estimated between $3 trillion and $6 trillion (Cicin-Sain 2015). But we don't know for sure.

In addition to this ocean-sized economy, we also want to know what could and should be encompassed in the *new* Blue Economy. The potential of our coasts and ocean to meet sustainable development needs is immense. And, if they can be maintained in and/or restored to a healthy and productive state, the ocean will play an even more important role in humanity's future. In many ways, the coasts and ocean are the final on-ramp to merge onto our road to sustainable development.

THE TRADITIONAL OCEAN ECONOMY

Much of the traditional ocean economy was short-sighted, unsustainable (it assumed we could dump as much in, and take out as much as we wanted) and put at risk water, food and energy security. The blue economy is not about old versus new in time scale; it is about unsustainable versus sustainable. Are there traditional ocean activities that generate economic returns but that are benign or regenerative for our coasts and ocean? Or, is it all about extraction, pollution and other activities that diminish the ocean's health?

Offshore Oil and Gas

Risks associated with offshore oil and gas exploration and extraction include the opportunity for harm during construction of infrastructure and accidental oil spills and release of gas at sea during storage and shipping. For example, a major oil spill in the Arctic would create an insurmountable clean-up issue if oil were to seep under the ice cover and comingle with ice forms. Oil harbors and terminals present the threat of accidental releases from storage or during off-loading. And, major transportation routes of other hazardous substances similarly carry the risk of harm to human infrastructure, water supply, and wildlife resulting from discharges and releases when accidents occur.

Recreation and Commercial Fishing

After ocean acidification and climate change, there is no bigger threat to the ocean than overfishing for the global seafood trade. In addition, there are 12 million recreational anglers in the U.S. alone (Conathan 2011). For years, we have used an estimate of $100 billion as our estimate of the scale of the fishing economy globally.

However, there are other numbers used. According to NOAA's 2012 report to Congress, "Fish processing, restaurants, grocery stores, sales of tackle and gas, icehouses, and a multitude of other businesses are involved with the seafood and fishing supply chain, generating $183 billion per year in the U.S. economy and more than 1.5 million full- and part-time jobs." And, yet the NOAA Office of Science and Technology says that in 2012 there were $199 billion in sales impacts generated by U.S. commercial and recreational fishing industries, supporting 1.7 million jobs. What is a sales impact, why is that number 16 billion more, and 200 thousand more jobs? And thus again, perhaps we don't really have a handle on the real scale of the sector.

Open pen aquaculture

Aquaculture production meets more than half the global seafood need now—and much of the production is land-based. Aquaculture will have to be scaled up to meet the basic protein needs of the expected 2 billion extra mouths by 2050. There are significant reasons to move away from the negative effects of in-ocean finfish and coastal production — both local (pollution, habitat destruction) and broader ecosystem impacts (escaping fish, diseases, parasites, chemical use, discharge of nutrients, microbial pathogens, drugs, herbicides and fungicides). Half of the fish imported into the U.S. in 2014 was a farmed product (given the escalating dietary needs of a booming global population, aquaculture will have to be part of the solution) (Pramod et al. 2014, 103). In this discussion of need, we should remember that the US had roughly 1.25 million metric tons of imported farmed seafood product in 2014 according to NOAA, of which about 870 thousand metric tons was salmon and shrimp, the vast majority of it farmed. So we have to be careful about how we're quantifying "need" to meet future food security. What we are really concerned about are the 1 in 7 people globally who obtain their protein from fish (World Health Organization 2016). In other words, fish are essential to over 1 billion people, and account for more than 50% of animal protein for 400 million individuals in the poorest countries. And, aquaculture attributes to 11 million jobs, mostly in developing countries (Allison 2011, 18); 50% for women (Mills et al.2011).

Shipping

Shipping is already the most carbon efficient means of transporting most goods across the world, but it is still a meaningful emitter of greenhouse gases, acoustic pollution, oil spills and other pollution. The International Maritime Organization estimates that CO2 emissions from shipping are about 3% of the global human caused emissions and expects them to continue to rise to meet demand for international trade. As with cruise ships, we are seeing improvements in fuels, propulsion systems, wastewater management, solid waste handling and emissions. This has included some return to high-tech hybrid sailing ships. So, we have an opportunity to make shipping ever cleaner. End of life of ships is another area for potential improvement.

Shipbreaking is the practice of recovering and recycling iron, copper and all sorts of other components from retired or derelict ships. From life jackets to electric cables, a surprising percentage of every ship can be repurposed or recycled, which is a good thing. Unfortunately, as practiced in certain countries, it is a very dangerous and poorly regulated industry with chronic labor abuses and minimal environmental mitigation. In these countries, shipbreaking pollutes the beaches and coastal waters, often at the expense of the seafood supply of local communities.

Coastal tourism

Simply stated, there is sustainable and responsible tourism; and there is unsustainable and disruptive tourism. Tourism infrastructure can seriously damage coastal areas if not planned with socially and environmentally recognized best practices. Coastlines around the world are under siege from the impacts of inappropriate tourism development. Conventional tourism often marginalizes and displaces local communities. This type of tourism can disturb and threaten local wildlife and their habitats, which attracted the tourist to the area in the first place. We know what the alternatives are, and we know how to pursue them.

Telecommunications

Submarine cables carry 95% of all global telecommunications, connecting 2.7 billion users and supporting global business, finance, entertainment, etc. (Cicin- Sain 2015). On one hand this facilitates commerce and communications without the need for postal air carrier emissions, but these cables do interact with the benthic zone and thus do cause some minimal harm to the seafloor. For an additional five to 10 percent of the total cost of any new cable system deployed, researchers are making a scientific and social case for "greening" new cables to be built to also collect information on tsunamis and to monitor global change in the deep ocean.

CHANGES DRIVING THE NEW BLUE ECONOMY

Why don't we know how big the ocean and maritime tech industries are today?

Traditional maritime industries such as fishing and shipbuilding no longer dominate the maritime sector in many countries. In addition to these, and the diverse component industries (e.g. fittings makers, engine builders, and other suppliers) that are part of the visible maritime sector, there are sectors that are less visible.

Fast growing blue technology companies have remained largely invisible, because

1. they typically sell outside of wherever they are located (and thus they do not belong to the local Chamber of Commerce or Economic Development Agency nor do politicians necessarily know they exist), and
2. because they are so diverse, it is not immediately obvious why they should participate in a larger regional cluster association representing companies that are linked only by being ocean-related.

Additionally, the human relationship with the ocean is changing, and the old ocean economy is adapting to respond to new demands, ecological needs, and the dynamics of global climate change. Goal 14, "*Conserve and Sustainability Use the Oceans, Seas and Marine Resources for Sustainable Development*," of the recently adopted UN Sustainable Development Goals (SDG) for the global ocean outlines seven targets and three means of implementation relating to the sustainable use of the ocean (see table 2). Particularly noteworthy in this context is target 14.7, which declares, "By 2030 increase the economic benefits to small island developing states (SIDS) and least developed countries (LDCs) from the sustainable use of marine resources, including through sustainable management of fisheries, aquaculture and tourism." This focus on economic development of SIDs and LDCs is starting to create a shift in management and protection of marine resources and their social and economic impact.

THE TRANSITION TO A BLUE ECONOMY

Sustainable development implies that economic development is both inclusive and environmentally sound, and to be undertaken in a manner that does not deplete the natural resources that societies depend on in the long term. The need to balance the economic, social, and environmental dimensions of sustainable development in relation to oceans is a key component of the blue economy. It is also a difficult balance to reach in practice, given that ocean resources are limited and the health of the oceans has drastically declined due to human activities—ranging from damage caused by carbon dioxide emissions to nutrient, chemical, and plastics pollution, unsustainable fishing, habitat degradation and destruction, and the spread of invasive species. The scientists and experts who prepared the First Global Integrated Marine Assessment (also known as the World Ocean Assessment) warned that the world's oceans face major pressures simultaneously with such great impacts that the limits of their carrying capacity are being reached—or in some cases have been reached—and that delays in implementing solutions to the problems that have already been identified as threatening to degrade the world's oceans will lead, unnecessarily, to greater environmental, social, and economic costs (United Nations 2016).

The importance of oceans for sustainable development is widely recognized by the international community and was embodied in, among others, Agenda 21, the Johannesburg Plan of Implementation, various decisions taken by the Commission on Sustainable Development, the Rio+20 outcome document The Future We Want, and the 2030 Agenda for Sustainable Development.

The 1982 United Nations Convention on the Law of the Sea (UNCLOS), together with its implementing agreements—the 1994 Agreement relating to the implementation of Part XI of UNCLOS and the 1995 United Nations Fish Stocks Agreement—sets out the legal framework within which all activities in the oceans and seas must be carried out and is of strategic importance as the basis for national, regional, and global action and cooperation in the marine sector. This includes the conservation and sustainable use of all areas of the oceans and their resources. The concept of a blue economy came out of the 2012 Rio+20 Conference and emphasizes conservation and sustainable management, based on the premise that healthy ocean ecosystems are more productive and form a vital basis for sustainable ocean-based economies (UN DESA 2014a).

Under "business as usual," the costs of marine ecosystem degradation from human uses should be high, but they are not quantified or accounted for. At the same time, the economic contribution of the ocean to humankind has been significantly undervalued (Economist

THE NEED FOR BLUE ECONOMY

Protecting our oceans is not a luxury. It is a necessity that contributes to our economy, our climate and our way of life. Working together, we can change the current course and chart a sustainable future. US Secretary of State, John Kerry(2014).

It is essential to standardize our methods and definitions for valuing the coasts and ocean. The world's population depends upon the ocean for its very existence. The ocean regulates our climate and our weather. It generates half of the oxygen we breathe (NOAA 2014). It provides food and income for billions of people. Covering almost three quarters of the planet, the ocean is the life support system for planet earth . As a proxy, we express this life support as "eco-system services:" provisioning (e.g. food, oxygen and water); regulating (e.g. climate/temperature regulation, coastal stabilization); supporting (e.g. pollution filtration, waste processing, transportation of goods); and cultural services (e.g. aesthetics, recreation, fun and inspiration).

FAST FACTS

- The worldwide ocean economy is valued at around valued at around US$1.5 trillion per year.
- Eighty per-cent of global trade by volume is carried by sea.
- 350 million jobs world-wide are linked to fisheries.
- By 2025 it is estimated that 34% of crude oil production will come from offshore fields.
- Aquaculture is the fastest growing food sector and provides about 50% of fish for human consumption.

THE ELEMENTS OF THE BLUE ECONOMY

Table 2.

Type of ecosystem services	Blue Economy sectors
Harvesting of living aquatic resources (seafood, plant marine organisms, and marine-biotechnological products)	Fishing (inland, coastal, and deep seas) Aquaculture Mariculture Pharmaceuticals, chemicals, cosmetics, genetic research
Extraction of nonliving resources and generation of new energy resources	Deep-sea and seabed mining Offshore oil and gas Renewable energy Marine salt harvesting Coastal mining of sand, gravel, and other construction materials
Commerce and trade in and around the ocean and rivers	Maritime transport and services Port infrastructure Shipbuilding and repairs River transport Tourism and recreation
Protection	Coastal protection Marine ecosystem protection Water resource protection
Cultural and religious values	Cultural and religious practices
Knowledge and information	Biophysical, socioeconomic, and political research

Source: International Bank for Reconstruction and Development, April 2016.

COMPONENTS AND PILLARS OF BLUE ECONOMY'S GROWTH:

"Blue Growth" consists of three pillars or components:

- A targeted approach to specific activities, such as aquaculture, coastal tourism, marine biotechnology, ocean energy and the exploitation of seabed.
- Specific integrated maritime policy measures, such as improving knowledge and access to maritime information, maritime spatial planning for the efficient and sustainable management of maritime activit ies and integrated maritime surveillance.
- Strategies for individual sea basins aiming at ensuring the most appropriate combination of sustainable development measures that take account of local climatic, oceanographic, economic, cultural and social factors, such as those which are closest to us of the Mediterranean Sea, the Adriatic Sea, the Ionian Sea and the Black

Figure 1.

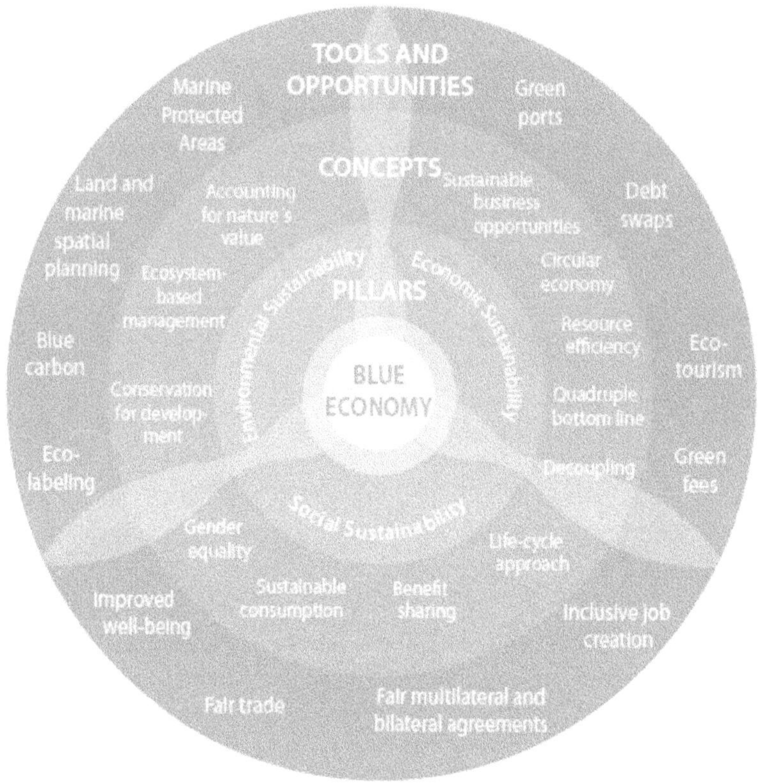

BLUE ECONOMY POLICY FORMULATION PROCESS

Blue Economy policy formulation process should take into consideration the following key principles:

- Sustainable use and sound management of aquatic and marine resources and ecosystems
- Shared benefits and prosperity for all through a progress-based development paradigm
- Value-based conservation and protection of aquatic and marine ecosystems
- Coherence with SDGs
- Systems thinking, lifecycle analysis, and value chain approaches
- Participatory, inclusive, broad-based and multi-stakeholder-based approach to policy formulation
- Intersectoral and holistic design and coordination
- Policy coherence at multiple levels
- Cooperation at all levels

Figure 2.
SOURCE: Africa's Blue Economy: A policy handbook

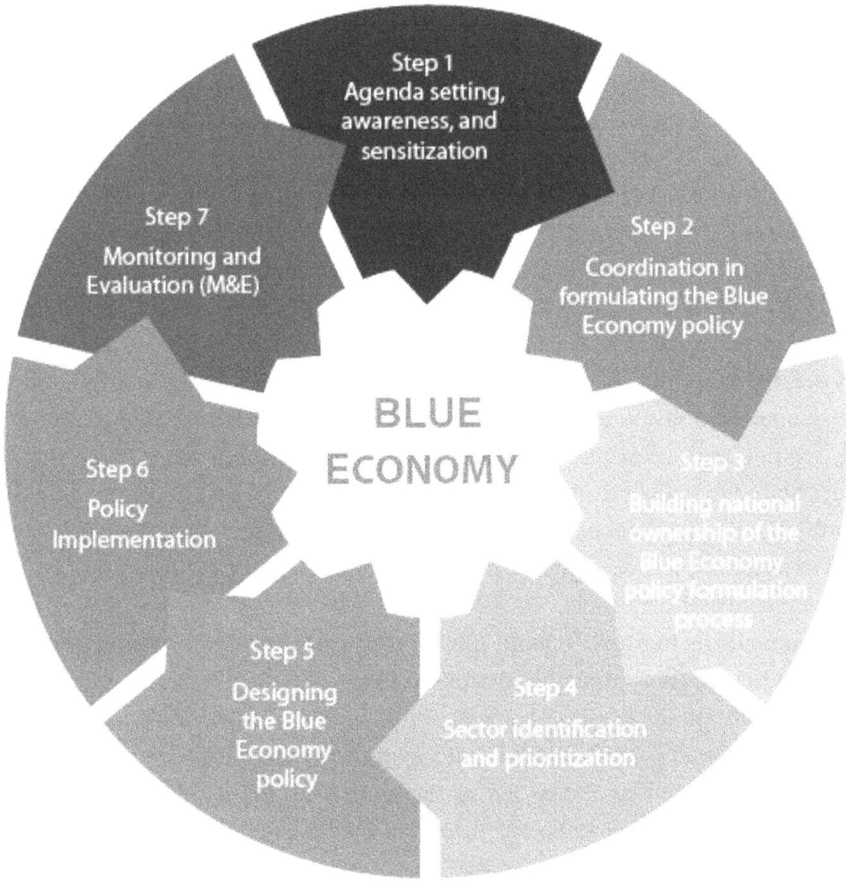

THE POTENTIALS OF BLUE ECONOMY

Although the term "blue economy" has been used in different ways, it is understood here as comprising the range of economic sectors and related policies that together determinewhether the use of oceanic resources is sustainable.

- An important challenge of the blue economy is thus to understand and better manage the many aspects of oceanic sustainability, ranging from sustainable fisheries to ecosystem health to pollution. A second significant issue is the realization that the sustainable management of ocean resources requires collaboration across nation-states and across the public-private sectors, and on a scale that has not been previously achieved. This realization underscores the challenge facing the Small Island Developing States (SIDS) and Least Developed Countries (LDCs) as they turn to better managing their blue economies.
- The "blue economy" concept seeks to promote economic growth, social inclusion, and the preservation or improvement of livelihoods while at the same time ensuring environmental sustain-

ability of the oceans and coastal areas. At its core it refers to the decoupling of socioeconomic development through oceans-related sectors and activities from environmentaland ecosystems degradation. It draws from scientific findings that ocean resources are limited and that the health of the oceans has drastically declined due to anthropogenic activities. These changes are already being profoundly felt, affecting human well-being and societies, and the impacts are likely to be amplified in the future, especially in view of projected population growth.

- The blue economy has diverse components, including established traditional ocean industries- such as fisheries, tourism, and maritime transport, but also new and emerging activities, such as offshore renewable energy, aquaculture, seabed extractive activities, and marine biotechnology and bioprospecting. A number of services provided by ocean ecosystems, and for which markets do not exist, also contribute significantly to economic and other human activity such as carbon sequestration, coastal protection, waste disposal and the existence of biodiversity.
- The mix of oceanic activities varies in each country, depending on their unique national circumstances and the national vision adopted to reflect its own conception of a blue economy. In order to qualify as components of a blue economy, as it is understood here, activities need to: provide social and economic benefits for current and future generations restore, protect, and maintain the diversity, productivity, resilience, core functions, and intrinsic value of marine ecosystems be based on clean technologies, renewable energy, and circular material flows that will reduce waste and promote recycling of materials.
- **The blue economy aims to move beyond business as usual and to consider economic development and ocean health as compatible propositions.**
- It is generally understood to be a long-term strategy aimed at supporting sustainable and equitable economic growth through oceans-related sectors and activities. The blue economy is relevant to all countries and can be applied on various scales, from local to global. In order to become actionable, the blue economy concept must be supported by a trusted and diversified knowledge base, and complemented with management and development resources that help inspire and support innovation.
- **A blue economy approach must fully anticipate and incorporate the impacts of climate change on marine and coastal ecosystems—impacts both already observed and anticipated.**
- Understanding of these impacts is constantly improving and can be organized around several main "vectors": acidification, sea-level rise, higher water temperatures, and changes in ocean currents. These different vectors, however, are unequally known and hard to model, in terms of both scope—where they will occur, where they will be felt the most—and severity. For instance, while not as well understood as the other impacts, and more difficult to measure, the impacts of acidification are likely to be the most severe and most widespread, essentially throughout any carbon-dependent ecological processes.
- Likewise, the effects of sea-level change will be felt differently in different parts of the world, depending on the ecosystems around which it occurs. Most importantly, however, and unlike in terrestrial ecosystems, further uncertainty results from the complex interactions within and between these ecosystems. In spite of this uncertainty, the current state of knowledge is sufficient to understand that these impacts will be felt on critical marine and coastal ecosystems throughout the world and that they fundamentally affect any approach to the management of marine resources, including by adding a new and increasing sense of urgency.

- **Healthy oceans and seas can greatly contribute to inclusiveness and poverty reduction, and are essential for a more sustainable future for SIDS and coastal LDCs alike.**
- Oceans and their related resources are the fundamental base upon which the economies and culture of many SIDS and coastal LDCs are built, and they are also central to their delivery of the 2030 Agenda for Sustainable Development, including the Sustainable Development Goals
- (SDGs). A blue economy provides SIDS and coastal LDCs with a basis to pursue a low-carbon and resource-efficient path to economic growth and development designed to enhance livelihoods for the poor, create employment opportunities, and reduce poverty. It is also clear that SIDS and coastal LDCs often lack the capacity, skills and financial support to better develop their blue economy.
- This report lays out steps for countries to follow to make the blue economy an important vehicle to sustain economic diversification and job creation in these countries.
- **In spite of all its promises, the potential to develop a blue economy is limited by a series of challenges.**
- First and foremost is the need to overcome current economic trends that are rapidly degrading ocean resources through unsustainable extraction of marine resources, physical alterations and destruction of marine and coastal habitats and landscapes, climate change, and marine pollution.
- The second set of challenges is the need to invest in the human capital required to harness the employment and development benefits of investing in innovative blue economy sectors. The third set of challenges relates to strengthening the concept and overcoming inadequate valuation of marine resources and ecosystem services provided by the oceans; isolated sectoral management of activities in the oceans, which makes it difficult to address cumulative impacts; inadequate human, institutional, and technical capacity; underdeveloped and often inadequate planning tools; and lack of full implementation of the 1982 United Nations Convention on the Law of the Sea (UNCLOS) and relevant conventions and instruments.
- While stimulating growth in individual oceanic sectors is comparatively straightforward, it is not always clear what a sustainable blue economy should look like and the conditions under which it is most likely to develop.

ELEMENTS OF PRINCIPLES TO BUILDING A SUSTAINABLE BLUE ECONOMY

- Promote economic activities per conservation and long run capability of the ocean, seas, lakes,and rivers to stay healthy and resilient.
- Apply relevant information and science to tell policy and decision-making
- Interact relevant stakeholders within the development and conservation of blue economy resources.
- Strengthen social and environmental company responsibility
- Develop information and understanding of the worth of the market and non-market merchandise and services of the blue economy
- Alien funding to support inclusive economic activities that enhance the health of blue economy resources.
- Support growth of little and medium enterprises within the blue economy.

Produce markets for rising and innovative blue economy connected industries

PRINCIPLES FOR A SUSTAINABLE BLUE ECONOMY

The world's oceans, seas, and coastal square measure are the most important ecosystems in the world and a precious a part of our natural heritage. They are additionally very important to the livelihoods and food security of billions of individuals around the world, and to the economic development of most countries (DESA, 2017).

- The ability of those marine environments to produce jobs and nutrition over the long run is, however, already fraught from human economic activities; and it is being more vulnerable by development approaches that square measure fragmented, uncoordinated, and infrequently in conflict with what science tells us is physically potential or ecologically sound.
- Fortunately, several governments, organizations, and communities in each developed and developing countries have become attentive to the necessity for a lot of coherent, integrated, fair, and science-primarily based approach to managing the economic development of the oceans.
- Humanity increasingly understands that we tend to square measure an integral part of the marine sector, which we tend to, should set up and implement our economic activities with care, equalization the will to enhance human living standards and eudemonia with the imperative to sustain scheme health.
- Visionary leadership is required, within the general public and private sectors, to steer the blue economy in an exceedingly sustain direction. This includes delivering on commitments already created–globally, regionally, nationwide and locally.

To ensure that the economic development of the ocean contributes to true sustainable and flexibility, these days and long into the future, with special recognition of the desires of developing countries, WWF is proposing the subsequent Principles for a sustainable Blue Economy (WWF Baltic Ecoregion Programme, 2015). These Principles offer a definition of a sustainable Blue Economy and a roadmap to assist us to get there. They're universal and may be applied to any part of the oceans, seas or coasts, still as utilized by any actor concerned within the economic development of the ocean, as well as governments, non-public and financial sector actors, international agencies, and civil society teams. WWF requests all Blue Economy actors to use these Principles for a sustainable Blue Economy and to embed these definitions, descriptions, and actions into marine policy and activities, all round the world. For clear, measurable, and internally consistent goals and targets for a sustainable Blue Economy, governments, economic sectors, individual businesses, and different actors should gear up relevant and measurable goals and targets for a sustainable blue economy to produce their designing, management, and activities with a transparent direction.

Goals and targets for various economic, social and ecological areas still as connected policies and activities should be created as integrated and coherent as potential, to avoid conflicts and contradictions.

SUSTAINABLE DEVELOPMENT AND AN EQUITABLE BLUE ECONOMY.

Sustainable development in any country could be achieved through an Equitable Blue Economy as explained in this figure

Figure 3.
Source: *Bennett, N.J., Cisneros-Montemayor, A.M., Blythe, J. et al. (2019). Towards a sustainable and equitable blue economy.*

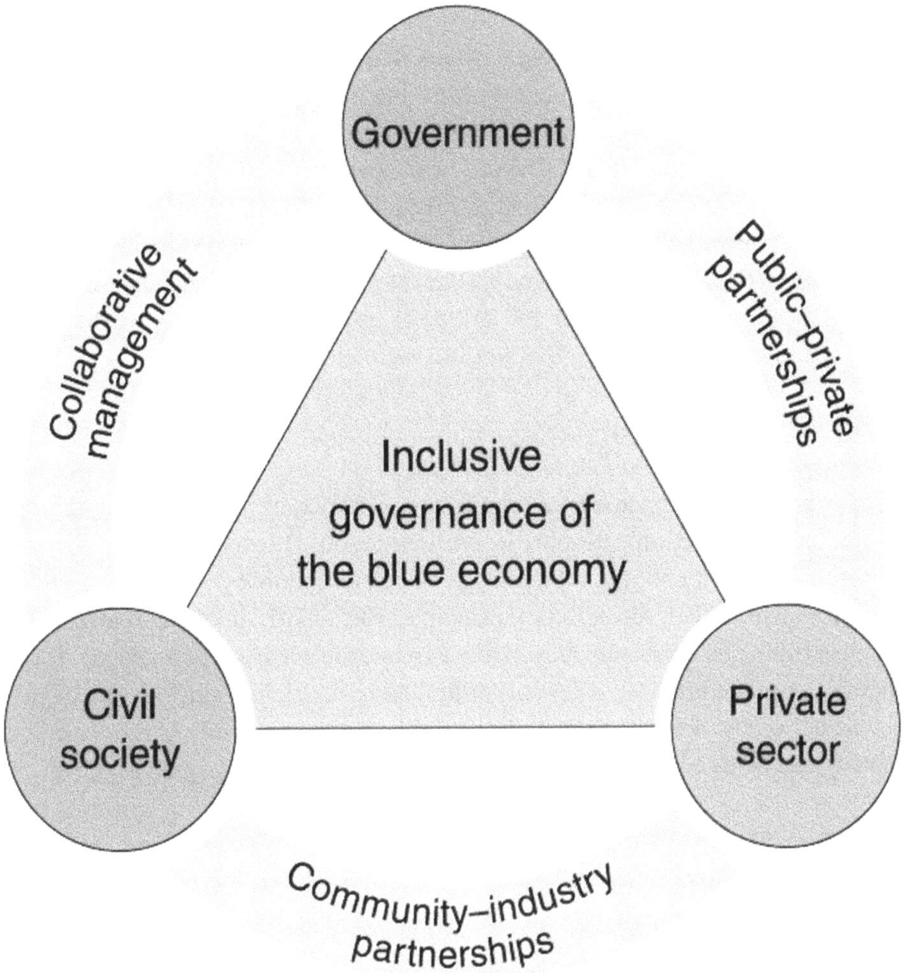

EMERGING INDUSTRIES BIRTHED BY OCEAN ECONOMY

These Include the Following:

Renewable energy

"Many new emerging technologies designed to address climate change through the development of alternative sources of energy are increasingly being deployed in marine ecosystems. The most promising of these technologies are also the most threatening to marine ecosystems: offshore wind farms; carbon sequestration; tidal and wave energy; and ocean thermal energy conversion (OTEC)," (Spalding and de Fontaubert 2007).

The ocean offers numerous types of renewable energy, including offshore wind, tidal, current, ocean thermal energy conversion, and wave energy. According to a 2008 report from the US Department of

Energy, the 28 states bordering the ocean and Great Lakes use 78 percent of the nation's electricity, thus we can locate production near markets and reduce long distance transmission losses (Conathan and Kroh 2012). For example, we expect offshore wind operations will produce 175 gigawatts of power by 2035. Harnessing the ocean's renewable energy capacity should be balanced against the potential harm it causes to natural habitats (changes in geomorphology and processes, sedimentation, erosion).

At the same time, we can also balance renewable energy against old school fossil fuel sourced energy. A January 2015 report from Oceana titled "Offshore Energy by the Numbers, An Economic Analysis of Offshore Drilling and Wind Energy in the Atlantic" notes that offshore wind would produce twice the number of jobs and twice the amount of energy as offshore drilling in the Atlantic Ocean.

This report also found that "offshore oil and gas development along the Atlantic could put at risk some of the nearly 1.4 million jobs and over $95 billion in gross domestic product that rely on healthy ocean ecosystems, mainly through fishing, tourism and recreation."

Seabed Mining (Still Potential)

Mining the seabed in any nation's exclusive economic zones (EEZs) or the deep sea within the high seas (Areas Beyond National Jurisdiction) presents us with numerous threats, including damaging seabed biomass and polluting the water column, which could harm communities dependent on that ecosystem for food. We should adhere to the precautionary principle, particularly in order to avoid the buildup of activities that deplete finite resources and irreversibly damage the ecosystem. As part of this, we need to consider whether or not seabed mining is less harmful than terrestrial mining (as some have asserted). In other words whether one is better than the other for the planet as a whole. And, if seabed mining is better, can we make it as benign as possible?

Remediation/restoration

Some businesses make money from ecosystem services, and some make money from restoring these ecosystem services. Remediation is a form of the latter. Design, construction, operation, and monitoring of large-scale coastal and marine restoration projects bear the potential for sustaining job creation and increasing ecosystem services vital to supporting existing coastal livelihoods. CAP-Oxfam's 2011 report "Beyond Recovery" found that every $1 million invested in wetland restoration can create 29 new jobs, which is nearly six times as many as the oil and gas industries for the same investment. Many of these jobs directly benefit the local community and cannot be outsourced.

According to *Estimating the Size and Impact of the Ecological Restoration Economy*, the domestic ecological restoration sector directly employs approximately 126,000 workers and generates about $9.5 billion in economic output (sales) annually (BenDor et al. 2015). This activity supports an additional 95,000 jobs and $15 billion in economic output through indirect (business-to-business) linkages and increased household spending.

Blue biotechnology

There is the risk of unintended extraction of marine species associated with blue biotechnologies. This field is yet ill defined and poorly regulated. The precautionary principle should be applied to bio-nano-technology, biomaterials and the introduction of genetically modified fish, shellfish and microorganisms.

Blue carbon

An entire new category of business is being formed to sell credits for carbon storage and sequestration in coastal and ocean living biomass and sediments. Concern has been raised about commodification of the ocean, but it may be offset by the value of restoring and protecting habitats that provide other benefits such as increased productivity in coastal areas and the attenuation of wave energy in the face of climate change driven sea level rise and storm surges.

Blue technology

The blue technology sector includes providers of infrastructure, including manufacturers of sensors, instruments, and platforms; those building, deploying, and operating observing systems; providers of the data infrastructure that manages and communicates ocean data; organizations that develop and maintain data management systems, software tools and models; environmental safety and compliance technology companies; marine robotics; and desalination.

Other examples

Other examples include nutrition, nutraceuticals, cosmetics, fisheries byproduct transformation, and the innovative marine molecules sector.

LEGAL FRAMEWORK OF THE BLUE ECONOMY

Blue economy activities are controlled by various laws and regulations (i.e national, regional and international). Government Departments and agencies have been given different mandates resulting in conflict of interest and poor governance due to lack of cooperation between the oversight agencies, compartmentalization and management. This leads to duplication of resources without clear goals of achieving a sustainable blue economy.

To achieve integrated approach and improved governance, the use of Integrated National Maritime Policy as a tool would offer solutions to oversee overarching issues that arose in the institutional, legal and regulatory regimes with a view of providing amicable solutions for the successive implementation of sustainable blue economy.

Within the confines of international law and the established legal regime for the rights, jurisdictions and responsibility of states parties on issues relating to the peaceful use of oceans, is the United Nations Convention on the Law of the sea (UNCLOS). It was adopted in 1982 but entered into force in 1994 outlining rights and obligations of states in carrying out activities in the oceans and seas (DOALOS, 2010). It answers the critical legal questions on the delineation of maritime zones and the extent of the territorial boundaries of adjoining coastal states. It also highlights other provisions, including- the exploitation of the living resources within the sea column and the exploration of non-living resources within the seafloor, the obligation for the protection and preservation of the marine environment, provisions on the transfer of marine technology, marine scientific research amongst others.

With a view to addressing arrays of issues, the legal framework within UNCLOS also provides for the adoption of other relevant agreements as complements to the convention. To this end, there were two agreements- firstly, the 1994 Agreement Relating to the implementation of Part XI of the Conventions of the Law of the Sea which relates to the exploitation and exploration of the resources in the international seabed area (Known according to the Convention as "the Area"), considered as the "common heritage of mankind" in section 2, Article 136 (UNCLOS, 1984, p. 70).

According to UNCLOS, the regulation of the activities in the Area is vested on the International SeabedAuthority (ISA) as an institution with this unique mandate (Zacharias, 2014). The other important agreement was the 1995 Agreement for the Management of Straddling Fish Stocks and Highly Migratory Fish Stocks (Also called, the United Nations Fish Stock Agreement), which provides guidelines and directions for the regional ooperation of parties on the management of fisheries and sustainable exploitation of the resources within the Exclusive Economic Zones (EEZ) and the high seas.

The Deep Sea Fisheries Management and Development Act, 2020, provides an important legal framework for Zanzibar's Blue Economy policy implementation. It provides among others, on how the EEZ can be explored,f acilities, incentives and scrutiny for its management.

As a supplement to UNCLOS, other equally binding international conventions and agreements exist within the broader legal frameworks of ocean governance regimes and conservation of marine ecosystems. Some of these include- the Convention on Biological Diversity (CBD) and Jakarta Mandate; Paris COP 21 Agreement;Convention on Wetlands of International Importance (Ramsar Convention); Convention for the Protection, Management and Development of the Marine and Coastal Environment of the Eastern African Region (NairobiConvention); International Convention for the Prevention of Pollution from Ships (MARPOL); World HeritageConvention; Africa Convention on the Conservation of Nature and Natural Resources; Africa Maritime Transport Charter amongst others (Folami, 2017).

Recently, there is a new development following a resolution of the United Nations General Assembly (UNGA) through Resolution 69/292 of 19 June 2015 which relates to developing an International Legally

Binding Instrument (ILBI) under UNCLOS on the conservation and sustainable use of Marine Biodiversity in Areas Beyond National Jurisdiction (ABNJ) (Konrad, 2017).

The development of legal and institutional frameworks is obviously still an ongoing process. However, there exists sufficient international legal and institutional regimes that allow for the integration of Blue Economy paradigms into existing hard and soft law instruments.

AFRICA'S BLUE ECONOMY

Africa's "Blue world" is made of vast lakes and rivers and an extensive ocean resource base. Thirty-eight of the fifty-four African States are coastal States. More than 90 percent of Africa's imports and exports are conducted by sea and some of the most strategic gateways for international trade are in Africa, underscoring the geopolitical importance of the region. Maritime zones under Africa's jurisdiction total about 13 million square kilometres including territorial seas and approximately 6.5 million square kilometres of the continental shelf. Mauritius with its 1850 square kilometres is one of the smallest countries in Africa and in the world. However, with its territorial waters, it becomes a country with 1.9 million square kilometres, the size of South Africa. Therefore, we have another Africa under the sea. Quite rightly, the African Union call the Blue Economy the "New Frontier of African Renaissance".

Africa's aquatic and marine spaces are an increasingly common topic of political discourse; its natural resources have remained largely underexploited but are now being recognized for their potential contribution to inclusive and sustainable development. This "Blue word" is more than just an economic space— it is part of Africa's rich geographical, social, and cultural canvas. Through a better understanding of the enormous opportunities emerging from investing and reinvesting in Africa's aquatic and marine spaces, the balance can be tipped away from illegal harvesting, degradation, and depletion to a sustainable Blue development paradigm, serving Africa today and tomorrow. If fully exploited and well managed, Africa's Blue Economy can constitute a major source of wealth and catapult the continent's fortunes.

Africa's economies continue to grow at remarkable rates, including through the exploitation of the rich endowment of land-based natural resources and commodity exports. Converting this growth into quality growth, through the generation of inclusive wealth, within environmental limits and respecting the highest social considerations, requires bold new thinking. It also involves the creation of jobs for a population on the rise. The Blue Economy offers that opportunity. For example, the International Energy Agency estimates that ocean renewable energy has a power potential sufficient to provide up to 400% of global current energy demand. Other estimates indicate that in 2010 the total annual economic value of maritime related activities reached 1.5 trillion euro. It is forecasted that by 2020, this figure will reach 2.5 trillion euro per year. Surely, Africa needs holistic and coherent strategies to harness this potential.

All water bodies, including lakes, rivers, and underground water, in addition to seas and the coast are unique resources, yet neglected and often forgotten. The largest sectors of the current African aquatic and ocean-based economy are fisheries, aquaculture, tourism, transport, ports, coastal mining, and energy. Additionally, the Blue Economy approach emphasizes interconnectedness with other sectors, is responsive to emerging and frontier sectors, and supports important social considerations, such as gender mainstreaming, food and water security, poverty alleviation, wealth retention, and jobs creation. The Blue Economy can play a major role in Africa's structural transformation.

The approach advocated in this Policy Handbook is premised in the sustainable use, management and conservation of aquatic and marine ecosystems and associated resources. It builds on principles of equity, low carbon footprint, resource efficiency, social inclusion and broad-based development, with the jobs agenda at the centre of it all. It is anchored on strong regional cooperation and integration, considers structural transformation as an imperative for Africa's development and advocates for a complete departure from enclave development models. Instead, through better linkages to other sectors of the economy, it situates the aquatic and marine economies as part of integrated ecosystem services based on the harvesting of living and non-living resources, benefitting both costal, island states and landlocked countries.

Biotic resources allow Africa to expand its fishing, aquaculture, mariculture sectors and foster the emergency of vibrant pharmaceutical, chemical and cosmetics industries. The extraction of mineral resources and the generation of new energy resources provide the feedstock to resource-based industrialisation and places Africa at the centre of global trade in value-added products, no longer a supplier of unprocessed raw materials. Central to this agenda, is the need to modernise Africa's maritime transport and logistics services, its port and railway infrastructure, improve its reliability and efficiency with the view to seamless link the continent's economies to national, regional and global value chains as well facilitate tourism and recreation activities, just to name a few.

Africa has salutary examples of maritime, riparian and river-based cooperation and dispute settlement. This includes examples of maritime and transnational aquatic boundary delimitation and demarcation. A collaborative approach for the development of the Blue Economy will create the foundation for the formulation of shared visions for transformation. The Blue Economy development approach is an integral part of African Agenda 2063. Building on the experience with implementing Green Economy principles for a transition to low-carbon development, we are seeing an increasing number of African member States formulating Blue Economy strategies to diversify their economic base and catalyze socioeconomic transformation.

There is a growing momentum to harness and utilize all the potential resources of the oceans, seas, rivers and lakes for the socio-economic emancipation of the African continent. The continent has a vantage geographical location being adjacent to some of the highly productive Oceanic and Sea environments such as the Atlantic Ocean, Indian Ocean, Red Sea and the Mediterranean Sea. These aquatic ecosystems present abundant opportunities for the African Union member states to participate in sustainable ocean (blue) economy by harnessing the potentials for improving productivity of the ocean environment, job creation, strengthening food and nutritional security, wealth creation opportunities and environmental sustainability toward sustainable blue economy development. The highly productive network of rivers and lakes, many of which are transboundary like; Lake Victoria, Lake Tanganyika, Lake Chad, Nile River, River Congo etc. also present avenues for blue economy growth in Africa.

Given the complexities associated with the governance of these water bodies and wetlands, a paradigm shift from the business-as-usual (or traditional ways of doing things) approach is needed to be able to fully amass the associated benefits in a sustainable manner for socio-economic emancipation and industrialization in Africa. However, despite the potentials benefits and opportunities associated with these aquatic resources, the resources of the oceans and inland waters are under serious threats due largely to governance and capacity issues as well as climate change and extreme weather events.

The Africa Blue Economy Strategy is consolidated based on the following five detailed thematic technical reports that are annexes to this Strategy:

1. Fisheries, aquaculture, conservation and sustainable aquatic ecosystems
2. Shipping/transportation, trade, ports, maritime security, safety and enforcement
3. Coastal and maritime tourism, climate change, resilience, environment, infrastructure
4. Sustainable energy and mineral resources and innovative industries
5. Policies, institutional and governance, employment, job creation and poverty eradication, innovative financing

AFRICA TODAY AND AT THE HORIZONS 2030 AND 2063

African BE sectors and components generate today a value of USD 296 billion with 49 million jobs. It is projected that by 2030, figures will be respectively USD 405 billion and 57 million jobs while in 2063 estimates would respectively be USD 576 billion of value created and 78 millions of jobs.

The number of jobs would correspond to about 5% of the active population in 2063. The main driving sectors of the BE are tourism, both in term of value added and jobs created; the mineral sector, and the Oil and Gas that have a strong contribution to the value added but a low participation in the job creation process. The fishery sector will remain stable, with a high number of people employed while the aquaculture will continue to grow in next decades. Port and shipping will grow at a constant rate. The value of blue carbon and other ecosystem services generated by coastal, marine and aquatic ecosystems will progressively increase as conservation efforts expand. Education and research will follow the same pattern due to a growing demand for knowledge, especially in the area of deep-sea mining, offshore exploration and climate change mitigation and adaptation.

Port and Shipping - Although Africa still has a relatively small impact in international trade(3% of world volumes), African shipping follows the upward trend in the world. As a result, traffic in African container ports has grown at an average annual rate of 8% over the past 5 years, compared to a global 5% change. The traffic in the African harbours should exceed 2 billion of tons by 2063 versus 500 million in 2018. The Increased port traffic will be done thanks to the modernization of the ports that can progressively accommodate the latest generation of large ships (more than 21 000 TFE). The creation of sub-regional maritime shipping companies, of cabotage companies and the development of transport corridors with the application of freight rates will furthermore allow African shippers to transport their cargoes at reasonable costs.

Fishery - The capture fisheries production, currently standing at 10 million tonnes, is expected to remain fairly constant throughout 2063 due to, inter alia, overfishing, overcapacity and poor governance. The total gross value-added of the fisheries in Africa is estimated at USD 21 billion or 1.26% of the GDP (USD1.9 trillion) of all African countries. Marine artisanal fisheries contribute the most at USD 8.1 billion, followed by marine industrial fisheries and inland fisheries at USD 6.8 billion and 6.3 billion respectively. In 2018, the fisheries sector employs about 13 million people of which 7 million were fishers and 6 million were processors.

More than half of the fishers are employed in inland fisheries and the largest share of processors work in marine artisanal fisheries.

Aquaculture - The African aquaculture sector records the fastest growth in the world between 2006-2018, averaging 10% or more and is expected to partially fill the growing fish supply-emand gap up to 2063. The value of aquaculture is estimated at USD 2.77 billion. Despite huge potential, the growth is confined to fewer countries with Egypt accounting for nearly 70% (1.37 million tonnes) of the total 1.98 million tonnes while Nigeria ranked second with 300 thousand tonnes. In 2018, there were about 1.2 million aquafarmers across the continent, an increase from 920 thousand in 2014.

Sustainable Blue Energy - Blue energy penetration has already started in many African countries such as Ghana (Wave Energy), Mauritius (FPV) and Offshore wind projects. Considering Ghana's electricity contribution to GDP of about 1.5% as our reference and assuming that progressively the share of the BE will be 5% of the total energy contribution in 2030 and 7% of the total energy contribution in 2063 the GDP contribution of the blue energy could reach about USD1.6 billion and USD2.3 billion, respectively.

Ocean Mining - Deep-seabed and seawater mining are the new frontier with huge potential. The value of top sea-bed mining minerals such as diamond, gold, cobalt, zinc and copper in Africa could reach a value added of about USD 6 billion. On the other hand, if African countries exploit about 2% of the market value from seawater mining of 10% of global production from seawater potential, it is worth about USD 50 billion of value added. This gives a combined value added of about USD 56 billion. It could reach about USD 76 by 2030 and USD 123 by 2063.

Oil and Gas - In 2018, the total GDP contribution of oil and gas in the major producing countries such as Angola, Congo. Dem. Rep., Cote d'Ivoire, Equatorial Guinea, Ghana, Mozambique, Nigeria and South Africa is about USD 80 billion. By 2030 and 2063, the value added could reach about USD 100 billion and USD 140 billion, respectively.

Coastal Tourism - In 2018 the sector contributed USD80 billion, about 3.4% of the GDP at annual growth rate of 1.3% over the last decade. The sector has potential for expansion and growth as most areas are yet to be exploited. The contribution to employment in 2018 was estimated at 24 million jobs in Africa at annual growth rate of 5.6% compared to global average of 3.9%. This provides potential opportunity for economic development. In 2030 the value added generated by the coastal tourism should exceed 100 billion with 28 million people employed while in 2063, it should generate 138 billion of value added with an employment figure of 35 million. The strong development of the continental tourism will boost the demand for tourism services and infrastructures. The development of eco-tourism will contribute to the conservation of ecosystems and reduce the ecological footprint.

Blue Carbon and Other Ecosystem Services - Blue Carbon is part of a Blue Economy with an opportunity to develop coastal wetland projects to mitigating climate change. The planning of blue carbon conservation projects and evaluating how ecosystems can be more effectively included within existing policy frameworks, carbon financing mechanisms such as Reducing Emissions from Deforestation and Land Degradation (REDD+) and other UNFCCC mechanisms are essential to restoring and protecting marine ecosystems. There is also a great opportunity for Nationally Determined Contributions (NDCs) for adapting and mitigating climate change in existing frameworks for carbon offsets referred to as carbon credits. Coastal protection, biomass production, water purification, etc., are among the most important ecosystem services delivered

by aquatic ecosystems. Their current value is estimated to the average monetary value of carbon sequestration of about USD 130 000 per km2 of mangrove, salt marshes and sea grasses. At the scale of Africa, the value is estimated at USD 40 billion in 2018 annually with a potential growth to USD 45 billion in 2030 to USD 70 billion in 2063 with an effective protection and restoration of coastal, marine and freshwater ecosystems.

Research and Education - Both are key pillars of the development of BE in Africa. Currently, the main research and education activities are linked to fisheries and aquaculture with a huge gap of expertise in renewable energy, deep sea mineral exploitation, oil and gas as these sectors are research driven by international companies with low connections to African education and research institutions. The growing importance of BE sectors and BE component such as Blue Carbon is currently pushing the development of new educational programs in pilot countries such as South Africa, Seychelles, Mauritius and Ghana. The current trend will be maintained until 2063.

NIGERIA'S BLUE ECONOMY

The Nigeria economy until the late 1960s relied on agricultural products for its foreign exchange alongside a few solid minerals. However, with the discovery of oil in abundance and following the boom in the oil industry in the 1970s, the other sectors that were predominant in economy notably; agriculture (blue economy) was abandoned (Adeyemi & Abiodun, 2013).

Blue economy (ocean) activities are globally acknowledged to play a key role in the alleviation of extreme poverty and hunger through employment and other economic opportunities. This includes the supply of seagoing personnel and ship recycling, ship owning and operating, shipbuilding and repair and port services, among others. Nigeria is blessed with a coastline of about 870km and about 3,000 kilometers of inland waterways with varieties of natural resources including petroleum, natural gas, tin, columbite, iron ore, coal, zinc, limestone, lead, and other minerals.

The unpredictable and harsh implications of over-dependence on oil heightened the need and call to diversify the Nigerian economy from oil towards the direction of the blue economy.

Proponents of an increase in the number of agricultural outputs think that the blue economy outputs have great capacities to stimulate the Niger Delta region and the Nigerian economy to the preferred growth and development. The blue economy is essential, not only to a wide array of biodiversity and ecosystems but also to the food chains, livelihoods and climate regulation for a human population heading towards nine billion individuals (Abdullahel, 2017).

The ocean (Blue economy) occupies about 75% of the Earth's surfaces and is home to more than half of all living things, which regularly makes a false impression that they are boundless resources. This prompts monstrous overexploitation and degradation, with an effect that comes to a long way past their shorelines. Ocean related issues are fundamental to a large portion of the Economic Development Goals and to the change towards the comprehensive green economy on which their sustainability depends. The complimentary "blue" component of that change known as the blue economy offers an inventive way to deal with monitoring the seas while receiving their rewards more impartially and sustainably.

Hoegh-Guldberg (2015) explained that it is increasingly obvious that without more sustainable management of the oceans, they, in turn, will be unable to sustain the population that depends on them. The blue economy integrates an innovative approach to the economic exploitation of the resources of oceans, lakes, rivers and different bodies of water.

CHALLENGES TO THE BLUE ECONOMY

The potential to develop the blue economy is limited by a series of challenges. For much of human history, aquatic ecosystems have been viewed and treated as limitless resources and largely cost-free repositories of waste. These resources, however, are far from limitless, and the world is increasingly seeing the impacts of this approach. The narrow coastal interface is oversubscribed by myriad sectors and is increasingly affected by climate change. Rising demand, ineffective governance institutions, inadequate economic incentives, technological advances, lack of or inadequate capacities, lack of full implementation of UNCLOS and other legal instruments, and insufficient application of management tools have often led to poorly regulated activities. This in turn has resulted in excessive use and, in some cases, irreversible change of valuable marine resources and coastal areas. In this increasingly competitive space, the interests of those most dependent and vulnerable (for example, small-scale artisanal fishers) are often marginalized, mostly for the benefit of other, more visible sectors (such as coastal tourism), where the actual economic benefits—while more clearly apparent at first—may actually be ephemeral or directly exported to foreign investors.The major human impacts include, among others, the following:

- **Unsustainable extraction from marine resources, such as unsustainable fishing** as a result of technological improvements coupled with poorly managed access to fish stocks and rising demand. FAO estimates that approximately 57 percent of fish stocks are fully exploited and another 30 percent are over-exploited, depleted, or recovering (FAO 2016). Fish stocks are further exploited by illegal, unreported, and unregulated fishing, which is responsible for roughly 11–26 million tons of fish catch annually, or US$10–22 billion in unlawful or undocumented revenue.
- **Physical alterations and destruction of marine and coastal habitats and landscapes** due largely to coastal development, deforestation, and mining. Coastal erosion also destroys infrastructure and livelihoods. Unplanned and unregulated development in the narrow coastal interface and near shore areas has led to significant externalities between sectors, suboptimal siting of infrastructure, overlapping uses of land and marine areas, marginalization of poor communities, and loss or degradation of critical habitats.

- **Marine pollution,** for example in the form of excess nutrients from untreated sewerage, agricultural runoff, and marine debris such as plastics.
- **Impacts of climate change, for example in the form of** both slow-onset events like sea-level rise and more intense and frequent weather events. The long-term climate Challenges to the Blue Economy change impacts on ocean systems are not yet fully understood, but it is clear that changes in sea temperature, acidity, and major oceanic currents, among others, already threaten marine life, habitats, and the communities that depend on them.
- **Unfair trade.** Exclusive Economic Zones, areas in which a state has sovereign rights over exploration and use of marine resources, are crucial to the economies of small island developing states and often dwarf their corresponding land mass and government's administrative capacity. (In Tuvalu, for instance, the EEZ is more than 26,000 times the size of the land mass.) In the case of fishing agreements allowing access to an EEZ, there is usually a low appropriation of fisheries export revenues by national operators and insufficient transfer to national stakeholders of specific fishing knowledge by foreign fishing companies, so the potential for national exploitation of those resources is reduced in the long run.

Despite a range of actors and large investments, current attempts to overcome these challenges have mostly been piecemeal, with no comprehensive strategy (for example, disparate efforts centered on fisheries governance, improving ports, marine litter efforts, and so on).

Even when one sectoral policy achieves some success, these results are often undermined by externalities from activities in another sector. For example, coastal zone management efforts, or support to coastal fishers, tend to be undermined by unbridled sand mining, ill-sited ports or aquaculture farms, or unregulated tourism development.

In coastal zones, declines in mangrove forest habitat resulting from habitat conversion, wood harvest, sea-level rise, destruction of dune systems from sand mining, and changes in sediment and pollutant loading from river basins combined with land reclamation for agriculture or infrastructure have serious negative impacts on fisheries by reducing or degrading spawning and feeding habitats.

Loss of mangrove forests, for instance, threatens profits from seafood harvests in excess of US$4 billion per year; in Belize, mangrove-rich areas produce on average 71 percent more fish biomass than areas with few mangroves.

In view of the challenges facing SIDS and coastal LDCs, partnerships can be looked at as a way to enhance capacity-building. Such partnerships already exist in more established sectors, such as fisheries, maritime transport, and tourism, but are found less in newer and emerging sectors.

There is thus an opportunity to develop additional partnerships around newer economic activities, such as marine biotechnology and renewable ocean energy.

A list of partnerships relating to the blue economy and its diverse sectors is available on the UN DESA website (https:www.un.org/development/desa/en/). The list of partnerships is dynamic and can be updated by users.

BLUE ECONOMY FUTURE TRENDS AND PROSPECTS

- Raise awareness to boost understanding of the Blue Economy idea still because of the relevant international rules, as well as recent UN agency tips on maritime cyber security threats and risk management.
- Introduction/establishment of coast guards among the waterways that.
- Develop an international framework and trade best practices to control and promote the adoption of blockchain technology in maritime transport.
- Developing and rolling out of maritime education and skills coaching policies supported comprehensive coaching, skills, and career gap analysis.
- Guaranteeing inclusivity in political beliefs and implementation processes of blue economy by incorporating native communities as well as autochthonic communities, girls and youth as real stakeholders.
- Pursue cooperation regionally and globally for sharing of experiences, info and best practices.
- Invest in simply accessible maritime info systems to facilitate educated and inclusive deciding.
- Implement sound urban designing as well as marine abstraction attending to conserve marine ecosystems.
- Promote business enterprise through diversification of business enterprise products.
- Produce necessary blue infrastructure, invest in relevant technologies, and strengthen funding mechanisms, build human capability and utilize talent, encourage analysis and innovation to drive sustainable energy and natural resources exploration and development of innovative industries among the blue economy.
- Empower women and youth to play the crucial role of championing the development of sustainable energy resources and mineral exploration among the blue economy as they account for about 60% of the Niger Delta and the world population at massive.
- Establish effective policy, regulative and institutional frameworks to safeguard the marine resources.
- Promote technology transfer and capability building for the little scale fisher-folks to foster their engagement in property fish production and process.
- Implement commitments created in maritime safety, security and regulative frameworks.
- Strengthen structures/frameworks for policy formulation, implementation, and analysis.

CONCLUSION

The ocean generates economic values that are not usually quantified (non-market data, including ecosystem services values). And, often there is no consensus on how to quantify these non- market values. In addition, the losses resulting from unsustainable use of coastal and marine resources and environmental degradation are not usually captured. We need a long-term effort to seek ways to measure natural capital to indicate whether the economic growth is sustainable over the long term (and value ecosystem goods and services), and agree to appropriate methodologies for each context. Thus, we need to start now on a balance sheet for ocean resources.

Our understanding of the ocean economy is changing as it is further studied and defined. In turn, industry sectors are being created or evolving to reflect demands for efficiency, sustainability and stewardship. Thus, this examination and categorization of the Blue Economy is timely. Let's make sure we rethink and define the *new* Blue Economy in such a way that ensures the sustainable economic growth and development of the resources and services of the ocean on which we all rely. At the core of the *new* Blue Economy concept is the de-coupling of socioeconomic development from environmental degradation. We are measuring as a subset of the entire ocean economy that has regenerative and restorative activities that lead to enhanced human health and well-being, including food security and creation of sustainable livelihoods.

The potential gains from realizing the African blue economy are substantial. While some nascent steps have been taken by a few countries to develop the blue economy, the acute security, maritime protection, environmental and other challenges facing African countries mean that much more is needed to spur progress. Several targeted, focused strategic initiatives, driven by strong African political leadership, including a new annual African Blue Economy Forum, may catalyze and sustain new momentum to build on early foundations.

Facts and figures originating from around the world present a scenario where women face enormous constraints in exercising their full potential in development programs. There are many factors, including those that are traditional, cultural, and mindset fixation among others because of which gender justice remains an elusive goal.

The situation is far more glaring in developing and least developed countries. Blue economy promises a new horizon for gender equality and women empowerment. The diverse nature of ocean-based industries and the rapidly developing blue growth programs can cater to economic prosperity for all and a fair share to women along the entire supply chain. Policy support will, however, be needed for inclusivity and a due share of women in stewardship of marine resources. The blue economy can provide them with gainful employment and a rare opportunity to establish many types of businesses of different scales to achieve economic independence, overcome poverty, and improve their well-being. Many of its newly emerging sectors require specific skills and advanced knowledge. Increasing the proportion of women in higher education will help them in meaningful employment that is critical for the success of the economy.

Existing national policies and development plans lack effective monitoring mechanisms and indicator frameworks to specifically show progress of the initiatives taken and to review their performance. There is a dire need for gender-differentiated data in all sectors of the blue economy.

Fisheries and aquaculture have a comparatively better record of gender-based jobs but that too has to be improved. Such data should be made available to policy-making institutions for assessment of the situation and formulating appropriate, evidence- based measures. Next important effort should be to facilitate data-policy integration to identify gaps in existing mechanisms and to address the problem(s). These are complex and intertwined issues that will require special integration tools to: (a) support structured policies of the national planning agencies and relevant ministries and (b) feed into development of industryspecific as well as national-level indicators to monitor effectiveness of the initiatives for gender equality.

An economy that is currently worth US$ 3–6 trillion/year deserves effective governance of the world's oceans to achieving a balance between development and ecosystem health and leveraging knowledge for integrating research, policy, and practice. Full potential of blue economy can only be realized if it is inclusive, allowing all sections of the society to contribute and share benefits. Developments in blue economy have used traditional as well as modern knowledge, and the programs for blue growth that are shaping up will require holistic and interdisciplinary knowledge rooted in the concept of sustainability.

REFERENCES

Abdullahel, B. (2017). Our Oceans and the blue economy: opportunities and challenges. *10th international conference on marine technology*. Available at https://www.sciencedirect.com/science/article/pii/S1877705817332447

About LDCs. (n.d.). https://www.oceanfdn.org/blog/looking-smalldetails

Adeyemi, K. S., & Abiodun, A. J. (2013). *Development of the non-oil sector in Nigeria*. Academic Press.

Allard, A., & Bauer, C. (2018). *The possible effects of the blue economy on gender quality in the republic of Seychelles* (Thesis). Linkoping University.

Amaechi, R. (2018). *Blue economy sustainability: Nigeria to partner other African countries*. Academic Press.

Asian Development Bank. (2014). Wave energy conversion and ocean thermal energy conversion potential in developing member countries. 2014 Asian Development Bank. Atlantic economy. *Marine Policy*, *64*, 72–81.

AUDA-NEPAD. (2019). *Development of the AUDA-NEPAD Blue Economy Programme*. Available at https://kippra.or.ke/kenyas-agenda-in-developing-the-blue-economy/

Bahar, H. (2019). *Ocean power: Tracking Clean Energy Progress*. IEA. doi:10.1016/j.proeng.2017.08.157

Barman, B. K., & Little, D. C. (2006). Nile tilapia (Oreochromis niloticus) seed production in irrigated rice fields in Northwest Bangladesh: An approach appropriate for poorer farmers. *Aquaculture (Amsterdam, Netherlands)*, *261*(1), 72–79. doi:10.1016/j.aquaculture.2006.06.018

Bennett, N. J., Cisneros-Montemayor, A. M., Blythe, J., Silver, J. J., Singh, G., Andrews, N., Calò, A., Christie, P., Di Franco, A., Finkbeiner, E. M., Gelcich, S., Guidetti, P., Harper, S., Hotte, N., Kittinger, J. N., Le Billon, P., Lister, J., López de la Lama, R., McKinley, E., ... Sumaila, U. R. (2019). Towards a sustainable and equitable blue economy. *Nature Sustainability*, *2*(11), 991–993. doi:10.103841893-019-0404-1

Brown, E. M. (2010). *A gender toolkit for educators*. United Nations Educational, Scientific and Cultural Organization.

Brugere, C., McAndrew, K., & Bulcock, P. (2001). Does cage aquaculture address gender goals in development? Results of a case study in Bangladesh. *Aquaculture Economics & Management*, *5*(3–4), 179–189. doi:10.1080/13657300109380286

CBD (Convention on Biological Diversity). (2010). Report on implementation of the programme challenges & lessons for less developed countries. *Covenant Journal of Business.*

Chan. (2019). Prospects and challenges of fish for food security in Africa. *Global Food Security, 20*, 17-25.

De Graaf, G., & Garibaldi, L. (2014). *The Value of African Fisheries.* FAO Fisheries and Aquaculture Circular No. 1093.

Diop. (2018). *The evolution of maritime transport in West and Central Africa*. The United Republic of Tanzania.

Economist Intelligence Unit. (n.d.). https://www.greengrowthknowledge.org/resource/blueeconomy-

Failler, P. (2018). *Demystifying the Sustainable Blue Economy*. International Conference on Sustainable Blue Economy, Nairobi, Kenya.

Failler, P. (2019). *Blue Economy of the Indian Ocean Region*. Third IORA Ministerial Blue Economy Conference "Promoting Sustainable Blue Economy- making the best use of opportunities from the Indian Ocean", Dhaka, Bangladesh.

Failler, P. (2019). *The Institutional Challenges for the Implementation of a Blue Economy Governance, The Law of the Blue Economy: International and South Asian Perspectives*. The Second Biennial Conference of the South Asia International Economic Law Network (SAIELN) will be held in Thiruvananthapuram, Kerala, India.

Failler, P., Touron-Gardic, G., & Traoré, M.-S. (2019). Is Aichi Target 11 Progress correctly measured for developing Countries? *Trends in Ecology & Evolution*, *34*(10), 875–879.

FAO. (2018). *The state of world fisheries and aquaculture: meeting the sustainable development goals*. Food and Agriculture Organization.

FAO. (2018). *The State of World Fisheries and Aquaculture – Meeting the Sustainable Development Goals*. FAO.

FAO (Food and Agriculture Organization). (2014a). *Securing Fish for the Caribbean*. FAO.

FAO, IFAD, UNICEF, WFP, & WHO. (2018). *The State of Food Security and Nutrition in the World 2018. Building climate resilience for food security and nutrition*. FAO.

Farr & Hall. (2015). *What is the environmental impact of a cruise holiday?* Presentation given at the Contemporary Perspectives in Tourism and Hospitality Research: Policy, Practice and Performance event, University of Brighton.

Hafner, M., Tagliapietra, S., & Strasser. L. (2018). *Energy in Africa Challenges and Opportunities*. Springer Briefs in Energy.

Harper, S., Grubb, C., Stiles, M., & Sumaila, U. R. (2017). Contributions by women to fisheries economies: Insights from five maritime countries. *Coastal Management*, *45*, 91–106.

Herr, D., Pidgeon, E., & Laffoley, D. (Eds.). (2012). *Blue carbon policy framework: based on the discussion of the international blue carbon policy working group. International Union for Conservation of Nature and Arlington Conservation International* Conservation International.

Hoegh-Guldberg, O. (2015). *Reviving the Ocean Economy: the Case for Action – 2015*. Academic Press.

Holmyard, N. (2018). *Seafood industry gender report highlights ongoing inequality*. Seafood Source News.

Hunt, B., & Vincent, A. C. (2006). Scale and sustainability of marine bioprospecting for pharmaceuticals. *Ambio*, *35*(2), 57–64.

Hussain Gulam, Al Karim, & Khurshed Alam. (2017). Major opportunities of blue economy development in Bangladesh. *Journal of the Indian Ocean Region, 13*(1), 111-118.

ILO. (2019). Work-related gender gaps persist but solutions are clear. *Journal of the Indian Ocean Region, 14*(1), 28–48.

Institute of African Studies. (2018). *International Symposium on Maritime Transport in Africa: Regional Integrations for Continental Development*. Author.

International Energy Agency. (2014). *Africa energy outlook—a focus on energy prospects in Sub-Saharan Africa* (World Energy Outlook Special Report). Author.

IPCC. (2014). *Climate Change 2014: Synthesis Report*. Contribution of Working Groups I, II and III to the Fifth Assessment Report of the Intergovernmental Panel on Climate Change. IPCC.

IRENA. (2015). *Africa 2030: Roadmap for A Renewable Energy Future*. www.irena.org/remap

IRENA. (2019). *Renewable Energy and Jobs. Annual Review 2019*. IRENA.

IRENA (International Renewable Energy Agency). (2016). *Innovation Outlook: Off shore Wind*. ITF Transport Outlook 2015.

IUCN. (2013). *Annual Report*. https://portals.iucn.org/library/efiles/documents/IUCN-2014-017.pdf

Jupiter, S. D., Cohen, P. J., Weeks, R., Tawake, A., & Govan, H. (2014). Locally-managed marine areas: Multiple objectives and diverse strategies. *Pacific Conservation Biology*, *20*(2), 165–179.

Kaup & Glavan. (2014). *Marine organisms produce half of the oxygen that land animals need to breathe*. https://oceanexplorer.noaa.gov/facts/oceanproduction.html

Kelleher, K. (2015). *Building the Blue Economy in the Western Indian Ocean*. Presented at the *8th Conference*.

Mele, G. (2014). *Mauritania Economic Update: 1*. World Bank. http://documents.worldbank.org/curated/en/2014/07/20133610/mauritania-economic-update

Mezher, T., Fath, H., Abbas, Z., & Khaled, A. (2011). Technoeconomic assessment and environmental impacts of desalination technologies. *Desalination*, *266*(1), 263–273.

Michel, K., & Noble, P. (2008). Technological Advances in Maritime Transportation. *The Bridge*, *38*(2), 33–40.

Middlebury Institute of International Studies at Monterey. (n.d.). https://www.oceaneconomics.org/market/coastal/coastalEconResults.asp?IC=N

Miller, K.A., Thompson, K.F., Johnston, P., & Santillo, D. (2019). *An Overview of Seabed Mining Including the Current State of Development, Environmental Impacts, and Knowledge Gaps*. Academic Press.

Mills, D. J., Westlund, L., de Graaf, G., Kura, Y., Willman, R., & Kelleher, K. (2011). Underreported and undervalued: Small-scale fisheries in the developing world. In Managing Small Scale Fisheries: Frameworks and Approaches. CABI.

Ministry of Natural Resources and Tourism. (2014). *An Overview of the Natural Resource Sector: Achievements, Challenges and Priorities for Financial Year 2014/2015*. Author.

Misko, J. (2008). *Combining formal, non-formal and informal learning for workforce skill development*. National Centre for Vocational Education and Research.

Modelevsky, M. S., & Modelevsky, M. M. (2016). Assessment of the discovered and undiscovered oil and gas of Africa. *Russian Geology and Geophysics*, *57*, 1342–1348. https://doi.org/10.1016/j.rgg.2016.08.019

Monfort, M. C. (2015). *The Role of Women in the Seafood Industry. GLOBEFISH Research Program 119*. Food and Agriculture Organization.

Monnereau & Failler. (2014). *Unlocking the full potential of the blue economy: Are African Small Island Developing States ready to embrace the opportunities?* African Climate Policy Center and Economic Commission for Africa. http://www.climdev-africa.org/sites/default/files/DocumentAttachments/Blue%20 Economy_19Sept14.pdf

Park, D., Seo, K., Kildow, D., & Judith, T. (2014). *Rebuilding the classification system of the ocean economy*. Academic Press.

Patil, P.G., Virdin, J., Colgan, C.S., Hussain, M.G., Failler, P., & Vegh, T. (2018). *Toward a Blue Economy: A Pathway for Bangladesh's Sustainable Growth*. The World Bank Group.

Patil, P. G., Virdin, J., Diez, S. M., Roberts, J., & Singh, A. (2016). *Toward A Blue Economy: A Promise for Sustainable Growth in the Caribbean; An Overview*. The World Bank.

Pauli, G. (2010). *The Blue Economy: 10 years-100 innovations-100 million jobs*. United State.

Pendleton, L., Donato, D. C., Murray, B. C., Crooks, S., Jenkins, W. A., Sifleet, S., Craft, C., & ... . (2012). Estimating global "blue carbon" emissions from conversion and degradation of vegetated coastal ecosystems. *PLoS One*, *7*(9), 1–7.

Pramod, G., Nakamura, K., Pitcher, T., & Delagran, L. (2014). Estimates of illegal and unreported fish in seafood imports to the USA. *Marine Policy*, *48*, 102–113. doi:10.1016/j.marpol.2014.03.019

Ragin, C. C. (2008). *What is Qualitative Comparative Analysis*. QCA.

Rakotondraompiana & Failler. (2015). Natural resources management and climate change in East Africa. In *Harnessing the Blue Economy for Eastern Africa's Development*. United Nations Economic Commission for Africa (UNECA).

Ramsar. (2015). *State of the World's Wetlands and Their Services to People: A Compilation of Recent Analyses*. Ramsar Briefing Note 7. Ramsar Convention on Wetlands.

Richard, M. (2019). *Blue Economy, Marine litter and pollution, Climate change and Environment, Talking points*. Office of the Vice President, Directorate of Environment and Climate Change.

Rodriguez-Delgado, C., Bergillos, R. J., & Iglesias, I. (2019, June). Dual wave farms for energy production and coastal protection under sea level rise. *Journal of Cleaner Production*, *222*(10), 364–372.

Rustomjee, C. (2016). *Financing the Blue Economy in Small States*. Center for International Governance Innovation.

Rutaisire, J., Kabonesa, C., Okechi, J. K., & Boera, P. N. (2010). Lake Victoria Basin: Gender issues in fish farming. In F. Flintan & S. Tedla (Eds.), Natural resource management. Academic Press.

Schumacher, K. P. (2014). Gender relations in global agrifood value chains: A review. *Die Erde J Geogr Soc Berlin*, *145*(3), 127–134.

Secretariat of the Pacific Community. (2010). *The Future of Pacific Island Fisheries*.

Senaratne, M., & Zimbroff, A. (2019). *The Blue Economy in the Indian Ocean. A Literature Review*. Academic Press.

Serrano, S. (2018). *Progressing women's economic empowerment enhancing user-producer engagement for policy responsive data and effective data-driven policies*. Economic and Social Commission for Asia and the Pacific.

Shaleh, S. R. M., Shapawi, R., Estim, A., & Mustafa, S. (2019). Leveraging scientific knowledge in aquaculture for entrepreneurship- case studies at Universiti Malaysia Sabah. *Borneo J Mar Sci Aquacult*, *3*(1), 25–32.

Shapawi, R., Shaleh, S. R. M., Annita-Yong, S. K., Abdullah, F. C., & Othman, R. (2019). Gender equality in blue growth. In S. Mustafa & A. Estim (Eds.), *Blue economy and blue growth in the context of development policies and priorities in Malaysia*. Penerbit UMS.

Shirajee, S. S., Salehin, M. M., & Ahmed, N. (2010). The changing face of women for small-scale aquaculture development in rural Bangladesh. *Aquaculture Asia Magazine*, *15*(2), 9–16.

Smith-Godfrey, S. (2016). Defining the Blue Economy. *Maritime Affairs*.

Tonazzini, D., Fosse, J., Morales, E., González, A., Klarwein, S., Moukaddem, K., & Louveau, O. (2019). *Blue Tourism. Towards a sustainable coastal and maritime tourism in world marine regions*. Eco-Union.

Torley, H. (2017). *Pharma, biotech and healthcare industries gender gap*. News Medical.

UNCTAD. (2014a). *Small Island Developing States: Challenges in Transport and Trade Logistics*. Background note to third session of Multi-Year Expert Meeting on Transport, Trade Logistics and Trade Facilitation. UNCTAD.

UNCTAD. (2018) Ocean economy and fisheries. *United Nations Conference on Trade and Development*.

UNCTAD. (2016). *Oceans economy and trade, Sustainable fisheries, transport and tourism*. UNCTAD.

UNCTAD. (2018). *Review of Maritime Transport Freight market 2017 and World seaborne trade 2017*. UNCTAD.

UNCTAD. (2018). *Sustainable freight transport in support of 2030 Agenda*. UNCTAD.

UNDESA. (2008). *Achieving Sustainable Development and Promoting Development Cooperation*. UNDESA.

UNDP. (2018). Blue Economy, Community Solutions. *UNDP.*

UNECA. (2016). *The Blue Economy.* UNECA.

UNECA. (2017). *Africa's Blue Economy: A policy handbook.* UNECA.

UNEP, FAO, IMO, UNDP, IUCN, & GRID-Arendal. (2012). *Green Economy in a Blue World.* Author.

UNEP. (2013). *Green Economy Definition.* https://www.unep.org/greeneconomy/AboutGEI/

UNEP. (2013). *Green Economy Definition.* UNEP.

UNESCO. (2013). *Girls' education – the facts.* United Nations Educational, Scientific and Cultural Organization.

UNESCO. (2016). *Facts and Figures on Marine Pollution.* UNESCO.

UNESCO. (2017). Education and the sustainable development goals. UNESCO.

United Nations. (2014). *United Nations Blue Economy Concept Paper.* Author.

United Nations. (2016). *The First Global Integrated Marine Assessment: World Ocean Assessment I.* Group of Experts of the Regular Process.

United Nations Conference on Sustainable Development. (n.d.). https://sustainabledevelopment.

United Nations Economic Commission for Africa. (2016). *Africa's blue economy: A policy handbook.* UNECA.

United Nations Environment Programme. (2012). *Green Economy in a Blue World Synthesis Report.* UNEP. www.unep.org/pdf/green_economy_blue.pdf

University of Arizona. (n.d.). https://eprints.ncrm.ac.uk/250/1/What_is_QCA.pdf

UNWTO. (2014). *Tourism in Small Island Developing States (SIDS): Building a More Sustainable Future for the People of Islands.* UNWTO.

UNWTO. (2013). *Tourism Highlights.* UNWTO.

U.S. Department of Energy. (2019). *Powering the Blue Economy: Exploring Opportunities for Marine Renewable Energy in Maritime Markets.* Author.

USAID. (2018). *Power Africa Gas Road Map to 2030.* USAID.

Veliu, A., Gessese, N., Ragasa, C., & Okali, C. (2009). *Gender analysis of aquaculture value chain in Northeast Vietnam and Nigeria.* Agriculture and rural development discussion paper 44. The World Bank.

Waheed, Z., Manjaji-Matsumoto, M., & Abdul-Basri, N. (2019a). Human capacity building and public education aligned with global perspectives for adaptation in coastal and ocean management- The role of the Borneo Marine Research Institute. In Ocean yearbook 33. Brill Nijhoff.

World Bank. (2017). *Girls' education.* The World Bank.

World Bank. (2019). *Creating a sustainable food future: a menu of solutions to feed nearly 10 billion people by 2050. World Resources Report*. The World Bank.

World Bank & Food and Agriculture Organization. (2008). *The Sunken Billions: The Economic Justification for Fisheries Reform*. Author.

World Bank & United Nations Department of Economic and Social Affairs. (2017). *The Potential of the Blue Economy: Increasing Long-term Benefits of the Sustainable Use of Marine Resources for Small Island Developing States and Coastal Least Developed Countries*. World Bank.

World Bank. (2019). *Where Sun Meets Water: An Introduction to Floating Solar*. World Bank, ESMAP and Solar Energy Research Institute of Singapore (SERIS).

WTTC. (2016). *Travel and Tourism Economic Impact Summary 2016*. WTTC.

Zhelyazkova, V. (2015). Green Banking-Definition, Scope and Proposed Business Model. *Journal of International Scientific Publications, 9,* 309-315.

Chapter 11
Environmental Accounting Impacts in Greening the Economy

Nima Norouzi
https://orcid.org/0000-0002-2546-4288
Bournemouth University, UK

ABSTRACT

Accounting has been increasing its importance. As time goes by, it has spread to sectors such as social, environmental, and others, in which they seek to have financial control of the resources that these sectors possess within. In these sectors, the one that has been most affected has been the environmental sector, largely due to the same social development, because people in their daily lives generate waste that is not friendly to the environment, or they do not have the habit of properly classifying these wastes, which is why this chapter seeks to analyze the importance of environmental accounting by inquiring into different sources of consultation on the subject, knowing the progress made by the implementation of environmental accounting in industrial companies and the positive or negative impact that it has had in different socio-economic environments.

INTRODUCTION

Human activities have led to damages to the environment, including depletion of natural resources, environmental pollution and abnormal climates. The global consensus at present is to promote sustainable development, among which corporate social responsibility (CSR) is most closely associated with business. Many countries around the world have mandated enterprises to establish green accounting and to disclose environmental information for the reference of interested parties. The Ministry of Environment Japan defined green accounting as "quantitative assessment of the expenditures and benefits in environmental protection activities" and specified "systematic records and reports, maintenance of a positive relationship between the enterprises and the natural ecology, and promotion of effective and efficient environmental activities, in order to achieve sustainable development". The green accounting system in EU countries,

DOI: 10.4018/978-1-6684-3393-5.ch011

such as Denmark and the Netherlands, is required by law to disclose environmental information to the government. Countries that have not legislated related laws, such as the U.S. and Japan, have mandated some enterprises to disclose environmental information. In Taiwan, the government has provided guidance to promote the green accounting system. In Vietnam, the government enacted the Environmental Taxation Act in 2010. Multinational corporations are increasingly concerned with whether their suppliers have disclosed green accounting information before proceeding with transactions. It is obvious that green accounting has become a mainstream trend in the world, and legislation of related laws is necessary. Once green accounting is enforced by the government, enterprises are required to internalize the external costs of the production activities, thus increasing the production and operational costs. Hence, in order to maintain the current profits or to lower costs, enterprises must make improvements in product design, such as green innovation or product redevelopment.

Accounting has been increasing its importance; as time goes by, it has spread to sectors such as social, environmental, and others, in which they seek to have financial control of the resources that these sectors possess. Within these sectors, the one that has been most affected has been the environmental sector, largely due to social development itself, because people in their daily lives generate waste that is not environmentally friendly or does not have the custom of properly classifying these wastes. Additionally, the increase in the trade of vehicles that run on fuel has increased, and this also causes environmental damage, and even in humans. The advance of this problem has increased, and it has been necessary to implement some corrective measures in which several social actors have intervened, such as the State, society, and companies, seeking to mitigate pollution and the risk that it represents for the same society.

Given the above, it is important to analyze. How is it possible to implement environmental accounting in industrial companies? This issue is focused on the high pollution that industrial companies produce to the environment in the country. The main causes of pollution are the chemicals and gases that these companies produce, for which it is important to raise awareness, obtaining a benefit for society and the environment; Therefore, the general objective of this work is to analyze the importance of environmental accounting by investigating different sources of consultation on the subject, knowing the progress made by the implementation of environmental accounting in industrial companies and the positive or negative impact that it has had in different socio-economic environments. Environmental accounting has been gaining importance in organizations since this, and it is possible to measure the costs and expenses incurred for the management of the waste disposal that the productive operation generates, thus becoming a source of information. That serves for decision making and, above all, to define the raw materials used in production.

With the implementation of this practice, a benefit is generated for companies (because the State provides tax benefits to companies with good environmental practices) and society since the risk of health conditions is reduced. Currently, it has become a common practice among companies to implement corporate social responsibility projects. Companies become aware of external factors; they seek to repair environmental damage through convenient benefits for all interested parties. The research project focuses on the study and analysis of environmental accounting in industrial companies in Columbia. In the productive development of these companies, waste is generated that negatively affects the environment, and this condition may represent an increase in the costs and expenses of these companies. Taking these increases into account, companies must implement models such as environmental accounting, which allow them to measure the financial impact that this pollution generates. Regarding the structure of this work, the reader will find a four-section analysis on the importance of environmental accounting, implementation of environmental accounting, environmental accounting in industrial companies, as well as the impact and evolution of environmental accounting, providing information found under investigation; In the same way, there will be some antecedents, at the same time the materials and methods that were used through the investigation, as well as a list of activities for the development of the general objective and specific objectives, providing analysis and discussion of the results obtained according to the conducting the interviews and later the discussion of the results, this to end with the respective conclusions.

BACKGROUND

Since the implementation of economic reform and opening-up policy in China, China has sacrificed nature while pursuing the economy's fast-growth. Although the economy has proliferated, the degree of damage to the ecological environment is also severe (Ebenstein et al. 2015). The economic activities of enterprises have created substantial economic profits and social value. However, these achievements have also generated some degree of harm to the natural environment.

Just like international agencies and countries, China attaches great importance to resource conservation and building an environment-friendly society. The concept of green development in China appeared for the first time in the 12th Five-Year Plan and was formulated as the goal of China's long-term sustainable development (Mol et al. 2011). As a tool for enterprises to provide information to information users, accounting has the responsibility of providing corporate environmental information. Using existing financial reports to supplement corporate environmental information disclosure is currently the most common way of environmental accounting information disclosure (Lu and Li 2020; Pien 2020; Tzouvanas et al. 2020). It increases how supplementary information is disclosed in the company's annual report (Iatridis 2013), listing announcement (Tang et al. 2020), prospectus (Pan et al. 2020), and information disclosure in interim reports (Goron 2018).

As China continues to lead the world with production (Wijsman et al. 2019; Taplin and Winterton 2019), production's side effect remains a significant problem (Chen et al. 2019; Sarkodie and Strezov 2019). In 2003, China issued the first environmental information guidelines (Mol et al. 2011). Three years later, the central government issued a public participation impact assessment on environmental disclosure (Hu and Karbhari 2015). In May 2008, enterprises were required to proactively disclose their environmental information (Zeng et al. 2010). Disclosure of environmental accounting information enables users to understand the environmental impact of corporate behavior.

Traditional accounting ignores the scarcity of natural environmental resources (Mather and Chapman 2018). But with the severe depletion of natural resources, environmental problems are becoming more prominent (Fondevila et al. 2019; Odoemelam and Okafor 2018), and traditional accounting can no longer meet the needs of information users. The extreme waste of natural environmental resources and the consequences of pollution has resulted in much attention to environmental protection (Acar and Temiz 2020; Odoemelam and Okafor 2018). Mining companies are facing unprecedented pressure due to innovative accounting methods of environmental cost (Jaskoski 2014; Martinico-Perez et al. 2018). As environmental problems continue to be a major concern of the globe (Lu and Li 2020; Tang et al. 2020; Chen et al. 2019), enterprises are facing pressure from the outside world in terms of minimizing production, which in turn will reduce pollution especially in heavily polluting industries such as mining. Environmental issues severely restrict the development of enterprises. Investors mostly pay attention to the company's financial situation, while little or less attention is paid on its corporate environmental performance (Deswanto and Siregar 2018; Newig et al. 2018). This has led to the need for the mining companies to strengthen environmental accounting so as to achieve coordinated development of economic and environmental benefits.

X. Meng et al. (2014a) compared corporate environmental information disclosure content ratings with environmental performance ratings. Through comparative analysis, it was found that changes in environmental performance would not affect the disclosure of environmental information. Later, Hassan and Romilly (2018) used Canadian companies as samples and found that companies' public decisions are positively correlated with pollution tendency. That is, corporate environmental information disclosure is negatively correlated with environmental performance. Tadros and Magnan (2019) found a significant and positive relationship between environmental performance and quality environmental disclosure. The mixed findings from the relationship between environmental information disclosure and environmental performance have resulted in a literature gap in this study area.

Taking into account the health impacts of environmental pollution, it is essential for companies that, through their activities, pollute the environment to take some actions to protect the environment. This study, therefore, seeks to (1) examine the compliance of environmental accounting reporting for listed mining companies and (2) explore the relationship that exists between environmental accounting information disclosure and environmental performance for mining companies listed in China.

The study adopted a quantitative research approach. Panel data extracted from a secondary source from the period 2000–2018 for listed mining companies of the two stock exchanges in China mainland were used for the empirical studies. Using Stata version 15 statistical package, Common Correlated Effects Mean Group (CCEMG) and Augmented Mean Group (AMG) estimators were used for the long-run relationship analysis. Our cointegration estimation analysis concluded that corporate environmental performance and environmental information disclosure has a positive and significant relationship at a 1% level. Trend analysis revealed that mining companies comply with environmental information disclosure in China.

Most of the previous studies on environmental accounting information disclosure focused on a particular company or city or province (Murdifin et al. 2019; Leung and Snell 2019). Few of the studies were able to take a whole industry of a country into consideration (Yao and Liang 2019; Tkachenko et al. 2019). Among the few studies, none of the studies considered the mining industry.

In Columbia, environmental problems have been increasing because human beings searching for satisfying their needs have been changing how they transform products. Since the 1990s and up to the present, laws have been enacted in which caring for the environment is beginning to become an obligation for both society and companies. The latter, in compliance with these standards, have been adapting to models that allow them to know the costs generated by the entire environmental issue "where the international financial information standards are born and among them a very important part that is concerning the protection and efficient management of natural resources and the importance of said impact on companies "(Cubides, 2017), there they begin to unify concepts and from there arises environmental accounting.

From the emergence of environmental accounting, it is becoming necessary for companies to generate information not only related to the economy within them, but also at the level of the environment "Accounting limited to disclosing information of a financial nature to users of interest; in this case, the accounting will only reflect the economic impacts of the company, ignoring the social and environmental impacts "(Rodríguez, 2011) generating information that is taken into account within its financial statements.

Currently, environmental accounting is already beginning to be part of companies. It becomes an important factor when presenting financial statements "it is pertinent to give rise to environmental accounting since it is no longer restricted only to figures and financial issues, but also the importance of accounting matters in aspects of Corporate Social Responsibility and sustainable development "(Bejarano & Chavarro, 2017) allowing the information they contain to be more truthful and real since many more factors are taken into account when assuming costs and expenses. Based on the reviews of the writings on environmental accounting, the text begins by talking about the importance of environmental accounting, and then an image is shown as a reference for environmental policies. They talk about environmental accounting in industrial companies and how they impact environmentally, then it is mentioned how accounting has been evolving in the environmental field to show basic aspects of environmental accounting and pollution finally.

As seen above, green accounting is to use lifecycle assessment to measure the environmental impacts of corporate activities, promote the use of clean production, adopt total cost assessment and combine traditional accounting to disclose the environmental financial information of the enterprises. The purpose is to urge enterprises to implement effective and efficient environmental activities, so as to achieve sustainable development.

Green accounting makes environmental expenditure a part of operational cost; thus, new thinking should be adopted for product design, in order to maintain the existing profits, enhance environmental performance or meet the green accounting rules. The new product design concept should meet the environmental requirements on product development and production. As the common goal of product design is to solve various problems, namely a concept of logical thinking instead of data computation of production technology, product design should be based on the thinking and analysis of the "concept", thus accomplishing the design according to the concept. The current green concept is to improve the environment, restore the ecology and maintain sustainable operation. Green design is environment oriented; in other words, environmental concerns carry the same weight as profitability in the product design and development process.

Importance of Enviromental Accounting

Globalization has allowed the world and mainly in companies, to broaden their vision of the benefit generated by the development of their activity, as they have been implementing policies that contribute to the growth of companies, it has also been generating the development of sustainability "sustainable development is the term given to the balance of the planet's management in three areas: environmental, social and economic" (Cortes & Peña, 2015). This has allowed companies to raise awareness of society.

To execute these sustainable development policies, companies implement information systems that allow them to know the benefit they are receiving from this. Hence, the importance of the implementation of environmental accounting within companies begins to be identified.

It is based on the fact that accounting-environmental information is a priority for business management. To quantify, record, and report the damage caused to the environment and the preventive or corrective actions necessary to avoid them. Environmental accounting is highly relevant to establish the degree of impact presented by applying policies and instruments for regulating and controlling the environment. Therefore it is necessary to establish the parameters to provide pertinent, feasible, and relevant information for its conformation within the world social sphere. (Londoño et al., 2009)

This importance has reached the point where its applicability has become law because the environment has become an important protagonist for companies, society, and even the State.

Considerations Regarding the Implementation of Environmental Accounting

Companies consider it important to show the results of environmental accounting management in their financial statements since the decisions made for the benefit of the companies' stakeholders depend on it. Environmental, depends on the quality of the information available to administrators since companies trust the most traditional types of financial information "(Urrea, 2015). In this financial information, companies show social balances in which the investment and/or the benefit of environmental accounting are detailed, and the transactions carried out with the environment.

Environmental accounting is part of the many processes that exist in companies. For its implementation, diagnoses must be made, in which they identify how they can contribute to this "implementation of policies that are complied with and not that remain embodied on paper, and our permanent collaboration, we will allow the environment in which we operate to be more prosperous and durable for future generations "(Arévalo, 2013) for this it is necessary that reviews of the processes are made. It is analyzed in which part of each of them that polluting factor is generated or that is not friendly to the environment; once this has been identified, the respective study can be carried out to find a way to implement corrective or improvement measures.

Environmental Accounting in Industrial Companies

The main pollutants occur in companies that transform raw materials into finished products because the process of transforming these products can generate polluting factors such as smoke, materials that are not biodegradable, large amounts of garbage with waste, among others. The work of this type of company, for the implementation of an environmental accounting system, is more arduous. Still, its implementation favors them, to the extent that its management can better measure costs and know the expenses incurred by companies after the production process; additionally, industrial companies must have the people in their environmental accounting system as their main actors. For this, they must generate sustainable development policies that allow both companies and the surrounding society to have a development that is not dependent and is maintained over time.

One of how industrial companies can mitigate environmental damage is:

For example, the replacement of machinery by one that consumes less energy and generates little noise, machines that reduce waste and maximize the use of raw materials, machines that trap pollution, others; It is thought that in this way Colombian companies will be able to maintain their profits and contribute to caring for the environment and have social and environmental responsibility. (Sánchez & Rodríguez, 2017)

For all this environmental inclusion to work in the best way, both companies and individuals must be part of this reduction to achieve a healthier environment. "It is necessary to overcome the business paradigm that considers the environmental variable as a source of problems associated with large expenses, which goes against the organization's profitability" (Bortone et al., 2004).

Environmental Impact and Evolution of Environmental Accounting

The environmental impact is one of the problems in the country that is caused by pollution, such as the use of natural resources and the soil, and this means that earth movements are no longer used for planting or a good use of resources, for this there are environmental assets, environmental liabilities and environmental costs, which are part of the accounting and environmental process. "Environmental assets represent the goods that serve for the preservation, protection, and environmental recovery" (Colmenares et al., 2015) With the help of technologies such as machines, which are called In accounting for property, plant, and equipment, with these new trends the costs of machinery expenses can be reduced to contaminate less the environment that is breathed.

Environmental liabilities are all those that are also found in the accounting and are debts for environmental damage, for investments and in their effect generate environmental costs that are those that facilitate the generation of projects that are carried out by the social and environmental responsibility of the companies.

DANE statistics show some asset investments made by some companies in industrial sectors to improve the environment.

Industrial establishments made investments in protecting and conserving the environment in 2016 for a value of $ 236,243 million. The environmental protection categories in which the largest investments were made were: air and climate protection (56.8%), wastewater management (32.6%), and waste management (3.9%), The groups of industrial divisions that made the largest investments in environmental protection and conservation in 2016 were: industries of other non-metallic mineral products (38.6%), food, beverages and tobacco (27.0%) and manufacture of substances and chemical products (10.0%). (DANE, 2016)

These statistics were made to quantify and verify whether industrial manufacturing companies in Colombia faced challenges to corporate social responsibility and thus have competitiveness with other companies in the sector. Within IAS 37, there are important costs that are environmental and are those that help to be reflected in the financial statements to demonstrate a real cost of the situation, such as, for example:

- By materials used.
- For supply costs.
- By manipulation and treatment of resources.
- For administrative actions.
- For premiums and insurance costs.
- For amortizations.
- Other costs for environmental action. (Álvarez, 2012)

Since these costs, what they do is reduce pollution and help to improve the operation of industrial companies in the future.

Literature review

In the communities, different social projects are developed that generate a positive impact, since they are thought for the benefit of different actors such as companies and the community itself, environmental accounting uses "different methods that allow evaluating the management that the organization exercises over environmental wealth "(Mejía & Vargas, 2012); it also helps to have costs that benefit these companies.

One of the most relevant aspects is that "environmental accounting allows to regain that trust that has been lost since it takes the company's financial statements as to its central information axis, but linking them with the environmental aspect" (Orrego, 2018), this approach can be seen reflected in the financial information of the organizations since within their costs and/or expenses the record of transactions associated with operations related to environmental aspects is shown.

Environmental costs are all those values incurred in those associated with the prevention of the environment "such as the consumption, necessary and duly valued, of productive factors related to natural resources essential for economic operations; the use of the natural environment of waste, generated by production and consumption activities "(Colmenares, 2015). These are all those resources that are not easy to classify and affect health and air.

Natural resources in the country are not consumed intentionally; although companies and society in general pay to use them, there is excessive consumption of them,

The reason why environmental goods are not properly valued is due, above all, that there is no defined market for their transaction and that no one would be willing to pay for something that could be obtained for free since environmental resources are not privately owned (Bello, 2015).

In society, awareness of the use of these resources must be created; only in this way can we contribute to improving environmental care in the different environments in which the community participates.

The public accountant, in addition to giving public faith and preparing financial statements, is also in the process of implementing environmental accounting, which provides a service to industrial companies and society since "in many companies, environmental policies and objectives are defined well enough by accountants, because they can begin to determine a role in measurement, analysis, and control, and therefore contribute to environmental improvement "(Lezca, 2019) and in its effect provides them an ecological and tax benefit in the country. At present, technology has evolved more and more, and environmental accounting is an issue that has not been left behind, it has been gaining importance over time; these two aspects have a certain relationship, as the author mentions in the following section:

Environment and technology should be considered, then, as two complementary and essential variables in development. In such a circumstance, the protection of the first should move as a unique possibility for human survival in permanent conditions of progress in levels of living standards. Community (Franco, 2009). Public accountants have an important challenge in the study and application of environmental accounting in organizations. It is an issue of utmost importance that must be considered since the environmental issue must be considered when developing new business units. Environmental pollution can be seen from various points of view, as is the environment through breathing and the consequences generated daily by the misclassification of said waste. It is also the incorporation into the receiving bodies of solid, liquid, or gaseous substances, or mixtures of them, provided that they adversely alter the natural conditions of the same or affect the health, hygiene, or well-being of the public (Ochoa et al., 2013; Norouzi, 2021). Due to this, high rates of garbage production are generated, reflected in the habitat daily.

MATERIALS AND METHODS

This work is qualitative because it collects several results to interpret speeches and observations that carry descriptive results. For this, literature reviews about accounting, the environment, and others were carried out that showed their relationship so that they allowed to identify the importance of environmental accounting in industrial companies. The methodology used for this research is analytical because it allows us to explore the investigated information to respond to the proposed objective, investigating the implications that environmental practices have in companies' accounting and how they influence the

Table 1. List of Activities for the Development of Objectives

Specific objectives	Performed activities
Analyze the importance of environmental accounting by inquiring into different sources of consultation on the subject, knowing the progress made in implementing environmental accounting in industrial companies.	Information gathering. Interviews with professionals who knew about the subject. Analysis of the information collected.
Compare information reported by different companies that apply environmental accounting, reviewing their financial reports.	Search in the business pages to give comparability to the investigated information. Analyze the information found to present a result comparable to that of other companies in the industrial sector.
Identify the main environmental accounting accounts by reviewing the literature on the use of these accounts in the accounting of industrial companies.	Queries in databases, graduate work, magazine articles, and web pages. Identification of the main accounts managed by industrial companies.
Explain the benefits that companies obtain using environmental accounting, investigating in magazine articles and laws the advantages obtained with applying this.	Review of information found where many companies, apart from having tax benefits, have implemented corporate social responsibility (CSR), being inclusive with society, the environment, and the environment in developing different projects.

construction of the statement's financial resources. The technique carried out for the investigation was the interview, which was carried out with five administrative professionals who work in the industrial field and know the basic aspects of environmental accounting. In this order and to develop the technique chosen for the investigation, the applied questionnaire was as follows:

Why is environmental accounting important?

How has the progress of industrial companies been in the implementation of environmental accounting?

What are the main accounting accounts and standards that must be considered in the environmental accounting implementation process?

What do you think should be the best way to disclose environmental information from an accounting perspective?

What are the benefits of companies when implementing environmental accounting?

RESULTS AND DISCUSSION

At this point, the results obtained through the application of the interviews are shown; from this, it begins by graphically showing how important professionals consider environmental accounting. The main accounting accounts related to the subject are shown, and then the progress they have been making in accounting disclosures is evidenced. Finally, and based on this, a brief analysis of each of these issues is made, fulfilling the established objectives.

The interviewees stated that Environmental accounting could measure the impacts (positive or negative) that companies have on the ecosystem or the environment in which the activities or development of the company's corporate purpose are carried out. It should be remembered that what is not measured cannot be controlled, and this is where environmental accounting becomes important, that is, in being able to measure the impacts that companies have on the environment, they are also those industrial companies that act in their process generation of resources through the transformation of natural raw materials, since

Figure 1. Importance of Environmental accounting

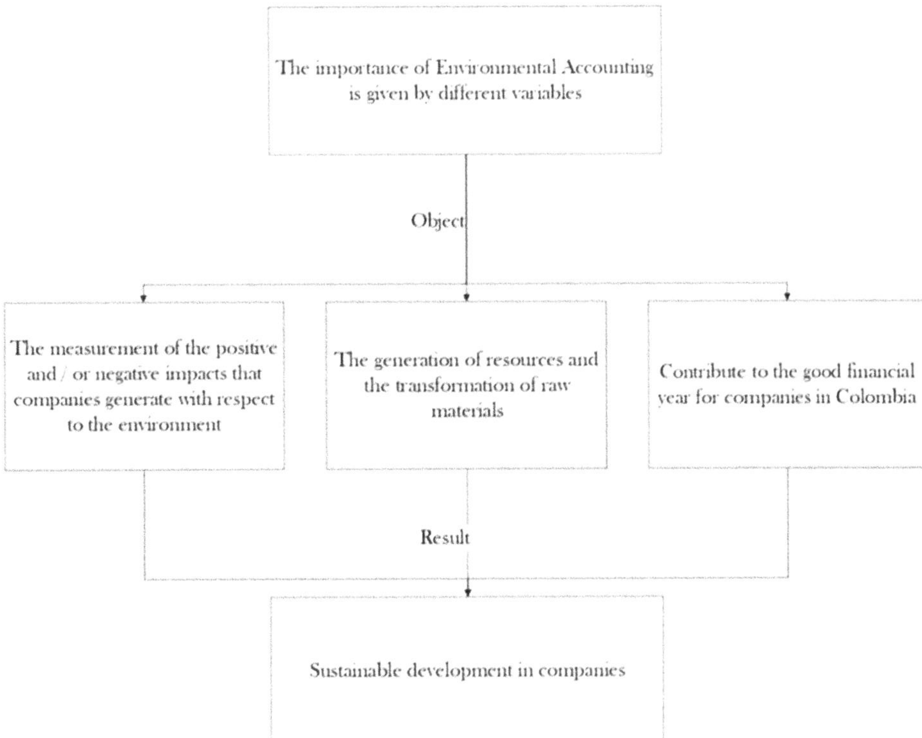

it allows to measure the sustainable development of companies, in addition to providing data that highlights the contribution of all-natural resources together with the good financial year(Norouzi et al., 2021).

From the previous evidence, the interviewees say that, although the IASB (IFRS issuing body) has already touched on the issue and there are regulations such as that referring to Biological assets, more than accounting accounts, it requires state intervention, with fines, sanctions, and benefits.

The following accounts have been observed in some companies:

- Environmental licenses.
- Lawsuits for contamination.
- Income from the sale of environmental goods.
- Environmental liabilities for lawsuits.
- provisions regarding equity and results.

The previous statements of the interviewees show that the best way to reveal this information is:

- Management reports and qualitative reports.
- Report through environmental indicators.
- Through the financial statements.
- Through the progress report and the correct application of the environmental management system.
- For recycled products.

Figure 2. Main accounting accounts

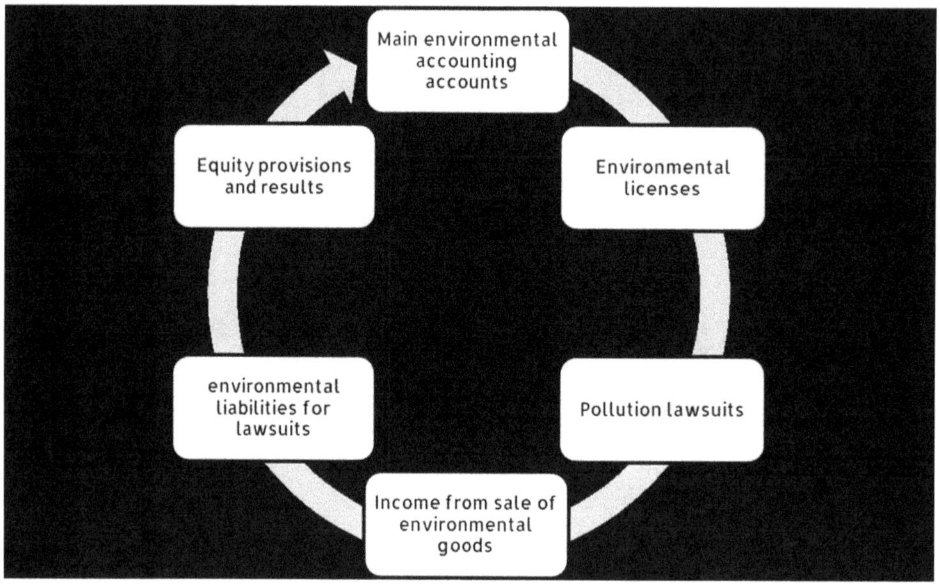

- By reducing the consumption of materials through recycling.
- Policies, advances, and methodologies that companies implement.

Under the results according to the information provided by the interviewees, it can be established that environmental accounting is considered an important tool for measuring the consumption of natural resources that aims to make the world sustainable, even though In Colombia, the existing environmental

Figure 3. Progress in the disclosure of Environmental accounting information

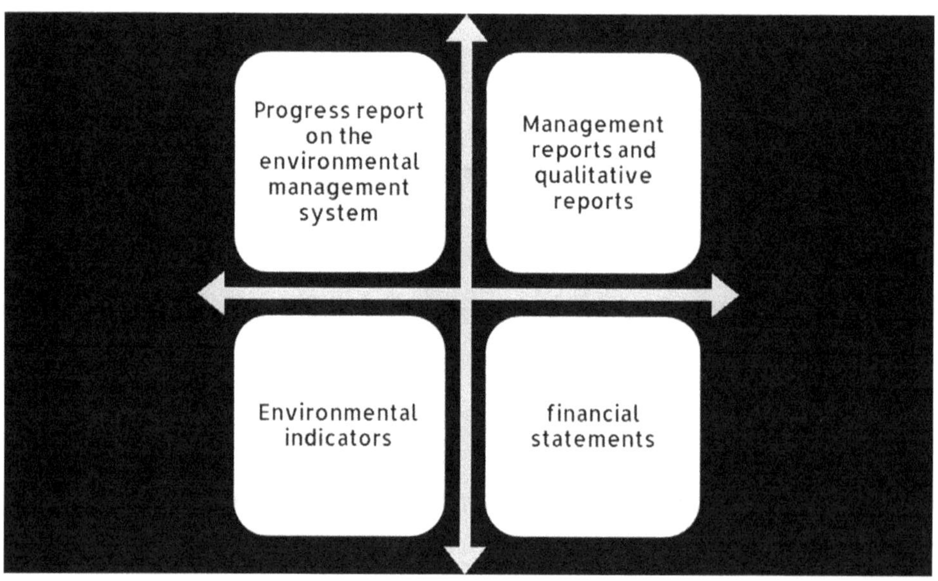

standards are not fully complied with; some organizations have adopted measures to contribute to caring for the environment as part of a corporate responsibility that occurs in the development of the corporate purpose of industrial companies in Colombia. As an incentive to the good practices of these organizations, the Colombian State offers tax benefits that are reflected in the financial statements and that account for environmental management. This helps managers become aware of giving great importance to the accounting environment within the company. For industrial companies, the implementation of new technologies in the transformation of raw materials contributes to minimizing waste, saving energy, and other important savings in production processes and environmental quality(Norouzi & Ataei, 2021).

In the search for several industrial companies, it was found that the information reported by the companies are sustainability reports where they speak in common about the importance of cost reduction and the most outstanding thing is the saving of energy that is called photovoltaic, which is where solar light is transformed into electricity utilizing panels that produce electric current, on the other, waste management reduces the generation of these and thus increases their use to reduce operating costs. For example, the Postobon and Grupo Nutresa companies focus mainly on the care of the hydrographic basins during the execution of their production process. Additionally, they seek to promote recycling projects so that they allow them to improve their packaging and packaging characteristics. Additionally, and taking this information into account, some of the main approaches they focus on to mitigate environmental impacts are listed. For this, a comparison is developed with the actions that each of the companies exercises or intends to carry out, seeking the greatest protection of the resources mentioned:

Additionally, a comparison of the assets of companies that apply environmental accounting is presented, this from the review of their financial statements, for this the companies Bioenergy SAS where it reflects in its Balance reports how it presents Biological assets.

According to the notes to the financial statements, Biological assets are measured at fair value fewer costs to selling at the point of harvest or collection, using the discounted cash flow methodology, which reliably represents the future economic benefits that the entity expects to receive the sale. The biological asset is compared with the book value, generating gains or losses due to recognizing the biological asset. In the event of not measuring fair value reliably, the provisions of paragraph 30 of IAS 41 will apply. (Bioenergy SAS, 2018)

It can be seen that the presentation of the information in the different companies varies, this because while some show their information from reports that project the management that has been carried out regarding environmental issues (in this case, the information shown from Postobon and Grupo Nutresa), others (Bioenergy SA) details its information regarding environmental accounting, in the movement that occurs within the accounts of biological assets and liabilities, which vary from one year to another according to the management that is carried out on environmental issues, or the benefits derived from the execution of environmentally friendly activities. Additionally, considering the conservation of assets involved in the operation contributes to the good management of compliance with the policies created from the implementation of environmental accounting(Norouzi & Kalantari, 2020).

Accounting accounts in companies allow the information generated by accounting to be classified in an orderly and easily accessible manner when making accounting reports and financial statements in general. These are adjusted as the needs within companies arise, creating new subaccounts that allow (as mentioned at the beginning of the text) to classify the information to show the company's reality at any time. In this case, the accounting accounts extend to the environmental sphere, within their main uses are in the assets account (biological assets) and liabilities (for example, provisions in case of disasters and accounts payable for environmental fines) that are managed in industrial companies, their

Table 2. Energy-saving comparison

Energy saving	Postobon	Nutresa
Transport fleet	Its main emission occurs in the use of the transport fleet, so its main focus is the reduction of the emission of gases that these generate; for this, they implemented strategies that were at the forefront of new technologies in transport fleets and additional acquisition of tools that will allow them to monitor the emissions that were being generated. One of its main strategies is the use of photovoltaic energy.	With the use of the transport fleet, in charge of distributing the finished product, there is high emission of gases. As a strategy to mitigate the generation of these gases, they implement strategies such as the constant maintenance of vehicles, the implementation of gas vehicles, and diesel fuel. But one of its main strategies is to look for alternative routes that reduce the circulation times of polluting vehicles.
Production plants	As a preventive measure in the production plants, they seek to largely reduce the reprocesses of the products, seeking to reduce the costs of energy consumption and contribute to the company's sustainable development. Additionally, through implementing a system, they seek to reduce the energy consumption that their customers produce by using the tools that the company provides them.	The Nutresa group, for its part, the production plants, requires the constant operation of machinery that generates high energy consumption. In their strategy to reduce this high consumption, they decide to implement solar panels in their production plants that contribute to the proper functioning of production tools and implement
Saving water	Postobon, for its part, in its sustainability report, shows strategies for reducing water consumption by increasingly minimizing said consumption for each product, going from consuming 3.1 liters per liter of drink to 2.5 liters, hoping to reach a consumption of 2 liters per liter of drink. Another of its strategies is that it is expected to eliminate the discharges of polluting waters that affect the environment.	One of the main resources that become necessary for the production process of this company is water, so one of its main strategic focuses in the conservation of resources should be towards the conservation of water. For this, the company implements within its production processes tools that allow a water recirculation process to be carried out for the activities that require it. For this, the plants have been adapting their infrastructure, contributing to reducing the consumption of these water resources.

good management is reflected in these reports, and with the help of technology, they help reduce costs and environmental impacts.

Accounting, as a socio-economic discipline, will provide information about the consumption of environmental goods through accounts; In this way, the participation of the productive sector in environmental matters will be determined, and the necessary information will be obtained to achieve what has been called sustainable development. (Barraza & Gómez, 2005)

With the use of these accounts, information is generated that, as shown in the previous points, allows companies to form sustainability reports. These reports show the management that companies have carried out seeking to mitigate environmental impacts. This is also based on the information shown in the financial statements so that the improvement can be compared or progress can be seen by comparing each of the results obtained in each year's operation.

This analysis will help future investigations of environmental accounts to interpret and regulate the needs of companies, both in social and community protection, for a specific purpose and commit to the environment. The benefit obtained by companies with the use of environmental accounting.

With the implementation and good management of environmental accounting, companies obtain benefits thanks to the good behavior and use of natural, renewable, and non-renewable resources to seek the tax benefit and in turn manage a good social responsibility with the community around it and its environment, resulting in a better quality of the environment in the habitat. The main benefits found are:

- Significantly reduce environmental costs.

Due to the use of new technologies in the different production processes, Colombian companies have allowed significant savings in costs and/or operating expenses. This has contributed to increasing investments in assets since this allows companies to be more competitive in the market, innovating with their products, and being friendly to the environment.

- More assertive financial statements.

Adequate accounting records in companies account for the transactions in developing their corporate purpose, which allows the disclosure of information to the different public of real interest that is useful for decision-making.

- Tax reduction for the application of clean technology.

The implementation of new technologies contributes to caring for the environment, benefits companies with a reduction in taxes, and is cost-effective in developing their products or services.

In the case of tax benefits, they are represented in the companies' profits since it is directly shown in the decrease in taxes, generating a greater profit beneficial for the company's partners.

With this, it can be said that with the implementation of environmental accounting in companies, several users are rescued who are benefited by the advantages that it generates. First, the same company obtains benefits such as recognition for natural resources, environmental certifications, and benefits at the tax level. There is a society, which benefits from creating sustainable development companies for the communities surrounding the production plants. And finally, it can be said that another of the biggest beneficiaries are the partners, a benefit that is reflected in the improvement of the results of the company's operation, which leads to improving the profits for the year and, in turn, what they receive for those profits.

Accounting in companies is a source of information necessary for decision-making. Its constant change has become a control entity in charge of the proper registration and analysis of all the information and the different economic transactions carried out within the companies.

Within these transactions are within them the operations that occur in environmental accounting, which becomes an important issue because in it what is sought is to have good environmental management, since it is in charge of the measurement economic-environmental facts that generate reliable and timely information for the creation of strategies that mitigate or prevent all these environmental impacts.

The conditions of production by any company and organization result in a series of elements that generate an impact on the social and environmental environment, which in some cases tends to be harmful and harmful; we are talking about pollutants or waste, among others; these by-products necessarily imply a reorientation by companies regarding the control and surveillance of their derivatives towards society and the environment in which it takes place and develops, hence the reflection and awareness around care for with the environment come from a specific area and discipline of companies, in this case, it is accounting in which recent case, there has been an evolution in conceptual terms towards areas such as ecology and social responsibility, to safeguard the common interests of both companies and people and their environment (Caicedo, Loaiza & Lugo, 2013)

Mentioning the importance of environmental accounting in companies, it can be highlighted that its main factor is in the relationship of accounting, the environment and costs, this because during the operation processes that require natural resources that in many Sometimes, it may not be used properly, therefore with the implementation of environmental accounting it is allowed to take corrective or preventive measures that contribute to the reduction of these and in turn generate policies that are of benefit to society or parties involved, since sometimes with the waste generated by the operation, the most affected are the communities that are close to the companies' locations, causing health effects or high risks of natural disasters, so one of the factors that contributes to environmental accounting being considered important, is that it can reduce both the risks of fines and others for the to the company, such as the risks of damage to third parties indirectly caused by the development of the operation.

CONCLUSION

Colombia is a country where a large part of the economy is in the primary sector; it is a producer of raw materials, so natural resources must be taken care of. These agricultural enterprises depend on biological assets for their subsistence, which are called environmental liabilities because they are resources that degrade the ecology. Environmental accounting must start to measure these environmental liabilities, and that is where the accountant's role enters the social sphere because it is a field of public interest. When talking about sustainability, they are spoken in environmental terms. Still, terms that the sector is sustained over time and the accelerated consumption of society, companies will not even have the resources to continue their operation in a very short time. Colombia must create laws that oblige these agricultural companies to implement environmental techniques with great impact. Otherwise, they should not be allowed to function. It is also the ethics of the accountant to allow and be part of these types of companies that affect society and the planet. Accountants must be trained more socially and not financially to impact the environment and help these types of companies be sustainable. During the investigation of this degree work, the greatest difficulty occurred in obtaining accounting information focused on the environmental part, since in some Financial Statements, the items with the execution of the entire environmental issue are not evidenced as such. However, Some information was obtained that served to reveal some of the financial aspects of the environmental issue.

ACKNOWLEDGMENT

This research received no specific grant from any funding agency in the public, commercial, or not-for-profit sectors.

REFERENCES

Acar, M., & Temiz, H. (2020). Empirical analysis on corporate environmental performance and environmental disclosure in an emerging market context: Socio-political theories versus economics disclosure theories. *International Journal of Emerging Markets.*

Agyemang, A. O., Yusheng, K., Ayamba, E. C., Twum, A. K., Chengpeng, Z., & Shaibu, A. (2020). Impact of board characteristics on environmental disclosures for listed mining companies in China. *Environmental Science and Pollution Research International, 27*(17), 21188–21201. doi:10.100711356-020-08599-2 PMID:32266625

Álvarez, A. (2012). *Study of Environmental Accounting National and International Legislation.* Academic Press.

Arévalo, V. (2013). *Environmental accounting in the Colombian socio-economic business environment.* Academic Press.

Barraza, C., & Gómez, M. (2005). *Approach to a concept of environmental accounting.* Cooperative University of Colombia.

Bejarano, Y. & Chavarro, J. (2017). *Analysis of the Contributions of Environmental Accounting to Business Management in the Framework of Social Responsibility in Colombia.* Academic Press.

Bello, A. (2015). *Cost accounting and environmental costs.* Academic Press.

Bioenergy SAS. (2018). *Separate Financial Statements.* Author.

Bortone, N. A., & Vergara, E. M. (2004). Accounting and Environment. A discipline and a field for knowledge and action. *FACES Accounting News, 7*(8), 7-22.

Caicedo, L., Loaiza, S., & Lugo, D. (2013). *Importance of Social Accounting and Environmental in Colombian Companies.* Academic Press.

Chen, Y., Wang, Z., & Zhong, Z. (2019). CO2 emissions, economic growth, renewable and non-renewable energy production and foreign trade in China. *Renewable Energy, 131*, 208–216. doi:10.1016/j.renene.2018.07.047

Colmenares, L., Adriani, R., & Valderrama, Y. (2015). Accounting representation from the perspective of business environmental impact. In the context of the development of industrial activities in Latin America. *Accounting Notebooks, 16*(41), 259–280.

Cortes, H., & Peña, J. (2015). From Sustainability to Sustainability. Development model Sustainable for its Implementation in Policies and Projects. *School of Business Administration Magazine, 78*, 40–55.

Cubides, A. (2017). *Importance and Applicability of Environmental Accounting in Colombian Companies.* Academic Press.

DANE. (2016). *Environmental Industrial Survey.* Academic Press.

Deswanto, R. B., & Siregar, S. V. (2018). The associations between environmental disclosures with financial performance, environmental performance, and firm value. *Social Responsibility Journal, 14*(1), 180–193. doi:10.1108/SRJ-01-2017-0005

Ebenstein, A., Fan, M., Greenstone, M., He, G., Yin, P., & Zhou, M. (2015). Growth, pollution, and life expectancy: China from 1991-2012. *The American Economic Review, 105*(5), 226–231. doi:10.1257/aer.p20151094

Fondevila, M. M., Moneva, J. M., & Scarpellini, S. (2019). Environmental disclosure and Eco-innovation interrelation. The case of Spanish firms: Divulgación ambiental y la interrelación de la ecoinnovación. El caso de las empresas españolas. *Revista de Contabilidad-Spanish Accounting Review, 22*(1), 73–87. doi:10.6018/rc-sar.22.1.354321

Franco, R. (2009). *Accounting and environmental control.* Academic Press.

Goron, C. (2018). Ecological civilisation and the political limits of a Chinese concept of sustainability. *China Perspectives, 2018*(4), 39-52.

Hassan, O. A., & Romilly, P. (2018). Relations between corporate economic performance, environmental disclosure and greenhouse gas emissions: New insights. *Business Strategy and the Environment, 27*(7), 893–909. doi:10.1002/bse.2040

Hu, Y. Y., & Karbhari, Y. (2015). Incentives and disincentives of corporate environmental disclosure: Evidence from listed companies in China and Malaysia. *Thunderbird International Business Review, 57*(2), 143–161. doi:10.1002/tie.21678

Iatridis, G. E. (2013). Environmental disclosure quality: Evidence on environmental performance, corporate governance and value relevance. *Emerging Markets Review, 14*, 55–75. doi:10.1016/j.ememar.2012.11.003

Jaskoski, M. (2014). Environmental licensing and conflict in Peru's mining sector: A path-dependent analysis. *World Development, 64*, 873–883. doi:10.1016/j.worlddev.2014.07.010

Leung, T. C. H., & Snell, R. S. (2021). Strategies for social and environmental disclosure: The case of multinational gambling companies. *Journal of Business Ethics, 168*(3), 447–467. doi:10.100710551-019-04190-z

Lezca, J. (2019). *Environmental accounting*. Academic Press.

Li, H., & Qi, A. (2008). Impact of corporate governance on voluntary disclosure in Chinese listed companies. *Corporate Ownership and Control, 5*(2), 360-366.

Londoño, F., Ochoa, C., Figueroa, S., & Hurtado, L. (2009). *Importance of Accounting Environmental.* Academic Press.

Lu, J., & Li, H. (2020). The impact of government environmental information disclosure on enterprise location choices: Heterogeneity and threshold effect test. *Journal of Cleaner Production, 277*, 124055. doi:10.1016/j.jclepro.2020.124055

Martinico-Perez, M. F. G., Schandl, H., Fishman, T., & Tanikawa, H. (2018). The socio-economic metabolism of an emerging economy: Monitoring progress of decoupling of economic growth and environmental pressures in the Philippines. *Ecological Economics*, *147*, 155–166. doi:10.1016/j.ecolecon.2018.01.012

Mather, A. S., & Chapman, K. (2018). *Environmental resources*. Routledge. doi:10.4324/9781315844305

Mejía, E. & Vargas, L. (2012). *Accounting for environmental and social sustainability*. Academic Press.

Meng, X. H., Zeng, S. X., Shi, J. J., Qi, G. Y., & Zhang, Z. B. (2014). The relationship between corporate environmental performance and environmental disclosure: An empirical study in China. *Journal of Environmental Management*, *145*, 357–367. doi:10.1016/j.jenvman.2014.07.009 PMID:25113230

Mol, A. P., He, G., & Zhang, L. (2011). Information disclosure in environmental risk management: Developments in China. *Journal of Current Chinese Affairs*, *40*(3), 163–192. doi:10.1177/186810261104000307

Mol, A. P., He, G., & Zhang, L. (2011). Information disclosure in environmental risk management: Developments in China. *Journal of Current Chinese Affairs*, *40*(3), 163–192. doi:10.1177/186810261104000307

Murdifin, I., Pelu, M. F. A., Perdana, A. A. H., Putra, K., Arumbarkah, A. M., Muslim, M., & Rahmah, A. (2019). Environmental disclosure as corporate social responsibility: Evidence from the biggest nickel mining in Indonesia. *International Journal of Energy Economics and Policy*, *9*(1), 115.

Newig, J., Challies, E., Jager, N. W., Kochskaemper, E., & Adzersen, A. (2018). The Environmental Performance of Participatory and Collaborative Governance: A Framework of Causal Mechanisms. *Policy Studies Journal: the Journal of the Policy Studies Organization*, *46*(2), 269–297. doi:10.1111/psj.12209 PMID:30034065

Norouzi, N. (2021). Post-COVID-19 and globalization of oil and natural gas trade: Challenges, opportunities, lessons, regulations, and strategies. *International Journal of Energy Research*, *45*(10), 14338–14356. doi:10.1002/er.6762 PMID:34219899

Norouzi, N., & Ataei, E. (2021). Covid-19 Crisis and Environmental law: Opportunities and challenges. *Hasanuddin Law Review*, *7*(1), 46–60. doi:10.20956/halrev.v7i1.2772

Norouzi, N., & Kalantari, G. (2020). The sun food-water-energy nexus governance model a case study for Iran. *Water-Energy Nexus*, *3*, 72–80. doi:10.1016/j.wen.2020.05.005

Norouzi, N., Khanmohammadi, H. U., & Ataei, E. (2021). The Law in the Face of the COVID-19 Pandemic: Early Lessons from Uruguay. *Hasanuddin Law Review*, *7*(2), 75–88. doi:10.20956/halrev.v7i2.2827

Ochoa, C., Mosquera, C., & Ruiz, C. (2013). *Environmental accounting model for the company Pedro Álvarez constructions SAS*. Academic Press.

Odoemelam, N., & Okafor, R. G. (2018). The influence of corporate governance on environmental disclosure of listed non-financial firms in Nigeria. *Indonesian Journal of Sustainability Accounting and Management*, *2*(1), 25–49. doi:10.28992/ijsam.v2i1.47

Orrego, J. (2018). *Connection between business economic growth and environmental protection*. Academic Press.

Pan, Y., Chen, Q., & Zhang, P. (2020). *Does policy uncertainty affect corporate environmental information disclosure: evidence from China*. Sustainability Accounting, Management and Policy Journal.

Pien, C. P. (2020). Local environmental information disclosure and environmental non-governmental organizations in Chinese prefecture-level cities. *Journal of Environmental Management*, *275*, 111225. doi:10.1016/j.jenvman.2020.111225 PMID:32889416

Postobon. (2018). *Sustainability Report 2018*. Academic Press.

Rodríguez, D. (2011). *Formulation of a theoretical structure for environmental accounting*. Academic Press.

Sánchez, H. M. & Rodríguez, C. (2017). *Determine the Hidden Environmental Costs of Hazardous Waste in Office Furniture Manufacturing Companies*. Academic Press.

Sarkodie, S. A., & Strezov, V. (2019). Effect of foreign direct investments, economic development and energy consumption on greenhouse gas emissions in developing countries. *The Science of the Total Environment*, *646*, 862–871. doi:10.1016/j.scitotenv.2018.07.365 PMID:30064112

Tadros, H., & Magnan, M. (2019). *How does environmental performance map into environmental disclosure? A look at underlying economic incentives and legitimacy aims. Sustainability Accounting, Management and Policy Journal.*

Tang, Y., Yang, R., Chen, Y., Du, M., Yang, Y., & Miao, X. (2020). Greenwashing of local government: The human-caused risks in the process of environmental information disclosure in China. *Sustainability*, *12*(16), 6329. doi:10.3390u12166329

Taplin, I. M., & Winterton, J. (2019). *Rethinking global production* (Vol. 26). Routledge. doi:10.4324/9780429444548

Tkachenko, I. N., Pervukhina, I. V., & Sokolovskaya, O. E. (2019), Environmental disclosure as a factor of sustainable development of the Russian business. In *The International Scientific and Practical Forum Industry. Science. Competence. Integration* (pp. 628–635). Springer.

Tzouvanas, P., Kizys, R., Chatziantoniou, I., & Sagitova, R. (2020). Environmental disclosure and idiosyncratic risk in the European manufacturing sector. *Energy Economics*, *87*, 104715. doi:10.1016/j.eneco.2020.104715

Urrea, M. (2015). *Implementation and Applicability of the Environmental Account for the Registry of Renewable Natural Resources in the Colombian Public Accounting Regime within the Framework of International Financial Reporting Standards*. Academic Press.

Wijsman, J. W. M., Troost, K., Fang, J., Roncarati, A., Smaal, A., Ferreira, J., & Strand, Ø. (2019). *Goods and services of marine bivalves*. Springer.

Yao, S., & Liang, H. (2019). Analyst following, environmental disclosure and cost of equity: Research based on industry classification. *Sustainability*, *11*(2), 300. doi:10.3390u11020300

Zeng, S. X., Xu, X. D., Dong, Z. Y., & Tam, V. W. (2010). Towards corporate environmental information disclosure: An empirical study in China. *Journal of Cleaner Production*, *18*(12), 1142–1148. doi:10.1016/j.jclepro.2010.04.005

ADDITIONAL READING

Deegan, C. (2013). The accountant will have a central role in saving the planet… really? A reflection on 'green accounting and green eyeshades twenty years later'. *Critical Perspectives on Accounting*, *24*(6), 448–458. doi:10.1016/j.cpa.2013.04.004

El Serafy, S. (1997). Green accounting and economic policy. *Ecological Economics*, *21*(3), 217–229. doi:10.1016/S0921-8009(96)00107-3

Gallhofer, S., & Haslam, J. (1997). The direction of green accounting policy: Critical reflections. *Accounting, Auditing & Accountability Journal*, *10*(2), 148–174. doi:10.1108/09513579710166703

Halberg, N., Verschuur, G., & Goodlass, G. (2005). Farm level environmental indicators; are they useful?: An overview of green accounting systems for European farms. *Agriculture, Ecosystems & Environment*, *105*(1-2), 195–212. doi:10.1016/j.agee.2004.04.003

Jahamani, Y. F. (2003). Green accounting in developing countries: The case of UAE and Jordan. *Managerial Finance*, *29*(8), 37–45. doi:10.1108/03074350310768418

Owen, D., Gray, R., & Bebbington, J. (1997). Green accounting: Cosmetic irrelevance or radical agenda for change? *Asia-Pacific Journal of Accounting*, *4*(2), 175–198. doi:10.1080/10293574.1997.10510519

Rubenstein, D. B. (1992). Bridging the gap between green accounting and black ink. *Accounting, Organizations and Society*, *17*(5), 501–508. doi:10.1016/0361-3682(92)90044-S

Vincent, J. R. (2000). Green accounting: From theory to practice. *Environment and Development Economics*, *5*(1), 13–24. doi:10.1017/S1355770X00000024

KEY TERMS AND DEFINITIONS

Circularity: A circular economy (also referred to as "circularity") is an economic system that tackles global challenges like climate change, biodiversity loss, waste, and pollution. Most linear economy businesses take a natural resource and turn it into a product that is ultimately destined to become waste because it has been designed and made. This process is often summarised by "take, make, waste." By contrast, a circular economy uses reuse, sharing, repair, refurbishment, remanufacturing, and recycling to create a closed-loop system, minimize resource inputs, and create waste, pollution, and carbon emissions. The circular economy aims to keep products, materials, equipment, and infrastructure in use for longer, thus improving the productivity of these resources. Waste materials and energy should become input for other processes through waste valorization: either as a component or recovered resource for another industrial process or as regenerative resources for nature (e.g., compost). This regenerative approach contrasts with the traditional linear economy, which has a "take, make, dispose of" production model.

Eco Commerce: Eco commerce is a business, investment, and technology-development model that employs market-based solutions to balancing the world's energy needs and environmental integrity. Through green trading and green finance, eco-commerce promotes the further development of "clean technologies" such as wind power, solar power, biomass, and hydropower.

Eco-Tariffs: An Eco-tariff, also known as an environmental tariff, is a trade barrier erected to reduce pollution and improve the environment. These trade barriers may take the form of import or export taxes on products with a large carbon footprint or imported from countries with lax environmental regulations.

Emissions Trading: Emissions trading (also known as cap and trade, emissions trading scheme, or ETS) is a market-based approach to controlling pollution by providing economic incentives for reducing the emissions of pollutants.

Environmental Enterprise: An environmental enterprise is an environmentally friendly/compatible business. Specifically, an environmental enterprise is a business that produces value in the same manner which an ecosystem does, neither producing waste nor consuming unsustainable resources. In addition, an environmental enterprise rather finds alternative ways to produce one's products instead of taking advantage of animals for the sake of human profits. To be closer to being an environmentally friendly company, some environmental enterprises invest their money to develop or improve their technologies which are also environmentally friendly. In addition, environmental enterprises usually try to reduce global warming, so some companies use environmentally friendly materials to build their stores. They also set in environmentally friendly place regulations. All these efforts of the environmental enterprises can bring positive effects both for nature and people. The concept is rooted in the well-enumerated theories of natural capital, the eco-economy, and cradle-to-cradle design. Examples of environmental enterprises would be Seventh Generation, Inc., and Whole Foods.

Green Economy: A green economy is an economy that aims at reducing environmental risks and ecological scarcities and that aims for sustainable development without degrading the environment. It is closely related to ecological economics but has a more politically applied focus. The 2011 UNEP Green Economy Report argues "that to be green, and an economy must be not only efficient but also fair. Fairness implies recognizing global and country-level equity dimensions, particularly in assuring a Just Transition to an economy that is low-carbon, resource-efficient, and socially inclusive."

Green Politics: Green politics, or ecopolitics, is a political ideology that aims to foster an ecologically sustainable society often, but not always, rooted in environmentalism, nonviolence, social justice, and grassroots democracy. It began taking shape in the western world in the 1970s; since then, Green parties have developed and established themselves in many countries around the globe and have achieved some electoral success.

Low-Carbon Economy: A low-carbon economy (LCE) or decarbonized economy is based on low-carbon power sources with minimal greenhouse gas (GHG) emissions into the atmosphere, specifically carbon dioxide. GHG emissions due to anthropogenic (human) activity are the dominant cause of observed climate change since the mid-20th century. Continued emission of greenhouse gases may cause long-lasting changes worldwide, increasing the likelihood of severe, pervasive, and irreversible effects for people and ecosystems.

Natural Resource Economics: Natural resource economics deals with the supply, demand, and allocation of the Earth's natural resources. One main objective of natural resource economics is to understand better the role of natural resources in the economy to develop more sustainable methods of managing those resources to ensure their future generations. Resource economists study interactions between economic and natural systems intending to develop a sustainable and efficient economy.

Sustainable Development: Sustainable development is an organizing principle for meeting human development goals while simultaneously sustaining the ability of natural systems to provide the natural resources and ecosystem services on which the economy and society depend. The desired result is a state of society where living conditions and resources are used to continue to meet human needs without undermining the integrity and stability of the natural system. Sustainable development can be defined as development that meets the needs of the present without compromising the ability of future generations to meet their own needs. Sustainability goals, such as the current UN-level Sustainable Development Goals, address the global challenges, including poverty, inequality, climate change, environmental degradation, peace, and justice.

Chapter 12
The Blue Economy and the Sustainable Development Goals:
The Blue Economy, the Sustainable Development Goals, and Corporate Social Responsibility

Muriel Lendoye
SOGEVAL, Gabon

ABSTRACT

The eco-responsible concept presents a new vision for the rational and sustainable exploitation of oceans, lakes, and rivers in the development literature. Arguably, the blue economy is very often cited as an example of a new development paradigm with the capability to fight against poverty, improve food diversification, and create added value in coastal countries of the African continent. To differentiate themselves and ensure long-lasting growth, established companies in Gabon have embraced sustainable development through several actions, some of which are CSR projects and interventions. This chapter presents a model of CSR action that impacts SDG 1 and shows how a vulnerable community has benefited from a project to improve its well-being and that of other populations.

INTRODUCTION

The blue economy has been foreseen as presenting huge economic opportunities for African countries within territorial coastlines and exclusive economic zones (EEZs) in the sea (Mohanty & Dash, 2020). The blue economy refers to a new development paradigm that advocates sustainable management, usage and conservation of ocean and ocean-related industrial activities such as fisheries, port and shipping, deep sea mining, ocean energy, coastal tourism, ecosystem services and marine services, among others, in a manner that offers huge potential for economic expansion, wealth creation and jobs to coastal nations and marine countries (Bueger & Wivel, 2018; Findlay, 2020; Mohanty & Dash, 2020). The oceans and ocean countries cannot be ignored because 80% of global trade is undertaken on the seas

DOI: 10.4018/978-1-6684-3393-5.ch012

and oceans, and they provide routes for global supply chains and global markets (UNEP, 2016; World Bank, 2017). Furthermore, the United Nations Conference on Trade and Development (UNCTAD, 2014) affirmed that if the blue economy is vigorously exploited, the world would benefit from almost 350 million jobs across critical sectors of the oceans, such as fishing, aquaculture, coastal and marine tourism and research activities. Moreover, as far back as a decade ago, the African Union (2012) stated that over 200 million Africans from 39 states and islands are coastal and littoral, an indication that they rely on the ocean for jobs, food and nutrition, and the fish industry in these enclaves provides over 10 million employees. The issue that requires more focus is the connection between the blue economy and sustainable development goals (SDGs).

To bridge the existing knowledge gap and poor understanding of the blue economy's connection with SDGs in the developing country context, this chapter explicates the prospects of the blue economy for driving sustainable development goals in Gabon. The objective of the chapter extends to examining the impact the real changes brought about by the CSR project of foundation called the FONDATION SUCAF GABON in the daily life of fishermen and its sustainability three years after its shutdown. In specific terms, the chapter through a survey provides answers to the following research questions: (a) What are the prospects of the CSR project of FONDATION SUCAF GABON in the daily life of fishermen? (b) What is the sustainability of the CSR project three years after its shutdown? This chapter intends to connect the blue economy and SDGs because the former, as a new development paradigm that focuses on ocean and ocean resources, has the capacity to boost economic development through food production and ocean industrialisation, increase the GDPs, and directly and indirectly strengthen the actualization of the 17 SDGs in the developing context.

Gabon was chosen for the blue economy discourse in this chapter contribution because of its strategic position as a coastal country with access to the Atlantic Ocean, including its encouraging records of forestry potential and agro-food industry in Central Africa (Yates, 2021). Moreover, Gabon is one of the countries with territorial coastlines and extensive kilometres of exclusive economic zones (EEZs) in the sea that have not been optimally tapped and harnessed for sustainable economic development (Akpomera, 2020; Yates, 2021).

Apart from the introduction above, the remaining parts of the chapter have 8 sections. Section 2 explains the background of the CSR project, including the hydrographic characteristics of Haut-Ogoué Province, where the CSR project that drives the blue economy is located. Section 3 presents the proof of the choice of intervention and connection with SDGs. Section 4 explicates the problems, issues and challenges facing the fishing province. Section 5 focuses on the methodology of the project. Section 6 presents the findings and discusses the thematic issues using the theory of change (ToC) framework. Section 7 concludes by contextualizing the findings, practical implications and conclusion.

BACKGROUND

To support the eradication of poverty, protection of the planet and inequalities in the world by 2030 without compromising the capacity of future generations, the Sustainable Development Goals were adopted in 2015 by the United Nations (Desa, 2016). In specific terms, the SDG agenda contained 17 veritable goals, 169 smart targets, and 230 measurable indicators that were well integrated and synchronized to help sustainably tackle the issues of poverty and hunger and abuse of the environment while fostering peace and inclusive economic development (Bello-Bravo & Lutomia, 2020; Raimi, Olowo & Shokunbi, 2021).

All actors, such as private companies, are concerned and called upon to mobilize to contribute to their implementation. Gradually, they appropriated them, and their commitments were felt at the level of internal functioning, at the level of their activities or in dialogueue with external stakeholders. In French-speaking countries, many multinationals in the industrial sector have embraced the ideals of sustainable entrepreneurship and sustainability by integrating social, environmental and economic concerns into their business strategies through a CSR approach. It is now fashionable to be ethical and socially responsible (Spence, Ben Boubaker Gherib & Ondoua Biwolé, 2011; Akinyemi et al., 2019).

This chapter discusses from practitioners' perspective a novel framework that connects the blue economy with the SDGs. Within this framework, the Society for the Organization, Management and Development of Food and Agricultural Industries (SOMDIAA), a major player in the agrofood industry in Central Africa, West Africa and Ocean India, has linked its activities to the SDGs by directly contributing to agricultural and industrial development, to the development of the economic fabric and to food security in the countries in which its subsidiaries are established. Indeed, the group's productions are benchmarks in the flour, animal feed, livestock and sugar sectors. In Gabon, the group has two subsidiaries, namely, a flour mill located in the capital Libreville called Société Meunière et Avicole du Gabon (SMAG) and a sugar complex called Sucrerie Africaine du Gabon (SUCAF GABON), located in the Haut-Ogooué province. Precisely in a village located between Franceville and Moanda.

In rural areas, its subsidiary SUCAF GABON participates in the industrialization of its implantation area and its facilities near rivers, among which the LEBOMBI LEYOU and other rivers have favored the arrival of a large workforce. This has created important social needs, such as the creation of housing, infrastructure for access to water, health care and education. Following a diagnosis carried out by the group's CSR commission in the outskirts of the sugar complex to know the different needs of local communities and to integrate the expectations of other external stakeholders expressed after the publication of articles as well as studies of several organizations, no governmental and external firms, community actions and projects have been put in place.

To manage the budget for smooth project operation, the group created a foundation called FONDATION SUCAF GABON, whose objectives are the management and optimization of resources dedicated to external social projects, the implementation of social actions, solidarity and health, the fight against precarious living conditions, the improvement of school, health, sociocultural structures and the promotion of income-generating activities. The areas of intervention include subsectors such as agriculture, livestock, arboriculture, processing, crafts, trade, health, hygiene education and fishing. The policy thrust was to support the community of artisanal fishermen in the village through the CSR project. The project has a lifeline of three years, after which it is expected that the objectives should have been achieved, especially the reduction of poverty in rural areas, in accordance with SDG 1.

Key Hydrographic Characteristics of Haut-Ogooue Province

The province has an extensive inland hydrographic network. The main rivers are the Ogooué, the Mpassa, the Lekoni, the Lebombi Leyou and the Sebe, supplemented by just over 400 ha of inland water, thus making the region a suitable site for artisanal fishing activities.

Potential of the Subsector

The province is accessible by land, rail and air. Unfortunately, it is frequently isolated from the rest of the country due to the poor condition of the access road network and the irregularity of train flows linked to frequent train derailments and the high cost of air transport. This situation disrupts the supply of fresh products, while since the decentralization of certain public administrations, the presence of SUCAF GABON and new mining players in other regions of the province, the demand for fresh fish has increased. Artisanal fishing therefore remains one of the main sources of fresh fish, and the development of this activity could allow the creation of income-generating activities and food diversification in the area.

Proof of the Choice of Intervention and Sustainable Development Goals

To contribute to the fight against poverty in rural areas corresponding to SDG1, the SUCAF GABON foundation has therefore chosen to intervene in this sector because it does not require very heavy investment capital. and is reserved for nationals. In addition, the activities of this subsector require little basic training in basic management on the job that can be done in a short time.

PRE-PROJECT SITUATION

The Village of Ouéllé

The locality is located in the Haut-Ogoué province, 40 km from Franceville and 30 km from Moanda on the banks of the Lekoko and Lebombi Leyou Rivers. A landlocked rural area, the village, was born upon the establishment of SUCAF GABON in 1974 and has developed in parallel with the sugar industry.

It is made up on the one hand of the SUCAF GABON sugar industrial complex, which includes 16,000 hectares of plantations, a factory, approximately fifty machines, an infirmary, a dispensary, a nursery school, a high school and four housing estates reserved for permanent workers. and temporary employees. On the other hand, groups set up around the complex.

For administrative reasons and to better distribute social assistance, political donations and other multifaceted support, the public authorities have divided the village into several districts, namely, Djoutou-center, Ouéllé 1, Ouéllé 2 and Ouéllé 3, Mossete, Mouinga and Moyabi.

Population Situation

The village has nearly 7,000 inhabitants, including 1,000 workers from SUCAF GABON. Most of the inhabitants outside SUCAF GABON are young and unemployed, particularly during the interseason period when the factory is shut down. More than half of the population lives there on € 2 per day and is responsible for large families. Among the local means of subsistence practiced for self-consumption and trade, we note the trade in tubers, bananas and fruits, local bushmeat and vegetables, and traditional fishing.

Figure 1. Map of Gabon
Google source 2021

Fishing Practice

Fishing activities in rivers and streams are carried out with traditional materials and equipment such as liana baskets, bamboo baskets and raffia baskets.

Some use small techniques to trap fish (spears and hooks) along the shores.

While others go on the rivers in groups or individually in canoes made of wood and use paddles.

Figure 2. Aerial View of the Sugar Industrial Complex in the Village of Ouéllé
source SOMDIAA portal network 2021

Figure 3. A fisherman making a bamboo basket and fishing baskets pattern
google photos and google 2021

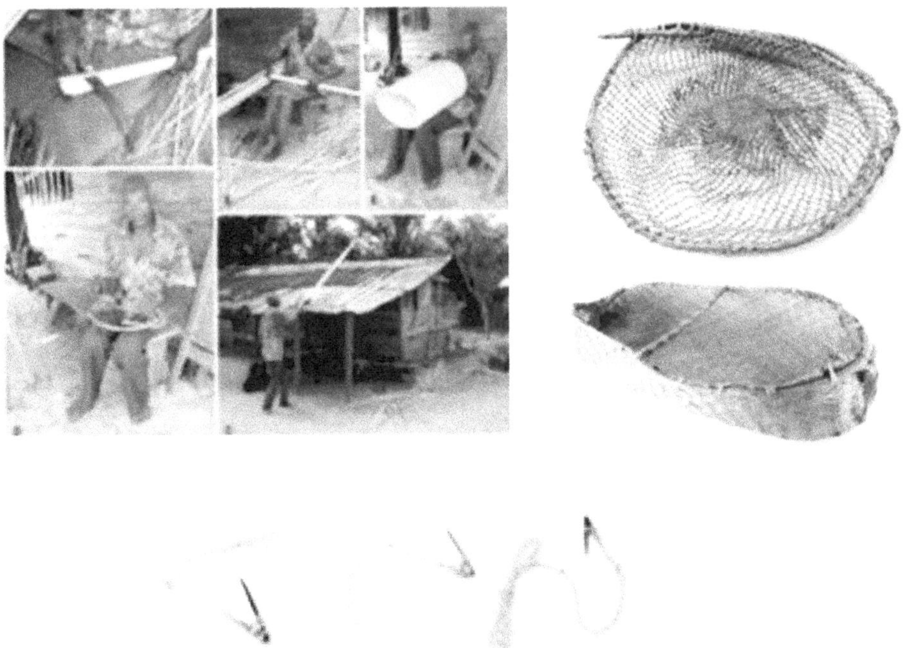

They also use mesh nets, and fishing operations take place in remote locations more than 1 km away in deep water.

As the access to the landing points is far from the main routes and the marketing is unstructured, the catches are sold informally in batches of bait on ropes and in basins, in crossroads and along the roads that lead to neighboring villages. and to the cited workers of SUCAF GABON.

Figure 4. Models of nets and canoes
Source google 2021

Table 1. Presentation of the different varieties

Name	The carpe	The silure	The mâchoiron	The lotte
Visual		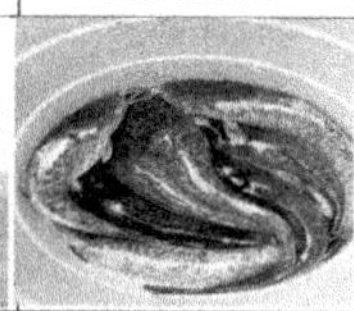	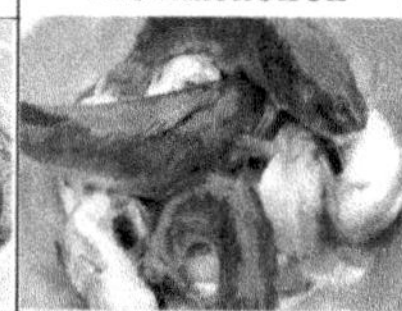	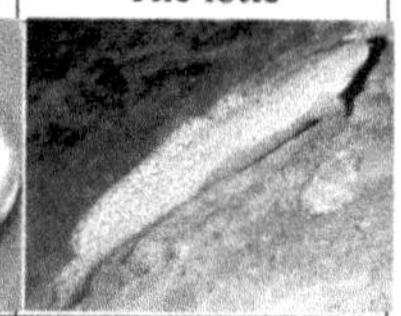
Description	Fish covered with large scales that are green or brackish yellow in color	Fish without scales with a very slippery skin with colors varying from light gray to green - brown.	Belonging to the same family as the catfish and otherwise called the jawbone, it is distinguished with a rosacea skin	Fish with a flat head, an elongated body covered with very small gray yellow marbled scales.

The Found Fish

The main species caught are carp, catfish, machoîron and burbot.

Fish trade

The catches are often sold fresh without processing in a local market (that of the city of Franceville) and are frequently found in large crossroads that bear the name of a village called Mvengué, located between the towns of Franceville and Moanda.

Sometimes they are transported by rail to the capital (Libreville) in large storage barrels filled with water to be sold in a specific market.

Fish price

The catches are shredded alive on a rope and sold on the basis of an estimate based on the size of the fish in the absence of scales. The prices in the area and the rest of the province are:

- 5,000 FCFA for carp
- 20 00 FCFA for the machoîron and catfish
- 20,000 FCFA for the monkfish

Problem, Issues and Challenges

The villagers who practice fishing constitute several significant communities but live in precariousness. They know some artisanal fishing techniques but practice the activity more by pleasure rather than by economic necessity due to a lack of suitable operating infrastructure, high-performance modern materials and equipment, secure boats, and appropriate means of conservation and funding. This situation makes the availability and trade of fish irregular on the one hand and the selling prices very high compared

Figure 5. Capture presentation

to the average local purchasing power on the other. Their incomes are extremely low, and they live in precariousness. Therefore, they cannot take care of their families.

Project description

The project in question began in 2016 and ended in 2018 for a duration of 02 years. It consisted of providing fishermen with training in simple management and the free provision of modern artisanal fishing materials and equipment. The objective of the project was to help those who practice small-scale fishing in the village to live better by giving them the means to increase their income to meet the basic needs of their families in terms of education, health and food. Specifically, the project was launched and funded to achieve the following:

- Improving the working conditions of fishermen
- This contributes to the development of fishing and related sectoral activities.
- Train fishermen in the handling of new fishing materials and preservation of biodiversity of the sea and ocean resources.

Project Expected Results

The desired results expected at the end of the project period include the following:

- Fishermen equipped with modern, more efficient materials
- Fishermen trained in the use of modern techniques that respect biodiversity
- Regular activity and available production
- Improved fishing conditions
- Trained fishermen made aware of respect for biodiversity
- Fishermen trained in elementary management principles for a sustainable activity
- The income of the beneficiaries improved and reinvested to expand the activity

Operating Sites and Beneficiaries

For environmental reasons, the waters near the industrial site, namely, the Lekoko and Lebombi Leyou Rivers, were excluded. The easily accessible river sites selected were the waters of Ogooué, M'passa and Poubara. However, the target beneficiaries were members of a community of 20 fishermen aged between 35 and 44, responsible for large families, extremely vulnerable and living in the Ouéllé 3 district, located near one of the sites. retained exploitation, which leads to the other rivers and near the cities of the sugar complex.

Other Stakeholders

The implementation of the project involved the involvement of several actors, namely:

- The SOMDIAA group
- The SUCAF GABON sugar industry
- The SUCAF GABON foundation
- A technical assistance firm for the fishing industry
- The heads of the Djoutou-Centre, Ouéllé 1, Ouéllé 2, Ouéllé 3 neighborhoods
- The customary chiefs of the village of Ouéllé
- Public authorities (the Ministry of Fisheries, the Ministry of Agriculture, the Ministry of Housing)

Figure 6. The foundation team
source SOMDIAA network portal 2021

Executing Body

The project was prepared by the SUCAF GABON foundation and implemented in collaboration with the assistance of a technical assistance firm specializing in fishing trades recruited through a national call for tenders.

Divided into two categories, the foundation's team was made up of a project selection committee set up during the constitutive general meeting in 2012, renewed each year, and two operational.

The positions of the members of the selection committee are filled by volunteers, and all employees of the SUCAF GABON company are vectors of internal communication on the company's CSR strategy.

The two field operators are direct employees of the foundation, including the following:

- A volunteer sent by a humanitarian aid association called International Solidarity
- An agent recruited locally as a local development coordinator, not an employee of the subsidiary

Funding and Expenses

Based on a survey conducted beforehand by the foundation's operational staff, the various needs identified, the priorities and the various quotations made it possible to set up a budget of €8.5K entirely supported by the SOMDIAA group.

The main categories of expenditure retained were as follows:

1. The development works
2. The purchase of fishing equipment and materials
3. The training

Activities

The work carried out was as follows:

1. Development works

Among the development work carried out as part of the project, there were:

a. The development of a disembarkation point
b. The rehabilitation of a house belonging to the SUCAF GABON company and sold as a temporary equipment storage location, damaged in a fire
c. Rehabilitation of access roads leading to rivers leading to the ogooué River

2. Capacity building

Consultants belonging to the team of the firm specializing in fishing trades requisitioned to provide training designed the training modules, which were validated by the foundation's executive committee and the General Management of the SOMDIAA group.

The components designed focused on four components, namely:

a. The development of a disembarkation point
b. Rehabilitation of access roads leading to rivers leading to the ogooué River
c. Training on handling modern fishing gear and techniques
d. Training in simplified management
e. Training on the maintenance of landscaped spaces
f. Training to preserve the environment

The learners all received know-how on modern fishing techniques, training in fisheries resource management methods and basic training in an activity and spaces. The apprenticeships were formalized by the issuance of an exercise certificate issued by the Ministry of Water, Forests, the Sea and the Environment jointly signed with the Ministry of Agriculture, Livestock, Fisheries and Food.

3. Installation support

The support therefore consisted of 05 canoes (made from hardwood) and accessories (machetes, boots, raincoats), 02 outboard motors, nylon nets, wheelbarrows, scales, 02 motorcycles, coolers, buckets, and 02 freezers.

To maintain group actions, beneficiaries were asked to operate equipment and materials collectively in rotation.

Expected Results

The expected results were as follows:

- fishermen trained in modern fishing techniques
- modern techniques that respect biodiversity used for catches
- higher catch volumes
- frequent supplies and available production
- the income of the beneficiaries improved and reinvested to expand the activity

Problems Encountered During the Implementation of the Project

The major problems encountered were as follows:

1. Slow comprehension at the time of theoretical training because of the educational level of the learners
2. Late delivery of deliverables
3. Recurring charges for certain expenses

Regular

The day-to-day management of the project was entrusted to the foundation's field operations. At the start of the project, they were responsible for mobilizing all the actors involved and beneficiaries and ensured the necessary collaborations with each of them. During the implementation of the project, they were responsible for coordinating the execution of activities and for making weekly reports and reports on expenditure management, addressed to the members of the foundation committee, to the General Management of SUCAF GABON. and to the General Management of the SOMDIAA group.

EVALUATION

Study Sponsor

As part of the development of the national strategy for reducing greenhouse gas emissions and protecting the environment (biodiversity), SOGEVAL took an interest in industrial pollution in rural areas and therefore assessed polluting Gabonese industrial companies, including SUCAF GABON. We were part of a delegation of experts as a junior consultant, and we worked on the CSR actions of this company from July to September 2021, i.e., 03 months.

Legal Obligations

The concept of social responsibility is still little known in Africa, such as Gabon, and is applied on a voluntary basis to avoid social demands in the areas in which they operate.

However, to give a legal and regulatory framework to CSR, the Gabonese legislature intervened through laws n ° 015/2005, n ° 017/2014, n ° 011/2014 and in 2018. All member states of the OHADA were assigned the obligation to provide information on CSR.

Regarding fishing activities, other texts frame the intervention operations, namely:

- Law n°015/2005 of August 8, 2005 on the Fisheries and Aquaculture Code in the Gabonese Republic
- Decree n°000176/PR/MEFEPEPN of 24 February 2005 relating to the monitoring of fishing vessel activities
- Decree n°000176/PR/MEFEPEPN of 24 February 2005 relating to the monitoring of vessel and fishing boat activities
- Decree n°0062/PR/MEFPE of January 10, 1994, which establishes the fishing zones and the type of equipment to be used
- Decree n° 00976/PR/MIN/AGRI of October 15, 1970 fixing the terms of application of the ordinance establishing producer groups, cooperative groups and cooperative societies - Gabon
- Ordinance n°44/70/PR/MEF/MAEER-MTPHU of August 12, 1970 organizing the fishing activity
- Council Regulation CE/450/2007 of April 16, 2007, partnership agreement in the fisheries sector - Gabon

General Objective of the Study

The general objective of the study was to learn about the real changes brought about by the project in the daily life of fishermen and their sustainability three years after its shutdown.

The results of this study will be transmitted to SOMDIAA and can be used during decision-making to renew the experience by involving women and young girl mothers for equality and respect for gender. a part. On the other hand, this example will contribute to the strengthening or adoption of new sectoral policies in fisheries, the environment and regulations on RSE.

Methodological Approach

Despite the fact that the health situation linked to the COVID-19 pandemic resulted in a series of preventive measures being observed, an adaptation was made for the collection of information. The evaluation work could be carried out as planned.

The methodology followed was first inspired by the theory of change, and then the evaluation framework was composed of key questions focusing on internationally recognized evaluation criteria applied to a sample.

Data Analysis and Presentation: The Theory of Change

It is a tool for describing how the activities carried out as part of an intervention, such as a project, program or policy, lead to results that will have intended or observed impacts. The evaluation of the impact of this community project was therefore based on an ex post reconstruction of the theory of change to describe the points of impact and define the evaluation framework, particularly the key evaluation questions relating to internationally recognized criteria and data collection.

Table 2.

<table>
<tr><th colspan="3">Production line</th><th colspan="3">Chain of effects</th></tr>
<tr><th>Inputs</th><th>Activities</th><th>Outputs</th><th>Direct effects</th><th>Intermediate effects</th><th>Ultimate Effects</th></tr>
<tr><td>Budget allocated</td><td>Provide fishing and storage facilities</td><td>Furnished facilities</td><td>Improvement of fishing exploitation facilities in the village of Ouéllé</td><td>Efficient fishermen</td><td rowspan="6">Improvement of fishermen's income</td></tr>
<tr><td>Equipment and support materials</td><td>Strengthen the capacities of fishermen</td><td>Trained fishermen</td><td>Increased knowledge of Ouéllé fishermen on fishing and rescue trades, elementary management principles, environmental preservation</td><td>Regular activity</td></tr>
<tr><td>Human resources mobilized</td><td>Handing over of equipment to learner fishermen</td><td>Learners are equipped with new materials</td><td>Improvement of the conditions for carrying out the activity</td><td>Increase in the volume of catches</td></tr>
<tr><td colspan="2" rowspan="3">Hypotheses</td><td>Access infrastructures are rehabilitated</td><td>The menalt roads at the disembarkation point are practicable and storage huts rehabilitated</td><td rowspan="3"></td></tr>
<tr><td>Educational materials are available</td><td>All fishermen benefited from the support</td></tr>
<tr><td>The budget positioned on time</td><td>Ownership of all training modules</td></tr>
</table>

Data Collection Strategy

1. Constitution of the sample

In accordance with the mission protocol, meetings were held between the consultants and the General Management of the SUCAF GABON company, the foundation managers and the village heads to explain to them the merits of the study carried out.

After agreements with the key people and the communication of the presence of the consultants in the area, 194 people were selected according to their degree of importance during the intervention while taking into account the number of inhabitants of the area. This sample was composed of (s):

- Fishermen benefiting from the support
- Families of fishermen
- Traders
- Agents of the SUCAF GABON foundation
- SUCAF GABON agents reside in the industrial site in Ouéllé
- Traditional village authorities
- Provincial representatives of public administration
- Groups of villagers from the Ouéllé district

2. Method adopted

To measure the effects of the project, particularly the changes made in the lives of the populations concerned, the mixed method combining the quantitative and qualitative methods was used, and a total of 180 respondents were recorded.

a. The quantitative method

It's a study technique that allows you to demonstrate facts by quantifying them. In our case, it consisted of verifying:

- The number of beneficiaries in activity
- The daily volume of catches
- The volume of fish sold
- Frequency of fish consumption
- The number of departures

In view of some difficulties identified, such as the establishment of a counterfactual scenario during the ex post reconstruction and the identification of a comparison group given the superimposition of other operations supported in the meantime by Technical and Financial Partners (JICA) not very far from the homes of our beneficiaries, a solution has nevertheless been found.

A comparison group could be identified, which is another fishing community living in the neighboring village commonly called Mvengué. The quantitative technique applied was therefore that of the quasi-experimental estimate given that the group of beneficiaries is known and the group of nonbeneficiaries of funding could be identified.

On this, the survey therefore brought out tagging questions, and a triangulation of data was done with those from the qualitative survey.

b. The qualitative method

It is a study technique that helps to understand the attitude and behavior of actors. In the case presented, in addition to understanding the production chain (resources and activities), it consisted of:

- determine the reasons for the departure of beneficiaries
- check if they are still in the fishing industry
- check the benefits of this intervention

The questions asked therefore called on memory and to find the contributions of the intervention, the combination of two methods was used, namely:

- Outcome mapping, which is an observation of changes in the behavior of one or more actors with whom the intervention has had direct contact and on whom it can expect to exert an influence;
- Outcome harvesting an observation and description of the main results generated following the intervention from the point of view of the stakeholders who participated in it to establish a link between the changes and the intervention.

3. Data collection instruments

Of the 180 respondents registered, the tool used for the quantitative method was as follows:

The Questionnaire

Questionnaires were administered anonymously to recipients of support and nonrecipients. Some of them could not write, and others were shy. They preferred that the questions be asked directly and the answers be filled in by the consultant.

For the qualitative method, the tools used were as follows:

Documentary Review

Reports containing information relating to the project were consulted, namely:

- The annual activity reports of the SUCAF GABON foundation for 2016, 2017 and 2018
- The annual activity report of SUCAF GABON for 2016
- SOMDIAA intersubsidiary reports for 2016, 2017 and 2018
- A press review dating from 2018

Observations

Field visits were made to:

- the fishermen's landing site to see if the canoes are active, how they work, the equipment used for catches, storage pending shipment for sale
- at the headquarters of the collective to obtain an idea of the storage of equipment
- at the Ouéllé market to see how the fish is sold, if requested

Interviews

On the basis of a semistructured interview guide, questions were asked of the actors involved in the implementation of the project, specifically:

- to the foundation's agents
- SUCAF GABON agents residing in Ouéllé
- traditional village authorities
- Some provincial representatives of the public administration
- women and traders

Evaluative Questions

Eight major questions were highlighted on the basis of criteria.

Analysis Method and Findings

Data entry and analysis were performed using Sphinx software (evaluation version V5) and Microsoft Excel. In terms of practices, the study was able to highlight the following:

Table 3.

Evaluation criteria	Main questions	Secondary questions
Efficiency	Have the initially assigned project objectives been achieved?	Did the mode of financing favor the realization of the planned activities? Did the participatory management of project implementation allow better monitoring?
Efficiency	Have resources been used optimally?	Did the people involved in the organization and implementation of the project do the best with the means at their disposal?
Consistency	Did the intervention agree with other projects?	Was the project compatible with the actions of other actors? Are there any similarities with what is done elsewhere, for example in other foundations of SOMDIAA?
Viability	Were the benefits of the intervention sustainable?	Are the beneficiaries of the support always in the same collective? Are they still practicing their activity three years after the end of the project?
Impact	what difference does the intervention make?	What changed after the end of the project and can now be observed in the behavior of funding recipients? In terms of productivity and comercialization ? In terms of consumption habits?
Empowerment	Did this intervention increase the incomes of the trainees?	Have the trainees been able to save and reinvest their income all this time?
Equality	Was the distribution of support fair?	
Kind	Did women play a role in the activity value chain at the end of the project?	

- A broken outboard motor has been handed over to a repairman since 2020. Thus far, it has not been recovered
- The rest of the materials delivered precisely to the canoes and paddles are still used
- Another outboard motor is mainly used by the group manager and his assistant.
- The rest of the trained fishermen use nets for their activities
- The fresh catches are kept in large bins used as coolers while awaiting delivery to their headquarters for temporary storage in 1 freezer before sale.
- Selling prices of 5,000 fcfa per kg for catfish and machoîron type fish, 10,000 fcfa per kg for carp
- Fishermen now transform fresh fish into smoked fish at the special request of their customer subscribers
- Fishing products are not sold in the village market because of their off-center geographical position from the main road, the poor condition of the access roads and weak
- The reported catches are sold and delivered directly to applicants throughout the sugar complex and village dwellings by 02 women who became involved in the activity after the project was terminated.

In terms of behavior, it has been observed that:

- The fishermen benefiting from the support formed a collective at the end of the project.
- All the trained fishermen are no longer part of the collective
- Some fishermen who are members of the collective live permanently in the camp by the water

- Other fishermen alternate between the camp and in the neighborhoods of the village where they now own second homes rented for financial transactions or family reasons
- Many will fish at least 01 times/week and more depending on the orders of their loyal customers; those who use the nets throw them during the night approximately 9 p.m. and at 4 a.m. that they will retrieve the catches
- They no longer exceed 1 kilometer in fishing width and use suitable materials and equipment to comply with the operating instructions and schedule transmitted by public authorities for the preservation of biodiversity.
- They often return to the neighborhoods of the village where some have rental commitments to carry out transactions that may be financial or social.

Project Effects

- 20 villagers were trained in fishing trades
- Seventeen villagers continue to carry out their activities by remaining members of the collective until now
- One thousand kilograms of fish are harvested per week, thus ensuring the supply of neighboring villages, SUCAF workers and their families as well as generating income for fishermen who are members of the collective.
- 03 resigning from the collective set up on their own account and carry on their activities without again benefiting from the support of the foundation

Answers to Evaluation Questions

1. Efficiency

Previous experiences of funding in other sectors have shown that actions are not carried out when the support is financial.

This is why the funding method chosen during the design of the project was the free provision of materials and equipment as well as capacity building, which took place without too many major incidents apart from the one stated at the start of the project. putting in practice. According to the results of the survey, this method of funding helped to carry out the planned activities.

The participatory management of the implementation of the project allowed better monitoring in the short term but proved to be costly in the long term, hence the withdrawal of the firm specializing in the trades of the shortly after the end of the project.

2. Efficiency

The people involved in the implementation of the project did their best with the allocated budget. In terms of equipment, it was still insufficient given the unit ratio per fisherman trained.

3. Coherence

The project was compatible with other projects, such as those carried out by Japanese cooperation consisting of the establishment of fishing centers in each locality. In addition, a similar project was implemented in one of the subsidiaries of the SOMDIAA group called SARIS CONGO in a region commonly called Kimpalanga located near the sugar factory.

4. Viability

Three beneficiaries of the support did not stay in the collective for lack of agreement with the two managers of the collective concerning the use of the outboard motor and on the daily amount as an operating tax to be paid to the Ministry of Peach. They preferred to continue their fishing activity independently.

5. Impact

The project contributed to the modernization of practices and techniques and contributed to the significant increase in the fishing production of the group of beneficiaries. The development of the unloading point as well as the rehabilitation of the headquarters for storage has improved the quality of storage.

In addition, capacity building enabled a good understanding of the issues related to the preservation of biodiversity and compliance with environmental instructions communicated on, such as the fishing period, the operating perimeter and the type of equipment needed.

6. Empowerment

Since the appropriation of new fishing materials, the increase in demand to be satisfied and the regular availability of fish, the fishermen of Ouéllé have seen an improvement in their sales and consequently their financial income.

In addition to their houses in the camp by the water, they also manage to provide rental charges in the neighborhoods of the village. Their children are all educated in the schools on the site; they are able to cover the rest of their family responsibilities and can travel to do financial transactions with other actors outside the site. Which is a significant change when you know that before the project this was not the case.

The study also revealed changes in access to certain microfinance services offered by a microcredit company called FINAM GABON, whose network of agencies extends to the provinces. This resulted in the opening of savings accounts for some members and the start of their investment in fish processing activities such as smoking.

The project has therefore certainly contributed to improving the incomes of the fishermen benefiting from the support (those from the village of Ouéllé), but when the level of their income is compared with that of the fishermen who did not benefit from the support. (the fishermen of Mvengué village), the nonbeneficiaries live better than the beneficiaries, and their income is higher.

This situation is explained by the fact that the beneficiaries sell almost all of their catches to the inhabitants of Ouéllé or, the latter mainly have low purchasing power. The village has no paved access roads and very often experiences deterioration in the condition of its roads. This is a barrier for other external customers wishing to come and obtain their supplies. Fishermen cannot present and sell their products in the fault stalls of large passages and the large dust released during car passages and are therefore obliged to operate by order deliveries.

Deliveries are not made outside the village because of multiple checks by the gendarmerie, possible taxes to pay, the price of fuel that has increased and which will be reflected in the final price of fish while the average prices are known.

Its geographical position is offset from the main roads leading to other neighboring villages and towns. There are no external clients. The majority of their customers are employees of the SUCAF GABON company.

The nonbeneficiary fishermen who live in the neighboring village called Mvengué use both traditional and modern fishing techniques. They go fishing at least once a week or more depending on the season. Their fishing products are fresh fish and smoked fish and involve women in their activities, whose role is in the sale.

Additionally, their fish are both sold on order and on proposal after presentation in a small space set up in large crossroads, leading to several small towns.

Figure 7. Ouéllé village market
source photography 2021

The location of their presentation space and the good condition of the road mean that their customers come from several cities and have a higher purchasing power. Most of the time, these are employees of a mining industry called COMILOG located in a neighboring town (Moanda), employees of local public administrations, service providers, residents, travelers, etc. These are therefore all requests, which means that the fishermen of the village of Mvengué have a higher level of income than those of the village of Ouéllé and consequently live better.

7. Gender

The project presented a weakness because it reached predominantly male beneficiaries. They are not part of the collective at the start and during the implementation of the project. Their involvement was requested by the head of the collective after the end of the gold project in the artisanal fishing sector, and their role was closely linked to that of men. Together, their actions form a chain.

Future Challenges

The next major challenges identified were as follows:

1. Encourage fishermen to become collective entrepreneurs
2. The renewal of experience with a more advanced budget taking into account other parameters such as external marketing, transport and logistics
3. the integration of women and unmarried mothers in fishing transformation activities
4. Maintaining free access to fishing equipment and materials
5. Retention of those trained
6. The establishment of partnerships
7. the satisfaction of other communities and stakeholders

Figure 8. Mvengué crossroads
source photography 2021

Practical Implications of the CSR project for the Blue Economy

First, the proactive management and optimization of resources earmarked for the implementation of social projects impact social and economic development in the areas of health, education, welfare and living conditions, the improvement of sociocultural structures and the promotion of income-generating activities. Second, the CSR project has enhanced the progression towards a blue economy and green economy at the same time. In particular, the intervention has positively impacted various subsectors, such as agriculture, livestock, arboriculture, processing, crafts, trade, health, hygiene education and fishing. She supported a community of artisanal fishermen in the village through a support project. Third, three years after the project, it has achieved the expected objectives, including the reduction of poverty in rural areas in accordance with SDG1. The project also has the potential to fight against poverty.

CONCLUSION

The eco-responsible concept presents a new vision for the rational and sustainable exploitation of oceans, lakes, rivers and rivers in the development literature. Arguably, the blue economy is very often cited as an example of a new development paradigm with the capability to fight against poverty, improve food diversification and create added value in coastal countries of the African continent. To differentiate themselves and ensure long-lasting growth, established companies in Gabon have embraced sustainable development through several actions, some of which are CSR projects and interventions. This chapter sets out to present a model of CSR action that impacts SDG 1 and shows how a vulnerable community has benefited from a project to improve its well-being and that of other populations. Ultimately, the two research questions were answered affirmatively. First, it was established that the CSR project of FONDATION SUCAF GABON positively impacts the daily life of fishermen. Second, the CSR project was found to be sustainable three years after its shutdown.

REFERENCES

African Union (AU). (2012). *2050 Africa's integrated maritime strategy*. Retrieved from http://www.au.int/maritime

Akinyemi, O., Efobi, U., Osabuohien, E., & Alege, P. (2019). Regional integration and energy sustainability in Africa: Exploring the challenges and prospects for ECOWAS. *African Development Review*, *31*(4), 517–528. doi:10.1111/1467-8268.12406

Akpomera, E. (2020). Africa's Blue Economy: Potentials and challenges for more locally beneficial development. *Review of African Political Economy*, *47*(166), 651–661. doi:10.1080/03056244.2020.1853517

Bello-Bravo, J., & Lutomia, A. N. (2020). Supporting Sustainability for a Decent Work and Economic Growth in Ghana. In Decent Work and Economic Growth, Encyclopedia of the UN Sustainable Development Goals. Springer Nature Switzerland. doi:10.1007/978-3-319-71058-7_120-1

Bueger, C., & Wivel, A. (2018). How do small island states maximize influence? Creole diplomacy and the smart state foreign policy of the Seychelles. *Journal of the Indian Ocean Region*, *14*(2), 170–188. doi:10.1080/19480881.2018.1471122

Desa, U. N. (2016). *Transforming our world: The 2030 agenda for sustainable development*. United Nations, Working Document, A/RES/70/1. https://stg-wedocs.unep.org/bitstream/handle/20.500.11822/11125/unepswiosm1inf7sdg.pdf?sequence=1

Findlay, K. P. (2020). Oceans and Blue Economies. In *Global Challenges in Maritime Security* (pp. 13–31). Springer. doi:10.1007/978-3-030-34630-0_2

Mohanty, S. K., & Dash, P. (2020). Economic Opportunities in Blue Economy in Africa. In *Asia-Africa Growth Corridor* (pp. 89–110). Springer. doi:10.1007/978-981-15-5550-3_6

Raimi, L., Olowo, R., & Shokunbi, M. (2021). A comparative discourse of sustainable finance options for agribusiness transformation in Nigeria and Brunei: Implications for entrepreneurship and enterprise development. *World Journal of Science, Technology and Sustainable Development*, *18*(4), 325–350. doi:10.1108/WJSTSD-05-2021-0051

Spence, M., Ben Boubaker Gherib, J., & Ondoua Biwolé, V. (2011). Sustainable entrepreneurship: Is entrepreneurial will enough? A north–south comparison. *Journal of Business Ethics*, *99*(3), 335–367. doi:10.100710551-010-0656-1

United Nations Conference of Trade and Development (UNCTAD). (2014). *The oceans economy: Opportunities and challenges for small island developing states, UNCTAD/DITC/TED/2014/5*. New York: UNCTAD.

United Nations Environment Programme. (2016). *Green Economy – Towards Greener and more inclusive economies.* UNEP Documents. https://www.unepfi.org/fileadmin/documents/greeneconomy_flyer.pdf

World Bank. (2017, July). *What is the Blue Economy?* The World Bank. https://www.worldbank.org/en/news/infographic/2017/06/06/blue-economy

World Bank and United Nations Department of Economic and Social Affairs. (2017). *The Potential of the Blue Economy: Increasing Long-term Benefits of the Sustainable Use of Marine Resources for Small Island Developing States and Coastal Least Developed Countries.* World Bank.

Yates, D. (2021). Testing the Illusion of Location Theory: Port-Gentil, Gabon. *Illusions of Location Theory: Consequences for Blue Economy in Africa*, 343.

Compilation of References

"Oral report of the Facilitator to the plenary" submitted during the BBNJ IGC1. (2018). Available from https://www.un.org/bbnj/sites/www.un.org.bbnj/files/final_oral_report_facilitator_abmts_mpas_final.pdf

"Group of 77 and China's Written submission" in response to the General Assembly Resolution 69/292. (2016). Available from https://www.un.org/depts/los/biodiversity/prepcom_files/rolling_comp/Group_of_77_and_China.pdf

Abdullahel, B. (2017). Our Oceans and the blue economy: opportunities and challenges. *10th International Conference on Marine Technology.*

Abdullahel, B. (2017). Our Oceans and the blue economy: opportunities and challenges. *10th international conference on marine technology.* Available at https://www.sciencedirect.com/science/article/pii/S1877705817332447

About LDCs. (n.d.). https://www.oceanfdn.org/blog/looking-smalldetails

Acar, M., & Temiz, H. (2020). Empirical analysis on corporate environmental performance and environmental disclosure in an emerging market context: Socio-political theories versus economics disclosure theories. *International Journal of Emerging Markets.*

Adeyemi, K. S., & Abiodun, A. J. (2013). *Development of the non-oil sector in Nigeria.* Academic Press.

Africa Blue Economy Strategy. (2019). Available online: https://www.au-ibar. org/ sites/ default/ files/ 2020-10/ sd_20200313_africa_blue_economy_strategy_en.pdf

African Union (AU). (2012). *2050 Africa's integrated maritime strategy.* Retrieved from http://www.au.int/maritime

Agyemang, A. O., Yusheng, K., Ayamba, E. C., Twum, A. K., Chengpeng, Z., & Shaibu, A. (2020). Impact of board characteristics on environmental disclosures for listed mining companies in China. *Environmental Science and Pollution Research International, 27*(17), 21188–21201. doi:10.100711356-020-08599-2 PMID:32266625

Akgüneş, G. (2020). *We must learn to live with blowfish.* Milliyet.

Akinyemi, O., Efobi, U., Osabuohien, E., & Alege, P. (2019). Regional integration and energy sustainability in Africa: Exploring the challenges and prospects for ECOWAS. *African Development Review, 31*(4), 517–528. doi:10.1111/1467-8268.12406

Akpomera, E. (2020). Africa's Blue Economy: Potentials and challenges for more locally beneficial development. *Review of African Political Economy, 47*(166), 651–661. doi:10.1080/03056244.2020.1853517

Allard, A., & Bauer, C. (2018). *The possible effects of the blue economy on gender quality in the republic of Seychelles* (Thesis). Linkoping University.

Álvarez, A. (2012). *Study of Environmental Accounting National and International Legislation.* Academic Press.

Amaechi, R. (2018). *Blue economy sustainability: Nigeria to partner other African countries*. Academic Press.

AMCEN. (2019). *Seventeenth Regular Session of the African Ministerial Conference on the Environment (AMCEN), UNEP—UN Environment Programme*. Available online: http://www.Unep .org/ events/conference/seventeenth-regular-session-african-ministerialconference-environment-amcen

Anuchitworawong, C., & Thampanishvong, K. (2015). Determinants of foreign direct investment in Thailand: Does natural disaster matter? *International Journal of Disaster Risk Reduction*, *14*, 312–321. doi:10.1016/j.ijdrr.2014.09.001

Arbow, T. (2019). *Washington Maritime Blue and the Blue Economy: Using diversity and inclusion to advance social justice in the maritime industry* (Doctoral dissertation).

Arctic Portal. (2012). *Aquaculture in the Arctic*. Retrieved October 22, 2021, from https://arcticportal.org/ap-library/yar-features/625-aquaculture-in-the-arctic

Arévalo, V. (2013). *Environmental accounting in the Colombian socio-economic business environment*. Academic Press.

Asian Development Bank. (2014). Wave energy conversion and ocean thermal energy conversion potential in developing member countries. 2014 Asian Development Bank. Atlantic economy. *Marine Policy*, *64*, 72–81.

Asimakopoulou, E., & Mohammed, E. Y. (2019). *Marine genetic resources in areas beyond national jurisdiction: a 'common heritage of mankind.'* IIED Briefing Papers. Retrieved January 14, 2022, from https://pubs.iied.org/17498iied

Attri, V. N. (2016). *An emerging new development paradigm of the blue economy in IORA; A policy framework for the future. Chair Indian Ocean Studies, Indian Ocean Rim Association (IORA)*. University of Mauritius.

AUDA-NEPAD. (2019). *Development of the AUDA-NEPAD Blue Economy Programme*. Available at https://kippra.or.ke/kenyas-agenda-in-developing-the-blue-economy/

Bahar, H. (2019). *Ocean power: Tracking Clean Energy Progress*. IEA. doi:10.1016/j.proeng.2017.08.157

Balogun, A. M. (2015). *The Fisheries subsector in a declining Oil-based Economy: Paradigm shift for Economic Diversification and Employment generation*. Keynote address at the 30th Annual Conference of Fisheries Society of Nigeria, Nigeria.

Barbour, P. (2005). *An assessment of South Africa's investment incentive regime with a focus on the manufacturing sector*. Economic and Statistics Analysis Unit (ESAU), ESAU Working Paper 14. Overseas Development Institute.

Bargh, M. (2014). A blue economy for Aotearoa New Zealand? *Environment, Development and Sustainability*, *16*(3), 459–470. doi:10.100710668-013-9487-4

Bari, A. (2017). Our oceans and the blue economy: Opportunities and challenges. *Procedia Engineering*, *194*, 5–11. doi:10.1016/j.proeng.2017.08.109

Barman, B. K., & Little, D. C. (2006). Nile tilapia (Oreochromis niloticus) seed production in irrigated rice fields in Northwest Bangladesh: An approach appropriate for poorer farmers. *Aquaculture (Amsterdam, Netherlands)*, *261*(1), 72–79. doi:10.1016/j.aquaculture.2006.06.018

Barraza, C., & Gómez, M. (2005). *Approach to a concept of environmental accounting*. Cooperative University of Colombia.

Bartenstein, K. (2017). Article 268. In United Nations Convention on the Law of the Sea: A Commentary. C.H. Beck/Hart/Nomos.

Baumann, T., Polyakov, I., Padman, L., Danielson, S., Fer, I., Janout, M., Williams, W., & Pnyushkov, A. (2020). Arctic Tidal Current Atlas. *Scientific Data*, *7*(1), 275. doi:10.103841597-020-00578-z PMID:32826909

Bax, N., Novaglio, C., Maxwell, K. H., Meyers, K., McCann, J., Jennings, S., Frusher, S., Fulton, E. A., Nursey-Bray, M., Fischer, M., Anderson, K., Layton, C., Emad, G. R., Alexander, K. A., Rousseau, Y., Lunn, Z., & Carter, C. G. (2021). Ocean resource use: Building the coastal blue economy. *Reviews in Fish Biology and Fisheries*, 1–19. doi:10.100711160-021-09636-0 PMID:33679009

Bejarano, Y. & Chavarro, J. (2017). *Analysis of the Contributions of Environmental Accounting to Business Management in the Framework of Social Responsibility in Colombia*. Academic Press.

Bello, A. (2015). *Cost accounting and environmental costs*. Academic Press.

Bello-Bravo, J., & Lutomia, A. N. (2020). Supporting Sustainability for a Decent Work and Economic Growth in Ghana. In Decent Work and Economic Growth, Encyclopedia of the UN Sustainable Development Goals. Springer Nature Switzerland. doi:10.1007/978-3-319-71058-7_120-1

Benkenstein, A., & Maposa, S. (2017). Governing the High Seas: Marine Genetic Resources in Areas Beyond National Jurisdiction. South African Institute of International Affairs Policy Insights, (51).

Bennett, N. J., Cisneros-Montemayor, A. M., Blythe, J., Silver, J. J., Singh, G., Andrews, N., Calò, A., Christie, P., Di Franco, A., Finkbeiner, E. M., Gelcich, S., Guidetti, P., Harper, S., Hotte, N., Kittinger, J. N., Le Billon, P., Lister, J., López de la Lama, R., McKinley, E., ... Sumaila, U. R. (2019). Towards a sustainable and equitable blue economy. *Nature Sustainability*, *2*(11), 991–993. doi:10.103841893-019-0404-1

Bennett, N. J., Cisneros-Montemayor, A. M., Blythe, J., Silver, J. J., Singh, G., Andrews, N., Calo, A., Christie, P., Di Franco, A., Finkbeiner, E. M., Gelcich, S., Guidetti, P., Harper, S., Hotte, N., Kittinger, J. N., Le Billon, P., Lister, J., Lopez De La Lama, R., Mckinley, E., ... Sumaila, U. R. (2019). *Towards a sustainable and equitable blue economy*. Nature Sustainability.

Bentlage, M., Wiese, A., Brandt, A., Thierstein, A., & Witlox, F. (2014). Revealing relevant proximities knowledge networks in the maritime economy in a spatial, functional, and relational perspective. *Raumforschung und Raumordnung*, *72*(4), 275–291. doi:10.100713147-014-0299-2

Bertelsen, R. G., & Gallucci, V. (2016). The Return of China, Post-Cold War Russia, and the Arctic: Changes on Land and at Sea. *Marine Policy*, *72*, 240–245. doi:10.1016/j.marpol.2016.04.034

Bhattacharya, P., & Dash, A. K. (2021). Determinants of Blue Economy in Asia-Pacific Island Countries: A Study of Tourism and Fisheries Sectors. *Ocean and Coastal Management*, *211*, 105774. doi:10.1016/j.ocecoaman.2021.105774

Bioenergy SAS. (2018). *Separate Financial Statements*. Author.

Blasiak, R., Jouffray, J.-B., Wabnitz, C. C., Sundström, E., & Österblom, H. (2018). Corporate control and global governance of Marine Genetic Resources. *Science Advances*, *4*(6). https://doi.org/10.1126/sciadv.aar5237

Blue Economy Department. (2018). *Seychelles Blue Economy, strategic policy framework and roadmap: charting the future*. Blue Economy Department.

Boczek, B. A. (1982). The Transfer of Marine Technology to Developing Nations in International Law. The Law of the Sea Institute, University of Hawaii.

Bogdan, A., Istudor, N., Gruia, R., Tobă, G. F., Bulz, N., Gâf-Deac, I., Chelmu, S., Găvan, C., Prică, I., & Paşalău, C. (2014). New holistic approach of bioeconomics and ecoeconomics theories, practical bridging from the green economy to blue economy, trough new integrated and innovative paradigm about "bioeco-geo-economy". *Procedia Economics and Finance*, *8*, 83–90. doi:10.1016/S2212-5671(14)00066-5

Bolarinwa, J. B. (2015). *The ichthyofauna Resources of The Coastal waters of Ondo State, Nigeria* (PhD Thesis). Federal University of Technology, Akure, Nigeria.

Bolarinwa, J. B. (2014). Role of Extension Services and Public Relations in Nigerian Fisheries Industry. *International Journal of Agricultural Research*, *9*(7), 325–330. doi:10.3923/ijar.2014.325.330

Boonstra, W. J., Valman, M., & Bjorkvik, E. (2018). A sea of many colours—How relevant is blue growth for capture fisheries in the Global North, and vice versa? *Marine Policy*, *87*, 340–349. doi:10.1016/j.marpol.2017.09.007

Bortone, N. A., & Vergara, E. M. (2004). Accounting and Environment. A discipline and a field for knowledge and action. *FACES Accounting News*, *7*(8), 7-22.

Breitburg, D., Levin, L., Oschlies, A., Grégoire, M., Chavez, F., Conley, D., Garçon, V., Gilbert, D., Gutiérrez, D., Isensee, K., Jacinto, G. S., Limburg, K. E., Montes, I., Naqvi, S. W. A., Pitcher, G. C., Rabalais, N. N., Roman, M. R., Rose, K. A., Seibel, B. A., ... Zhang, J. (2018). Declining Oxygen in the Global Ocean and Coastal Waters. *Science*, *359*(6371), eaam7240. Advance online publication. doi:10.1126cience.aam7240 PMID:29301986

Brookes, G., & Barfoot, P. (2016). Global income and production impacts of using GM crop Technology 1996–2014. *GM Crops and Food: Biotechnology in Agriculture and the Food Chain*, *7*(1), 38–77. doi:10.1080/21645698.2016.1176817 PMID:27116697

Brouder, P. (2013). *Tourism Development in Peripheral Areas: Processes of Local Innovation and Change in Northern Sweden*. Mid Sweden University.

Brown, C. J., Smith, S. J., Lawton, P., & Anderson, J. T. (2011). Benthic habitat mapping: A review of progress towards improved understanding of the spatial ecology of the seafloor using acoustic techniques. *Estuarine, Coastal and Shelf Science*, *92*(3), 502–520. doi:10.1016/j.ecss.2011.02.007

Brown, E. M. (2010). *A gender toolkit for educators*. United Nations Educational, Scientific and Cultural Organization.

Brugere, C., McAndrew, K., & Bulcock, P. (2001). Does cage aquaculture address gender goals in development? Results of a case study in Bangladesh. *Aquaculture Economics & Management*, *5*(3–4), 179–189. doi:10.1080/13657300109380286

Bryman, A. (2008). *Social Research Methods* (Vol. 3). Oxford University Press Inc.

Bryman, A., & Bell, E. (2007). *Business research methods* (Vol. 2). Oxford University Press Inc.

Bueger, C., & Wivel, A. (2018). How do small island states maximize influence? Creole diplomacy and the smart state foreign policy of the Seychelles. *Journal of the Indian Ocean Region*, *14*(2), 170–188. doi:10.1080/19480881.2018.1471122

Buheji, M., & Ahmed, D. (2021). Forward: The Pandemic Calls for More Colours Economies. *Forward: The Pandemic Calls for More Colours Economies*, *5*(1), 1–3. doi:10.5923/j.ijire.20210501.01

Buhl-Mortensen, L., Olsen, E., Røttingen, I., Buhl-Mortensen, P., Hoel, A. H., Ringheim, L., & Cheke, A. O. (2012). Establishment of model Fish Market For Women. Fish handling and processing methods in Nigeria. NAFDAC Workshop on Fish Imports and Exports Procedures.

Buiatti, M., Christou, P., & Pastore, G. (2013). The application of GMOs in agriculture and in food production for a better nutrition: Two different scientific points of view. *Genes & Nutrition*, *8*(3), 255–270. doi:10.100712263-012-0316-4 PMID:23076994

Burgess, M. G., Clemence, M., McDermott, G. R., Costello, C., & Gaines, S. D. (2018). Five rules for pragmatic blue growth. *Marine Policy*, *87*, 331–339. doi:10.1016/j.marpol.2016.12.005

Caicedo, L., Loaiza, S., & Lugo, D. (2013). *Importance of Social Accounting and Environmental in Colombian Companies*. Academic Press.

Cantwell, M. (2009). *The blue economy: the role of the Oceans in our Nation's Economic Future*. U.S. Committee on Commerce, Science, and Transportation United States Senate One Hundred Eleventh Congress. Government Printing Office.

Cao, Y., Yu, M., Hui, F., Zhang, J., & Cheng, X. (2021). Review of Navigability Changes in Trans-Arctic Routes. *Chinese Science Bulletin*, *66*(1), 21–33. doi:10.1360/TB-2020-0596

Caswell, B. A., Klein, E. S., Alleway, H. K., Ball, J. E., Botero, J., Cardinale, M., & Thurstan, R. H. (2020). Something old, something new: Historical perspectives provide lessons for blue growth agendas. *Fish and Fisheries*, *1246*(4), 774–796. Advance online publication. doi:10.1111/faf.12460

Cavalieri, D. J., & Parkinson, P. (2012). Arctic Sea Ice Variability and Trends, 1979-2010. *The Cryosphere*, *6*(4), 881–889. doi:10.5194/tc-6-881-2012

CBD (Convention on Biological Diversity). (2010). Report on implementation of the programme challenges & lessons for less developed countries. *Covenant Journal of Business.*

Census of Marine Life. (2011). *Scientific Results to Support the Sustainable Use and Conservation of Marine Life*. Author.

Chakrabarti, S., Paul, A., & Ghosh, I. (2014). FDI and Retail Regulation in India. *From the Editors Desk*, 111.

Chan. (2019). Prospects and challenges of fish for food security in Africa. *Global Food Security, 20*, 17-25.

Chang. (2015). *A Preliminary Assessment of the Blue Economy in South Korea*. Powerpoint presented in the Inception Workshop on Blue Economy Assessment, Manila.

Charter of the United Nations (UN Charter). (1945). Available from https://www.un.org/en/about-us/un-charter/full-text

Chen, Y., Wang, Z., & Zhong, Z. (2019). CO2 emissions, economic growth, renewable and non-renewable energy production and foreign trade in China. *Renewable Energy*, *131*, 208–216. doi:10.1016/j.renene.2018.07.047

Cheung, W. W., Lam, V. W., & Wabnitz, C. C. (2019). *Future scenarios and projections for fisheries on the high seas under a changing climate.* IIED Working Paper. IIED. https://pubs.iied.org/16653IIED

Chircop, A., Dzidzornu, D., & Oguamanam, C. (2016). Ocean law reform: A multilevel comparative law analysis of nigerian maritime zone legislation. *Marine Policy*, *67*, 60–75.

Choi, Y. R. (2017). The blue economy as governmentality and the making of new spatial rationalities. *Dialogues in Human Geography*, *7*(1), 37–41. doi:10.1177/2043820617691649

Çinar, M. E., Bilecenoğlu, M., Yokeş, M. B., Öztürk, B., Taşkin, E., Bakir, K., Doğan, A., & Açik, Ş. (2021). Current status (as of end of 2020) of marine alien species in Turkey. *PLoS One*, *16*(5), e0251086. doi:10.1371/journal.pone.0251086 PMID:33945562

Clark, N. A. (2020). Institutional arrangements for the new BBNJ agreement: Moving beyond global, regional, and hybrid. *Marine Policy*, *122*, 104–143. https://doi.org/10.1016/j.marpol.2020.104143

Clegg, P., Mahon, R., McConney, P., & Oxenford, H. A. (Eds.). (2020). *The Caribbean blue economy*. Routledge. doi:10.4324/9780429342233

Cliffe, P. T., & Akinrotimi, O. A. (2015). The Role of Women in Fisheries activities in Some Coastal communities of Rivers State. *International Journal of Agricultural Research*, *10*(1), 24–32. doi:10.3923/ijar.2015.24.32

Cochrane, K. (2000). Reconciling Sustainability, Economic Efficiency and Equity in Fisheries: The One That Got Away? *Fish and Fisheries*, *1*(1), 3–21. doi:10.1046/j.1467-2979.2000.00003.x

Colmenares, L., Adriani, R., & Valderrama, Y. (2015). Accounting representation from the perspective of business environmental impact. In the context of the development of industrial activities in Latin America. *Accounting Notebooks*, *16*(41), 259–280.

Concepcion, G. P. (2008). *Marine Biodiversity and Marine Biotechnology: A Philippine Competitive Advantage. In Selected Essays on Science and Technology for Securing a Better Philippines*. Department of Science and Technology.

Conde, E., & Sanchez, S. I. (2016). *Global Challenges in the Arctic Region: Sovereignty, Environment and Geopolitical Balance*. Routledge., doi:10.4324/9781315584768

Conger, T., & Chang, S. E. (2019). Developing indicators to identify coastal green infrastructure potential: The case of the Salish Sea region. *Ocean and Coastal Management*, *175*, 53–69. doi:10.1016/j.ocecoaman.2019.03.011

Conley, H., Pumphrey, D., Toland, T., & David, M. (2013). *Arctic Economics in the 21st Century. The Benefits and Costs of Cold. A Report of the CSIS Europe Program*. Center for Strategic and International Studies.

Corbett, J. J., & Winebrake, J. (2008, November). The impacts of globalization on international maritime transport activity. In *Global forum on transport and environment in a globalizing world* (Vol. 31). Academic Press.

Cortes, H., & Peña, J. (2015). From Sustainability to Sustainability. Development model Sustainable for its Implementation in Policies and Projects. *School of Business Administration Magazine*, *78*, 40–55.

Costa, J. A. V., de Freitas, B. C. B., Lisboa, C. R., Santos, T. D., de Fraga Brusch, L. R., & de Morais, M. G. (2019). Microalgal biorefinery from CO_2 and the effects under the blue economy. *Renewable & Sustainable Energy Reviews*, *99*, 58–65. doi:10.1016/j.rser.2018.08.009

Costanza, R. (1999). The ecological, economic, and social importance of the oceans. *Ecological Economics*, *31*(2), 199–213. doi:10.1016/S0921-8009(99)00079-8

Crane, B., Albrecht, C., Duffin, K. M., & Albrecht, C. (2018). China's special economic zones: An analysis of policy to reduce regional disparities. *Regional Studies, Regional Science*, *5*(1), 98–107. doi:10.1080/21681376.2018.1430612

Cristiani, P. (2017). New challenges for materials in the blue economy perspective. *MetallItaliana*, *7–8*, 7–10.

Cubides, A. (2017). *Importance and Applicability of Environmental Accounting in Colombian Companies*. Academic Press.

DANE. (2016). *Environmental Industrial Survey*. Academic Press.

Dankelman, I. (2002). Climate change: Learning from gender analysis and women's experiences of organising for sustainable development. *Gender and Development*, *10*(2), 21–29. doi:10.1080/13552070215899

Danladi, I. B., Kore, B. M., & Gül, M. (2017). Vulnerability of the nigerian coast: An insight into sea level rise owing to climate change and anthropogenic activities. *Journal of African Earth Sciences*, *134*, 493–503. doi:10.1016/j.jafrearsci.2017.07.019

Dawson, J., Maher, P., & Scott, S. (2007). Climate Change, Marine Tourism, and Sustainability in the Canadian Arctic: Contributions from Systems and Complexity Approaches. *Tourism in Marine Environments*, *4*(2-3), 69–83. doi:10.3727/154427307784772057

De Graaf, G., & Garibaldi, L. (2014). *The Value of African Fisheries*. FAO Fisheries and Aquaculture Circular No. 1093.

Denscombe, M. (2017). *EBOOK: The Good Research Guide: For Small-Scale Social Research Projects*. McGraw-Hill Education.

Desa, U. N. (2016). *Transforming our world: The 2030 agenda for sustainable development*. United Nations, Working Document, A/RES/70/1. https://stg-wedocs.unep.org/bitstream/handle/20.500.11822/11125/unepswiosm1inf7sdg.pdf?sequence=1

Deswanto, R. B., & Siregar, S. V. (2018). The associations between environmental disclosures with financial performance, environmental performance, and firm value. *Social Responsibility Journal*, *14*(1), 180–193. doi:10.1108/SRJ-01-2017-0005

Diop. (2018). *The evolution of maritime transport in West and Central Africa*. The United Republic of Tanzania.

Djavidnia, S., Ott, M., & Seeyave, S. (2014). *Oceans and society: Blue planet*. Cambridge Scholars Publishing.

Dolan, A. H., Taylor, M., Neis, B., Ommer, R., Eyles, J., Schneider, D., & Montevecchi, B. (2005). Restructuring and Health in Canadian Coastal Communities. *EcoHealth*, *2*(3), 195–208. doi:10.100710393-005-6333-7

Druel, E., & Gjerde, K. M. (2014). Sustaining marine life beyond boundaries: Options for an implementing agreement for Marine Biodiversity Beyond National Jurisdiction under the United Nations Convention on the law of the sea. *Marine Policy*, *49*, 90–97. https://doi.org/10.1016/j.marpol.2013.11.023

Dunne, T., Kurki, M., & Smith, S. (Eds.). (2010). *International Relations Theories: Discipline and Diversity* (2nd ed.). Oxford University Press.

DW Recommends. (2017). *Invasive venomous fish spotted off Italy's coast*. https://www.dw.com/en/invasive-venomous-fish-spotted-off-italys-coast/a-38213006

Ebenstein, A., Fan, M., Greenstone, M., He, G., Yin, P., & Zhou, M. (2015). Growth, pollution, and life expectancy: China from 1991-2012. *The American Economic Review*, *105*(5), 226–231. doi:10.1257/aer.p20151094

Eckersley, R. (2010). Green Theory. In International Relations Theories Disciplines and Diversity (2nd ed.). New York: Oxford University Press.

Economist Intelligence Unit. (2015). *The blue economy: Growth, opportunity and a sustainable ocean economy*. https://www. eiuperspectives. economist. com/sustainability/blue-economy/white-paper/blue-economy

Economist Intelligence Unit. (n.d.). https://www.greengrowthknowledge.org/resource/blueeconomy-

Edwards, P., & Roberts, I. (2009). Population adiposity and climate change. *International Journal of Epidemiology*, *1*, 1–4. PMID:19377099

Eikeset, A. M., Mazzarella, A. B., Davíðsdóttir, B., Klinger, D. H., Levin, S. A., Rovenskaya, E., & Stenseth, N. C. (2018). What is blue growth? The semantics of "Sustainable Development" of marine environments. *Marine Policy*, *87*, 177–179. doi:10.1016/j.marpol.2017.10.019

Elliot, M. (2002). *The role of women on fisheries*. Internet.

Enright, M. J. (2002). Trends in multinational strategies and organizations in the Asia-Pacific. In *Japanese foreign direct investment and the East Asian industrial system* (pp. 41–68). Springer. doi:10.1007/978-4-431-66990-6_3

Enright, M. J. (2016). *Developing China: The remarkable impact of foreign direct investment*. Routledge. doi:10.4324/9781315393346

Erokhin, V. (2018). Northern Sea Route as an Infrastructure Framework of the Russia-China Arctic Blue Economic Corridor. *Marketing and Logistics*, *15*(1), 12–29.

Erokhin, V., Gao, T., & Zhang, X. (2018). Arctic Blue Economic Corridor: China's Role in the Development of a New Connectivity Paradigm in the North. In L. Heininen & H. Exner-Pirot (Eds.), *Arctic Yearbook 2018* (pp. 456–474). Northern Research Forum.

Erokhin, V., Gao, T., & Zhang, X. (Eds.). (2019). *Handbook of Research on International Collaboration, Economic Development, and Sustainability in the Arctic*. IGI Global., doi:10.4018/978-1-5225-6954-1

European Commission. (2012, August). *Blue Growth Study - Scenarios and drivers for Sustainable Growth from the Oceans, Seas and Coasts*. European Commission, DG MARE. https://webgate.ec.europa.eu/maritimeforum/system/files/Blue%20Growth%20Final%20Report%2013092012.pdf

European Commission. (2020). *The EU blue economy report*. Publications Office of the European Union. .2771/073370 doi:https://doi.org/10

European Commission. (2020). *The EU blue economy report*. Publications Office of the European Union., doi:10.2771/073370

European Environment Agency (EEA). (2021). *Indicator Assessment, Trends in marine non-indigenous species*. https://www.eea.europa.eu/data-and-maps/indicators/trends-in-marine-alien-species-mas-3/assessment

Fagerberg, J. (2018). Mobilizing innovation for sustainability transitions: A comment on transformative innovation policy. *Research Policy*, *47*(9), 1568–1576. doi:10.1016/j.respol.2018.08.012

Fahrudin, A. (2015). *Indonesian Ocean Economy and Ocean Health*. Powerpoint presented in the Inception Workshop on Blue Economy Assessment, Manila.

Failler, P. (2018). *Demystifying the Sustainable Blue Economy*. International Conference on Sustainable Blue Economy, Nairobi, Kenya.

Failler, P. (2019). *Blue Economy of the Indian Ocean Region*. Third IORA Ministerial Blue Economy Conference "Promoting Sustainable Blue Economy- making the best use of opportunities from the Indian Ocean", Dhaka, Bangladesh.

Failler, P. (2019). *The Institutional Challenges for the Implementation of a Blue Economy Governance, The Law of the Blue Economy: International and South Asian Perspectives*. The Second Biennial Conference of the South Asia International Economic Law Network (SAIELN) will be held in Thiruvananthapuram, Kerala, India.

Failler, P., Touron-Gardic, G., & Traoré, M.-S. (2019). Is Aichi Target 11 Progress correctly measured for developing Countries? *Trends in Ecology & Evolution*, *34*(10), 875–879.

Fairbridge, R. W. (2004). Classification of coasts. *Journal of Coastal Research*, *201*, 155–165. doi:10.2112/1551-5036(2004)20[155:COC]2.0.CO;2

FAO (Food and Agriculture Organization of the United Nations). (2020). *The State of Mediterranean and Black Sea Fisheries 2020*. General Fisheries Commission for the Mediterranean. doi:10.4060/cb2429en

FAO (Food and Agriculture Organization of the United Nations). (n.d.a). *Geographical subareas (GSAs)*. https://www.fao.org/gfcm/data/maps/gsas

FAO (Food and Agriculture Organization of the United Nations). (n.d.b). *General Fisheries Commission for the Mediterranean – GFCM, Fisheries*. https://www.fao.org/gfcm/activities/fisheries

FAO (Food and Agriculture Organization of the United Nations). (n.d.c). *Aquaculture*. https://www.fao.org/gfcm/activities/aquaculture/

FAO (Food and Agriculture Organization of the United Nations). (n.d.d). *Fisheries and Aquaculture*. https://www.fao.org/figis/servlet/SQServlet?file=/usr/local/tomcat/8.5.16/figis/webapps/figis/temp/hqp_460716040742363493.xml&outtype=html

FAO (Food and Agriculture Organization of the United Nations). (n.d.e). *GFCM capture production (1970-2019)*. https://www.fao.org/gfcm/data/capture-production

FAO (Food and Agriculture Organization). (2014a). *Securing Fish for the Caribbean*. FAO.

FAO, IFAD, UNICEF, WFP, & WHO. (2018). *The State of Food Security and Nutrition in the World 2018. Building climate resilience for food security and nutrition*. FAO.

FAO. (2012). Strategies for Sustainable Animal Agriculture in Developing countries. *Proceedings of the FAO Expert Consultation, Animal Production and Health*.

FAO. (2016). The state of world fisheries and aquaculture 2016. *Contributing to food security and nutrition for all, 200.*

FAO. (2016). The State of World Fisheries and Aquaculture 2016. FAO.

FAO. (2018). *Blue Economy Project*. FAO.

FAO. (2018). *The State of World Fisheries and Aquaculture – Meeting the Sustainable Development Goals*. FAO.

FAO. (2018). *The state of world fisheries and aquaculture: meeting the sustainable development goals*. Food and Agriculture Organization.

Farr & Hall. (2015). *What is the environmental impact of a cruise holiday?* Presentation given at the Contemporary Perspectives in Tourism and Hospitality Research: Policy, Practice and Performance event, University of Brighton.

Farre, A. B., Stephenson, S. R., Chen, L., Czub, M., Dai, Y., Demchev, D., ... Wighting, J. (2014). Commercial Arctic Shipping through the Northeast Passage: Routes, Resources, Governance, Technology, and Infrastructure. *Polar Geography*, *37*(4), 298–324. doi:10.1080/1088937X.2014.965769

Fartash, K., Jahangirnia, M., & Sadabadi, A. A. (2018). Three frames for innovation policy: R&D, systems of innovation and transformative change. *Research Policy*, *47*(9), 1554–1567. doi:10.1016/j.respol.2018.08.011

Fauchald, P., Arneberg, P., Debernard, J. B., Lind, S., Olsen, E., & Hausne, V. H. (2021). Poleward Shifts in Marine Fisheries under Arctic Warming. *Environmental Research Letters*, *16*(7), 074057. doi:10.1088/1748-9326/ac1010

FDF. (2010). *Fisheries Statistics of Nigeria* (5th ed.). Federal Department of Fisheries.

Federal Department of Fisheries. (n.d.). *Fisheries statistics of Nigeria; 1995 – 2007*. Author.

Findlay, K. P. (2020). Oceans and Blue Economies. In *Global Challenges in Maritime Security* (pp. 13–31). Springer. doi:10.1007/978-3-030-34630-0_2

Finkl, C. W. (2004). Coastal classification: Systematic approaches to consider in the development of a comprehensive scheme. *Journal of Coastal Research*, *201*, 166–213. doi:10.2112/1551-5036(2004)20[166:CCSATC]2.0.CO;2

FishBase. (2015). *Species in the Mediterranean Sea*. https://www.fishbase.se/TrophicEco/FishEcoList.php?ve_code=13

Fisher, B., Turner, R. K., & Morling, P. (2009). Defining and classifying ecosystem services for decision making. *Ecological Economics*, *68*(3), 643–653. doi:10.1016/j.ecolecon.2008.09.014

Fitt, E. (2020). *For the Mediterranean, the Suez is a wormhole bringing in alien invaders*. https://news.mongabay.com/2020/04/for-the-mediterranean-the-suez-is-a-wormhole-bringing-in-alien-invaders/

Flake, L. E. (2013). Russia and China in the Arctic: A Team of Rivals. *Strategic Analysis*, *37*(6), 681–687. doi:10.1080/09700161.2013.847048

Fondevila, M. M., Moneva, J. M., & Scarpellini, S. (2019). Environmental disclosure and Eco-innovation interrelation. The case of Spanish firms: Divulgación ambiental y la interrelación de la ecoinnovación. El caso de las empresas españolas. *Revista de Contabilidad-Spanish Accounting Review*, *22*(1), 73–87. doi:10.6018/rc-sar.22.1.354321

Food and Agriculture Organisation, International Fund for Agricultural Development, United Nations International Children's Emergency Fund, World Food Program, & World Health Organisation. (2018). The State of Food Security and Nutrition in the World 2018. Building Climate Resilience for Food Security and Nutrition. Rome: FAO.

Franckx, E., Gustafson Juras, K., & Noyes, J. (2010). *Law of the Sea in a Nutshell*. West Publishing Company.

Franco, R. (2009). *Accounting and environmental control*. Academic Press.

Freestone, D. (2019). The UN process to develop an international legally binding instrument under the 1982 law of the Sea Convention: Issues and Challenges. *Conserving Biodiversity in Areas beyond National Jurisdiction*, 3–46. doi:10.1163/9789004391703_002

Funk, C., Jensen, P. E., & Skjermo, J. (2021). Blue Economy in the North: Scandinavian Algal Biotechnology to the Rescue. *Physiologia Plantarum*, *173*(2), 479–482. doi:10.1111/ppl.13534 PMID:34528273

Galil, B. (2014). *How to stop the Mediterranean's invasive species*. https://www.weforum.org/agenda/2014/12/how-to-stop-the-mediterraneans-invasive-species/

Gao, T. (2019). Going North: China's Role in the Arctic Blue Economic Corridor. In V. Erokhin, T. Gao, & X. Zhang (Eds.), *Handbook of Research on International Collaboration, Economic Development, and Sustainability in the Arctic* (pp. 133–161). IGI Global. doi:10.4018/978-1-5225-6954-1.ch007

Gao, T., Bobylev, N., Gadal, S., Lagutina, M., Sergunin, A., & Erokhin, V. (2021a). Planning for Sustainability: An Emerging Blue Economy in Russia's Coastal Arctic? *Sustainability*, *13*(9), 4957. doi:10.3390u13094957

Gao, T., & Erokhin, V. (2020a). China-Russia Collaboration in Arctic Shipping and Maritime Engineering. *The Polar Journal*, *10*(2), 353–374. doi:10.1080/2154896X.2020.1799612

Gao, T., & Erokhin, V. (2020b). Widening the Scope of Responses to Environmental Concerns in the High North: Arctic Countries' Policies and the Role of China. In L. Heininen, H. Exner-Pirot, & J. Barnes (Eds.), *Climate Change and the Arctic: Global Origins, Regional Responsibilities? Arctic Yearbook 2020* (pp. 357–397). Arctic Portal.

Gao, T., & Erokhin, V. (2021). China-Russia Research and Education Collaboration in the Arctic: Opportunities, Challenges, and Gaps. *The Polar Journal*, *11*(1), 188–207. doi:10.1080/2154896X.2021.1889837

Gao, T., Erokhin, V., Arskiy, A., & Khudzhatov, M. (2021b). Has the COVID-19 Pandemic Affected Maritime Connectivity? An Estimation for China and the Polar Silk Road Countries. *Sustainability*, *13*(6), 3521. doi:10.3390u13063521

Gautier, D., Bird, K., Charpentier, R., Grantz, A., Houseknecht, D., Klett, T., Moore, T. E., Pitman, J. K., Schenk, C. J., Schuenemeyer, J. H., Sørensen, K., Tennyson, M. E., Valin, Z. C., & Wandrey, C. (2009). Assessment of Undiscovered Oil and Gas in the Arctic. *Science*, *324*(5931), 1175–1179. doi:10.1126cience.1169467 PMID:19478178

Geissdoerfer, M., Savaget, P., Bocken, N. M., & Hultink, E. J. (2017). The circular economy—A new sustainability paradigm? *Journal of Cleaner Production*, *143*, 757–768.

Geology.com. (2022). *Nigeria Map and Satellite Image*. https://geology.com/world/nigeria-satellite-image.shtml

Gharbaoui, D., & Blocher, J. (2016). The reason land matters: Relocation as adaptation to climate change in Fiji Islands. In *Migration, risk management and climate change: Evidence and policy responses* (pp. 149–173). Springer. doi:10.1007/978-3-319-42922-9_8

Ghoshal, S. (2014). Understanding food mile: An qualitative study on the concept of food mile. *TSM Business Review.*, *2*(2), 55–70.

Glasson, J., & Wood, G. (2009). Urban regeneration and impact assessment for social sustainability. *Impact Assessment and Project Appraisal*, *27*(4), 283–290. doi:10.3152/146155109X480358

GoArctic. (2020). *Alternative Energy in the Arctic.* Retrieved October 22, 2021, from https://goarctic.ru/work/alternativnaya-energetika-v-arktike/

Golden, J. S., Virdin, J., Nowacek, D., Halpin, P., Bennear, L., & Patil, P. G. (2017). Making sure the blue economy is green. *Nature Ecology & Evolution*, *1*(2), 1–3. doi:10.103841559-016-0017 PMID:28812613

González, A. W. (2007). Cutting a gordian knot? Towards a practical and realistic scheme for the transfer of Marine Technology. *Law, Science & Ocean Management*, 345–380. doi:10.1163/ej.9789004162556.i-850.100

Gorman, G., & Clayton, P. (2005). Qualitative Research for the Information Professional, a practical handbook (2nd ed.). London: Facet Publishing.

Goron, C. (2018). Ecological civilisation and the political limits of a Chinese concept of sustainability. *China Perspectives, 2018*(4), 39-52.

Górski, J. (2019). Northern Sea Route: International Law Perspectives. In V. Erokhin, T. Gao, & X. Zhang (Eds.), *Handbook of Research on International Collaboration, Economic Development, and Sustainability in the Arctic* (pp. 292–313). IGI Global. doi:10.4018/978-1-5225-6954-1.ch014

Grati, F., Carlson, A., Carpentieri, P., & Cerri, J. (2021). *Handbook for data collection on recreational fisheries in the Mediterranean and the Black Sea.* FAO Fisheries and Aquaculture Technical Paper No. 669. FAO. doi:10.4060/cb5403enThe

Graziano, M., Alexander, K. A., Liesch, M., Lema, E., & Torres, J. A. (2019). Understanding an emerging economic discourse through regional analysis: Blue economy clusters in the US Great Lakes basin. *Applied Geography (Sevenoaks, England)*, *105*, 111–123.

Green Economy Coalition. (2021, June). *The 5 Principles of Green Economy.* https://www.greeneconomycoalition.org/news-and-resources/the-5-principles-of-green-economy

Groww. (2022). *Foreign Direct Investment (FDI).* https://groww.in/p/foreign-direct-investment

Grunberg, L. (1991). The Changing International Political Economy of Multinational Corporations. In *Introduction to International Political Economy.* Prentice Hall.

Gryka, A., Broom, J., & Rolland, C. (2012). Global warming: Is weight loss a solution? *International Journal of Obesity*, *36*(3), 474–476. doi:10.1038/ijo.2011.151 PMID:21792168

Gudners, D. (2012). *Wasted: How America Is Losing Up to 40 Percent of Its Food from Farm to Fork to Landfill.* NRDC. August iP:12-06-B.

Gulseven, O. (2020). Measuring achievements towards SDG 14, life below water, in the United Arab Emirates. *Marine Policy*, *117*, 103972. doi:10.1016/j.marpol.2020.103972

Gustafsson, B., Hermerén, G., & Petterson, B. (2011). *God Forskningssed.* Bromma: Vetenskapsrådet.

Guy, E., & Lasserre, F. (2016). Commercial Shipping in the Arctic: New Perspectives, Challenges, and Regulations. *The Polar Record*, *52*(3), 294–304. doi:10.1017/S0032247415001011

Haber. (2020). *The invasive took its place among 2 species of Mediterranean fish.* News.

Habitat, U. N. (2018). *Tracking progress towards inclusive, safe, resilient and sustainable cities and human settlements.* https://apo.org.au/node/182836

Hadjimichael, M. (2018). A call for a blue degrowth: Unravelling the European Union's fisheries and maritime policies. *Marine Policy*, *94*, 158–164. doi:10.1016/j.marpol.2018.05.007

Hafner, M., Tagliapietra, S., & Strasser. L. (2018). *Energy in Africa Challenges and Opportunities.* Springer Briefs in Energy.

Hagbert, P., & Bradley, K. (2017). Transitions on the home front: A story of sustainable living beyond eco-efficiency. *Energy Research & Social Science*, *31*, 240–248. doi:10.1016/j.erss.2017.05.002

Hall, K. D., Guo, J., Dore, M., & Chow, C. C. (2009). The Progressive Increase of Food Waste in America and Its Environmental Impact. *PLoS One*, *4*(11), e7940. doi:10.1371/journal.pone.0007940 PMID:19946359

Hamisu, A. H. (2019). *A study of Nigeria's blue economy potential with particular reference to the oil and gas sector.* World Maritime University Dissertations. 1234. https://commons. wmu.se/all_ dissertations/1234

Harper, S., Grubb, C., Stiles, M., & Sumaila, U. R. (2017). Contributions by women to fisheries economies: Insights from five maritime countries. *Coastal Management*, *45*, 91–106.

Hassan, O. A., & Romilly, P. (2018). Relations between corporate economic performance, environmental disclosure and greenhouse gas emissions: New insights. *Business Strategy and the Environment*, *27*(7), 893–909. doi:10.1002/bse.2040

Heininen, L., Everett, K., Padrtova, B., & Reissell, A. (2020). *Arctic Policies and Strategies – Analysis, Synthesis, and Trends.* International Institute for Applied Systems Analysis.

Heller, A., & Debre, I. (2020). *Experts say Med Sea altered by Suez Canal's invasive species.* https://apnews.com/article/climate-change-science-invasive-species-mediterranean-sea-europe-bc435ffbf4618b917b1181fb51ad4a8f

Heller, M. C., & Keoleia, G. A. (2000). Life Cycle-Based Sustainability Indicators for Assessment of the U.S. Food System. University of Michigan.

Hemsath, J. (2010). *The Arctic Energy Summit: The Arctic as an Emerging Energy Province.* The Institute of the North.

Henriksen, K., Bjerre, M., Maria Almasi, A., & Damgaard-Grann, E. (2012). *Green Business Model Innovation-Conceptualisation report. Nordic Council of Ministers.* Nordic Innovation Publication.

Herr, D., Pidgeon, E., & Laffoley, D. (Eds.). (2012). *Blue carbon policy framework: based on the discussion of the international blue carbon policy working group. International Union for Conservation of Nature and Arlington Conservation International* Conservation International.

High Sea Alliance, Guiding Questions: Environmental Impact Assessments (EIAs) with a focus on Strategic Environmental Assessments (SEAs). (2021). UN.

Highet, K. (1997). Maritime Boundary Disputes and Settlement. In Sustainable Development and Preservation of the Oceans: The Challenges of UNCLOS and Agenda 21 (p. 775). The Law of the Sea Institute, University of Hawaii.

Hinrich Foundation Case Study. (2017). *Maersk's contribution to China through FDI.* https://www.hinrichfoundation.com/media/snfhzwm3/hinrich-foundation-fdi-in-china-maersk-case-study-9-8-17.pdf

Hoegh-Guldberg, O. (2015). *Reviving the Ocean Economy: the Case for Action – 2015*. Academic Press.

Hoegh-Guldberg, O., Beal, D., Chaudhry, T., Elhaj, H., Abdullat, A., & Etessy, P. (2015). *Reviving the ocean economy: the case for action*. WWF International.

Holmyard, N. (2018). *Seafood industry gender report highlights ongoing inequality*. Seafood Source News.

Hongur, A. (2019). *The blowfish damaged the ecology and economy of the Mediterranean*. AA.

Hsieh, H.-F., & Shannon, S. E. (2005). Three Approaches to Qualitative Content Analysis. *Qualitative Health Research*, *15*(9), 1277–1288. doi:10.1177/1049732305276687 PMID:16204405

Hughes, T., Kerry, J., Baird, A., Connolly, S., Dietzel, A., Eakin, M., Heron, S. F., Hoey, A. S., Hoogenboom, M. O., Liu, G., McWilliam, M. J., Pears, R. J., Pratchett, M. S., Skirving, W. J., Stella, J. S., & Torda, G. (2018). Global Warming Transforms Coral Reef Assemblages. *Nature*, *556*(7702), 492–496. doi:10.103841586-018-0041-2 PMID:29670282

Hunt, B., & Vincent, A. C. (2006). Scale and sustainability of marine bioprospecting for pharmaceuticals. *Ambio*, *35*(2), 57–64.

Huo, J. (2015). *How nations innovate* (Vol. 1). Oxford University Press. doi:10.1093/acprof:oso/9780198735847.001.0001

Hussain Gulam, Al Karim, & Khurshed Alam. (2017). Major opportunities of blue economy development in Bangladesh. *Journal of the Indian Ocean Region, 13*(1), 111-118.

Hussain, M. G., Failler, P., Al Karim, A., & Alam, M. K. (2017). Review on opportunities, constraints and challenges of blue economy development in Bangladesh. *Journal of Fisheries and Life Sciences*, *2*(1), 45–57.

Hu, Y. Y., & Karbhari, Y. (2015). Incentives and disincentives of corporate environmental disclosure: Evidence from listed companies in China and Malaysia. *Thunderbird International Business Review*, *57*(2), 143–161. doi:10.1002/tie.21678

Iatridis, G. E. (2013). Environmental disclosure quality: Evidence on environmental performance, corporate governance and value relevance. *Emerging Markets Review*, *14*, 55–75. doi:10.1016/j.ememar.2012.11.003

Ibrahim, H. D. (2018). *Harnessing the potentials of blue economy for sustainable development of Nigeria*. Academic Press.

IISD. (2018). *IGC-1 Summary report, 4–17 September 2018*. Retrieved January 14, 2022, from https://enb.iisd.org/events/1st-session-intergovernmental-conference-igc-international-legally-binding-instrument-12

IISD. (2019). *IGC-2 Summary report, 25 March – 5 April 2019*. Retrieved January 14, 2022, from https://enb.iisd.org/events/2nd-session-intergovernmental-conference-igc-conservation-and-sustainable-use-marine/summary

IISD. (2019). *IGC-3 Summary report, 19–30 August 2019* [web log]. Retrieved January 14, 2022, from https://enb.iisd.org/events/3rd-session-intergovernmental-conference-igc-conservation-and-sustainable-use-marine/summary

ILO. (2019). Work-related gender gaps persist but solutions are clear. *Journal of the Indian Ocean Region*, *14*(1), 28–48.

Inclusive and Sustainable Industrial Development (ISID) Reporting Service. (2019a, September 2). Third Session: Summary and Analysis. *Earth Negotiations Bulletin*, *25*(218), 1–2. https://enb.iisd.org/download/pdf/enb25218e.pdf

Institute of African Studies. (2018). *International Symposium on Maritime Transport in Africa: Regional Integrations for Continental Development*. Author.

Intergovernmental Panel on Climate Change. (2013). Summary for Policymakers. In T. F. Stocker, D. Qin, G.-K. Plattner, M. Tignor, S. K. Allen, & J. Boschung (Eds.), *Climate Change 2013: The Physical Science Basis. Contribution of Working Group I to the Fifth Assessment Report of the Intergovernmental Panel on Climate Change*. Cambridge University Press.

International Energy Agency. (2014). *Africa energy outlook—a focus on energy prospects in Sub-Saharan Africa* (World Energy Outlook Special Report). Author.

International Energy Agency. (2018). *Status of Power System Transformation 2018: Advanced Power Plant Flexibility*. International Energy Agency. doi:10.1787/9789264302006-

Investopedia. (2021). *Foreign Direct Investment (FDI)*. https://www.investopedia.com/terms/f/fdi.asp

IPCC. (2014). *Climate Change 2014: Synthesis Report*. Contribution of Working Groups I, II and III to the Fifth Assessment Report of the Intergovernmental Panel on Climate Change. IPCC.

Irazábal, C. (2018). Coastal urban planning in the 'Green Republic': Tourism development and the nature–infrastructure paradox in Costa Rica. *International Journal of Urban and Regional Research*, *42*(5), 882–913. doi:10.1111/1468-2427.12654

IRENA (International Renewable Energy Agency). (2016). *Innovation Outlook: Off shore Wind*. ITF Transport Outlook 2015.

IRENA. (2015). *Africa 2030: Roadmap for A Renewable Energy Future*. www.irena.org/remap

IRENA. (2019). *Renewable Energy and Jobs. Annual Review 2019*. IRENA.

ISID Reporting Service. (2019b, September 2). Summary of the Third Session of the Intergovernmental Conference (IGC) on the Conservation and Sustainable Use of Marine Biodiversity of Areas Beyond National Jurisdiction: 19-30 August 2019. *Earth Negotiations Bulletin*, *25*(218). https://enb.iisd.org/download/pdf/enb25218e.pdf

Ite, A. E., Ibok, U. J., Ite, M. U., & Petters, S. W. (2013). Petroleum exploration and production: Past and present environmental issues in the Nigeria's Niger delta. *American Journal of Environmental Protection*, *1*(4), 78–90.

IUCN. (2013). *Annual Report*. https://portals.iucn.org/library/efiles/documents/IUCN-2014-017.pdf

James, C. A. (2010). Global overview of biotech (GM) Crops: Adoption, impact and future prospects. *GM Crops*, *1*(1), 8–12. doi:10.4161/gmcr.1.1.9756 PMID:21912206

Jaskoski, M. (2014). Environmental licensing and conflict in Peru's mining sector: A path-dependent analysis. *World Development*, *64*, 873–883. doi:10.1016/j.worlddev.2014.07.010

Jensen, R. (2012). Do labor market opportunities affect young women's work and family decisions? Experimental Evidence from India. *The Quarterly Journal of Economics*, *127*(2), 753.

Joroff, M. (2009). The Blue Economy: Sustainable industrialization of the oceans. *International Symposium on Blue Economy Initiative for Green Growth*, 173–181.

Jouffray, J. B., Blasiak, R., Norström, A. V., Österblom, H., & Nyström, M. (2020). The blue acceleration: The trajectory of human expansion into the ocean. *One Earth*, *2*(1), 43–54. doi:10.1016/j.oneear.2019.12.016

Jouili, T. (2018). Determinants of foreign investment in maritime nations. *International Journal of Advanced and Applied Sciences*, *5*(5), 43–47. doi:10.21833/ijaas.2018.05.006

Jupiter, S. D., Cohen, P. J., Weeks, R., Tawake, A., & Govan, H. (2014). Locally-managed marine areas: Multiple objectives and diverse strategies. *Pacific Conservation Biology*, *20*(2), 165–179.

Kabil, M., Priatmoko, S., Magda, R., & Dávid, L. D. (2021). Blue Economy and Coastal Tourism: A Comprehensive Visualization Bibliometric Analysis. *Sustainability*, *13*(7), 3650. doi:10.3390u13073650

Kaczynski, W. (2011). The future of the blue economy: Lessons for the European Union. *Found Manag*, *3*(1), 21–32. doi:10.2478/v10238-012-0033-8

Kadafa, A. A. (2012). Oil exploration and spillage in the Niger Delta of Nigeria. *Civil and Environmental Research*, *2*(3), 38–51.

Kahle, L. R., & Gurel-Atay, E. (Eds.). (2014). *Communicating Sustainability for the Green Economy*. M.E. Sharpe.

Karlsson, M., Trygg, L., & Elfström, B. O. (2004). Measuring R&D productivity: Complementing the picture by focusing on research activities. *Technovation*, *24*(3), 179–186. doi:10.1016/S0166-4972(03)00111-1

Kathijotes, N. (2013). Keynote: Blue economy-environmental and behavioural aspects towards sustainable coastal development. *Procedia: Social and Behavioral Sciences*, *101*, 7–13. doi:10.1016/j.sbspro.2013.07.173

Kaup & Glavan. (2014). *Marine organisms produce half of the oxygen that land animals need to breathe*. https://oceanexplorer.noaa.gov/facts/oceanproduction.html

Kaur, M., & Dhillon, S. S. (2017). Determinants of foreign direct investment in India: An empirical analysis. *Asian Journal of Research in Business Economics and Management*, *7*(8), 244–260. doi:10.5958/2249-7307.2017.00142.6

Keen, M.R., Schwarz, A.-M., & Wini-Simeon, L. (2017). Towards defining the Blue Economy: practical lessons from Pacific Ocean governance. *Mar. Pol.*

Kelleher, K. (2015). *Building the Blue Economy in the Western Indian Ocean*. Presented at the *8th Conference.*

Kent, H. (1954). The Historical Origins of the Three-Mile Limit. *The American Journal of International Law*, *48*(4), 537–553.

Khan, T. M., Bai, G., Fareed, Z., Quresh, S., Khalid, Z., & Khan, W. A. (2020). CEO Tenure, CEO Compensation, Corporate Social & Environmental Performance in China. The Moderating Role of Coastal and Non-Coastal Areas. *Frontiers in Psychology*, *11*, 3815. PMID:33551900

Kituyi, M., & Thomson, P. (2018, July 13). *90% of fish stocks are used up – fisheries subsidies must stop* [web log]. Retrieved January 14, 2022, from https://unctad.org/news/90-fish-stocks-are-used-fisheries-subsidies-must-stop

Klein, N. (2009). *Dispute settlement in the UN Convention on the law of the sea*. Cambridge University Press.

Klümper, W., & Qaim, M. A. (2014). Meta-Analysis of the impacts of genetically modified crops. *PLoS One*, *9*(11), e111629. doi:10.1371/journal.pone.0111629 PMID:25365303

Knol, M. (2010). Scientific advice in integrated ocean management: The process towards the Barents Sea plan. *Marine Policy*, *34*, 252–260.

Kolesnikova, M. (2018). Promoting the Blue Economy in the Mediterranean Region. *Scientific and Analytical Herald of the Institute of Europe of the Russian Academy of Sciences*, *5*(5), 121–127. doi:10.15211/vestnikieran52018121127

Komarova, I., Kopteva, E., & Kondakov, A. (2015). Marine Clusters as a Management Tool of Blue Economy. *Modern Production Forces*, *2*, 145–354.

Kondratiev, V. (2020). Mineral Resources and Future of the Arctic. *Russian Mining Industry*, *1*(1/2020), 87–96. doi:10.30686/1609-9192-2020-1-87-96

Kourantidou, M., Cuthbert, R. N., Haubrock, P. J., Novoa, A., Taylor, N. G., Leroy, B., Capinha, C., Renault, D., Angulo, E., Diagne, C., & Courchamp, F. (2021). Economic Costs Of Invasive Alien Species In The Mediterranean Basin. *Neobiota, 67*, 427-458. doi:10.3897/neobiota.67.58926

Kumar, K. (1982). Third World Multinationals. International Studies Quarterly, 26(3), 397 – 424.

Lanteigne, M. (2019). *China's Emerging Strategies in the Arctic.* Retrieved October 23, 2021, from https://www.high-northnews.com/en/chinas-emerging-strategies-arctic

Lanteigne, M. (2014). *China's Emerging Arctic Strategies: Economics and Institutions.* University of Iceland Press.

Lasserre, F. (2014). Case Studies of Shipping along Arctic Routes. Analysis and Profitability Perspectives for the Container Sector. *Transportation Research Part A, Policy and Practice*, *66*, 144–161. doi:10.1016/j.tra.2014.05.005

Leary, D. (2019). Agreeing to disagree on what we have or have not agreed on: The current state of play of the BBNJ negotiations on the status of Marine Genetic Resources in areas beyond national jurisdiction. *Marine Policy*, *99*, 21–29. https://doi.org/10.1016/j.marpol.2018.10.031

Leech, B. L. (2002). Asking questions: Techniques for semistructured interviews. *PS, Political Science & Politics*, *35*(4), 665–668.

Leedy, P. D., & Ormrod, J. E. (2010). *Practical Research: Planning and Design* (Vol. 9). Pearson Education, Inc.

Lee, K. H., Noh, J., & Khim, J. S. (2020). The Blue Economy and the United Nations' sustainable development goals: Challenges and opportunities. *Environment International*, *137*, 105528. doi:10.1016/j.envint.2020.105528 PMID:32014791

Leung, T. C. H., & Snell, R. S. (2021). Strategies for social and environmental disclosure: The case of multinational gambling companies. *Journal of Business Ethics*, *168*(3), 447–467. doi:10.100710551-019-04190-z

Lewis-Brown, E., Reid, P., Andersson, A., Arthurton, R., Bates, N., Barange, M., … Wood, R. (2008). The Impacts of the Oceans on Climate Change. *IEEE*, 29-32. . doi:10.1109/ESTC.2008.4684318

Lezca, J. (2019). *Environmental accounting.* Academic Press.

Li, H., & Qi, A. (2008). Impact of corporate governance on voluntary disclosure in Chinese listed companies. *Corporate Ownership and Control, 5*(2), 360-366.

Liu, N., Lin, L., Kong, B., Wang, Y., Zhang, Z., & Chen, H. (2016). Association between Arctic Autumn Sea Ice Concentration and Early Winter Precipitation in China. *Acta Oceanologica Sinica*, *35*(5), 73–78. doi:10.100713131-016-0860-7

Live Science Staff. (2011). *Wave Of Alien Species Invade Mediterranean Sea.* https://www.livescience.com/14339-wave-alien-species-invade-mediterranean-sea.html

Llamzon, A. P. (2007). Jurisdiction and compliance in recent decisions of the International Court of Justice. *European Journal of International Law*, *18*(5), 815–852. https://doi.org/10.1093/ejil/chm047

Londoño, F., Ochoa, C., Figueroa, S., & Hurtado, L. (2009). *Importance of Accounting Environmental.* Academic Press.

Lu, J., & Li, H. (2020). The impact of government environmental information disclosure on enterprise location choices: Heterogeneity and threshold effect test. *Journal of Cleaner Production*, *277*, 124055. doi:10.1016/j.jclepro.2020.124055

Lukin, A., Bogdanova, V., Kostyunichev, V., & Korolev, A. (2016). Prospects for Development of Aquaculture in the Western Part of the Russian Arctic. *Arctic: Ecology and Economy*, *24*(4), 100–108.

Lyou, B.-H. (1997). *International Law Ii.* CUPL Press.

Madiraju, K. S. (2019). Contemplating a Domestic Regulatory and Enforcement Framework for Deep Seabed Mining. *Natural Resources and Environment*, *34*(2), 17–21.

Maersk. (2014). *Exploring Maersk in China.* Sustainability Report.

Maersk. (2015). *Maersk Line orders seven ice-class container vessels.* http://www.maerskline.com/ro-ro/countries/int/news/news-articles/2015/03/seven-iceclass-container-vessels

Maersk. (2015a). *Maersk to move China office from HK to Beijing.* Maersk Press Release.

Mah, A. (2021). Future-proofing capitalism: The paradox of the circular economy for plastics. *Global Environmental Politics, 21*(2), 121–142. doi:10.1162/glep_a_00594

Mann, R. F. (2017). Controlling the Environmental Costs of Obesity. *Environmental Law (Northwestern School of Law), 2007*, 47.

Mappr. (n.d.). *Mediterranean Map/List of Mediterranean Countries.* https://www.mappr.co/thematic-maps/mediterranean-countries/

Martinez-Vazquez, R. M., Milan-Garcia, J., & Jaime de Pablo, V. (2021). Challenges of the Blue Economy: Evidence and research trends. *Environmental Sciences Europe, 33*(1), 61. doi:10.118612302-021-00502-1

Martinico-Perez, M. F. G., Schandl, H., Fishman, T., & Tanikawa, H. (2018). The socio-economic metabolism of an emerging economy: Monitoring progress of decoupling of economic growth and environmental pressures in the Philippines. *Ecological Economics, 147*, 155–166. doi:10.1016/j.ecolecon.2018.01.012

Mather, A. S., & Chapman, K. (2018). *Environmental resources.* Routledge. doi:10.4324/9781315844305

McCauley, D., Pinsky, M., Palumbi, S., Estes, J., Joyce, F., & Warner, R. (2015). Marine Defaunation: Animal Loss in the Global Ocean. *Science, 347*(6219), 6219. doi:10.1126cience.1255641 PMID:25593191

Mediterranean 2017 Quality Status Report. (n.d.). *The Mediterranean Marine and Coastal Environment.* https://www.medqsr.org/mediterranean-marine-and-coastal-environment

Mediterranean Blue Economy Stakeholder Platform. (n.d.). *Blue Eonomy.* https://medblueconomyplatform.org/about/blue-economy/

Mejía, E. & Vargas, L. (2012). *Accounting for environmental and social sustainability.* Academic Press.

Mele, G. (2014). *Mauritania Economic Update: 1.* World Bank. http://documents.worldbank.org/curated/en/2014/07/20133610/mauritania-economic-update

Melia, N., Haines, K., & Hawkins, E. (2017). *Future of the Sea: Implications from Opening Arctic Sea Routes.* Government Office for Science.

Meng, Q., Zhang, Y., & Xu, M. (2017). Viability of Transarctic Shipping Routes: A Literature Review from the Navigational and Commercial Perspectives. *Maritime Policy & Management, 44*(1), 16–41. doi:10.1080/03088839.2016.1231428

Meng, X. H., Zeng, S. X., Shi, J. J., Qi, G. Y., & Zhang, Z. B. (2014). The relationship between corporate environmental performance and environmental disclosure: An empirical study in China. *Journal of Environmental Management, 145*, 357–367. doi:10.1016/j.jenvman.2014.07.009 PMID:25113230

Mezher, T., Fath, H., Abbas, Z., & Khaled, A. (2011). Technoeconomic assessment and environmental impacts of desalination technologies. *Desalination, 266*(1), 263–273.

Michael, Y. M. A. K., & Peacock, C. J. (2011, January). Social sustainability: A comparison of case studies in UK, USA and Australia. In *17th Pacific Rim Real Estate Society Conference, Gold Coast* (pp. 16-19). Academic Press.

Michel, K., & Noble, P. (2008). Technological Advances in Maritime Transportation. *The Bridge, 38*(2), 33–40.

Middlebury Institute of International Studies at Monterey. (n.d.). https://www.oceaneconomics.org/market/coastal/coastalEconResults.asp?IC=N

Miller, K.A., Thompson, K.F., Johnston, P., & Santillo, D. (2019). *An Overview of Seabed Mining Including the Current State of Development, Environmental Impacts, and Knowledge Gaps*. Academic Press.

Mills, D. J., Westlund, L., de Graaf, G., Kura, Y., Willman, R., & Kelleher, K. (2011). Underreported and undervalued: Small-scale fisheries in the developing world. In Managing Small Scale Fisheries: Frameworks and Approaches. CABI.

Ministry of Family Affairs. (2018). *The National Gender Policy, Republic of Seychelles*. Gender Equality Department.

Ministry of Foreign Affairs. (2010). *Seychelles Millennium Development Goals, status report 2010*. Ministry of Foreign Affairs.

Ministry of Foreign Affairs. (2014). The Blue Economy. Ministry of the Environment.

Ministry of Natural Resources and Tourism. (2014). *An Overview of the Natural Resource Sector: Achievements, Challenges and Priorities for Financial Year 2014/2015*. Author.

Misko, J. (2008). *Combining formal, non-formal and informal learning for workforce skill development*. National Centre for Vocational Education and Research.

Modelevsky, M. S., & Modelevsky, M. M. (2016). Assessment of the discovered and undiscovered oil and gas of Africa. *Russian Geology and Geophysics*, *57*, 1342–1348. https://doi.org/10.1016/j.rgg.2016.08.019

Moe, A., & Oystein, J. (2010). *Opening of New Arctic Shipping Routes. Standard Briefing*. Directorate-General for External Policies of the Union / European Parliament.

Moffitt, C. M., & Cajas-Cano, L. (2014). Blue growth: The 2014 FAO state of world fisheries and aquaculture. *Fisheries (Bethesda, Md.)*, *39*(11), 552–553. doi:10.1080/03632415.2014.966265

Mohammad, M. T. S. H. (2010). Principles of sustainable development in Ibn Khaldun's economic thought. *Malaysian Journal of Real Estate*, *5*(1), 1–18.

Mohanty, S. K., & Dash, P. (2020). Economic Opportunities in Blue Economy in Africa. In *Asia-Africa Growth Corridor* (pp. 89–110). Springer. doi:10.1007/978-981-15-5550-3_6

Mol, A. P., He, G., & Zhang, L. (2011). Information disclosure in environmental risk management: Developments in China. *Journal of Current Chinese Affairs*, *40*(3), 163–192. doi:10.1177/186810261104000307

Molenaar, E. (2007). Managing biodiversity in areas beyond National Jurisdiction. *International Journal of Marine and Coastal Law*, *22*(1), 89–124. https://doi.org/10.1163/157180807781475263

Momsen, J. (2010). *Gender and Development* (Vol. 2). Routledge.

Monfort, M. C. (2015). *The Role of Women in the Seafood Industry. GLOBEFISH Research Program 119*. Food and Agriculture Organization.

Monnereau & Failler. (2014). *Unlocking the full potential of the blue economy: Are African Small Island Developing States ready to embrace the opportunities?* African Climate Policy Center and Economic Commission for Africa. http://www.climdev-africa.org/sites/default/files/DocumentAttachments/Blue%20Economy_19Sept14.pdf

Morawicki, R. O. (2012). *Handbook of Sustainability for the Food Sciences*. Wiley-Blackwell. doi:10.1002/9780470963166

Morrissey, K. (2017). It's not just a blue economy moment…. *Dialogues in Human Geography*, *7*(1), 42–44. doi:10.1177/2043820617691651

Mortensen, D. T., & Pissarides, C. A. (1998). Technological progress, job creation, and job destruction. *Review of Economic Dynamics*, *1*(4), 733–753.

Mossop, J. (2019). Dispute settlement in the New Treaty on marine biodiversity in areas beyond national jurisdiction. *SSRN Electronic Journal*. doi:10.2139/ssrn.3508734

Motyka, M., Slaughter, A., & Amon, C. (2018). *Global Renewable Energy Trends. Solar and Wind Move from Mainstream to Preferred.* Retrieved October 22, 2021, from https://www2.deloitte.com/us/en/insights/industry/power-and-utilities/global-renewable-energy-trends.html?id=gx:2el:3dc:4direnenergy:5awa:6di:09132018

Mulazzani, L., & Malorgio, G. (2017). Blue growth and ecosystem services. *Marine Policy*, *85*, 17–24. doi:10.1016/j.marpol.2017.08.006

Murdifin, I., Pelu, M. F. A., Perdana, A. A. H., Putra, K., Arumbarkah, A. M., Muslim, M., & Rahmah, A. (2019). Environmental disclosure as corporate social responsibility: Evidence from the biggest nickel mining in Indonesia. *International Journal of Energy Economics and Policy*, *9*(1), 115.

Nagy, H., & Nene, S. (2021). Blue Gold: Advancing Blue Economy Governance in Africa. *Sustainability*, *13*(13), 7153. doi:10.3390u13137153

Nation. (2013). *Seychelles ranks second in Africa for gender equality*. Retrieved 10 28, 2017, from Nation: https://www.nation.sc/article.html?id=239473

National Snow and Ice Data Center. (2016). *Arctic Sea Ice News and Analysis*. Retrieved October 21, 2021, from https://nsidc.org/arcticseaicenews/2016/10/

Nature Seychelles. (2014). *Blue Economy, nature inspired technologies to drive the economy forwards*. Retrieved 04 02, 2018, from Nature Seychelles: http://natureseychelles.org/what-we-do/blue-economy

Nelson, D. (2002). *Statement on the Commemoration of the 20th Anniversary of the Opening for Signature of the 1982 United Nations Convention on the Law of the Sea at the Plenary of the fifty-seventh Session of the United Nations General Assembly*. https://www.itlos.org/fileadmin/itlos/documents/statements_of_president/nelson/ga_091202_eng.pdf

Nelson, D. (2005). *Statement on the occasion of the presentation of the Report of the Tribunal at the fifteenth Meeting of States Parties*. https://www.itlos.org/fileadmin/itlos/documents/statements_of_president/nelson/msp_160605_eng.pdf

Newig, J., Challies, E., Jager, N. W., Kochskaemper, E., & Adzersen, A. (2018). The Environmental Performance of Participatory and Collaborative Governance: A Framework of Causal Mechanisms. *Policy Studies Journal: the Journal of the Policy Studies Organization*, *46*(2), 269–297. doi:10.1111/psj.12209 PMID:30034065

Nicoletti, G. (2001). *Regulation in services: OECD patterns and economic implications*. OECD.

Nikandrov, V., Pavlisov, A., Schindavina, N., Lukin, A., Golod, V., & Lipatova, M. (2018). Arctic Char (Salvelinus alpinus L.) – A Perspective Aquaculture Object for the North of Russia. *Arctic: Ecology and Economy*, *31*(3), 137–143. doi:10.25283/2223-4594-2018-3-137-143

NIMASA. (2018). *Nigeria's Maritime Industry Forecast. Emerging opportunities and Challenges.* Author.

Ninawe, A. S. (2017). Blue economy is the economic activities that directly or indirectly take place in the ocean and seas, use outputs, goods and services into ocean and land based activities. *Examines in Marine Biology & Oceanography*, 1-3.

Nordquist, M. H., Rosenne, S., & Sohn, L. B. (Eds.). (1989). *United Nations Convention on the Law of the Sea, 1982: A Commentary* (Vol. 5). Nijhoff.

Norouzi, N. (2021). Post-COVID-19 and globalization of oil and natural gas trade: Challenges, opportunities, lessons, regulations, and strategies. *International Journal of Energy Research*, *45*(10), 14338–14356. doi:10.1002/er.6762 PMID:34219899

Norouzi, N., & Ataei, E. (2021). Covid-19 Crisis and Environmental law: Opportunities and challenges. *Hasanuddin Law Review*, *7*(1), 46–60. doi:10.20956/halrev.v7i1.2772

Norouzi, N., & Kalantari, G. (2020). The sun food-water-energy nexus governance model a case study for Iran. *Water-Energy Nexus*, *3*, 72–80. doi:10.1016/j.wen.2020.05.005

Norouzi, N., Khanmohammadi, H. U., & Ataei, E. (2021). The Law in the Face of the COVID-19 Pandemic: Early Lessons from Uruguay. *Hasanuddin Law Review*, *7*(2), 75–88. doi:10.20956/halrev.v7i2.2827

North Pacific Fishery Management Council. (2009). *Fishery Management Plan for Fish Resources of the Arctic Management Area*. North Pacific Fishery Management Council.

Nourzad, F., Greenwold, D. N., & Yang, R. (2014). The interaction between FDI and infrastructure capital in the development process. *International Advances in Economic Research*, *20*(2), 203–212. doi:10.100711294-013-9457-5

Nuttall, M., & Callaghan, T. (Eds.). (2019). *The Arctic: Environment, People, Policy*. Routledge., doi:10.4324/9780429340475

Nwabueze, Eric, Ifejika, Ayanda, & Tafida. (2007). Strengthening Fisheries extension under a unified Agricultural Extension System. *UAES Proceeding of Fisheries Society of Nigeria*.

Nwabueze, A. A. (2010). The role of women in sustainable aquacultural development in Delta state. *Journal of Sustainable Development in Africa*, *12*(5), 23–25.

Nwankwpala, H. O. (2011). Coastal aquifers of Nigeria: An overview of its management and sustainability considerations. *Journal of Applied Technology in Environmental Sanitation*, *1*(4).

Nwilo, P. C., & Badejo, O. T. (2006). *Impacts and management of oil spill pollution along the Nigerian coastal areas*. Academic Press.

Nwilo, P. C., & Badejo, O. T. (2006a). *Impacts and management of oil spill pollution along the Nigerian coastal areas*. Academic Press.

Ochoa, C., Mosquera, C., & Ruiz, C. (2013). *Environmental accounting model for the company Pedro Álvarez constructions SAS*. Academic Press.

Odili, O. E., Nwabeze, G. O., & Tafida, A. A. (2012). Contribution of women to Fisheries Development in Nigeria: A review. *27th Annual Conference of Fisheries Society of Nigeria Proceedings*, 435-437.

Odoemelam, N., & Okafor, R. G. (2018). The influence of corporate governance on environmental disclosure of listed non-financial firms in Nigeria. *Indonesian Journal of Sustainability Accounting and Management*, *2*(1), 25–49. doi:10.28992/ijsam.v2i1.47

OECD. (2011, May). *Towards green growth A summary for policy makers*. Brochure of OECD Meeting of the Council at Ministerial Level, Paris, France. https://www.oecd.org/greengrowth/48012345.pdf

OECD. (2016). *Blue Economy*. OECD.

OECD. (2016). *The ocean economy in 2030*. OECD. https://www.oecd.org/ocean/data/

OEDDiLibrary. (2022). *Foreign direct investment (FDI)*. https://www.oecd-ilibrary.org/finance-and-investment/foreign-direct-investment-fdi/indicator-group/english_9a523b18-en

Offshore Technology. (2018). *Nigeria tops countries with largest remaining deepwater oil reserves.* Offshore Technology. Available at https://www.offshore-technology.com/comment/nigeria-tops-countries-largestremaining-\deepwater-oil-reserves/

Ogola, P. (2007). *Environmental Impact Assessment General Procedures.* Paper presented at Short Course II on Surface Exploration for Geothermal Resources, organized by UNU-GTP and KenGen, at Lake Naivasha, Kenya.

Okafor-Yarwood, I., Kadagi, N. I., Belhabib, D., & Allison, E. H. (2022). Survival of the Richest, not the Fittest: How attempts to improve governance impact African small-scale marine fisheries. *Marine Policy*, *135*, 104847. doi:10.1016/j.marpol.2021.104847

Omole, D. O., & Isiorho, S. A. (2011). Waste management and water quality issues in coastal states of Nigeria: The ogun state experience. *Journal of Sustainable Development in Africa*, *13*(6), 207–217.

Oonincx, D. G. A. B., van Itterbeeck, J., Heetkamp, M. J. W., van den Brand, H., van Loon, J. J. A., & van Huis, A. (2010). An Exploration on Greenhouse Gas and Ammonia Production by Insect Species Suitable for Animal or Human Consumption. *PLoS One*, *5*(12), e14445. doi:10.1371/journal.pone.0014445 PMID:21206900

Orrego, J. (2018). *Connection between business economic growth and environmental protection.* Academic Press.

Özacar, İ.U. (2020). *Climate change is also increasing invasive species in the seas.* TRT News.

Özkan, M. (2021). Invasive species harm ecosystems, human health and the economy. *Tarım ve Orman Dergisi.*

Öztürk, B. (2021). *Non-indigenous species in the Mediterranean and the Black Sea.* Studies and Reviews No. 87 (General Fisheries Commission for the Mediterranean). FAO. doi:10.4060/cb5949en

Pan, Y., Chen, Q., & Zhang, P. (2020). *Does policy uncertainty affect corporate environmental information disclosure: evidence from China.* Sustainability Accounting, Management and Policy Journal.

Park, D., Seo, K., Kildow, D., & Judith, T. (2014). *Rebuilding the classification system of the ocean economy.* Academic Press.

Patil, P.G., Virdin, J., Colgan, C.S., Hussain, M.G., Failler, P., & Vegh, T. (2018). *Toward a Blue Economy: A Pathway for Bangladesh's Sustainable Growth.* The World Bank Group.

Patil, P. G., Virdin, J., Diez, S. M., Roberts, J., & Singh, A. (2016). *Toward A Blue Economy: A Promise for Sustainable Growth in the Caribbean; An Overview.* The World Bank.

Pauli, G. (2010). *The Blue Economy: 10 years-100 innovations-100 million jobs.* United State.

Pauli, G. A. (2010). *The blue economy: 10 years, 100 innovations, 100 million jobs.* Paradigm publications.

Pelc, R., & Fujita, R. M. (2002). Renewable energy from the ocean. *Marine Policy*, *26*(6), 471–479. doi:10.1016/S0308-597X(02)00045-3

Pelyasov, A., Galtseva, N., & Atamanova, E. (2017). Economy of the Arctic "Islands": The Case of Nenets and Chukotka Autonomous Okrugs. *Economy of Region*, *13*(1), 114–125. doi:10.17059/2017-1-11

Pendleton, L., Donato, D. C., Murray, B. C., Crooks, S., Jenkins, W. A., Sifleet, S., Craft, C., & … . (2012). Estimating global "blue carbon" emissions from conversion and degradation of vegetated coastal ecosystems. *PLoS One*, *7*(9), 1–7.

Peng, J., & Wegge, N. (2015). China's Bilateral Diplomacy in the Arctic. *Polar Geography*, *38*(3), 233–249. doi:10.1080/1088937X.2015.1086445

Phelan, A., Ruhanen, L., & Mair, J. (2020). Ecosystem services approach for community-based ecotourism: Towards an equitable and sustainable blue economy. *Journal of Sustainable Tourism*, *28*(10), 1–21. doi:10.1080/09669582.2020.1747475

Pichon, E. (2019). *The African Union's Blue Strategy*. European Parliamentary Research Service. Available online: https://www. europarl. europa. eu/RegData/etudes/ ATAG/2019/635574/ EPRS_ATA(2019)635574_EN.pdf

Pien, C. P. (2020). Local environmental information disclosure and environmental non-governmental organizations in Chinese prefecture-level cities. *Journal of Environmental Management*, *275*, 111225. doi:10.1016/j.jenvman.2020.111225 PMID:32889416

Pierre, C., & Olivier, F. (2015). Relevance of the Northern Sea Route (NSR) for Bulk Shipping. *Transportation Research*, *78*, 337–346. doi:10.1016/j.tra.2015.05.020

Pinsky, M., Eikeset, A., McCauley, D., Payne, J., & Sunday, J. (2019). Greater Vulnerability to Warming of Marine versus Terrestrial Ectotherms. *Nature*, *569*(7754), 108–111. doi:10.103841586-019-1132-4 PMID:31019302

Poloczanska, E., Brown, C., Sydeman, W., Kiessling, W., Schoeman, D., Moore, P., Brander, K., Bruno, J. F., Buckley, L. B., Burrows, M. T., Duarte, C. M., Halpern, B. S., Holding, J., Kappel, C. V., O'Connor, M. I., Pandolfi, J. M., Parmesan, C., Schwing, F., Thompson, S. A., & Richardson, A. (2013). Global Imprint of Climate Change on Marine Life. *Nature Climate Change*, *3*(10), 919–925. doi:10.1038/nclimate1958

Postobon. (2018). *Sustainability Report 2018*. Academic Press.

Potgieter, T. (2018). Oceans economy, blue economy, and security: notes on the South African potential and developments. *J Indian Ocean Region, 14*(1), 49–70. .2018.14109 62 doi:10.1080/19480881

Pramod, G., Nakamura, K., Pitcher, T., & Delagran, L. (2014). Estimates of illegal and unreported fish in seafood imports to the USA. *Marine Policy*, *48*, 102–113. doi:10.1016/j.marpol.2014.03.019

President of the Russian Federation. (2020). *Decree #645 from October 26, 2020, "On the Strategy for the Development of the Arctic Zone of the Russian Federation and Ensuring National Security up to 2035"*. Retrieved October 18, 2021, from http://static.kremlin.ru/media/events/files/ru/J8FhckYOPAQQfxN6Xlt6ti6XzpTVAvQy.pdf

Pretorius, R., & Henwood, R. (2019). Governing Africa's blue economy: The protection and utilisation of the continent's blue spaces. Studia Univ. *Babes-Bolyai Studia Eur.*, *64*(2), 119–148. doi:10.24193ubbeuropaea.2019.2.05

Priven, V., Sacks, R., Seppänen, O., & Savosnick, J. (2014, June). A lean workflow index for construction projects. In *22nd Annual Conference of the International Group for Lean Construction: Understanding and Improving Project Based Production, IGLC 2014* (pp. 715-726). Academic Press.

Purvis, M.-T. (2015). Seychelles blue economy Strategy. *Island Stud.: Indian Ocean*, 14–19.

Qi, X., & Xiao, W. (2019). Identifying the evolutionary path of maritime industries from the perspective of super network. *Journal of Coastal Research*, *97*(sp1), 131–135. doi:10.2112/SI97-018.1

Quested, T., & Johnson, H. (2009). *Household Food and Drink Waste in the UK*. Report prepared by WRAP. Banbury.

Ragin, C. C. (2008). *What is Qualitative Comparative Analysis*. QCA.

Raimi, L., Olowo, R., & Shokunbi, M. (2021). A comparative discourse of sustainable finance options for agribusiness transformation in Nigeria and Brunei: Implications for entrepreneurship and enterprise development. *World Journal of Science, Technology and Sustainable Development*, *18*(4), 325–350. doi:10.1108/WJSTSD-05-2021-0051

Rakotondraompiana & Failler. (2015). Natural resources management and climate change in East Africa. In *Harnessing the Blue Economy for Eastern Africa's Development*. United Nations Economic Commission for Africa (UNECA).

Ramsar. (2015). *State of the World's Wetlands and Their Services to People: A Compilation of Recent Analyses*. Ramsar Briefing Note 7. Ramsar Convention on Wetlands.

Request for an advisory opinion submitted by the Sub-Regional Fisheries Commission (SRFC), Advisory Opinion, ITLOS Case No 21. Available from https://www.itlos.org/index.php?id=252

Revised draft text of an agreement under the United Nations Convention on the Law of the Sea on the conservation and sustainable use of marine biological diversity of areas beyond national jurisdiction ("Draft HST"). (2019). Available from https://www.un.org/bbnj/sites/www.un.org.bbnj/files/revised_draft_text_a.conf_.232.2020.11_advance_unedited_version.pdf

Ricart, J. E., Enright, M. J., Ghemawat, P., Hart, S. L., & Khanna, T. (2004). New frontiers in international strategy. *Journal of International Business Studies*, *35*(3), 175–200. doi:10.1057/palgrave.jibs.8400080

Richard, M. (2019). *Blue Economy, Marine litter and pollution, Climate change and Environment, Talking points*. Office of the Vice President, Directorate of Environment and Climate Change.

Rochette, J., Wright, G., Chabason, L., Unger, S., Ardron, J., & Houghton, K. (2015). *Advancing governance of marine areas beyond national jurisdiction* (Brief for Global Sustainable Development Report 2015). Retrieved January 14, 2022, from https://sustainabledevelopment.un.org/content/documents/5774Brief%20ABNJ%20GSDR_rev.pdf

Rodríguez, D. (2011). *Formulation of a theoretical structure for environmental accounting*. Academic Press.

Rodriguez-Delgado, C., Bergillos, R. J., & Iglesias, I. (2019, June). Dual wave farms for energy production and coastal protection under sea level rise. *Journal of Cleaner Production*, *222*(10), 364–372.

Rose-Ackerman, S. (1997). The political economy of corruption. *Corruption and the Global Economy*, *31*, 60.

Roy, A. (2019). Blue Economy in the Indian Ocean: Governance perspectives for sustainable development in the region. *Observer Research Foundation Occasional Paper*, (181).

Roy, A. (2019). *Blue economy in the Indian Ocean: Governance perspectives for sustainable development in the region.* ORF Occasional Paper, 181.

Rustomjee, C. (2016). *Developing the blue economy in Caribbean and other small states*. Academic Press.

Rustomjee, C. (2016). *Financing the Blue Economy in Small States*. Center for International Governance Innovation.

Rustomjee, C. (2018). *Green shoots for the African blue economy?* Academic Press.

Rutaisire, J., Kabonesa, C., Okechi, J. K., & Boera, P. N. (2010). Lake Victoria Basin: Gender issues in fish farming. In F. Flintan & S. Tedla (Eds.), Natural resource management. Academic Press.

Ruys, T., & Soete, A. (2015). 'Creeping' Advisory Jurisdiction of International Courts and Tribunals? The Troublesome Case of the International Tribunal for the Law of the Sea. *Leiden Journal of International Law*. doi:10.2139/ssrn.2645895

Sala, E., Mayorga, J., Costello, C., Kroodsma, D., Palomares, M. L., Pauly, D., Sumaila, U. R., & Zeller, D. (2018). The economics of fishing the High Seas. *Science Advances*, *4*(6). https://doi.org/10.1126/sciadv.aat2504

Sánchez, H. M. & Rodríguez, C. (2017). *Determine the Hidden Environmental Costs of Hazardous Waste in Office Furniture Manufacturing Companies*. Academic Press.

Sanusi, L. S. (2010). Growth prospects for the Nigerian economy. Eighth Convocation Lecture of the Igbinedion University, Okada, Nigeria.

Sareen, S., & Haarstad, H. (2018). Bridging sociotechnical and justice aspects of sustainable energy transitions. *Applied Energy, 228*, 624–632. doi:10.1016/j.apenergy.2018.06.104

Sarker, S., Ara Hussain, F., Assaduzzaman, M., & Failler, P. (2019). Blue economy and climate change: Bangladesh perspective. *Journal of Ocean and Coastal Economics, 6*(2), 6. doi:10.15351/2373-8456.1105

Sarker, S., Bhuyan, M. A. H., Rahman, M. M., Islam, M. A., Hossain, M. S., Basak, S. C., & Islam, M. M. (2018). From science to action: Exploring the potentials of Blue Economy for enhancing economic sustainability in Bangladesh. *Ocean and Coastal Management, 157*, 180–192. doi:10.1016/j.ocecoaman.2018.03.001

Sarkodie, S. A., & Strezov, V. (2019). Effect of foreign direct investments, economic development and energy consumption on greenhouse gas emissions in developing countries. *The Science of the Total Environment, 646*, 862–871. doi:10.1016/j.scitotenv.2018.07.365 PMID:30064112

Saunders, M., Lewis, P., & Thornhill, A. (2016). *Research Methods for Business Students* (7th ed.). Pearson Education.

Schartup, A., Thackray, C., Quershi, A., Dassuncao, C., Gillespie, K., Hanke, A., & Sunderland, E. (2019). Climate Change and Overfishing Increase Neurotoxicant in Marine Predators. *Nature, 572*(7771), 648–650. doi:10.103841586-019-1468-9 PMID:31391584

Scherer, M. E., & Asmus, M. L. (2021). Modeling to evaluate coastal governance in Brazil. *Marine Policy, 129*, 104501. doi:10.1016/j.marpol.2021.104501

Schumacher, K. P. (2014). Gender relations in global agrifood value chains: A review. *Die Erde J Geogr Soc Berlin, 145*(3), 127–134.

Schutter, M. S., & Hicks, C. C. (2019). Networking the blue economy in Seychelles: Pioneers, resistance, and the power of influence. *J Political Eco, 26*(1), 425–447.

Schutter, M. S., & Hicks, C. C. (2019). Networking the blue economy in Seychelles: Pioneers, resistance, and the power of influence. *Journal of Political Ecology, 26*(1), 425–447.

Schutter, M. S., & Hicks, C. C. (2019). Networking the Blue Economy in Seychelles: Pioneers, resistance, and the power of influence. *Journal of Political Ecology, 26*(1), 425–447.

Secretariat of the Pacific Community. (2010). *The Future of Pacific Island Fisheries.*

Secretariat, C. (2018). *Commonwealth Blue Charter.* Shared Values, Shared Ocean. A Commonwealth Commitment to Work Together to Protect and Manage Our Ocean.

Senaratne, M., & Zimbroff, A. (2019). *The Blue Economy in the Indian Ocean. A Literature Review.* Academic Press.

Serrano, S. (2018). *Progressing women's economic empowerment enhancing user-producer engagement for policy responsive data and effective data-driven policies.* Economic and Social Commission for Asia and the Pacific.

Sevastiyanov, D., Colpaert, A., Korostelyov, E., Mulyava, O., & Shitova, L. (2014). Management of Tourism and Recreation Possibilities for the Sustainable Development of the North-Western Border Region in Russia. *Nordia Geographical Publications, 43*(1), 27–38.

Sexton, W. J., & Murday, M. (1994). The morphology and sediment character of the coastline of Nigeria: The Niger delta. *Journal of Coastal Research, •••*, 959–977.

Shakman, E., Eteayb, K., Taboni, I. & Ben Abdalha, A. (2019). Status of Marine Alien Species Along The Libyan Coast. J. Black Sea/Mediterranean Environment, 25(2), 188-209.

Shaleh, S. R. M., Shapawi, R., Estim, A., & Mustafa, S. (2019). Leveraging scientific knowledge in aquaculture for entrepreneurship- case studies at Universiti Malaysia Sabah. *Borneo J Mar Sci Aquacult*, *3*(1), 25–32.

Shapawi, R., Shaleh, S. R. M., Annita-Yong, S. K., Abdullah, F. C., & Othman, R. (2019). Gender equality in blue growth. In S. Mustafa & A. Estim (Eds.), *Blue economy and blue growth in the context of development policies and priorities in Malaysia*. Penerbit UMS.

Shirajee, S. S., Salehin, M. M., & Ahmed, N. (2010). The changing face of women for small-scale aquaculture development in rural Bangladesh. *Aquaculture Asia Magazine*, *15*(2), 9–16.

Shojaei, A., Ketabi, R., Razkenari, M., Hakim, H., & Wang, J. (2021). Enabling a circular economy in the built environment sector through blockchain technology. *Journal of Cleaner Production*, *294*, 126352. doi:10.1016/j.jclepro.2021.126352

Shuvalova, T., & Glubokov, A. (2015). Aquatic Bioresources Development in the Arctic Zone: Problems and Prospects. *Fisheries (Bethesda, Md.)*, *4*, 11–13.

Silver, J. J., Gray, N. J., Campbell, L. M., Fairbanks, L. W., & Gruby, R. L. (2015). Blue economy and competing discourses in international oceans governance. *Journal of Environment & Development*, *24*(2), 135–160. doi:10.1177/1070496515580797

Simionov, I.-A., Cristea, D. S., Petrea, Ş.-M., Mogodan, A., Jijie, R., Ciornea, E., Nicoară, M., Turek Rahoveanu, M. M., & Cristea, V. (2021). Predictive Innovative Methods for Aquatic Heavy Metals Pollution Based on Bioindicators in Support of Blue Economy in the Danube River Basin. *Sustainability*, *13*(16), 8936. doi:10.3390u13168936

Simpson, J. L., & Fox, H. (1959). International Arbitration: Law and Practice. *The American Journal of International Law*, *54*(2), 433–435. https://doi.org/10.2307/2195272

Smale, D., Wernberg, T., Oliver, E., Thomsen, M., Harvey, B., Straub, S., Burrows, M. T., Alexander, L. V., Benthuysen, J. A., Donat, M. G., Feng, M., Hobday, A. J., Holbrook, N. J., Perkins-Kirkpatrick, S. E., Scannell, H. A., Sen Gupta, A., Payne, B. L., & Moore, P. (2019). Marine Heatwaves Threaten Global Biodiversity and the Provision of Ecosystem Services. *Nature Climate Change*, *9*(4), 306–312. doi:10.103841558-019-0412-1

Smith-Godfrey, S. (2016). Defining the blue economy. *Maritime Affairs: Journal of the National Maritime Foundation of India, 12*(1), 58-64.

Smith-Godfrey, S. (2016). Defining the Blue Economy. *Maritime Affairs.*

Snyder, H., & Erbaugh, J. (2020). Fishery Observers Address Arctic Fishery Discards. *Environmental Research Letters, 15*, 0940c4. . doi:10.1088/1748-9326/aba57d

Sohn, L. B. (1983). The Future of Dispute Resolution. In The Structure and Process of International Law: Essays in Legal Philosophy, Doctrine and Theory (Vol. 6, p. 1131). Martinus Nijhoff Publishers.

South China Sea Arbitration, *Philippines v China*, Award, PCA Case No 2013-19

Southern Bluefin Tuna Cases (*New Zealand v Japan; Australia v Japan*), Provisional Measures, ITLOS Case Nos 3 and 4, (1999) 38 ILM 1624

Spence, M., Ben Boubaker Gherib, J., & Ondoua Biwolé, V. (2011). Sustainable entrepreneurship: Is entrepreneurial will enough? A north–south comparison. *Journal of Business Ethics*, *99*(3), 335–367. doi:10.100710551-010-0656-1

State Council Information Office of the People's Republic of China. (2020). *Energy in China's New Era.* The State Council of the People's Republic of China.

State Council of the People's Republic of China. (2017). *Vision for Maritime Cooperation under the Belt and Road Initiative*. Retrieved October 18, 2021, from http://english.www.gov.cn/archive/publications/2017/06/20/content_281475691873460.htm

State Council of the People's Republic of China. (2018). *China's Arctic Policy*. The State Council of the People's Republic of China.

Steblyanskaya, A., Ai, M., Bocharnikov, V., & Denisov, A. (2021). Strategies for Green Economy in China. *Foresight and STI Governance, 15*(1), 74–85. doi:10.17323/2500-2597.2021.1.74.85

Steinfeld, H. (2006). *Environment and Development (LEAD) Initiative Livestock, and Food and Agriculture Organization. Animal Production and Health Division. Livestock's Long Shadow: Environmental Issues and Options*. FAO.

Stephenson, S. R., Brigham, L., & Smith, L. C. (2013). Marine Accessibility along Russia's Northern Sea Route. *Polar Geography, 37*(2), 111–133. doi:10.1080/1088937X.2013.845859

Sterligova, O., Kuchko, Y., Savosin, E., & Ilmast, N. (2019). Prospects of Cultivation of Aquaculture Objects in the Lakes of Karelia. *Problems of Fisheries, 20*(2), 216–224. doi:10.36038/0234-2774-2019-20-2-216-224

Stille, M., Gasteratos, I., & Stille, B. (2021). Alien and invasive terrestrial vertebrate species on Corfu, Ionian Islands, Greece. *J. of Vertebrate Biology, 70*(1). doi:10.25225/jvb.20126

Sunesen, E. R., Jeppesen, T., Henriksen, J. J., & Grunfelder, J. (2018). *The World in Europe, global FDI flows towards Europe. Intra-European FDI*. ESPON EGTC.

Su, P., & Lanteigne, M. (2015). China's Developing Arctic Policies: Myths and Misconceptions. *Journal of China and International Relations, 3*(1), 2. doi:10.5278/ojs.jcir.v3i1.1144

Tadros, H., & Magnan, M. (2019). *How does environmental performance map into environmental disclosure? A look at underlying economic incentives and legitimacy aims. Sustainability Accounting, Management and Policy Journal.*

Taheri, F., Azadi, H., & D'Haese, M. A. (2017). World without Hunger: Organic or GM Crops? *Sustainability, 9*(4), 580. doi:10.3390u9040580

Tanaka, Y. (2015). Reflections on the advisory jurisdiction of ITLOS as a full court: The Itlos Advisory Opinion of 2015. *The Law and Practice of International Courts and Tribunals, 14*(2), 318–339. doi:10.1163/15718034-12341296

Tang, Y., Yang, R., Chen, Y., Du, M., Yang, Y., & Miao, X. (2020). Greenwashing of local government: The human-caused risks in the process of environmental information disclosure in China. *Sustainability, 12*(16), 6329. doi:10.3390u12166329

Taplin, I. M., & Winterton, J. (2019). *Rethinking global production* (Vol. 26). Routledge. doi:10.4324/9780429444548

Techera, E. J. (2018). Supporting blue economy agenda: Fisheries, food security and climate change in the indian ocean. *Journal of the Indian Ocean Region, 14*(1), 7–27. doi:10.1080/19480881.2017.1420579

Teletchea, F., & Beisel, J. N. (2018). *Alien Fish Species in France with Emphasis on the Recent Invasion of Gobies, Biological Resources of Water, Sajal Ray*. IntechOpen. Available from: https://www.intechopen.com/chapters/59375

The Commonwealth. (2018). *Seychelles Blue Economy Strategic Roadmap and Implementation*. Retrieved 02 09, 2018, from The Commonwealth: https://thecommonwealth.org/project/seychelles-blue-economy-strategic-roadmap-and-implementation

The Commonwealth. (2021a). *Blue economy*. Commonwealth Secretariat. https://thecommonwealth.org/blue-economy

The Commonwealth. (2021b). *Aquaculture*. Commonwealth Secretariat https://thecommonwealth.org/aquaculture

The Commonwealth. (n.d.). *Blue Economy.* https://thecommonwealth.org/blue-economy

The Economist. (2015a). *Coastal Governance Index 2015.* An index and study by The Economist Intelligence Unit. https://www.oceanprosperityroadmap.org/wp-content/uploads/2015/05/EIU_CGIndex_WEB-revised-June-4.pdf

The Economist. (2015b). *The Blue Economy: Growth, Opportunity and a Sustainable Ocean Economy.* https://www.oceanprosperityroadmap.org/wp-content/uploads/2015/05/2.-State-of-the-Blue-Economy_briefing-paper_WOS2015.pdf

The Economist. (2019). *Coastal Governance Index 2019.* An index and study by The Economist Intelligence Unit. https://www.oceanprosperityroadmap.org/wp-content/uploads/2015/05/EIU_CGIndex_WEB-revised-June-4.pdf

The Ocean Foundation. (2021). *Ocean and Climate Change.* Retrieved October 20, 2021, from https://oceanfdn.org/ocean-and-climate-change/

The World Bank. (2013). *Shared prosperity; a new goal for a changing world.* Retrieved 05 29, 2018, from World Bank: https://www.worldbank.org/en/news/feature/2013/05/08/shared-prosperity-goal-for-changing-world

The World Bank. (2016a). *Blue Economy Project.* Author.

The World Bank. (2016b). *The Components of The Blue Economy.* Author.

Thiel, H. (2003). *Approaches to the Establishment of Protected Areas on the High Seas.* Kluwer Law International.

Thomas, K. P. (2009). *Subnational FDI competition in developing countries: The case of Viet Nam.* APSA 2009 Toronto Meeting Paper. https://papers.ssrn.com/sol3/papers.cfm?abstract_id=1450115

Tillman, H., Yang, J., & Nielsson, E. T. (2018). The Polar Silk Road: China's New Frontier of International Cooperation. *China Quarterly of International Strategic Studies*, *4*(3), 345–362. doi:10.1142/S2377740018500215

Tilman, D., & Clark, M. (2014). Global diets link environmental sustainability and human health. *Nature*, *515*(7528), 518–522. doi:10.1038/nature13959 PMID:25383533

Tirole, J. (2017). *Economics for the Common Good.* Princeton University Press.

Tkachenko, I. N., Pervukhina, I. V., & Sokolovskaya, O. E. (2019), Environmental disclosure as a factor of sustainable development of the Russian business. In *The International Scientific and Practical Forum Industry. Science. Competence. Integration* (pp. 628–635). Springer.

Tonazzini, D., Fosse, J., Morales, E., González, A., Klarwein, S., Moukaddem, K., & Louveau, O. (2019). *Blue Tourism. Towards a sustainable coastal and maritime tourism in world marine regions.* Eco-Union.

Torley, H. (2017). *Pharma, biotech and healthcare industries gender gap.* News Medical.

Tortsev, A. (2018). Efficiency of Management of Fishery Resources in the Arctic Zone of the Russian Federation: Features of Assessment. *Arctic: Ecology and Economy*, *30*(2), 131–141. doi:10.25283/2223-4594-2018-2-131-141

Treves, T. (2004). Flags of Convenience before the Law of the Sea Tribunal. *San Diego International Law Journal, 6*(1). doi:https://doi.org/https://digital.sandiego.edu/ilj/vol6/iss1/9/

Treves, T. (2015). Historical Development of the Law of the Sea. In D. Rothwell, A. Oude Elferink, K. Scott, & T. Stephen (Eds.), *The Oxford Handbook of the Law of the Sea.* OUP.

Turnbull, J., Keller, E., Norris, M., & Wiltshire, R. (2016). Independent Evaluation of Point Source Fossil Fuel CO_2 Emissions to Better than 10%. *Proceedings of the National Academy of Sciences of the United States of America*, *113*(37), 10287–10291. doi:10.1073/pnas.1602824113 PMID:27573818

Tzouvanas, P., Kizys, R., Chatziantoniou, I., & Sagitova, R. (2020). Environmental disclosure and idiosyncratic risk in the European manufacturing sector. *Energy Economics*, *87*, 104715. doi:10.1016/j.eneco.2020.104715

U.S. Department of Energy. (2019). *Powering the Blue Economy: Exploring Opportunities for Marine Renewable Energy in Maritime Markets*. Author.

UN General Assembly Resolution 72/249, *International legally binding instrument under the United Nations Convention on the Law of the Sea on the conservation and sustainable use of marine biological diversity of areas beyond national jurisdiction.* (2017). Available from https://undocs.org/A/RES/72/249

UNCTAD. (2014). *The state of commodity dependence 2014. United Nations Conference on Trade and Development*, Geneva, Switzerland.

UNCTAD. (2014a). *Small Island Developing States: Challenges in Transport and Trade Logistics*. Background note to third session of Multi-Year Expert Meeting on Transport, Trade Logistics and Trade Facilitation. UNCTAD.

UNCTAD. (2016). *Oceans economy and trade, Sustainable fisheries, transport and tourism*. UNCTAD.

UNCTAD. (2016). *Review of Maritime Transport 2016*. United Nations.

UNCTAD. (2016). World Investment Report 2016: Investor Nationality: Policy Challenges. New York: United Nations Conference on Trade and Development, United Nations United Nations Blue Economy Concept Paper. *Conference on Sustainable Development.*

UNCTAD. (2018) Ocean economy and fisheries. *United Nations Conference on Trade and Development.*

UNCTAD. (2018). *Review of Maritime Transport Freight market 2017 and World seaborne trade 2017*. UNCTAD.

UNCTAD. (2018). *Sustainable freight transport in support of 2030 Agenda*. UNCTAD.

UNDESA. (2008). *Achieving Sustainable Development and Promoting Development Cooperation*. UNDESA.

UNDP. (2018). Blue Economy, Community Solutions. *UNDP*.

UNDP. (2018). *Leveraging the Blue Economy for Inclusive and Sustainable Growth.* https://www.undp. org/content/dam/kenya/docs/UNDP%20Reports/Policy%20 Brief%20%202018%20-%206-%20%20Blue% 20Economy%20for%20 Inclusive%20and%20Sustainable%20Growth.pdf

UNDP. (2018). Policy Brief. *Harnessing the Blue Economy for Sustainable Development in Nigeria.* Retrieved from; https://www.ng.undp.org/content/nigeria/en/home/library/poverty/policy-briefharnessing-the-blue-economy-for-sustainable-develop.html

UNECA. (2016). *The Blue Economy*. UNECA.

UNECA. (2017). *Africa's Blue Economy: A policy handbook*. UNECA.

UNEP, FAO, IMO, UNDP, IUCN, & GRID-Arendal. (2012). *Green Economy in a Blue World.* Author.

UNEP. (2013). *Green Economy Definition*. https://www.unep.org/greeneconomy/AboutGEI/

UNEP. (2013). *Green Economy Definition*. UNEP.

UNESCO. (2013). *Girls' education – the facts*. United Nations Educational, Scientific and Cultural Organization.

UNESCO. (2016). *Facts and Figures on Marine Pollution*. UNESCO.

UNESCO. (2017). Education and the sustainable development goals. UNESCO.

United Nations Blue Economy Concept Paper. (2014). Available at https://sustainabledevelopment.un.org/concent/documents/2978BEconcept.pdf

United Nations Conference of Trade and Development (UNCTAD). (2014). *The oceans economy: Opportunities and challenges for small island developing states, UNCTAD/DITC/TED/2014/5*. New York: UNCTAD.

United Nations Conference on Sustainable Development. (n.d.). https://sustainabledevelopment.

United Nations Conference on Trade and Development. (2021). *Oceans Economy and Fisheries*. Retrieved October 23, 2021, from https://unctad.org/topic/trade-and-environment/oceans-economy

United Nations Convention on the Law of the Sea (UNCLOS). (1982). Available from https://www.un.org/depts/los/convention_agreements/texts/unclos/unclos_e.pdf

United Nations Development Program (UNDP). (1998). Baseline Survey of Agriculture. Rural Development, Health and Mass Literacy of States of Nigeria. conducted by Gothards-IHLS Consortium.

United Nations Development Programme. (2018). *Millennium Development Goals*. Retrieved 05 26, 2018, from UNDP: http://www.undp.org/content/undp/en/home/sdgoverview/mdg_goals.html

United Nations Economic Commission for Africa. (2016). *Africa's blue economy: A policy handbook*. UNECA.

United Nations Environment Programme and Gender and Water Alliance (2019). *Gender Mainstreaming in the Management of Marine and Coastal Ecosystems*. Author.

United Nations Environment Programme. (2012). *Green Economy in a Blue World Synthesis Report*. UNEP. www.unep.org/pdf/green_economy_blue.pdf

United Nations Environment Programme. (2015). *Blue Economy: Sharing Success Stories Inspire Change*. UNEP Regional Seas Report.

United Nations Environment Programme. (2016). *Green Economy – Towards Greener and more inclusive economies*. UNEP Documents. https://www.unepfi.org/fileadmin/documents/greeneconomy_flyer.pdf

United Nations Environment Programme. (2016). *Green Economy – Towards Greener and more inlusibe economies*. https://www.unepfi.org/fileadmin/documents/greeneconomy_flyer.pdf

United Nations Environment Programme. (2021). *Green Economy*. https://www.unep.org/explore-topics/green-economy

United Nations. (2014). *United Nations Blue Economy Concept Paper*. Author.

United Nations. (2016). *Africa's Blue Economy a Policy Handbook*. Available online: https://wedocs. unep.org/bitstream/handle/20.500.11822/30130/AfricasBlueEconomy.pdf ?sequence=1&isAllowed=y

United Nations. (2016). *The First Global Integrated Marine Assessment: World Ocean Assessment I*. Group of Experts of the Regular Process.

United Nations. (2017). Goal 14: Conserve and sustainably use the oceans, seas and marine resources. United Nations.

United Nations. (2021). *Illegal wildlife trade/fishing/logging/mining. Interagency taskform on financing for development*. https://developmentfinance.un.org/illegal-wildlife-tradefishingloggingmining

United Nations. (2021a). *Goal 14. Conserve and Sustainably Use the Oceans, Seas and Marine Resources for Sustainable Development*. Retrieved October 18, 2021, from https://sdgs.un.org/goals

United Nations. (2021b). *The 17 Goals*. Retrieved October 18, 2021, from https://sdgs.un.org/goals

United Nations. (n.d.a). *Sustainable Development Goals*. Retrieved 10 28, 2017, from United Nations: https://www.un.org/sustainabledevelopment/sustainable-development-

United Nations. (n.d.b). *Goal 5: Achieve gender equality and empower all women and girls*. Retrieved 04 02, 2018, from United Nations: https://www.un.org/sustainabledevelopment/gender-equality/

United States Geological Survey. (2021). *Data and Tools*. Retrieved October 22, 2021, from https://www.usgs.gov/products/data-and-tools/data-and-tools-topics

University of Arizona. (n.d.). https://eprints.ncrm.ac.uk/250/1/What_is_QCA.pdf

University of Gävle. (2018a). *Ecological sustainability*. https://www.hig.se/Ext/En/University-of-Gavle/About-the-University/Environmental-Work/What-is-sustainable-development-at-HiG/Ecological-sustainability.html

University of Gävle. (2018b). *Economic sustainability*. https://www.hig.se/Ext/En/University-of-Gavle/About-the-University/Environmental-Work/What-is-sustainable-development-at-HiG/Economic-sustainability.html

Unutmaz, Ş. (2021). *14 of the world's 100 worst invasive species are in Turkey*. Hurriyet.

UNWTO. (2013). *Tourism Highlights*. UNWTO.

UNWTO. (2014). *Tourism in Small Island Developing States (SIDS): Building a More Sustainable Future for the People of Islands*. UNWTO.

Urrea, M. (2015). *Implementation and Applicability of the Environmental Account for the Registry of Renewable Natural Resources in the Colombian Public Accounting Regime within the Framework of International Financial Reporting Standards*. Academic Press.

USAID. (2018). *Power Africa Gas Road Map to 2030*. USAID.

van Ginneken, V., & de Vries, E. (2016). Towards a Seaweed Based Economy": The Global Ten Billion People Issue at the Midst of the 21st Century. *Journal of FisheriesSciences.Com*, *10*(2), 1–11.

Veliu, A., Gessese, N., Ragasa, C., & Okali, C. (2009). *Gender analysis of aquaculture value chain in Northeast Vietnam and Nigeria*. Agriculture and rural development discussion paper 44. The World Bank.

Vierros, M. K., & Harden-Davies, H. (2020). Capacity building and technology transfer for improving governance of marine areas both beyond and within National Jurisdiction. *Marine Policy*, *122*. doi:10.1016/j.marpol.2020.104158

Visbeck, M. (2018a). Ocean science research is key for a sustainable future. *Nature Communications*, *9*(1), 690. doi:10.103841467-018-03158-3 PMID:29449661

Visbeck, M., Kronfeld-Goharani, U., Neumann, B., Rickels, W., Schmidt, J., Van Doorn, E., & Quaas, M. F. (2014). Securing blue wealth: The need for a special sustainable development goal for the ocean and coasts. *Marine Policy*, *48*, 184–191.

Voyer, M., Schofield, C., Azmi, K., Warner, R., Mcilgorm, A., Quirk, G. (2018). Maritime security and the blue economy: Intersections and interdependencies in the Indian ocean. *J. Indian Ocean Reg.*, 1–21.

Voyer, M., Farmery, A. K., Kajlich, L., Vachette, A., & Quirk, G. (2020). Assessing policy coherence and coordination in the sustainable development of a Blue Economy. A case study from Timor Leste. *Ocean and Coastal Management*, *192*, 105187. doi:10.1016/j.ocecoaman.2020.105187

Voyer, M., Quirk, G., McIlgorm, A., & Azmi, K. (2018a). Shades of blue: What do competing interpretations of the Blue Economy mean for oceans governance? *Journal of Environmental Policy and Planning*, *20*(5), 595–616. doi:10.1080/1523908X.2018.1473153

Waheed, Z., Manjaji-Matsumoto, M., & Abdul-Basri, N. (2019a). Human capacity building and public education aligned with global perspectives for adaptation in coastal and ocean management- The role of the Borneo Marine Research Institute. In Ocean yearbook 33. Brill Nijhoff.

Wallinga, D. (2010). Agricultural policy and childhood obesity: A food systems and public health commentary. *Health Affairs (Project Hope)*, *29*, 405–410.

Wang, C. (2021). On the Legal Status of Marine Genetic Resources in Areas beyond National Jurisdiction. *Sustainability*, *13*(14), 7993. https://doi.org/10.3390/su13147993

Webb, J., Williams, A. G., Hope, E., Evans, D., & Moorhouse, E. (2013). Do foods imported into the UK have a greater environmental impact than the same foods produced within the UK? *The International Journal of Life Cycle Assessment*, *18*(7), 1325–1343.

Weber, C. L., & Matthew, H. S. (2008). Food-Miles and the Relative Climate Impacts of Food Choices in the United States. *Environmental Science & Technology*, *42*(10), 3508–3513.

Wenhai, L., Cusack, C., Baker, M., Tao, W., Mingbao, C., Paige, K., Xiaofan, Z., Levin, L., Escobar, E., Amon, D., Yue, Y., Reitz, A., Neves, A. A. S., O'Rourke, E., Mannarini, G., Pearlman, J., Tinker, J., Horsburgh, K. J., Lehodey, P., ... Yufeng, Y. (2019). Successful blue economy examples with an emphasis on international perspectives. *Frontiers in Marine Science*, *6*, 261. doi:10.3389/fmars.2019.00261

Wenwen, X., Bingxin, Z., & Lili, W. (2016). Marine industrial cluster structure and its coupling relationship with urban development: A case pf Shandong Province. *Polish Maritime Research*, *23*(s1), 115–122.

Wiederer, C. K. (2018). *Logistics Infrastructure Along the Belt and Road Initiative Economies*. World Bank Group.

Wijsman, J. W. M., Troost, K., Fang, J., Roncarati, A., Smaal, A., Ferreira, J., & Strand, Ø. (2019). *Goods and services of marine bivalves*. Springer.

Williams, T. A., & Shepherd, D. A. (2017). Mixed method social network analysis: Combining inductive concept development, content analysis, and secondary data for quantitative analysis. *Organizational Research Methods*, *20*(2), 268–298. doi:10.1177/1094428115610807

World Bank & Food and Agriculture Organization. (2008). *The Sunken Billions: The Economic Justification for Fisheries Reform*. Author.

World Bank & United Nations Department of Economic and Social Affairs. (2017). *The Potential of the Blue Economy: Increasing Long-term Benefits of the Sustainable Use of Marine Resources for Small Island Developing States and Coastal Least Developed Countries*. Washington, DC: World Bank.

World Bank & United Nations Department of Economic and Social Affairs. (2017). *The Potential of the Blue Economy: Increasing Long-term Benefits of the Sustainable Use of Marine Resources for Small Island Developing States and Coastal Least Developed Countries*. World Bank.

World Bank and United Nations Department of Economic and Social Affairs. (2017). *The Potential of the Blue Economy: Increasing Long-term Benefits of the Sustainable Use of Marine Resources for Small Island Developing States and Coastal Least Developed Countries*. World Bank.

World Bank and United Nations. (2017). *Blue Economy: Increasing Long-term benefits of the sustainable use of marine resources for small island developing states and coastal least developed countries.* https://documents.worldbank.org/curated/en/523151496389684076/pdf/115545-1-6-2017-14-48-41-BlueEconomyJun.pdf

World Bank. (2013). *Fish to 2030—prospects for fisheries and aquaculture.* World Bank Report Number 83177-GLB.

World Bank. (2017). *Girls' education.* The World Bank.

World Bank. (2017). *The potential of the Blue Economy: Increasing long-term benefits of the sustainable use of marine resources for Small Island Developing States and Least Developed Countries.* www.worldbank.org

World Bank. (2017). *What is the Blue Economy?* Available from: https://www.worldbank.org/en/news/infographic/2017/06/06/blueeconomy

World Bank. (2017, July). *What is the Blue Economy?* The World Bank. https://www.worldbank.org/en/news/infographic/2017/06/06/blue-economy

World Bank. (2019). *Creating a sustainable food future: a menu of solutions to feed nearly 10 billion people by 2050. World Resources Report.* The World Bank.

World Bank. (2019). *Where Sun Meets Water: An Introduction to Floating Solar.* World Bank, ESMAP and Solar Energy Research Institute of Singapore (SERIS).

World Economic Forum. (2017). *83 countries are more ocean than land.* https://www.weforum.org/agenda/2017/10/global-ocean-governance-all-at-sea/

World Health Organization. (2018). *Obesity and overweight.* Available from: http://www.who.int/mediacentre/factsheets/fs311/en/

World Ocean Council. (2019). *The Law of the Sea "BBNJ Agreement" and Ocean Business Activities.* World Ocean Council. Retrieved January 14, 2022, from https://www.oceancouncil.org/resources/the-law-of-the-sea-bbnj-agreement-and-ocean-business-activities/

World Ocean Initiative. (2018). *Economist Intelligence Unit reveals leaders and laggards on coastal governance.* The Economist Newspaper Limited. https://ocean.economist.com/governance/articles/economist-intelligence-unit-reveals-leaders-and-laggards-on-coastal-governance

World Population Review. (2019). *Nigeria Population 2019.* World Population.

World Population Review. (2021). *Mediterranean Countries 2021.* https://worldpopulationreview.com/country-rankings/mediterranean-countries

World Wildlife Fund. (2021). *Oceans.* Retrieved October 20, 2021, from https://www.wwf.org.uk/where-we-work/oceans

WTTC. (2016). *Travel and Tourism Economic Impact Summary 2016.* WTTC.

Xi, J. (2017). *The Governance of China II.* Foreign Languages Press.

Xinhua. (2017). *Vision for Maritime Cooperation under the Belt and Road Initiative.* Retrieved October 23, 2021, from http://news.xinhuanet.com/english/2017-06/20/c_136380414.htm

Xu, G. (2016). China's Arctic Interests and Policy: History, Legal Ground and Implementation. *World Economy and International Relations, 60*(2), 52–62. doi:10.20542/0131-2227-2016-60-2-52-62

Xu, H., Yin, Z., Jia, D., Jin, F., & Ouyang, H. (2011). The Potential Seasonal Alternative of Asia-Europe Container Service via Northern Sea Route under the Arctic Sea Ice Retreat. *Maritime Policy & Management, 38*(5), 541–560. do i:10.1080/03088839.2011.597449

Yang, J., & Zhao, L. (2019). Opportunities and Challenges of Jointly Building of the Polar Silk Road: China's Perspective. *Outlines of Global Transformations: Politics, Economics, Law, 12*(5), 130–144. doi:10.23932/2542-0240-2019-12-5-130-144

Yao, S., & Liang, H. (2019). Analyst following, environmental disclosure and cost of equity: Research based on industry classification. *Sustainability, 11*(2), 300. doi:10.3390u11020300

Yates, D. (2021). Testing the Illusion of Location Theory: Port-Gentil, Gabon. *Illusions of Location Theory: Consequences for Blue Economy in Africa*, 343.

Yildirim, S., & Kaplan, M. (2020). Seafood Security and Sustainability Through Sustainable Development: A Review of Turkish Seafood Market. In A. Obayelu & O. Obayelu (Eds.), Developing Sustainable Food Systems, Policies, and Securities (pp. 16–36). IGI Global. https://doi.org/10.4018/978-1-7998-2599-9.ch002

Yıldırım, S., & Yıldırım, D. C. (2021). Achieving Seafood Security in the Mediterranean Region: A Case of Turkey. In R. Castanho & J. Martín Gallardo (Eds.), *Management and Conservation of Mediterranean Environments* (pp. 175–195). IGI Global. doi:10.4018/978-1-7998-7391-4.ch011

Yu, X., & Li, Y. (2020). Effect of environmental regulation policy tools on the quality of foreign direct investment: An empirical study of China. *Journal of Cleaner Production, 270*, 122346. doi:10.1016/j.jclepro.2020.122346

Zalyvsky, N. (2015). The Northern Sea Route: The Potential of Expectations and the Real Functioning Problems. *Arctic and North, 20*, 37–57. doi:10.17238/issn2221-2698.2015.20.37

Zenetos, A., Çinar, M.E., Crocetta, F., Golani, D., & Rosso, A. (2017). Uncertainties and validation of alien species catalogues: the mediterranean as an example. *Estuarine, Coastal And Shelf Science, 191*, 171-187. .Ffhal-01976050 doi:10.1016/J.Ecss.2017.03.031ff

Zeng, S. X., Xu, X. D., Dong, Z. Y., & Tam, V. W. (2010). Towards corporate environmental information disclosure: An empirical study in China. *Journal of Cleaner Production, 18*(12), 1142–1148. doi:10.1016/j.jclepro.2010.04.005

Zhang, X., & Daly, K. (2011). The determinants of China's outward foreign direct investment. *Emerging Markets Review, 12*(4), 389–398. doi:10.1016/j.ememar.2011.06.001

Zhao, H., Hu, H., & Lin, Y. (2016). Study on China-EU Container Shipping Network in the Context of Northern Sea Route. *Journal of Transport Geography, 53*, 50–60. doi:10.1016/j.jtrangeo.2016.01.013

Zhao, Q., Zhu, Z., Zeng, H., Zhao, W., & Myneni, R. B. (2020). Future greening of the Earth may not be as large as previously predicted. *Agricultural and Forest Meteorology, 292*, 108111. doi:10.1016/j.agrformet.2020.108111

Zhelyazkova, V. (2015). Green Banking-Definition, Scope and Proposed Business Model. *Journal of International Scientific Publications, 9*, 309-315.

Zheng, H., Liu, X., Xu, Y., & Mu, H. (2021). Economic Spillover Effects of Industrial Structure Upgrading in China's Coastal Economic Rims. *Sustainability, 13*(7), 3855. doi:10.3390u13073855

Zheng, X., Lu, Y., Yuan, J., Baninla, Y., Zhang, S., Stenseth, N., Hessen, D. O., Tian, H., Obersteiner, M., & Chen, D. (2020). Drivers of Change in China's Energy-Related CO_2 Emissions. *Proceedings of the National Academy of Sciences of the United States of America, 117*(1), 29–36. doi:10.1073/pnas.1908513117 PMID:31871172

Zhu, S., Fu, X., Ng, A., Luo, M., & Ge, Y.-E. (2018). The Environmental Costs and Economic Implications of Container Shipping on the Northern Sea Route. *Maritime Policy & Management*, *45*(4), 456–477. doi:10.1080/03088839.2018.1443228

Zmieva, K. (2020). Problems of Energy Supply in the Arctic Regions. *Russian Arctic*, *8*, 5–14. doi:10.24411/2658-4255-2020-00001

Zvorykina, J., & Teteryatnikov, K. (2019). The Northern Sea Route as a Tool of Arctic Development. *Russian Economic Journal*, *4*(4), 21–44. doi:10.33983/0130-9757-2019-4-21-44

About the Contributors

Lukman Raimi is an Assistant Professor of Entrepreneurship at the American University of Nigeria. Previously, he was a Principal Lecturer/Coordinator of Training & Part-Time Programme at the Centre for Entrepreneurship Development (CED), Yaba College of Technology, Lagos. His research interests include: Entrepreneurship, Development Economics, Corporate Social Responsibility, General Management and Human Resources Management. Raimi is an alumnus of both Cumberland Lodge, Windsor, United Kingdom and Entrepreneurship Development Institute (EDI), Ahmedabad, India. He had undergone special training in Enterprise Education for Employability facilitated by the Oxford Brookes University and the Pan African University Nigeria under the British Council's sponsorship. University Degree: Ph.D., De Montfort University, Leicester (UK); M.Sc., Industrial Relations & Personnel Management, University of Lagos (Nigeria); M.Sc.., Economics, University of Lagos (Nigeria); B.Sc., Economics, Obafemi Awolowo University (Nigeria); and Certificate; Small Business Promotion, Entrepreneurship Development Institute (India).

Jainaba M. L. Kah has a Ph.D. in Urban Planning and Policy Development from the Edward J. Bloustein School, Rutgers – The State University of New Jersey, USA. She also earned a Masters in Development Economics (M.D.E.) from Dalhousie University, Canada, and a Bachelor of Commerce (Cum Laude) from St. Mary's University in Halifax, Canada. Prof. Jainaba M. L. Kah (née: Saho) is the Director General of the Department of Strategic Policy & Delivery (DSPD) at Office of The President in The Gambia. DSPD is the technical arm of the Office of The President, functioning to assist and enable the President to develop, implement and monitor the vision of the government and to provide strategic leadership for cross-sectoral policies or programmes. As the Director General of DSPD, Professor Jainaba M.L. Kah is responsible for leadership, strategic management, innovations, talent management and functionality of the Department in liaison with the Office of the Secretary General, the Cabinet Office and other Ministries, Departments and Agencies (MDAs) and other stakeholders. Prof. Kah has extensive practitioner experience having worked for the World Bank as an Urban/Transport Specialist and also served as a consultant for the USA Federal Transit Administration; Financial Analyst for Amnesty International; and Audit Senior at KPMG. Prof. Kah served for four years as the Chairperson of the Adjudication Committee of the All Africa Public Sector Innovation Awards (AAPSIA), which is the first Africa wide ministerial initiative celebrating innovation in the Public Sector.

* * *

Taoreed Amodu is currently a Second-Mate in the Merchant Navy Fleet. He began his academic pursuit from Federal College of Fisheries and Marine Technology, Lagos, Nigeria, during which he secured a scholarship to study Maritime Transport in far away North Africa-Egypt. A highly motivated maritime transport graduate and member of the Nautical Institute, UK. As a certified navigator, he has been able to complete many voyages around the world from the Mediterranean Sea to Atlantic Ocean to the Red Sea through the Suez Canal. These explorations has inspired his interest in writing to help others see the world through him.

Vasilii Erokhin is an Associate Professor at Harbin Engineering University, School of Economics and Management, Polar Development and Northeast Asian Economic Research Center (PAERC). His spheres of research interests: international trade, globalization, trade integration and liberalization, sustainable development, economies in transition, food security issues. Dr. Erokhin is an author of over 150 research works in international economics, international trade, sustainable rural development and regionalization. Vasily Erokhin is a member of editorial review boards of several international journals: International Journal of Sustainable Economies Management (IJSEM); Economies; Journal of World Economic Research; Economics of Agriculture (Ekonomika poljoprivrede), editor of international book projects "Global Perspectives on Trade Integration and Economies in Transition" (IGI Global, USA, 2016) and "Establishing Food Security and Alternatives to International Trade in Emerging Economies" (IGI Global, USA, 2017). He is a holder of the honorary awards from the Ministry of Agriculture of the Russian Federation (2010), Ministry of Education and Science of the Russian Federation (2012).

Gao Tianming is a Professor, School of Economics and Management, Harbin Engineering University, China. He is a Director and Chief Expert of the Center for Russian and Ukrainian Studies (CRUS) and Arctic Blue Economy Research Center (ABERC) at Harbin Engineering University, Deputy Head of the Heilongjiang International Economic and Trade Association, leading consultant of governmental bodies and commercial organizations in the sphere of economic collaboration between China, Russia, and the Republic of Korea.

Merve Kaplan was born in 1986. She was graduated her master's degree from Kocaeli University in Turkey. The subject of her thesis was "Effects of shucking and cooking of striped venus clam (Chamelea gallina L.,1753) collected from Kandira Beach with different thermal methods on meat yield chemical composition". She is an aquaculture engineer, and she has been working in Kocaeli Provincial Directorate of Agriculture and Forestry, Turkey. Also, she is a PhD student at Canakkale Onsekiz Mart University in Turkey. Also, she is preparing her PhD thesis.

Muriel Lendoye, holder of a Master in Political Science course Consulting and Expertise in Public Action, is a junior consultant in Evaluation of programs and public policies. She is also a member of the Gabonese Society for the Evaluation of Public Policies and the Quebec Society for Program Evaluation. In these capacities, she has contributed to studies and participated in forums. She has just completed the basic training for a certification in development evaluation provided by the International Development Evaluation Training Program in partnership with the National School of Administration of Quebec.

Nima Norouzi does research in techno-economic, techno-environmental, techno-social, and legal aspects of energy and natural resources economics.

Moshood Sanni is a seasoned researcher, assistant lecturer and doctorate student at University of Ibadan, Ibadan Nigeria. He is author of "The impact of management information system (M.I.S) on corporate performance and The impact of skill acquisition and empowerment programmes on the participation of youth in Ikeja Local Government Lagos. His current research looks at eradicating poverty among the youth via Skills Acquisition and Entrepreneurship Training thus creating employment opportunities for others.

Muhammad Usman Tariq has more than 14+ years of experience in industry and academia. He has been working as a consultant and trainer for industries representing six sigma, quality, health and safety, environmental systems, project management, and information security standards. His work has encompassed sectors in aviation, manufacturing, food, hospitality, education, finance, research, software and transportation. He has diverse and significant experience working with accreditation agencies of ABET, ACBSP, AACSB, WASC, CAA, EFQM and NCEAC. Additionally, Dr. Tariq has operational experience in incubators, research labs, government research projects, private sector startups, program creation and management at various industrial and academic levels. He is Certified Higher Education Teacher from Harvard University, USA, Certified Online Educator from HMBSU, Certified Six Sigma Master Black Belt, Lead Auditor ISO 9001 Certified, ISO 14001, IOSH MS, OSHA 30, and OSHA 48. He is member of Harvard Business Review Advisory Council. Dr. Tariq earned his Doctor of Business Administration from California Southern University with distinction. He holds a Master of Science in Computing Science, with a specialization in Software Engineering from SZABIST, and a Bachelor of Science degree in Computing from Bahria University. He has more than 51 research publications in international journals, one book, and 4 patents. His research interests include six sigma, knowledge management, information technology, economics, organizational change, facial recognition, biomedical devices, and computer science. Dr. Tariq has a passion for learning and development, project management, and training.

Seda Yıldırım currently works at Tekirdag Namık Kemal University in Turkey. She studies on sustainable development, 2030 sustainable development goals, sustainable consumption patterns, Islamic finance and banking, consumption patterns, environmental quality and food security. She is married and has one child. ORCID: https://orcid.org/0000-0003-4367-6652, https://twitter.com/sdayildr?s=08, https://www.researchgate.net/profile/Seda-Yildirim-10.

Index

U

www.ingramcontent.com/pod-product-compliance
Lightning Source LLC
LaVergne TN
LVHW062145300926
849161LV00010B/2635